18

TEACHERS' EDITION

USING GOOD ENGLISH 11

COMPOSITION and GRAMMAR

JOHN E. BREWTON
Chairman, English Department
George Peabody College for Teachers
Nashville, Tennessee

R. STANLEY PETERSON
Head of the English Department
New Trier Township High School
Winnetka, Illinois

B. JO KINNICK
Teacher of Creative Writing
Oakland High School
Oakland, California

LOIS McMULLAN
Formerly Teacher of English, Laboratory School
George Peabody College for Teachers
.Nashville, Tennessee

LAIDLAW BROTHERS • PUBLISHERS

River Forest, Illinois

SUMMIT, NEW JERSEY   PALO ALTO, CALIFORNIA   DALLAS, TEXAS   ATLANTA, GEORGIA

CONTENTS

1. The Materials of Instruction

The students' text, with the title *Using Good English* accompanied by an arabic numeral indicating its grade designation, is the basic material of instruction. The students' practice book, *Practice for Using Good English*, is designed to accompany the students' text. Test booklets, which are available in individual booklets under separate cover, are also useful to the teacher in evaluating student progress. To assist the teacher in making the most effective use of the text, a complete teachers' edition is included as part of the series. Each of these materials of instruction is discussed in some detail in the paragraphs that follow.

STUDENTS' TEXT

One of the outstanding attributes of *Using Good English*, Grade 11, is its scope of coverage. Because the demands for English skills today go beyond the teaching of grammar, usage, and mechanics, *Using Good English*, Grade 11, is organized into two general areas. The first area, composition and communication, emphasizes listening, speaking, reading, and writing. The second, the Handbook for Study and Reference, presents the study of the sentence from the points of view of grammatical structure and of usage and the study of the mechanics of writing—form, spelling, capitalization, punctuation, and syllabication—in a form that is readily usable in teaching and learning situations and that provides the convenience of a ready reference when used as a handbook.

Composition and communication

The first seven units, characterized by the pages on which blue is the predominant color, provide experiences in composition and in the other areas of communication—listening, speaking, and reading. Although the emphasis in each unit is on a particular communication skill, provision is made in all units for developing and refining all the communication skills. The over-all plan of the composition and communication portion of the text is such that within each unit the teaching of both basic and advanced skills is co-ordinated with the presentation of the subject matter. Although these units are arranged in a logical sequential order, their independent organization allows the teacher to select for study any unit that he feels will best meet the needs of a class at a particular time.

Unlimited writing opportunities are presented throughout the entire text, but particular emphasis is placed on creative writing in Unit 7. Since not all students can express themselves in poetry or in the short-story form, provision is made for creative expression in other forms, as well. Another major opportunity for writing is provided in the study of Unit 6, The Research Paper.

If weaknesses in grammar, usage, capitalization, spelling, or punctuation become apparent at any time during the study of composition and communication, the Handbook is available for both reference and study.

Handbook

The strict organization and convenient reference qualities of a handbook have long been recognized by teachers. The limitations of a handbook for the English teacher have centered around the lack of developmental material in all the areas of communication. For this reason, the grammar and the mechanics of using the language have been put in the Handbook of *Using Good English* and the composition and communication skills in a separate section. The Handbook pages in the text may be easily recognized as those on which red is the predominant color.

The Handbook is preceded by a Key on pages 183-190, which are tinted red so that they can be found easily in the book. In addition to the fact that students find security in the strict organization of a handbook, teachers will find the Handbook with its Key particularly valuable in grading written work. For example, students often commit faults that are difficult to explain because of space limitations at the point of the error on the paper and because of the amount of teacher-time involved in the writing of a detailed explanation. The student should know, however, what error he has committed, how the error can be corrected, and how to avoid making the same mistake in the future. Using the Handbook Key, the teacher may write the appropriate number on the student's paper. The student may then find the number in the Key, refer to the page indicated, and find an explanation of his error along with examples and exercises. The error has ceased to be a demerit; it has become a constructive teaching aid. Familiarization with the Handbook Key will come quickly to teachers. Teachers who teach more than one grade level will also appreciate the fact that every rule or definition in any text of the *Using Good English* series for Grades 9-12 is keyed with the same number in every other Handbook of the series.

The plan of the Handbook is flexible to allow particular areas to be studied whenever the teacher feels that the study is necessary. However, a sound approach to teaching grammar and usage would be to start with the study of the sentence at the beginning of Unit 8. A natural progression from an understanding of sentences to the words, phrases, and clauses that make up a sentence follows. Unit 9, Usage Skills, would logically follow Unit 8. Unit 10 may be taught at the most opportune time for the study of form in writing and mechanics in writing.

You will notice that the rules in this book are not presented in numerical order but are organized to present broad areas of study that incorporate related topics and subtopics. The purpose of this arrangement is to enable students to study grammatical concepts of the English language from another point of view.

Organization of individual units

The basic organization of each of the units in the text includes an introduction that states the purpose of the unit and the reasons that the study of the unit is important to the students. Following the introduction is a section titled Check Yourself, printed in color. By answering the questions in this section, the student will become aware of his own weaknesses, an awareness that will provide additional motivation for the study of the unit. It is the intent of the authors that the Check Yourself questions not be graded by the teacher. Ample opportunity for evaluation is provided throughout the remainder of the unit.

The major divisions of a unit are signified by the numbered headings in large type that are centered on the page. These main sections are divided into topics, indicated by boldface side headings. Each topic, and sometimes the subtopics within topics, will be followed by Developing Your Skill exercises. These skills exercises ordinarily begin with discussion questions to establish understandings prior to written application. Because the exercises generally increase in difficulty within a Developing Your Skill section, teachers may choose those exercises that meet the special needs of particular classes. Provisions for review activities are included at the end of each of the main sections of the unit.

The blue and red edges on certain pages designate end-of-unit review activities. A brief Unit Summary aids recall for the students before they begin the Unit Review Exercises. These exercises are divided into four areas

—Discussion Topics, to help establish understandings; Written Work, to provide written application of understandings; Vocabulary, to strengthen understandings of words that should be a part of the student's working vocabulary; and Spelling, to help students spell correctly the words in their vocabulary. The five vocabulary words are taken from the unit and are presented in different contexts. The first five spelling words are the words from the vocabulary section, the second five words are taken from the unit, and the remaining ten words are those words often misspelled by students at the particular grade level. Each unit ends with a Unit Self-Test, designed to be self-administered by students.

TEACHERS' EDITION

The first section of the teachers' edition is printed on tinted paper to separate it from the pages found in the students' text. Each page number in this section begins with *T*, for *T*eachers' edition.

1. *Materials of Instruction.* Pages T3-T7 present an explanation of the students' text, the teachers' edition, the students' practice book, and the test booklet—the materials that comprise the *Using Good English* series for each grade.

2. *Unit Previews.* Pages T8-T41 contain an overview of each of the ten units in the students' text. The information on these pages will be particularly valuable to the inexperienced teacher. Even experienced teachers will appreciate new suggestions or additional ideas that will help him use the text more effectively. The suggestions in the unit previews are divided into two categories—*Background and Interest* and *General Teaching Suggestions.*

3. *Unit Tests.* A test has been included in the teachers' edition for each of the ten units in the students' text to aid the teacher in objective evaluation. These tests are in addition to the Unit Self-Test at the end of each unit in the students' text. Teachers in school systems where *Using Good English* has been adopted as the basic text are granted permission to reproduce these tests in full or modified form.

4. *Audio-Visual Aids.* Listed on page T52 are audio-visual aids that teachers may be interested in securing for use in class.

5. *Bibliography.* The references on page T53 include professional books on teaching composition, communication, grammar, and usage. This list may be used as a guide for acquiring professional books.

6. *Additional Answers.* Wherever possible, answers to exercises are printed on the pages of the students' text contained in the teachers' edition. Obviously, many exercises require answers for which there is not sufficient space on the students' page. These answers are listed on pages T54-T80. A cross reference is included on the students' page to guide the teacher to the exact page in the teachers' edition where the answer may be found. Answers are included for the teacher's convenience and are particularly helpful when large numbers of papers must be graded.

7. *Annotated Students' Text.* The teachers' edition of the *Using Good English* series is unique in that each page of the students' text is reproduced in full size with helpful annotations in color. The marginal notes offer helpful suggestions and ideas to the teacher. In no way are the notes intended to limit the teacher's approach in presenting the subject matter. Interesting side lights, additional suggestions, and some of the main ideas are realistically presented in the convenient annotated form. An additional convenience for teachers in the *Using Good English* teachers' edition is the printing of answers directly on the page where the exercise occurs. If more space than is available on a page is needed for an answer, a cross reference has been supplied to direct the teacher to the exact page in this teachers' edition where the answer occurs.

OBJECTIVE TESTS

The objective tests which are under the heading Unit Tests on pages T42-T51 are intended to carry evaluation one step further than the Unit Review Exercises and the Unit Self-Test at the end of each unit of the students' text. Teachers in school systems where *Using Good English* has been adopted as the basic text are granted permission to reproduce the tests in full or in modified form. For teachers' convenience, the tests also are published separately and may be purchased from the publisher of the *Using Good English* series.

STUDENTS' PRACTICE BOOK

The practice book *Practice for Using Good English* is planned to enrich the learnings of the text by providing an abundance of additional exercises. Although *Practice for Using Good English* is a valuable aid to the teacher, the text is not dependent upon the practice book and alone can provide a full, satisfactory instructional program.

2. Unit Previews

Unit 1—Movies and Stage Plays

BACKGROUND AND INTEREST

If a student learns to view movies and stage plays critically, they can become a vital part of his education. He can learn to be discriminating in his tastes, selective in his viewing, and critical in his analyses, so that instead of being soporifics, movies and plays become valuable, living experiences.

The opening paragraphs of the unit offer a good silent reading exercise, to be done either at home or in the classroom. The questions in the Check Yourself on page 2 are designed to enable the teacher to determine students' attitudes toward and critical awareness of movies and plays. The discussion should not be prolonged, because the material of the Check Yourself is anticipatory and is not meant to be exhaustive. Questions raised here will be explored throughout the unit.

GENERAL TEACHING SUGGESTIONS

Pages 2-8   1. Choosing Movies and Plays

Pages 2-4   Some Aids to Finding Good Movies and Plays

Discuss with students the techniques for selecting movies and plays suggested on page 3. Point out to them that they cannot rely on one of these devices, alone. For example, an actor's having won an award—or even several awards—does not guarantee that every movie or play in which he appears will be worth seeing or that the actor's performance will be equally good in all movies or plays. Repeated outstanding performances, however, are an indication that one may anticipate consistent excellence.

Local newspapers, weekly magazines, and any other reputable sources of information should be exploited to provide students with reliable critical material. The bulletin board should be used extensively for the posting of significant reviews of local movies and forthcoming television programs. School plays and local theater offerings should also be publicized in the classroom. The aim is to make the students aware of and, at the same time, critical of what is going on in the theater world.

Pages 4-8   Critical Reviews

The habit of reading critical reviews has to be cultivated. At the same time students must be cautioned against indiscriminate acceptance of reviewers' opinions. Reviews serve only as a guide and, then, only when at least several reviews are compared. Reading and analyzing a number of reviews of well-known motion pictures and plays will train your students in what to look for and how to evaluate what they read in the reviews. As students learn to discriminate between objective reviews and prejudiced reviews, they will also increase their own critical perceptions and will, as a result, develop greater selectivity in their choices of movies and plays.

Pages 9-14   2. Judging Movies and Plays

Pages 9-11   Evaluate the Story

Concentrate first on the story. The story may not be the most important aspect of a play or a movie, but it is always significant. Although the plot of a story may not achieve great originality, it should not be so trite that the audience can foretell all the characters' actions before they are carried out. The story should not be too complex and thus promote confusion, nor should it be so simple as to become dull. The conflicts must spring from reasonable causes, preferably out of the complexity of the characters' lives; and the solutions must be probable rather than merely possible. The author's intention must carry through the action of the story, for there must be some purpose, some theme, some significant truth about man, that the author wishes to convey. ·

The discussion of the stereotypes in Exercise B on page 11 will undoubtedly elicit various responses from students since the terms are rather general. For example, *gangster* may call to mind several stereotypes, depending upon the area of crime in which the gangster operates. There will also be some variation in the types of viewing experiences students have had.

Pages 11-12   Evaluate Direction, Acting, and Photography

A movie or a stage play is a combined enterprise: author, director, set designer, actors, stage hands, lighting and sound-effects men, cameramen— all are important. The critical viewer will take into consideration the over-all effect of good or bad direction, the appropriateness of the actors for their roles, the quality of the acting, and the illusion of reality that these elements create for the viewer.

Students should understand that incompetent direction, stilted acting, or faulty photography can destroy a good story.

Pages 12-14   Evaluate Background Elements

The mood or atmosphere of a movie or stage play springs partly from the settings, costumes, sound, music, and color. In garish musical comedies these elements may be the most significant part of the show, but in serious drama they are adjuncts to the acting and should never be so conspicuous that they detract from the main purpose of the performance. The standards listed on page 13 will require considerable study and call for discussion. In view of the many movies and certainly some stage plays that students have seen, they will be able to elaborate on each of the ten points listed.

The questions in Exercise B on pages 13-14 should be discussed beforehand so that students are aware of what they are looking for in the motion picture that they are analyzing. You may wish to have slower students comment only on as many aspects as you feel their capabilities will permit.

Page 14   Unit Summary

The following suggestions for using the end-of-unit material, denoted by the blue strips and the red strips at the edge of the pages, may be followed in administering the material at the end of each unit.

It is suggested that students read the Unit Summary silently. As they read each point, they should be encouraged to think through the details of the information that applies in preparation for the Unit Review Exercises.

Page 15   Unit Review Exercises

These exercises afford an opportunity for summary and review of the unit. The oral review is presented before the written applications so that, through discussion, students can pin-point the main ideas and the important details of the unit. In carrying out the Discussion Topics, permit students to refer to the text whenever they are in doubt about some of the points covered.

The Written Work exercises should be carried out by the students, working independently. Students should be encouraged to reread and study any material in the unit about which they are uncertain. The purpose of these exercises is not only to review the unit coverage but also to insure retention of the subject matter. Some of the checking of the Written

Work may be done through class discussion, thus lightening the teacher's paper load.

The Vocabulary study is designed to increase the student's vocabulary through the recognition of words used in context. The comparison of the two uses of each word—the use in the text of the unit and the use in the exercise sentence—will help the student recognize the importance of context to word meaning. The number in brackets following the Vocabulary sentence refers to the page of the unit on which the word being studied appears.

The incorporation of the Spelling section into the unit will make spelling more meaningful to the students. The first five words of the spelling list are those used in the Vocabulary section; the second group of five words appeared in the unit; the remainder are commonly misspelled words. Students should be able to pronounce the words correctly and use them in sentences, as well as spell them correctly. Encourage students to continue using the words in speaking and in writing.

Page 16   Unit Self-Test

The Unit Self-Test, as its name implies, is designed to permit students to evaluate their comprehension of the unit. It is recommended that the test be done in class and that students not be permitted to refer to the text of the unit. The papers can be checked quickly in class with each student checking his own paper to discover his areas of weakness. Time may then be given for additional review before the final Unit Test is given. Those students who find that they are weak in certain areas should be directed to study the pages that cover the material they missed. The teacher may wish to designate a special section of the student's notebook for notes on areas of weakness. Such a section will give the student a special study help. A copy of a suggested final Unit Test for each unit is included on pages T42-T51 of this teachers' edition.

Unit 2—Listening

BACKGROUND AND INTEREST

Listening is an active, not a passive, experience. Whether the student listens for information or for appreciation, he must be an active participant; he must not merely hear or half-listen.

The world, unfortunately perhaps, is a sea of noises, noises that increase rather than lessen as time goes on. Education must provide training in how to be selective—how to shut out the undesirable sounds and how to focus attention on those sounds that are important. It is the purpose of this unit to teach students how to listen effectively.

GENERAL TEACHING SUGGESTIONS

Pages 18-23   1. Informational Listening

Pages 18-22   Listen Actively

Students should memorize and learn to apply the formula for good listening: (1) make a conscious effort to follow what is being said; (2) organize the ideas; and (3) ask intelligent questions about or make intelligent comments on what has been said.

Class situations provide many opportunities for practice in listening to assignments and to directions, explanations, and announcements. Students must be made to understand from the start that you will answer intelligent questions and will try to clarify any misunderstandings, but that you will not repeat information that was missed because of inattention on the student's part. If students know that you will repeat information whenever they ask, they are less likely to listen carefully from the start. When the subject matter permits, lecture to the class occasionally and allow them to take notes.

Pages 22-23   Take Notes

The mistake students make most frequently in taking notes is that they try to record too much of what is being said. Emphasize the importance of summarizing and organizing material while listening. Provide as many opportunities as possible for note taking—class lectures, recorded speeches, assembly speeches. Until students have developed skill in taking notes, follow each note-taking situation with a discussion: What were the main ideas? What were the important supporting details? If you found it difficult to take notes, did the fault lie with the speaker or with you? Explain. Occasionally, a speech may be poorly organized or poorly presented so that it is almost impossible to take notes. Consider this point in your discussion.

Students will find it helpful to know some of the short cuts to good note taking. Illustrate the use of key words and phrases, outlining, and abbreviations in a class session. Stress the fact that notes should be revised and expanded as soon as possible, while the material is still fresh in the listener's mind.

Pages 23-33   **2. Appreciative Listening**

Pages 24-27   *Enjoying Poetry*

This part of the unit can be used in connection with Unit 7 on creative writing. You may feel, as do many other teachers, that the road to good creative writing is to be found in training the ear to listen to the language. Such matters as rhythm, melody, and imagery need to be investigated before students learn to appreciate poetry. The E. E. Cummings poem on page 26 is an excellent one to teach appreciative listening. Students would undoubtedly enjoy hearing Cummings and other poets read their own poetry in the album called *Pleasure Dome* (Columbia Master Works, ML 4259).

Pages 27-33   *Enjoying Choral Speaking*

A well-motivated class in choral speaking can be a rewarding experience for students and teacher alike. The structure of poems will become clear, the dramatic possibilities will show themselves, and the power of language to move the emotions should demonstrate itself. Before attempting a choral reading of a poem, discuss the selections in detail as suggested in Exercise A on page 31.

Pages 33-36   *End-of-Unit Material*

For suggestions for administering the end-of-unit material, see pages T10-T11 of the teachers' edition.

Unit 3—Discussion and Debate

BACKGROUND AND INTEREST

Discussion and debate make strong demands upon the student: seriousness of purpose, good reasoning, and a mastery of communication skills. The teacher will be able to judge from his knowledge of his students whether all or only part of this unit may be profitably used. With slower classes the section on debate may have to be curtailed, since it does call for rather advanced thinking and speaking. Even slow learners, however, can profit from learning what a debate is and what the general procedures are in preparing for a debate.

The Check Yourself questions on pages 37-38 will reveal the students' background in discussion and debate. Questions 2-13 and 15-16 provide a diagnostic self-analysis of students' attitudes as participants in discussion and may serve as a guide for setting up standards for participating in discussions.

GENERAL TEACHING SUGGESTIONS

Pages 38-45   1. Discussion

Pages 38-39   Selecting and Analyzing a Discussion Subject

An appropriate subject for a discussion is one that arouses a difference of opinion or one that is multi-faceted and thought provoking. Questions that elicit a *Yes* or *No* answer are not suitable, nor are questions that have obvious answers to which nearly everyone in class agrees. As subjects are suggested for Exercise A on page 39, consider each one in terms of its suitability as a discussion topic. Work toward Exercise B on page 39, in which the student is to select a subject and make an analysis and an outline.

Pages 40-42   Participating in Discussion

Total participation should be the aim of any discussion. Since there are always those students who are reluctant to speak in public, motivation is important. Subjects should be fresh, stimulating, interesting to the students, and within the students' experience and comprehension. If everyone is interested, if everyone is informed, if everyone makes an honest effort to contribute his share of information, then the discussion will be a success. Insist upon observance of the amenities of good discussion: attentive listening and polite co-operation. Otherwise the discussion may degenerate into a free-for-all session in which nothing can be accomplished.

Pages 42-43   Leading a Discussion

The selection of a discussion leader should be based on the capabilities of the person chosen rather than on his popularity. Discuss the qualifications of a good leader before the class votes on a discussion leader. Encourage students to select as many different students as possible to serve as chairmen for successive assignments. Practice in leading class discussions will give students an opportunity to develop qualities of class leadership.

Pages 43-45   Special Types of Discussion

Distinguish among the following terms: *round-table, panel, forum,* and *symposium.* If possible, work toward a class demonstration of each type. Refer to Exercise C on page 45 for a summary of standards against which all discussions will be evaluated.

Pages 46-58   2. Debate

Page 46   The Form of Debate

Debate is a formal argument conducted according to established rules. Insist upon students' learning the terms that apply to traditional debating.

Pages 47-49   Selecting and Analyzing the Proposition

The choice of a subject is extremely important in debate. The subject must be timely, interesting, and debatable. Apply to each topic suggested for debate the tests given on page 47. Analysis of the proposition calls for complete understanding of both sides of the question; otherwise the debater may be caught without adequate defense for his own arguments or without rebuttals for his opponents' arguments. Notice that beginning with the exercises on page 49, a series of cumulative exercises has been planned, culminating in an actual debate.

Pages 49-50   Collecting and Organizing Debate Material

One of the most valuable skills learned in debating is the marshaling of evidence to prove a point of view. What is sufficient? What is the best arrangement? What is the best presentation? To what extent should one resort to the opinions of experts for supporting argument? These are important questions to settle in class discussion periods. The method of collecting material is treated briefly in this unit. For further instructions on doing library research work, the student should be referred to Unit 6.

Exercise B on page 50 is another in the series of cumulative exercises.

Pages 50-53   Constructing the Brief

The analysis of the brief should be worked over in class, with all members contributing. When the time comes for Exercise A on page 53, all students will be ready for the development of the brief. The teacher should understand, however, that making a formal brief is a time-consuming process, requiring extensive research. If time is short, the complete brief should not be attempted. You may wish to have students prepare only part of a brief. Exercises A and B on page 53 are part of the cumulative series of exercises.

Pages 53-56   Logical Reasoning

The successful debater must be able to reason clearly; above all, he must avoid the common errors of faulty reasoning. The teacher can illuminate the faulty-reasoning pitfall for debaters by bringing into class examples of radio, television, and magazine commercial advertising that will illustrate most of the common errors in argument. It is only through an understanding of the common fallacies in reasoning that students can detect these fallacies in their opponents' reasoning and avoid them in their own reasoning.

Pages 56-58   Refuting Your Opponent's Arguments

Rebuttal speeches call for alert minds. To see through the false arguments of the opposition, to pierce the apparent shield of logic that they have set up, to detect any omissions or irregularities—these require even more astuteness than do the initial arguments. The successful debater is the one who can anticipate his opponents' arguments and be ready with counter arguments. The Developing Your Skill exercise on pages 57-58 is the last of the series of cumulative exercises.

The Review Exercise on page 58 is the culminating activity if you have time for class or inter-class debates.

Pages 59-60   End-of-Unit Material

For suggestions for administering the end-of-unit material, see pages T10-T11 of the teachers' edition.

Unit 4—Words and Meanings

BACKGROUND AND INTEREST

This unit is based on the premise that an understanding of language— knowing how language develops and grows—will enable students not only to build better vocabularies but also to use language appropriately and selectively. The approach to the unit, then, should be from the point of view of increasing one's knowledge of language rather than only from the point of view of adding words to one's vocabulary.

The Check Yourself exercises on page 62 do not, of course, explore all the areas where language is important, but they will serve as a good motivating force to carry your pupils over into the particular studies on increasing knowledge of words and using language selectively.

GENERAL TEACHING SUGGESTIONS

Pages 63-76   1. Increasing Your Knowledge of Words

Pages 63-64   *Words as Symbols*

All words are symbols, and they take on meaning according to the intentions of the people who use them. Man has created language to serve his purposes, and he has altered language whenever he has needed to make changes in his ways of thinking. There has always been, however, a conservative tendency to keep the major body of a language from altering too swiftly; man's need to communicate with his fellows has made him recognize that he must maintain a certain consistency or he would fail to communicate. But man also has been inventive. As new experiences have taught new lessons and new discoveries have brought new concepts, man has had to keep his language alive to keep pace with his own growth. With improved methods of communication, modern man is finding that his language is growing in complexity along with his society. There is still the conservative tendency, but new words come into the language and quickly achieve almost universal acceptance; old words are used in new and different ways. In presenting this material on language, stress the point that a word is a symbol for something; it is not the thing itself.

Pages 64-67   *Language Changes and Growth*

Little motivation is needed to interest students in the histories of words that they take for granted. They are amused by some of the changes that have taken place and are fascinated by others. Some of your more advanced students—and perhaps even some of your slower students—may be interested in doing research on word histories and reporting to the class.

Through the study of what has happened to individual words, the eleventh-grade student will begin to have some knowledge of the problems of linguistics. His knowledge will lead him to further study later on.

Exercise A on page 67 may suggest other similar pairs of words. Perhaps some of your students can be motivated to write a similar paragraph.

Pages 68-70   Concrete and Abstract Words

If man had only concrete words with which to communicate, he would live on a plane only slightly above the animals. He could see and name the objects about him, but he could go no further in expressing himself. It is the abstract words that man has invented that enable him to express concepts beyond the concrete. The exercises on page 70 provide practice not only in the recognition of concrete and abstract terms but also in the awareness of the varying degrees of exactness that exist within categories of words.

Pages 71-73   Connotation and Denotation

There are few words in the language that are merely denotative, because almost everyone, when he speaks or writes, gives some personal meaning to the words he uses. You may wish to use the word *house* as an example. To most people *house* denotes a building for lodging a family, but if the person speaking personalizes the house, the word takes on richer significance. The word *home* is richer in connotation, but it can lose much of its fringe meaning if the speaker uses it without feeling; for example, *He established a home for stray mutts*. Where exact meaning is most important in communication, words are likely to be denotative: in law briefs, in scientific documents, in mathematical analyses. But wherever the emotions are stirred, wherever fine shades of feeling must be distinguished, whenever literature rather than pure communication of information is the aim, connotations play an important part.

The study of propaganda words, suggested in the exercises on page 73, will help students to understand the role of connotation in spoken and written language. Students will see not only the power in connotative words but also the danger.

Pages 73-76   Words in Context

The concept that is stressed in this section is that a word has meaning only as it is used in a particular sentence, or in its context. Both the author and the reader must see that within a given context a word takes on only one possible meaning or certain limited meanings (in case a pun, a figure of speech, or irony is intended).

Good reading depends largely on an understanding of context. Misreading often results from the failure to recognize the possibilities of multiple meanings and the failure to choose the right meaning to fit the specific context.

Exercise B at the top of page 76 will help students to realize the various elements that may combine to create context—ideas, time, place, circumstances, and so on.

Pages 77-85   2. Using Language Selectively

Pages 77-81   *Words that Fit the Occasion*

Students must be brought to the scientific view that different levels of language usage exist; that no level of language is in itself wrong, but that certain usages are more appropriate than others in particular situations. The emphasis in the teaching of this section of the unit should be on appropriateness of language rather than on accuracy of language. Formal language is not always appropriate, and substandard language may not always be wrong. The aim for most students should be the level of English used by educated persons in informal speaking and writing situations. At the same time, students should be able to elevate their language to formal style in their reports, and they should be allowed a certain latitude in their friendly conversational periods, where slang and adolescent idiom have an appreciable value. Students may show enough interest in Exercise B on page 81 that you may wish to make the lists longer than the suggested five words.

Pages 81-84   *Idioms*

A consideration of the literal translations of idioms will help students to understand why idioms lose meaning when translated into other languages. Some of your language students may be able to contribute idioms from foreign languages and give their literal translations. Expressions that students will recognize as being peculiar to the English language are *up in the air, to fall asleep, to get used to, to catch cold, well-to-do, ill at ease, odds and ends, to give in, to take heart,* and *to take to heart.* Students may suggest others. Lively idioms add spice to a student's writing, but the student must be cautioned to avoid trite and dull idoms. Usually good idioms will improve his style by giving naturalness and ease to it.

Pages 85-88   End-of-Unit Material

For suggestions for administering the end-of-unit material, see pages T10-T11 of the teachers' edition.

Unit 5—Reading for Appreciation

BACKGROUND AND INTEREST

Students often fail fully to appreciate imaginative literature, particularly the short story, if they do not have some knowledge of the devices employed by writers and also if they do not have a mastery of some kind of analysis technique. Both these aspects of reading for appreciation are presented in this unit.

The Check Yourself exercises on page 90 are designed both to test the student's knowledge of basic devices and techniques used in writing and to indicate some of the elements that must be recognized and understood if one is to read appreciatively. Students must realize from the start that the ability only to recognize devices is not enough; they must understand how an author employs various devices to achieve particular effects.

GENERAL TEACHING SUGGESTIONS

Pages 90-100   1. Recognizing the Author's Devices

Pages 90-94   Figurative Language

Students who fail to recognize an author's use of figurative language often lose not only the primary meanings of sentences, but also the overtones of suggestion.

Make students aware of the importance of freshness and appropriateness in the use of figures of speech. Point out to them that trite or strained figures may destroy rather than enhance writing. However, caution students to consider the period during which the work they are reading was written. What may now appear to be trite may have been fresh and effective when the author first used it.

Pages 95-99   Irony

A discussion of the derivation of the word *irony* may help students better to understand what is meant by the ". . . deliberate twisting of facts, events, or meanings to imply something different from, sometimes even the opposite of, what is actually said." *Irony* comes from the Greek *eirōneia* meaning *dissimulation* in the sense of hiding or covering up.

Pages 100-114   2. Reading Critically

Page 100   Aspects of Style

Style is a difficult aspect of writing to handle in the classroom. It is sometimes too subtle for young students to appreciate; therefore expect from your students only a general appreciation of what an author's style is. It is the total impression; it is the man himself who is writing; it is his attitude toward his material and toward his audience; it is his language. Exposing students to literature that is noted for its style is perhaps the best way to impress on students what the term means. Choose works by men whose styles are distinctive, as Poe, Mark Twain, Lardner, and Hemingway.

Pages 101-105   A Method of Analysis

There is always some resistance to analysis of literature. Students mistakenly feel that a critical discussion of a piece of literature detracts from their enjoyment of the literary work. The analogies suggested between the student's problem and the doctor's or the mechanic's may be sufficient to convince them otherwise; if not, the analyses they do should result in so much more understanding of the stories analyzed that the students will accept the method. You will win over most of the objectors if the principles set forth in this unit are made vivid through application.

Pages 105-114   An Analysis

"The Emperor's New Clothes" is a good short story to train your students in the art of analysis. It is simple enough for everyone to read and understand; yet it illustrates well all the classic characteristics of a good short story. For the active reader it is filled with humor and suggestions; for the slower reader it offers many opportunities for guided reading. The teacher will be able to use the side-column commentary to bring out the essential short-story techniques that sometimes are difficult concepts for many students. Mastery of the principles of criticism and analysis will make the next story read a more satisfying intellectual and emotional experience.

In the discussion that follows the reading of "The Emperor's New Clothes," refer to the question raised in the opening paragraph of this section on page 105. While it is true that the story can be accepted purely at the "fairy tale" level, students should also be aware of the adult satire in the story. You may wish to make this point after students finish their first reading of the story but before they consider the analysis of the story. Recognizing the adult qualities in "The Emperor's New Clothes" may serve as a motivational device.

When students write analyses, insist that their compositions be true analyses and not merely plot summaries. However, specific reference should be made to the text of the story wherever necessary to illustrate or substantiate a point.

Pages 114-116   End-of-Unit Material

For suggestions for administering the end-of-unit material, see pages T10-T11 of the teachers' edition.

Unit 6—The Research Paper

BACKGROUND AND INTEREST

Your students have already learned a great deal about the use of the library. They perhaps know in a general way where the important reference books are shelved; they know how to use various encyclopedias and are undoubtedly familiar at least with the purpose and organization of *Readers' Guide*. It is the objective of this unit to extend their knowledge of the research facilities of the library and to help them develop techniques of investigation that they will be able to use the rest of their lives. Particularly in college, students will be called upon to write long papers based on library materials, and they will find the disciplines taught in this unit invaluable.

Students should always avail themselves of the help of a librarian, but they should gradually become independent and be able to carry through an investigation with a minimum of help.

GENERAL TEACHING SUGGESTIONS

Pages 118-121   **1. The Research Topic**

Pages 118-119   *Selecting a Topic*

Topics selected for research should be within the scope of eleventh-graders' interests and capabilities. If possible, include topics about which there is open difference of opinion available to the students doing the investigating. Subjects which are purely biographical should be eliminated, except, perhaps, for slower students.

Pages 119-121   *Limiting the Topic*

Students should be advised against assuming too great a task. A small canvas is infinitely better than a large mural for the beginner in research. Since a paper of this kind should be limited to 1,000–1,500 words, the topic must be carefully restricted. Purely technical subjects, straight biographical subjects—in fact any subject that will result only in an amassing of facts—are probably not good topics for papers. In Exercise A on page 120, search for aspects of the broad subject matter that will interest students, that will be workable, and that will promote some controversy.

Exercise B on page 121 begins a series of cumulative exercises that culminate in the writing of a research paper.

Pages 121-138   **2. Doing Research**

Pages 121-129   **Library Resources**

Students will not be able to master all this material at once. They should be brought together in the library or in a special room near the library, and the librarian or the teacher should acquaint them with as many of these resources as possible. They should, if possible, have time to open the vertical files and to look through some of the reference books.

Students will find that the bibliography on pages 122-128 will prove invaluable as they do research. Exercise C on page 129 will insure the students' at least scanning the annotations and acquiring some knowledge of the contents of various references.

Pages 130-134   *The Working Bibliography*

After class time has been spent studying the correct way to prepare bibliography cards, students should carry out Exercise B on p. 134, another of the cumulative exercises. Emphasize the fact that students are to find every available source of information on their topics. Insist upon absolute accuracy in making out bibliography cards. There are many different methods of preparing bibliography cards; the system employed in this unit is one that is widely accepted. Whatever system you use, insist that students follow it consistently. Let the student understand that he may add to his cards as he finds new material or that he may discard a reference if the material later turns out to be unusable.

Pages 134-138   Reading and Taking Notes

If time permits, work with students in developing techniques of skimming. One way of doing this is to have students skim a page from one of their textbooks and list the main ideas without again referring to the page. Follow this procedure by having students reread for details and take notes. Each student should have practice in writing direct quotation cards, précis cards, and abbreviated summary cards so that when he comes to the actual reading and taking of notes on his project, he will know how to proceed.

Exercise C on page 137 is another of the cumulative exercises leading to the writing of the research paper.

Pages 138-152   3. Writing the Paper

Pages 138-140   Preparing an Outline

If students have been systematic and consistent in preparing their note cards, they should have no difficulty in working out an outline. It is suggested that the procedures described on pages 138-139 be followed step by step. Emphasize the importance of the statement of theme. When the student knows the direction his paper is to take, he will be better able to develop an outline. Point out to students that the preliminary outline may undergo changes as the writing of the paper progresses, but that a basic outline must be prepared before any writing of the paper is done.

Exercise A on page 140 provides preliminary practice in outlining; Exercise B is another in the series of cumulative exercises.

Pages 140-142   Writing a First Draft

If your schedule does not allow time for the actual writing of a research paper, you may wish to study the remainder of the unit, beginning with this section, without requiring the completion of the paper. Students will at least have learned and practiced the techniques involved in carrying out a research project.

For classes in which this paper is to be written, Exercise B on page 142 is another in the series of cumulative exercises. If note taking and outlining have been well executed, the writing of the first draft of the paper will be comparatively easy. Emphasize the importance of students' completing the first draft without interruptions if possible. Caution students about the slavish imitation of the style of the authors they have used; demand, rather, the students' own words and phrasing. Students should understand the purpose of and need for footnotes.

Pages 142-143   Making Revisions

You may wish to prepare a check list based on the material included in this section of the unit. This list will call the student's attention to those things which he should keep in mind while making revisions. Stress the importance of reading the paper several times, each time for a different purpose. The habit of good copy reading will prove invaluable to the student in his writing of all future papers.

Exercise B on page 143 is another of the series of cumulative exercises for classes in which the research paper is to be written.

Pages 143-150   Preparing the Final Draft

Assembling the final paper should not be difficult if each of the previous steps has been carried out effectively. The major difficulty will be the tendency on the part of some students to leave the work until the final moment and then rush through it, with the result that the paper will be hurriedly assembled and will be filled with numerous mechanical errors. This situation can be avoided if the teacher can find the time to check the research project at each step.

The sample pages on pages 146-149 will provide students with a model for key sections of their own papers. Exercise B on page 149 represents the final step in the series of cumulative exercises for classes in which the research paper is to be written.

Pages 150-152   End-of-Unit Material

For suggestions for adminstering the end-of-unit material, see pages T10-T11 of the teachers' edition.

Unit 7—Creative Writing

BACKGROUND AND INTEREST

As students become more aware of and alert to the world of ideas, they should better understand the enthusiasm that writers feel for ideas. They will, in their study of other writings and in their own attempts to create, learn to have an appreciation of language—of its power to move the emotions or to convince the intellect—and they will sense its beauty.

Read the introduction to this unit aloud, stopping after each paragraph for discussion of the points made. Students may question the statement in the last paragraph on page 153 that creative writing is largely self-taught. This is an important point. One can be taught the terminology and the techniques of creative writing, and one can be exposed to models of good creative writing; but fluency and skill come only through one's own awareness and application.

GENERAL TEACHING SUGGESTIONS

Pages 155-160   1. The World Around You

Pages 155-156   *Wake Up Your Senses*

Two rules for successful writing have to do with awareness: the senses must be alert, and the familiar must be the source of inspiration. Create in the classroom as many opportunities as possible for training the sensory faculties of your students. For example, one student might describe a classmate without identifying him and call on someone to make the identification. A blindfold test might be used for the identification and description of odors such as fruits, cleaning supplies, and so on. The blindfold test might also be used to test tactile sensitivity. Students will probably be eager to suggest other sense tests. In all these tests the important thing is not the correct identification of the person or thing involved but the vivid verbalization of the impression received.

Pages 156-160   *Write About the Familiar*

Students frequently feel that if they draw upon their own experiences, they must relate those experiences exactly as they happened. The discussion and example on pages 157-159 are designed to show students that compatible elements of different situations may be combined.

The exercises on page 160 are designed to make students base their writing upon their own experiences and observations.

Pages 161-172   2. Informal Prose

Informal prose writing, such as the letter, the diary, and the essay, is spontaneous and personal. It is the kind of writing which most students will do in their adult life. It should therefore occupy a great share of the time that students devote to writing.

Pages 161-163   *The Letter Writer*

Difficulties always arise in teaching the letter-writing technique. Students are sometimes self-conscious about writing to non-existent people or they may resent having their personal letters read by the teacher or by classmates. Using real situations wherever possible will help to overcome the problem of self-consciousness. The teacher-student'and the student-student rapport in each class will determine what approach you can take to having letters read aloud and discussed in class.

Pages 163-166   *The Diarist*

Point out to students that despite the dangers inherent in using the diary form for creative writing, the diary can be restrained, thoughtful and effective. You may wish to introduce the term *journal* before students carry out the exercises on page 166. Using the diary or journal form will force the student to look inward and draw from his own experiences the material for composition. The more he looks, the more he will discover about himself.

Pages 166-172   *The Essayist*

The essay, whether informal or formal, will introduce form into the student's writing. Unlike the letter or the diary entry, the essay has more evident structure: there is a beginning, a middle, and an end. The intention of the writer can be discerned at all times. The essay can be personal and not differ greatly from the diary, except that the writer knows he has an audience that he is trying to please, to cajole, to frighten, to dismay, or to influence in some other way.

Before students attempt the exercise on page 169, discuss with them the importance of naturalness in humor. Humor that is strained is not effective. You may wish to make this exercise optional.

Pages 173-180   3. Poetry

Pages 173-174   Awareness

The training for writing poetry starts at the same place as that for writing prose—with awareness. As the study of poetry progresses, students should recognize the differences in language and interpretation that distinguish poetry from prose.

Pages 174-176   Compression

The use of compression is the poet's secret. He can say much in few words. Along with the Japanese *haiku* given in this unit, you may wish to use Carl Sandburg's poem "Fog," which was inspired by his reading of these short lyrics. Discuss at length the effect of understatement in poetry. In carrying out Exercise C on page 176, emphasize effective language rather than form.

Pages 176-180   Form

Just as the essay introduced the element of form into the writing of prose, the use of stanzas, meter, and rhyme bring the concept of form and structure to the writing of poetry. The elements studied here are not too complex to be mastered by eleventh graders; in fact, with some classes the teacher may wish to amplify the study of form by introducing other stanzas and other elements of prosody.

Pages 180-182   End-of-Unit Material

For suggestions for administering the end-of-unit material, see pages T10-T11 of the teachers' edition.

Unit 8—Sentence Skill

BACKGROUND AND INTEREST

The grammar of the sentence is the basic material for Unit 8. Part 1 deals with the structure of sentences; Part 2, with aspects of style: completeness, clarity, and unity.

The nomenclature employed in this unit on grammar is conventional. There is no introduction of new terms to confuse students already brought up on traditional grammar. The purpose of this unit is to make those traditional terms and their applications clear and understandable to eleventh-grade students. The authors of *Using Good English* have thought it wise to preserve the fundamental outlines of traditional grammar, at the same time recognizing many of the principles of the new approaches to grammar wherever possible. The aim has been to give a solid body of information about the language and to create a solid background upon which later studies of linguistics can be based.

The teacher will find the Key to the Handbook on pages 183-190 useful as a time-saver in the correction of student themes. Suppose, for example, that a student has written the following sentence, which contains four major errors:

> John and me hadn't went a mile before he suddenly griped my arm, the look on his face startled me.

The possibilities for marking the errors are many. The teacher could cross out the error and write in the correct form. Not only is this time-consuming, but students tend to look at the correction without learning the reason for it. A second technique would involve writing in the margin *case of pronoun used as subject, past participle used with auxiliary, spelling, comma splice.* This method indicates to the student what types of errors he has made but does not lead him to a means of understanding how to correct his errors. Many teachers save time by using a system of symbols. For the example being used to illustrate this point, the symbols might read, in order, *gr, gr, sp, ss.* The student would know that he had made two errors in grammar, one in spelling, and one in sentence structure. He would not necessarily know how to proceed to correct the errors. Using the Handbook Key, the teacher would mark the errors *35, 27, 54d, 57n.* By referring to the Key, the student would be directed to the page on which an explanation of the error is given. Following the rule will be examples and exercises. The Handbook Key, then, not only saves the teacher time but also leads the student to the information necessary for correcting his errors. Teachers will find that, with use, the rule numbers will be learned quickly. Since the same numbers are used to refer to these rules in all the books in Grades 9-12, teachers and students will not be faced with a completely new set of numbers each year. Only additional numbers for new material have been introduced in the later books.

GENERAL TEACHING SUGGESTIONS

Pages 193-283   1. Structure in Sentences

Pages 193-221   *Subjects and Predicates*

The organization of the unit is such that related grammatical topics are presented together as a way of relating the study of grammar more closely to the actual problems of speaking and writing. The study of subjects and predicates, for example, includes the study of nouns, pronouns, verbs and their related subtopics.

Students should already be familiar with most of the material presented in the study of nouns and pronouns (pages 197-204), although some new rules have been added. The teacher will have to determine from his knowledge of his classes which material the students can review on an individual basis, which must be reviewed in class, which must be retaught, and which must be presented as new grammatical concepts. In teaching pronouns, stress the basic assumption underlying the use of most pronouns: that they are substitutes in a relatively complex language for nouns that have been explicitly stated or implied in previous conversation or writing. Just how far the teacher will wish to go in teaching all the aspects of the verb presented on pages 204-220 will depend upon the make-up of the class. Some students will find the subjunctive too difficult to cope with. If this is the case, the teacher may wish to limit the study of the subjunctive to one or two common examples of present day usage.

Diagraming is a mechanical device used to illustrate the structure of sentences. It should not be used as an end in itself; but, carefully handled, it will make clear to students the fundamental structures of English sentences that no amount of finger pointing and verbal analyzing can accomplish. The great danger in diagraming is that students may be led to believe that every English sentence can be so analyzed, and the teacher will have to be ready with the explanation that modern usage, informal idiom, and invention of writers often make scientific analysis very difficult. Basically, English sentences are capable of such diagramatic analysis; there are, however, sentences that defy such analysis.

Pages 222-232   *Modifiers*

Students should understand single adjectives and adverbs before any attempt is made to teach the larger modifying units. Emphasize the point made on page 222 that there are only two parts of speech that modify—adjectives and adverbs—and that any word or word group that modifies performs the function of one of these two parts of speech.

By working from the precept that the use of a word in a sentence determines its part of speech, you can make clear to students the difference between parts of speech out of context and parts of speech in context—for example, a pronoun and a pronominal adjective (adj.) and a noun and an adverbial objective (adv.).

Pages 233-240   Complements

Stress the meaning of the word *complement*—a word that completes the meaning of a verb that, in itself, does not carry out a completed action or predication. Complements that follow linking verbs are easiest to recognize when taught with the verb *be,* which should be studied in all its forms so that students will recognize it immediately. Extend your teaching to include forms of verbs such as *seem, become, appear, grow, remain, sound, feel, taste,* and *smell.* Point out distinctions such as *He grew tall* (predicate adjective) and *He grew rapidly* (adverb). The retained object is a usage that students tend to employ naturally. Emphasize the point made on page 238 that, while the retained object completes the meaning of a passive verb, the subject of the sentence receives the action of the passive verb.

Pages 240-247   Connectives

The proper and exact use of connectives lends clarity and vigor to both oral and written expression. This is particularly true of conjunctions, which are the links that promote or destroy the logical progressions of ideas. Spend considerable time in class on the precise meanings of all the conjunctions; for example, the difference between *and* and *but* and the fine shades of distinction between *while* and *as,* between *since* and *while,* and between *however* and *nevertheless.* After students have completed Exercise B on page 247, discuss with them the differences in meaning produced by combining the sentences with various conjunctions.

Pages 247-249   Appositives

Appositives are parenthetical in nature, always following a noun or pronoun that needs further explanation. The exercise on page 249 illustrates the degree of separation that exists between the noun or pronoun and the appositive. Discuss the reasons for the punctuation (or lack of punctuation) in each case.

Pages 249-262   Clauses in Sentences

Be sure that students are clear regarding the nomenclature of this section. You may wish to point out that the terms *independent* and *main* clause are interchangeable, as are *dependent* and *subordinate* clause. Adjective clauses will be easiest for students to identify and to use in their writing. One possible difficulty in identification may arise in the use of the subordinating conjunctions *where, when,* and *why,* which ordinarily carry adverbial connotations. When these conjunctions are used to introduce clauses that limit or describe a preceding noun or pronoun, the subordinate clauses are to be considered adjectival in function. Other difficulties in teaching the dependent clause are to be found in the omitted relative pronoun or in the use of a preposition preceding the relative pronoun *(to whom, upon which,* etc.). Elliptical adverb clauses may give some difficulty, also, until the student learns to complete the intended predication of the clause. Noun clauses are most easily taught by observing that the pronoun *it, him,* or *her* can usually be substituted for the complete clause. Emphasize the point made on page 260 that a noun clause is always part of an independent clause.

Pages 262-273   Phrases in Sentences

In structure, phrases may be classified as verbal or prepositional. In function they may be used as nouns, adjectives, or adverbs. Students have little difficulty with prepositional phrases but often encounter trouble with verbals. Since the exercises move from the study of individual verbals into phrases containing verbals, the student should have little difficulty if he pays attention to each step of the development in the text. The chart on page 269, the diagraming exercises that follow, and the Developing Your Skill exercises on page 273 are arranged for the cumulative effect of helping the student to achieve mastery of this aspect of grammar.

Pages 274-276   Inverted Order

As a stylistic device to secure variety in sentence patterns, inverted order is sometimes desirable. In older, more rhetorical days, the practice was perhaps more prevalent than it is today, but inverted order is still common, and students will find that the ability to vary the patterns of sentences will help make their style supple and interesting. The chief reason for the study of inverted order, however, is to make the student conscious of the subject-verb relationship in such sentences so that he will avoid the solecism of mixing singular and plural subjects and predicates. Emphasize the point that sentences to be analyzed or diagramed should be restated in natural order.

Pages 276-277   *Elliptical Sentences*

Elliptical sentences are intentional on the part of the author when he seeks the informality of conversational speech. They are not to be confused with fragments that spring from ignorance of grammatical construction. Except for grammatically correct elliptical sentences, such as those illustrated under rule 1 on pages 276-277, the use of either elliptical or fragmentary sentences should be limited to creative writing in which the writer is reproducing the exact speech of characters in informal dialogue.

Pages 278-281   *Independent Elements*

Interjections and words in direct address do not have direct grammatical relationship to any other words in a sentence. They are therefore thought of as being independent. Such is the case, too, with the absolute expression. Since the absolute expression is rapidly passing out of use in modern English, students should be warned against using such expressions, except perhaps in formal situations such as reports or reviews. The use of a subordinate clause is preferable in modern informal style. Students should, however, be able to identify the absolute expression.

Pages 283-295   2. Style in Sentences

Since the aim of the study of grammar is better speech and better writing, this study of style in sentences comes appropriately after the study of the formal aspects of grammar.

Pages 283-285   *Completeness in Sentences*

This topic has already been mentioned in the study of elliptical sentences on pages 276-277. It is introduced here as a further incentive to students to establish good habits of speech and writing and to eliminate the too casual and awkward expressions that often occur when sentences are not complete. The exercise on page 285 requires that students not only recognize sentence fragments but also correct such fragments by rewriting them as complete sentences.

Pages 286-293   *Clarity in Sentences*

Grammatical correctness is no assurance of good style. The student who has learned to write grammatically correct sentences is now ready to learn some of the refinements of style that will lend clarity to his writing. The student must avoid wordiness, trite expressions, misplaced and dangling modifiers, and illogical constructions. This section of the unit on style is very important and should not be slighted. Exercises A and B on page 289 afford practice in writing concise sentences; the exercises on pages 291-292 and 293, in writing clear and logical sentences.

Pages 293-294   *Unity in Sentences*

Effective writing demands close attention to the principle of unity. A sentence must be thought of as a unit in which one main purpose is achieved. Proper co-ordination between sentence elements; proper subordination when one element is less important than another or when there is a logical cause and effect relationship between the parts; complete separation when the parts of a statement are not related—these are principles of unity which every student must master in order to develop a mature style of writing.

Pages 295-300   *End-of-Unit Material*

For suggestions for administering the end-of-unit material, see pages T10-T11 of the teachers' edition.

You may wish to duplicate the chart on page 296 or have students copy it into their notebooks. This summary chart will prove helpful in demonstrating to students the relationships among single words, phrases, and clauses that function interchangeably in sentences.

Unit 9—Usage Skills

BACKGROUND AND INTEREST

Language is a part of man's social inheritance. People tend to speak as they live—or as they would like to live—and correct usage varies according to the time, the place, and the occasion. The form of English that is suitable in most instances is the form usually referred to as *informal usage;* yet there are times—and students must recognize this injunction—when formal English is the only kind that is suitable. The authors of *Using Good English* have tried to avoid as many dilemmas as possible for both teacher and student and, at the same time, have tried to present a realistic picture of the language as it is used, both in written and oral usage. When discussing the Check Yourself exercise on pages 301-302, you may wish to point out to students that the level for which they should strive is that of standard usage—the forms accepted and used by most educated persons.

GENERAL TEACHING SUGGESTIONS

Pages 302-319   1. Usage in Sentences

Pages 302-306   *Subject-Verb Agreement*

Errors in subject-verb agreement spring largely from poor speech habits. Where students have had a good background of speech patterns, no problem should arise, and much of this unit may be used solely for review and reference. Where errors are frequent, the teacher should make every effort to establish correct habits of oral and written usage. Every rule should be discussed; additional sentences should be invented to illustrate the principles; constant repetition and practice should be made part of the English program until the patterns become fixed.

Pages 307-310   *Pronoun-Antecedent Agreement*

As with subject-verb agreement, the amount of teaching, review, and practice necessary will vary according to the backgrounds and abilities of the class. Mastery of clear pronoun reference and pronoun-antecedent agreement is essential to mature use of language. After students have written the exercise on page 310, you may wish to discuss with your students the reasons for the changes made in the sentences.

Pages 310-318   *Other Usage Problems*

Here again the key to success lies in the habit of correct speech. When areas of difficulty are discovered, the teacher should direct students to exercises for practice in using the correct forms. You may wish to use the exercises on pages 313, 314, 316, 317-318, and 318-319 for oral as well as written practice.

Pages 319-341   2. Specific Word Forms

Pages 319-322   *Troublesome Pronouns*

The *who-whom* problem is difficult for some students. The approach in this section is through an analysis of the grammatical construction of the sentence. Before teaching the material in this section, review with students the parts of the sentence, the functions of words in sentences, and the principles of agreement. The exercise on pages 321-322 may be used for both written and oral practice.

Pages 322-327   *Troublesome Verbs*

The main verbs and auxiliaries discussed on these pages are those that cause the most difficulty in usage. As with other usage problems, provide as many opportunities as possible for oral practice. Students frequently learn to write the correct forms but continue to use the incorrect forms in speaking. Ear training, then, is necessary. When the ear recognizes the correct forms, errors will cease. The *shall-will* and *should-would* distinctions discussed on pages 325-326 have almost entirely disappeared in informal usage. You may wish to omit the teaching of these fine distinctions with slower classes. More advanced students, however, should be aware of the differences in usage.

Pages 327-328   *Troublesome Modifiers*

Many of the usages presented on these pages as substandard and illiterate are frequently heard in informal usage and in the speech of some radio and TV performers. You may wish to point out to students that these forms have not yet been accepted into the standard vocabulary of English usage and, therefore, must still be considered substandard.

Pages 329-331   *Troublesome Connectives*

The emphasis here is on the use of easily confused prepositions and idiomatic propositional phrases. Each rule should be discussed thoroughly and then practiced until students use the forms easily and naturally. If you have any foreign-born students in your classes, they will probably need special help in the use of idioms. The same connectives are often used in different ways in different languages. Again the approach should be through oral example and repetition wherever students have difficulty.

Pages 331-340 Easily Confused Words

These words are demons in the English language. Pronunciation, recognition of the fine distinctions in meanings, and attention to spelling will make these words clear. Stress the point made on page 331 that the only way to overcome difficulties in the use of such words is to master each word. The definitions and examples are arranged to serve as a ready reference for both teachers and students.

Pages 341-344 End-of-Unit Material

For suggestions for administering the end-of-unit material, see pages T10-T11 of the teachers' edition.

Unit 10—Mechanics In Writing

BACKGROUND AND INTEREST

Students may argue that the mechanics of writing are not nearly so important as the ideas expressed in the writing. Thus they try to excuse their poor manuscript, careless spelling, improper capitalization, faulty punctuation, and incorrect syllabication. Now is the time to disabuse them of any such idea.

Form in writing is absolutely essential to clarity. Discuss with your students the ideas presented in the introduction on page 345. The Check Yourself exercises on pages 346-347 will help teachers to decide which areas of the mechanics of writing need only to be reviewed and which must be developed in detail.

GENERAL TEACHING SUGGESTIONS

Pages 347-360 1. Form in Writing

This section deals with paragraphs, outlining, and letter writing, in all of which form is important. Stress the point that the form of the writing indicates the writer's plan to the reader.

Pages 348-349 Paragraphs

Surprisingly, some students in the eleventh grade continue to make errors in the simple rules of what constitutes a paragraph. Insist on margins, indention, and a single topic. The jumbled paragraph on page 349 can be worked out in class, then written neatly and correctly on paper. The clues to solving the puzzle of the jumbled paragraph lie in the transition words and phrases.

Pages 349-353   Outlines

Students should learn the difference between sentence and topic outlines, the correct use of numbers and letters in outlines, and the consistent use of periods after each number and letter. Make clear the idea of parallelism in outlining. You may wish to teach this section in conjunction with the section on outlining the research paper on pages 138-140.

Pages 353-360   Letter Writing

A trial letter form, in which the student simply fills in the heading, inside address, salutation, and complimentary close, will tell you whether your students need a refresher course in letter-writing form. You may wish to use one of the exercises on page 360 for this purpose. If students put punctuation in the wrong places, use a semicolon after the salutation, or omit the comma after the complimentary close, review the material in this section carefully.

Pages 361-368   2. Spelling

In addition to the spelling words at the end of each unit, this section stresses some principles that, if applied thoroughly, will help a student to improve his spelling. Some students seem to be naturally poor spellers, but experience shows that when they make up their minds to improve their spelling, they can do it. The procedures suggested on page 361 will help students develop habits that will enable them to spell more accurately. Special provision should be made for poor spellers to practice. Students who are good spellers may be asked to volunteer to work with those who need help. It is important that students who help others be able to pronounce words correctly and have an understanding of syllabication and of the spelling rules.

Pages 368-376   3. Capitalization

A short test may tell you which of your students still have trouble with capitalization. It may be that your students can omit parts of this section entirely or simply review some parts by themselves. Slower classes will probably need the full treatment given in this section. All classes can use this section for reference. Point out to students the fact that not all publishing and printing houses use exactly the same style of capitalization, but that essentially the practice of capitalization in English language publications follows the rules prescribed in this text.

Pages 376-414   4. Punctuation

Punctuation, like capitalization, is a printer's device to make writing clear; it improves communication and should therefore be presented as an essential part of written composition. The introduction to this section on pages 376-377 is worth reading aloud and discussing in class. Emphasize the last paragraph of the introduction, particularly the last sentence—"Overpunctuation is just as bad as too little punctuation."

Pages 377-390   Comma

The comma is not only the most used of all punctuation marks but is also often the most misused. Students tend to use commas indiscriminately, particularly when the comma is equated with a pause in speaking. Unless you plan to present a detailed discussion of juncture, it is suggested that the approach to the teaching of the comma be solely from the point of view of logical meaning and clarity.

You will, of course, want to make the teaching of punctuation functional by correlating it with the work in writing. You may also want to correlate the teaching of specific rules with the teaching of other areas of language study; for example, rule 57b with the teaching of adverbial clauses, rule 57c with the teaching of verbal phrases, rule 57d with the teaching of prepositional phrases, and so on. The material on restrictive and nonrestrictive elements on pages 383-385 should be carefully developed.

Pages 391-393   Semicolon

As it is most frequently used, the semicolon connects two or more parts of a balanced structure. Students should understand that the use of a semicolon instead of a conjunction and a comma should be a deliberate choice. The semicolon should be used to connect ideas that are so closely related that they belong in the same sentence but that would be weakened by the use of a co-ordinating conjunction. Point out to students that two independent clauses that are linked only by a semicolon could also be written as two simple sentences, but that the ideas frequently lose force when they are separated. Point out, too, that the substitution of a semicolon for a co-ordinating conjunction and a comma can lend greater force to ideas. Illustrate by writing two closely related clauses in all three ways.

Where semicolons are used for clarity, as in rules 58b, 58c, and 58d, illustrate the reason for their use by substituting commas for the semicolons in the example sentences.

Pages 393-395   Colon

The colon is a formal type of punctuation mark. It is associated with lists of things introduced by formal expressions; it is used in formal letters, but not in friendly letters; it is used in certain conventional usages to indicate chapter and verse, clock time, etc. More subtle is the use of the colon to indicate that what is to follow is an explanation of what has just been said. In this last usage students must understand that there is a difference between the semicolon used in balanced structure and the colon used to introduce a conclusion, a result, or an effect.

Pages 395-399   End Punctuation

End, or terminal, punctuation offers few difficulties for most students. The new concepts introduced in this unit include the use of the period in an ellipsis and the use of the question mark to indicate a doubt concerning a statement which has been made and the use of the question mark after elliptical questions in a series. These uses of punctuation should give the average student no trouble after he has studied the rules and the examples.

Pages 400-403   Quotation Marks

The chart suggested on page 400 should be used frequently to give students a graphic picture of the different kinds of sentence patterns that involve quotation marks. A new rule in this section involves the use of quotation marks to enclose words used in a special sense. Emphasize the point made on page 402 that this usage should not be overdone.

Pages 403-405   Apostrophe

The apostrophe, strictly speaking, is an adjunct of spelling, rather than a punctuation mark, but since so many errors are made even by good students, the apostrophe should receive considerable attention. The use of the apostrophe in spelling is discussed in greater detail on pages 226-227 of the text.

Pages 406-407   Dash

The dash is a very useful mark of punctuation, but it should not be over-worked. In very informal prose it can be used to approximate the informal patterns of conversation, but in formal writing it should be used sparingly.

Pages 407-408   Hyphen

The hyphen is most often used as a printer's device to divide a word at the end of a line or it is used as a spelling aid in forming compound words. The use of the hyphen within words is rather fluid, and students should consult recent dictionaries for the most recent authority in spelling, particularly for compound words.

Pages 409-410   Italics (Underlining)

Stress the point made on page 409 that underlining in handwritten and typewritten material corresponds to italic type in printed material. You may wish to teach the use of italics in conjunction with the research unit.

Pages 410-412   Parentheses

Parentheses have a wide variety of uses, from informal personal essays to formal research-type treatises. The examples should be studied carefully. Emphasize the discussion of punctuation of parenthetical material on pages 410-411.

Pages 412-413   Brackets

Students should learn the two main uses for brackets, particularly before they write a long investigative paper.

Pages 414-416   Syllabication

If your students have not learned the principles of syllabication, they should concentrate on the rules discussed here. These rules are basic to correct syllabication and are almost infallible. Emphasize the point made on page 414 that one should avoid carrying over fewer than three letters when dividing a word.

Pages 417-422   End-of-Unit Material

For suggestions for administering the end-of-unit material, see pages T10-T11 of the teachers' edition.

3. Unit Tests

Unit Test

Unit 1—Movies and Stage Plays

A. Read each of the following statements. If the statement is true, write *T* in the space that precedes the number; if the statement is false, write *F* in the space.

  F   1. A good reviewer limits his comments to the plot and the acting.

  T   2. Several reviews should be compared before one makes a decision about seeing a movie or play.

  F   3. Reviewers' comments quoted in advertisements are a good guide for selecting movies and plays.

  F   4. The story of a movie or play is always of primary importance.

  F   5. Characters in good movies and plays are easily recognizable stereotypes.

  T   6. The director is involved in all phases of a production.

  F   7. A cameraman is concerned solely with achieving unusual effects.

  T   8. The background elements of a movie or play help to develop the mood or atmosphere.

  T   9. A good movie or stage-play story presents some significant truth about man.

  F 10. There should be no moments of silence in a good movie or play.

B. On the line preceding each of the following statements about movies and plays, write whether the statement is a standard for evaluating the *story, direction, acting, photography,* or *background.*

  background   1. The settings are appropriate to the cultural, social, and financial status of the characters in the story.

  story   2. The theme is interesting and significant.

  acting   3. The interpretation is natural and believable.

  story   4. Interest is maintained throughout by a series of conflicts leading directly to a climax and a logical ending.

  direction   5. There is evidence that both the stars and the supporting actors were chosen for their fitness for the roles.

  photography   6. Long shots and close-ups are used to increase interest.

  background   7. Sound and music are used for their dramatic value.

  story   8. The characters and situations are not hackneyed.

  acting   9. Characterization is consistent throughout.

  background 10. Costumes are appropriate and authentic.

Unit Test

Unit 2—Listening

A. In the space that precedes each of the numbered definitions, write the term from the following list to which the definition applies.

melody	notes	unison	informational
refrain	antiphonal	tempo	sequential
part	choral speaking	imagery	appreciative
theme	transitional	poetry	mood

informational   1. The kind of listening that is done to acquire facts.

notes   2. A record of key words and phrases.

theme   3. The central idea of a speech.

transitional   4. Words and phrases such as *first, second, as a result*.

poetry   5. Rhythmic language that appeals to the emotions.

choral speaking   6. The oral group interpretation of poetry.

refrain   7. The kind of group speaking in which a soloist tells the story and the entire group responds in the chorus.

antiphonal   8. Two-part speaking.

sequential   9. This kind of group speaking is particularly appropriate for selections that present a series of ideas, images, or experiences.

part   10. The kind of group speaking whose arrangement is comparable to an orchestral arrangement.

imagery   11. Word pictures in poetry.

melody   12. The flow of consonants and vowels in poetry.

mood   13. The feeling produced by the rhythm, melody, and tempo of the lines in poetry.

appreciative   14. Listening whose primary purpose is enjoyment.

unison   15. The kind of speaking in which an entire group speaks as one person.

B. In the space preceding each of the following, write whether one listens primarily for *main ideas* or for *details* in the specific listening situations.

details   1. Listening to assignments

main ideas   2. Listening to class lectures

details   3. Listening to announcements

details   4. Listening to directions

main ideas   5. Listening to speeches

Unit Test

Unit 3—Discussion and Debate

A. Complete the following statements by writing the appropriate words in the blanks.

   1. A **round-table** discussion is best suited to small groups.
   2. A discussion in which the audience participates following a direct speech is called a **forum**.
   3. The participants in a **panel** discussion direct all their remarks to the other participants but keep their audience in mind.
   4. A contest in which formal arguments are presented for and against a proposal is called a **debate**.
   5. In a **symposium** each speaker is usually an authority on one phase of the subject under discussion.

B. Place a check (✔) in front of those resolutions that are debatable.

   ____ 1. Resolved: That higher education should be compulsory.
   ✔ 2. Resolved: That a single international language be adopted.
   ____ 3. Resolved: That time should not be taken from the school day for athletics; however, athletics is important.
   ____ 4. Resolved: That the jury system should not be abolished.
   ✔ 5. Resolved: That the school year be extended to twelve months.

C. In the space preceding each of the terms in the left-hand column, write the letter of the definition in the right-hand column that best applies.

d	1. proposition	a. sufficient evidence for accepting a proposition
h	2. brief	
a	3. proof	b. the team that supports the proposition
i	4. rebuttal	c. reasoning from a generalization to a specific instance
b	5. affirmative	
j	6. negative	d. a formal statement of a debate subject
e	7. inductive reasoning	e. reasoning from specific instances to a generalization
c	8. deductive reasoning	
f	9. syllogism	f. a form of reasoning in which a logical conclusion is drawn from two premises
g	10. hasty generalization	g. a general statement based on too few observations
		h. an outline of arguments and evidence
		i. argument to answer opposing argument
		j. the team that opposes the argument

Unit Test

Unit 4—Words and Meanings

A. In the space preceding each of the following statements, write the name of the process of language change described.

elevation	1. Words acquire more favorable meanings.
transference	2. Words go through a series of changes that result in additional meanings.
degeneration	3. Words acquire less favorable meanings.
specialization	4. Word meanings move from broad to narrow.
generalization	5. Limited word meanings become more general.

B. Write a single concrete word that could be applied to the entire group of words in each of the following lists.

vegetable(s)	1. celery, carrot, green pepper, lettuce, asparagus
spice(s)	2. ginger, cinnamon, black pepper, cloves, paprika
meat(s)	3. steak, veal, lamb chops, ground beef, mutton
fabric(s)	4. silk, linen, nylon, wool, cotton
tool(s)	5. saw, hammer, drill, plane, awl

C. Select the word from the parentheses that will make the sentence correct and write it in the blank that precedes the sentence.

of	1. No one has ever died (with, of) that ailment.
in	2. The children were completely absorbed (in, by) the game they were playing.
with	3. Their uniforms are almost identical (with, to) ours.
at	4. Was there anybody (to, at) home when you called?
from	5. I always find it difficult to part (with, from) friends.
of doing	6. He is capable (to do, of doing) that job well.
from	7. Your ideas have always been different (from, than) mine.
over	8. Jean and Dianne differed (with, over) the plans.
of cutting	9. We used a new method (to cut, of cutting) patterns.
graduating from	10. My sister is (graduating, graduating from) college this year.
for	11. Please wait (for, on) me after school.
with	12. As compared (to, with) you, I am short.
with	13. I shall comply (to, with) your request at once.
of	14. They are going out in search (of, for) wild flowers.
to go	15. I plan (to go, on going) with you.

Unit Test

Unit 5—Reading for Appreciation

A. Identify each of the following figures of speech as *simile, metaphor, personification, metonymy,* or *hyperbole.*

personification	1. The leaves spoke of the end of summer.
metaphor	2. Laura has drawn back into her shell.
hyperbole	3. I am starved.
metonymy	4. Labor and management met to discuss the dispute.
metaphor	5. Her face mirrored her emotions.
simile	6. The icicles hung like unsheathed daggers.

B. Complete the following sentences by writing the appropriate words in the blanks.

1. **Irony** is the deliberate twisting of facts, events, or meanings to imply something different from what is actually said.
2. The clues an author gives to characters, events, and situations are called **foreshadowing.**
3. Another term for *point of view* is **focus of narration.**
4. The mood or **atmosphere** of a story is established through setting, characterization, plot, and the style of writing.
5. The part of a story that establishes the background is called the **exposition.**
6. **Conflict** refers to the problem to be solved in a story.
7. The point at which a story reaches its moment of greatest tension is called the **climax.**
8. A seeming contradiction that has an underlying truth is called a **paradox.**
9. The key moment, or **moment of illumination,** is that point at which all previous events come into focus and their meanings become clear.
10. The moment at which the problem has been solved and when the fate of the protagonist is clear is called the **denouement.**
11. **Sarcasm** is a device that involves the making of stinging remarks for the express purpose of wounding someone's feelings.
12. The device that holds up to ridicule mankind's vices and follies is called **satire.**
13. **Style** is everything about a piece of writing that makes the writing distinctive.
14. Before one can successfully analyze a work of fiction, one must cultivate an attitude of **suspension of disbelief.**

Unit Test

Unit 6—The Research Paper

A. List in order the five parts of a research paper.

1. **Title page**
2. **A blank page**
3. **Table of contents (outline)**
4. **Body of the paper**
5. **Bibliography**

B. Complete the following statements by writing the correct words in the blanks.

1. All the books available in a library are listed in the **card catalog**.
2. The **vertical (or clipping)** file is often the source of the most recent information on a current topic.
3. The number used on bibliography and note cards to identify a reference is called a **source number**.
4. Two kinds of notes are taken for research papers—the **summary** and the **direct quotation**.
5. An **ellipsis** in quoted material is indicated by three dots.
6. The word **sic** indicates that an error in quoted material appeared in the original.
7. Explanatory material within a direct quotation is set off by **brackets**.
8. Direct quotations and borrowed facts and opinions are credited in **footnotes** at the bottom of the page.
9. A complete list of sources used in writing a research paper is called a **bibliography**.

C. Number the following steps in preparing a research paper according to the order in which they are carried out.

  3   1. Prepare a working bibliography
10   2. Proofread
  8   3. Prepare the final draft
  5   4. Prepare an outline
  9   5. Compile the final bibliography
  2   6. Limit the topic
  6   7. Write the first draft
  4   8. Read and take notes
  1   9. Select a topic
  7 10. Make revisions

Unit Test

Unit 7—Creative Writing

A. On the line preceding each of the following descriptions, write the letter of the appropriate term from the following list.

a. letter   e. pentameter   i. meter   m. foot
b. compression   f. couplet   j. essay   n. trimeter
c. *haiku*   g. senses   k. familiar   o. diary
d. dimeter   h. rhyme scheme   l. quatrain   p. hexameter

  g   1. Stimulating these will increase your awareness of the world.
  k   2. An important characteristic of subjects for writing.
  a   3. A form of writing that depends on the personal rapport between the writer and his audience.
  o   4. A danger in using this form is that writing sometimes becomes over-emotional.
  j   5. Informal prose that has definite form.
  b   6. Understatement in poetry.
  i   7. The rhythmical arrangement of words in a line of poetry.
  m   8. A group of syllables in poetry, usually containing one accented and one or more unaccented syllables.
  h   9. The pattern in which the ends of lines of poetry rhyme.
  l 10. A four-line stanza.
  f 11. Two successive lines of poetry that rhyme with each other.
  c 12. A Japanese poetic form.
  e 13. A five-foot line of poetry.

B. In the space preceding each of the following patterns, write the name of the metrical feet illustrated.

iamb   1. ∪ /
trochee   2. / ∪
dactyl   3. / ∪ ∪
anapest   4. ∪ ∪ /

C. Assume that the following words represent the ends of lines of poetry. On the lines preceding the words, write the rhyme scheme of the two-stanza poem.

        a sight   **c** new
        b dread   **d** bold
        a right   **c** true
        b red   **d** gold

Unit Test

Unit 8—Sentence Skill

A. Draw one line under each subject and two lines under each predicate verb in the following sentences. Enclose each complement in parentheses. Above the complement write *DO* for *Direct Object, IO* for *Indirect Object, PN* for *Predicate Nominative, PA* for *Predicate Adjective, OC* for *Objective Complement* or *RO* for *Retained Object.*

1. The court <u>clerk</u> <u>read</u> the (jury) the (testimony) in question.
2. The <u>students</u> on the committee <u>will be given</u> special (badges.)
3. <u>Has</u> <u>Louise</u> <u>become</u> a (member) of the choir?
4. Never before <u>have</u> <u>I</u> <u>heard</u> (Yvonne) so (serious.)
5. My new <u>luggage</u> <u>is</u> (slim) in line and (lightweight.)

B. In the space below write a synopsis of the verb *see* in the third person singular, masculine gender, active and passive voices.

Present	he sees	he is seen
Past	he saw	he was seen
Future	he will see	he will be seen
Present Perfect	he has seen	he has been seen
Past Perfect	he had seen	he had been seen
Future Perfect	he will have seen	he will have been seen

C. In the space preceding each of the following, write the form of the verb in parentheses that will make the sentence correct.

taken	1. You should not have (take) me so seriously.
shall have read	2. By the end of the week, I (read) both books.
brought	3. He has (bring) a gift for you.
chosen	4. Have you (choose) a card yet?

D. Underscore each dependent clause in the following sentences. If the clause is used as a modifier, write the word it modifies in the space that precedes the sentence; if the clause is used as a noun, write its noun function.

ask	1. <u>When Bill calls</u>, ask him to leave a message.
one	2. The one <u>I mean</u> is on the top shelf.
objective complement	3. No one could convince him <u>that he should see his doctor about the chest pains</u>.
made	4. <u>While visiting her aunt</u>, she made many new friends.
subject	5. <u>What Claire said yesterday</u> was unfair.

Unit Test

Unit 9—Usage Skills

A. In the space preceding each of the following sentences, write the word from the parentheses that makes the sentence correct.

are	1. Neither Lou nor her sisters (is, are) going with us.
has	2. Michael, as well as Doug, (has, have) called you.
is	3. Five dollars (is, are) a lot to pay for that.
themselves	4. They decided to complete the project (themselves, theirselves).
anybody	5. Hasn't (nobody, anybody) told Ed about the meeting?
as if	6. Don't treat me (like, as if) I were a child.
Let	7. (Let's, Let) us plan the program carefully.
as	8. Have you asked for extra help (like, as) I suggested?
Who	9. (Who, Whom) do you think will be nominated?
lain	10. The broken gate has (laid, lain) there for months.
Whose	11. (Whose, Who's) coats are those?
Lend	12. (Borrow, Lend) me one of your pencils.
taught	13. Haven't you been (learned, taught) to say "Please"?
may	14. Do you think it (may, might) rain this afternoon?
take	15. When you go to the office, (bring, take) this report with you, please.

B. Some of the following sentences contain errors in usage. If a sentence is correct, write *correct* in the space preceding the sentence; if the sentence contains an error, cross out the incorrect word or words and write them correctly in the space provided.

correct	1. Several students were excepted from the final examination.
advice	2. I do not feel that I am qualified to give you ~~advise.~~
fewer	3. There are ~~less~~ members attending the meeting than there are visitors.
correct	4. The student council has already effected many worthwhile changes in the school government.
annoy	5. Please do not ~~aggravate~~ me this way.
continually	6. My little brother interrupts me ~~continuously~~ when I am trying to study.
counsel	7. Mr. Cross has been appointed ~~council~~ for the defendant.
famous	8. The pianist was internationally ~~notorious~~ for his technique.
correct	9. His speech contained numerous literary allusions.
imply	10. Do you mean to ~~infer~~ that he has been unfair?

Unit Test

Unit 10—Mechanics in Writing

A. Correct all errors in capitalization and punctuation. (1 point for each capital letter and for each punctuation mark—64 points total)

1. "I shall try to be there by 3:15," said debbie, "but I may be a little late."
2. The last address I have for dr. and mrs. gonzalez is 501 east 32 street, lansing 12, michigan.
3. "Wow!" shouted Ted. "when you talked me into running for office, I didn't think I stood a chance of winning."
4. Mrs. Barton, that is her name isnt it? will discuss three of Charles Dickens's books: a tale of two cities, oliver twist, and david copperfield.
5. Although it was a bright, sunny day, the woods appeared dark and forbidding; we therefore skirted the area.
6. He agreed to an inter-class meeting, didn't he?
7. A paragraph must have the following three essentials: (1) unity, (2) clarity, and (3) coherence.

B. Place a check (✔) in front of those words that are hyphenated only where they may be broken at the ends of lines. (1 point each)

___	1. a-long	___	6. ca-pa-ble
✔	2. spa-ghetti	✔	7. buzz-ers
___	3. fun-ction	✔	8. re-com-mend
___	4. par-all-el	___	9. pit-y
✔	5. ac-com-mo-date	✔	10. oc-cur-rence

C. Write correctly the misspelled words in the following sentences. (2 points each)

1. I apreciate you're telling me about the change in plans.
   appreciate   your
2. We were decieved by the aparrent similiarity between the two plans that were suggested.
   deceived   apparent   similarity
3. My brother-in-laws planed a suprise party for my sisters.
   brothers-in-law   planned   surprise
4. His cour, agous atitude won him everybodys respect.
   courageous   attitude   everybody's
5. The architect is makeing a minature model of the house he has designed for the Joneses.
   making   miniature

4. Audio-Visual Aids

FILMS

Corral, The Shepherd, Street to the World, The Chairmaker and the Boys, Railroaders (International Film Bureau) constitute a series of films produced by the National Film Board of Canada. These films may be used to stimulate oral and written expression. The first three films have no spoken sound and permit free range of the students' imaginations.

Improve Your Punctuation (Coronet Films) demonstrates the importance of punctuation to sentence meaning. The film discusses troublesome problems in punctuation: run-on sentences, the comma splice, commas in a series, direct quotations, and restrictive and nonrestrictive clauses.

FILMSTRIPS

Communication of Ideas and Ideals (Educational Audio Visual, Inc.), prepared by Bess Sondel, Ph.D., consists of eight filmstrips with the following titles: 1. *Relation of a Personality to Communication;* 2. *Relation of Interests to Communication;* 3. *How to Read: To Understand, Evaluate, Use;* 4. *How to Write; Four Uses of Words;* 5. *How to Converse;* 6. *How to Prepare a Speech;* 7. *How to Deliver a Speech;* 8. *Relation of Ideals to Communication.*

How to Listen (Educational Audio Visual, Inc.), prepared by Bess Sondel, Ph.D., consists of four filmstrips with the following titles: 1. *Tell the Difference Between Essentials, Details;* 2. *Discover the Purpose of a Speaker;* 3. *Tell the Difference Between Facts, Opinions;* 4. *Information; Persuasion; Propaganda.*

RECORDS

The Anatomy of Language by Morris Schrieber (Folkways) contains seven records, five of which deal with vocabulary study. The remaining two records discuss writing and reading: types of composition development, common errors in sentence structure and usage, reading and interpreting literature, recognizing an author's devices.

One Language for the World by Mario Pei (Folkways) discusses and illustrates the various languages, including constructed tongues, that have been proposed for international use.

T52

5. Bibliography

Bamman, Henry A., Ursula Hogan, and C. Greene, *Reading Instruction in the Secondary School.* New York: Longmans, Green and Company Inc. 1961.

Gordon, Edward J. and Edward S. Noyes, eds., *Essays on the Teaching of English: Reports of the Yale Conferences on the Teaching of English.* Champaign, Illinois: National Council of Teachers of English, 1960.

Laird, Charlton and Robert M. Gorrell, eds., *English As a Language: Backgrounds, Development, Usage.* New York: Harcourt, Brace and World, Inc., 1961.

Loban, Walter, Margaret Ryan, and James R. Squire, *Teaching Language and Literature.* New York: Harcourt, Brace and World, Inc., 1961.

Long, Ralph B., *The Sentence and Its Parts.* Chicago: The University of Chicago Press, 1961.

Mencken, Henry L., *The American Language,* 4th ed. New York: Alfred A. Knopf, 1960.

————, *The American Language, Supplement I.* New York: Alfred A. Knopf, 1960.

————, *The American Language, Supplement II.* New York: Alfred A. Knopf, 1960.

Mersand, Joseph, *Attitudes Toward English Teaching.* Philadelphia: Chilton Company—Book Division, 1961.

National Association of Secondary School Principals Committee on Curriculum Planning and Development, *English Language Arts in the Comprehensive Secondary School.* Champaign, Illinois: National Council of Teachers of English, 1961.

The National Interest and the Teaching of English. Champaign, Illinois: National Council of Teachers of English, 1961.

Pooley, Robert C., ed., *Perspectives on English.* New York: Appleton-Century-Crofts, Inc., 1960.

Roberts, Paul, *English Sentences.* New York: Harcourt, Brace and World, Inc., 1962.

Strom, Ingrid M., *Research in Grammar and Usage and Its Implications for Teaching Writing.* Bloomington, Indiana: Indiana University Bookstore, 1961.

6. Additional Answers

Page 3

A. The following items are of greatest value: the *stars* and the *director*, if they have established themselves in their fields and are noted for their consistent excellence in those fields; the *story*, if one can determine its worth beforehand; the recommendations of *parents*, *teachers*, and *friends*, depending upon common interests and attitudes toward movies and stage plays. The *title* of a movie or play may be misleading; *advertising* may be slanted; *"nothing else to do"* as a reason for seeing a movie or a play may indicate a limited outlook; a *double feature* is a poor reason for selecting a movie.

Page 4

B. 3. The criteria for judging various types of films and plays are different. For example, a full-length comedy must have elements that are believable, since live actors and realistic settings are usually involved; a cartoon may be pure fantasy, since it achieves its aims through animated drawings.

C. The discussion here should include more than just a listing of the elements on which the award was based. If, for example, the award was given for the story, the discussion should include the qualities that make the story an outstanding one.

Page 22

A. One listens for information when taking down *assignments*, when *directions* and *explanations* are being given, when *announcements* are being made, and when *lectures* and *speeches* are being given. Details are of primary importance in listening to assignments, directions and explanations, and announcements; main ideas are of primary importance in lectures and speeches.

B. The skills involved in informational listening include the following: active listening, organization of ideas, retention of information, writing summaries. Develop these ideas in discussion, applying each to the specific listening situations discussed in the text.

Page 27

B. After students have listened once to the poem selected for discussion, discuss with them the elements of melody, tempo, mood, and imagery for which they are to listen. Play the recording of the poem again and even a third time, if necessary. Then proceed with the discussion. Following the discussion, play the recording once more for fuller appreciation.

Page 33, Review Exercises

A. *Melody, tempo, mood* and *imagery* are the means by which the poet appeals to the senses and to the emotions and through which he reveals meaning. A greater awareness of these elements increases the listener's understanding and, therefore, appreciation of poetry.

B. Through choral interpretation of poetry one develops an awareness of what poetry is and of how the various elements combine to lend beauty and meaning to poetry. As a result, one learns to listen with greater appreciation.

C. Yeats's point, of course, is that poetry is meant to be heard. However, it must be interpreted sensitively if it is to be fully appreciated. A poor reading can destroy a poem. It is likely that most students will agree. Insist that all students give reasons for agreeing or disagreeing with Yeats.

Page 34

A. Informational listening skills are important in school and in the business and professional world. The ability to absorb, organize, and use important data is essential to success, whether the individual be a student, a laborer, an office worker, or a professional person. Appreciative listening skills broaden one's cultural outlook, whether one's interests lie with poetry, music, or one of the other oral arts.

B. Summarize ideas as they are presented and relate them to what is already known about the subject; take notes, if possible; discuss and evaluate the information acquired; write a summary of the ideas presented by a speaker. Information is usually acquired so that it may be used; without accurate retention, one cannot use what has been heard.

Page 36, Unit Self-Test

1. Assignments, directions, explanations, announcements, lectures, speeches. **4.** Attentive listening, organizing speaker's material, reducing ideas to key words and phrases, keeping up with the speaker. **5.** Notes can be used for study purposes and as a source of ideas for writing and speaking assignments. **6.** It is the conductor who keeps the group working as unit. He signals the rhythm, tempo, beginnings, pauses, and endings.

Page 42

Students should reject the following statements: 1, 2, 4, 5, 8, 9, 10. **1.** One's presence in a suburb does not prove the suburb better than the city or any other area. **2.** This is opinion, not fact. **4.** This is opinion again. **5.** This is a personal preference. **8.** While this may have validity for the person who has pets, it is not a generally applicable statement of fact. **9.** This is important to the suburbanite, but it does not make the suburbs the best place to live. **10.** Even if it were true, this fact does not make the suburbs the best place to live.

Page 43

B. The major point to be made in the composition is that all participants in a discussion must be aware of the rights of others. The point is not who can monopolize the discussion for the longest period of time but, rather, how many phases of a subject and points of view concerning the subject can be presented and analyzed.

Page 45, Review Exercises

A. Other pitfalls include the following: inattention to what others are saying, a closed mind, argument on a personal level rather than a lively exchange of opinion, lack of participation by some members of the group, a contradictory attitude, an all-knowing attitude, agreement for the sake of being agreeable, partiality on the part of the chairman, digression.

Page 46

A. 1. *Debate* means a contest in which formal arguments are presented for and against a proposal. **2.** The *affirmative* team favors the proposal. **3.** The *negative* team opposes the proposal. **4.** *Constructive speeches* are those in which both teams present arguments for and against the proposal. **5.** *Rebuttal speeches* are those in which both teams attempt to refute their opponents' arguments.

B. The major differences between group discussion and formal debate lie in the presentation of arguments. In group discussion, ideas and opinions may be exchanged freely and informally. In formal debate, opponents are restricted to a set order and must work within a given time limit.

Page 49

A. 1. This is a *debatable* proposition. Arguments for and against may be offered. **2.** *Not debatable* as stated. *Minimum* is an ambiguous term. **3.** *Not debatable* as stated. A proposition must be stated in the affirmative. **4.** *Not debatable* as stated since it incorporates two separate propositions. **5.** *Not debatable*. This proposition is too one-sided to be debatable. The affirmative would have the advantage from the start.

Page 50

A. Students must be made aware of the importance of evidence in debate. *Sufficient* is the key word. Sufficient evidence for debate means enough to counteract evidence that might be produced by the opposing team, as well as sufficient evidence to make one's point initially. The gathering of evidence involves thorough, detailed research. Pertinent, authentic, significant, and up-to-date facts are the best evidence. Opinions of recognized experts may be introduced to lend validity to the arguments presented, but should not be relied upon as proof.

Page 55

A. 1. His being well informed would depend upon the subject-matter areas in which James reads and upon his absorption of what he reads. **2.** Because Mary learned quickly, it does not necessarily follow that knitting is easily learned. **3.** One would have to know Sara's reason for not walking under ladders. Even if she were superstitious about this one thing, she would not necessarily be a superstitious person.

Page 56

4. Rhubarb does not make everyone ill. **5.** Punishment is usually deserved; it is not based upon dislike.

Page 59, Discussion Topics

D. A successful debater must be able to (1) *analyze* a proposition to determine the issues, (2) do *research*, (3) *organize* material, (4) *brief* his arguments, both constructive and rebuttal, (5) *reason* logically, (6) *think* on his feet, (7) *speak* convincingly.

Page 59, Written Work

A. Paragraphs will vary. However, the emphasis should be on discussion as a means of thinking through problems and arriving at solutions.

B. Paragraphs will vary. However, points such as learning to think critically, to reason logically, to do research, to organize material, and to speak effectively should be included.

Page 64

A. 1. They do not refer to known things. **2.** That for which a word stands. **3.** Men need symbols to communicate with each other about new concepts, discoveries, or inventions. **4.** As a new word gains widespread acceptance through usage, the word becomes a part of the language. **5.** It might indicate that thought, discovery, and invention were at a standstill. It could also signify a dying-out of the civilization of the English-speaking world.

B. *Picture window*, a large window, usually one that frames an attractive exterior view; *cold war*, a war that is carried on by means of propaganda and economic and political strategy rather than by combat; *carport*, a roofed automobile shelter, open on three sides, that extends from the side of a building; *sound* *barrier*, the sudden tremendous force that is exerted upon an aircraft as its speed approaches the speed of sound; *freeway*, an expressway on which no tolls are charged; *exurbanite*, a former city dweller who chooses to live outside the city, usually beyond the suburbs, but maintains an urban way of life; *brainwash*, to use forcible means to cause an individual to accept a set of political standards different from the ones he originally held; *fluoridate*, to use a fluoride with; *egghead*, an intellectual; *split-level*, a house so divided that the floor level in one part is about halfway between the levels of two adjoining stories; *ballistic missile*, a self-propelled missile that follows a planned trajectory and is guided in its ascent but is free-falling in its descent; *tranquilizer*, a medication designed to reduce tensions in people and in animals; *fallout*, the particles that drop through the air after a nuclear explosion; *nuclear fission*, the splitting of an atomic nucleus; *sputnik*, a man-made satellite.

Page 67

A. *Alarums* and *alarms* have the same derivation. Chesterton's distinction lies in the difference between the early meaning of *alarum*, which was the call "To arms!" and a current meaning of *alarm*, which is *a feeling of fear and apprehension*. *Villa* and *villain* both come from the same root, meaning *village*. However, *villa* has come to mean *a rather ostentatious residence* whereas *villain* has degenerated from meaning *one who lives on a farm or in a country house*, through *a low-born person*, to its present meaning of *scoundrel*. *Chivalrous* originally came from a word meaning *a horseman*.

B. 1. *Meat* originally had the general meaning of *food*. **2.** *Hypocrite* originally meant *one who played a part on a stage*. **3.** *Shoulder* originally was only the noun that refers to *the part of the body where the arm joins the trunk*. **4.** *Steward* originally meant *a sty warden* or *a house warden*. **5.** *Pastor* comes from a word whose meaning was *to pasture* or *to feed*. **6.** *Pioneer* originally meant *a foot soldier*. **7.** *Manuscript* originally meant *something written by hand*. **8.** *Villain* originally meant *one who lives on a farm or in a country house*. **9.** *Prime* meant *first*, particularly as in *prima hora*, the *first hour of the day*. **10.** *Pen* originally meant *a feather* or *a quill*.

Page 81

A. The correct use of language is usually what is appropriate to the situation. Even substandard English has its place. Slang is often used to achieve a particular effect. Other substandard usages may be appropriate in certain situations. For example, it is sometimes better to repeat a substandard usage that someone has uttered rather than risk embarrassing the individual by pointedly interjecting the standard usage. Speakers, particularly politicians, often adjust their level of language to the level employed by the members of the audience.

Page 86, Discussion Topics

A. Since the English language is constantly changing and growing, English is a living language. As the need for new words arises, such words are created to fill the need. As words become obsolete, they fall into disuse. Word meanings change through usage. The five most common means by which word meanings change are *generalization*, *specialization*, *elevation*, *degeneration*, and *transference*. Many students will probably be interested in word changes that are the result of accident. Students should cite examples studied or new examples found as a result of their study of language.

B. Since abstract words have different meanings for different people, the use of such words often generates misunderstanding. Such misunderstanding can be avoided if the speaker defines his terms.

C. Connotative meanings are sometimes used to mislead in politics, in advertising, and in other situations in which the aim is to play on the emotions. Connotative meanings may also be used to achieve effects beyond the literal meanings of words. Creative writers frequently use connotation in this way.

D. Context means the surrounding words or the situations through which words reveal their meaning. A change of context can change the meaning of a word. Students should be encouraged to cite examples other than those given in the text.

E. One must understand how language works in order to use language effectively. Discuss the importance of current usage as opposed to obsolete and archaic usage. Selectivity in the use of language is a sign of maturity. Emphasize appropriateness here. Draw from students illustrations of how various situations require the use of various levels of language.

Page 86, Written Work

A. The original meanings of the words follow: **1.** *Manufacture*, to make by hand. **2.** *Saloon*, hall. **3.** *Bank*, bench. **4.** *Undertaker*, entrepreneur. **5.** *Menial*, household. **6.** *Disease*, discomfort. **7.** *Nervous*, vigorous. **8.** *Carnival*, literally, "O flesh, farewell!" **9.** *Enthusiasm*, inspired by the gods. **10.** *Thimble*, thumb.

Page 94

A. A *simile* is a direct comparison of two unlike things that have one element in common; it is introduced by *like* or *as*. A *metaphor* is an implied comparison between unlike things. *Personification* is a particular kind of metaphor that attributes the qualities or characteristics of a human being to an abstract idea or an inanimate object. *Metonymy* is the substitution of one word for another closely associated word. *Hyperbole* is deliberate exaggeration to emphasize a point or situation or to create humor.

Page 98

A. 1. *Irony* is the deliberate twisting of facts, events, or meanings to imply something different from, sometimes even the opposite of, what is actually said. **2.** *Sarcasm* is ironical when it depends upon the reversed meaning of the words. **3.** *Satire* is a device used to criticize or ridicule mankind for his vices and his foibles. **4.** The *scope* of satire is from the gentle to the bitter, from the trifling to the momentous. **5.** A *paradox* appears to be a contradiction; the irony lies in the reversed meaning of the words.

B. The irony lies in the situation. After ten years of struggling to pay for the diamond necklace she had lost, Mathilde discovers that the jewels were paste.

C. Saxe directs his satire against woman's propensity for getting her own way; that is, for exercising her will over man. The satire in the Goldsmith quotation is obvious: dog bites man; man recovers; dog dies.

Page 99

D. 1. The paradox lies in the words *sweet sorrow*. The lovers are sorrowful at parting; yet, since they are lovers, there is sweetness in the parting. See *Romeo and Juliet*, II: 2, l. 184. **2.** The paradox lies in the seeming contradiction of *cruel* and *kind*. The reference here is to Hamlet's deliberate unkindness to Queen Gertrude, his mother. He feels he is being harsh to her for her own sake. See *Hamlet*, III:4, l. 178.

Page 115, Discussion Topics

A. Figurative language makes writing more colorful, more expressive, and more forceful. However, if the figures are strained or are trite, they can destroy rather than enhance the effectiveness of the writing.

B. Irony depends for its effect upon the deliberate twisting of facts, events, or meanings to imply something different from, sometimes even the opposite of, what is actually said. Its force lies in the contrast between the actual words and the implied meaning. Since sarcasm, satire, and paradox all depend upon reversed meanings, they are forms of irony.

C. Style is everything about a piece of writing that makes it distinctive. Since it is a reflection of the author's patterns of language, his tastes, habits, attitudes, and emotions, style necessarily reflects the author's personality.

D. Style, methods of developing subject matter. In fiction, for example, one must consider the *focus of narration*, the *exposition*, the *setting*, the *atmosphere*, *foreshadowing*, *character development*, development of *conflict*, method of building to *climax* and *key moment* through *complications*, the resolution or *denouement*. Critical reading requires thoughtful analysis of a work—its development and the relationship among its parts. With such analysis comes greater understanding and, therefore, increased appreciation.

Page 118

1. The third topic is the only one sufficiently limited for a research topic. **2.** *Card catalog, stacks, vertical or clipping file, general reference books* (encyclopedias, yearbooks, dictionaries), *special reference books* (biography, geography, history, music, etc., and magazine, newspaper, and document indexes). **3.** *Call number, source number* (if this system is used), *author, title, place of publication, publisher, date of publication.* **4.** A card on which notes are recorded. *Source number* corresponding to number on bibliography card, *heading* indicating topic, *page reference, body.* **5.** Summary or direct quotation. **6.** An omission of part of the material, ellipsis is indicated by three dots. **7.** *Sic* indicates that an error in quoted material occurred in the original material. **8.** Brackets. **9.** *Ibid.* is used to refer to a source in the footnote immediately preceding; *op. cit.* is used for references to a work if other sources intervene. The author's last name must be used with *op. cit.* **10.** The final bibliography serves as a reference guide for the reader.

Page 129

C. The most appropriate references are given here; others may be cited. **1.** *Information Please Almanac, World Almanac* **2.** *Statesman's Year-book* **3.** *The American Language* **4.** *Current Biography* **5.** *Essay and General Literature Index* **6.** *Industrial Arts Index* **7.** *Dramatic Index* **8.** *Agricultural Index* **9.** Bartlett's *Familiar Quotations* **10.** *Statistical Abstract of the United States, World Almanac, Information Please Almanac.*

Page 134

A. 1. A list of possible sources. **2.** Call number, source number, author, title, place of publication, publisher, date of publication. **3.** *Magazine article*—source number, author, title of article, title of periodical, volume number, if any, date, pages. *Newspaper article*—source number, author and title of article, if given, name of newspaper, date, volume, page, column. *Encyclopedia article*—source number, author's name, if given, title of article, title of encyclopedia, edition, volume number, pages. **4.** The source number is the number used throughout the research project to identify the source listed. It saves writing bibliographical data each time. **5.** Using a 3-by-5 card for each source, list all possible sources of information. Read one or two encyclopedia articles to get an overview of the subject. List references given in encyclopedia. Check card catalog, *Readers' Guide, New York Times Index*, and any other indexes that apply. Check vertical file. List any known experts in the field to whom letters may be written or with whom interviews may be arranged. Follow whatever form has been established for recording bibliographical data.

Page 137, Developing Your Skill

A. 1. Check table of contents, select chapters that seem to apply, skim these chapters, reread applicable material and take notes. **2.** *Source number* that corresponds to number on bibliography card; *heading*, which tells topic to which note is related; *page reference; body* of note. **3.** Summary or direct quotation. The summary is a paraphrase of the writer's material; the direct quotation is a verbatim quote from the writer's material. **4.** Abbreviated notes are made up of key words and phrases; a précis is written in sentences. **5.** An ellipsis is an omission in quoted material. *Sic* indicates that an error in quoted material appeared in the original. Explanatory material is set off in brackets.

Page 137, Review Exercises

A. 1. Complete bibliographical data on books. **2.** Pictures, charts, pamphlets, circulars, bulletins, current newspaper clippings. **3.** Summaries and surveys of broad topics. **4.** Maps of the world and tables of special statistical information. **5.** Miscellaneous information. **6.** Index to articles in periodicals catalogued by author, subject, and, occasionally, title. **7.** Index to articles in the *New York Times* and guide to articles of current interest in other newspapers. **8.** Index to essays in collections. **9.** Contains statistics on political, social, industrial, and economic organization of the United States. **10.** *U. S. Catalog* contains books published by American publishers. Index contains listings of all English language books. Both are indexed by author, title, and subject.

Page 141

A. 2. Since the introduction must lead naturally into the body of the paper, some writers prefer to write the introduction after they have developed their ideas. **3.** Interruptions can break the chain of thought and keep one from developing his theme logically. **4.** Subject matter for footnotes should be marked so the writer will know where footnotes are needed. This cannot be left for the final draft since such material is not always readily recognized again, as not all of it is quoted material. Even if the material were readily recognizable, leaving the marking for the final draft would be more time consuming and less accurate than marking material in the first draft. **5.** One cannot ethically take credit for facts that are not one's own. Whenever facts and opinions are borrowed from other sources, credit should be given. Exceptions are facts that are general knowledge.

Page 150, Review Exercises

A. The following is a suggested outline:

Writing the Paper

I. Preparing an outline
   A. Sort note cards by headings
   B. Write statement of theme
   C. Select main topic and subtopics
      1. Sort cards by main topics
      2. Decide on subtopics
      3. Set aside unrelated cards
   D. Mark cards with outline numerals and letters
   E. Write outline
   F. Check for overlapping and for form

II. Writing a first draft
   A. Expand statement of theme
   B. Write body of paper
      1. Concentrate on content
      2. Write without interruption
      3. Write on one side of paper
      4. Leave space between lines for corrections and revisions

III. Making revisions
   A. Allow time lapse for objectivity
   B. Content
      1. Reread
         a. Ideas
         b. Order
         c. Gaps
      2. Revise
         a. Cut and paste for major changes
         b. Make minor changes in space between lines
   C. Mechanics
      1. Reread and mark with colored pencil
         a. Style
         b. Usage
      2. Revise
   D. Reread for final edit
      1. Unnecessary words
      2. Overstatement
      3. Emphasis

4. Other details of style

IV. Preparing the final draft
   A. Margins
   B. Indentions
   C. Spacing
      1. Text
      2. Quotations
   D. Page numbers
   E. Footnotes
      1. Superior numbers in text
      2. Notation at bottom of page
         a. Original entries
         b. Subsequent entries
   F. Title page
   G. Table of contents
   H. Bibliography
   I. Final proofreading
   J. Binding

Page 150, Discussion Topics

A. Select topic, limit topic, make working bibliography, read and take notes, outline, write first draft, revise, write final draft, prepare title page, table of contents, bibliography, proofread, bind.

B. Interest, research potential, material available.

Page 151, Discussion Topics

C. Research projects in other subjects, taking notes in other courses, writing business and professional reports. Students should be encouraged to cite specific examples.

Page 151, Written Work

A. Blair, Walter and W. K. Chandler, *Approaches to Poetry*. New York, London: D. Appleton-Century Company, Inc., 1935, pp. 9-77.

Canby, Henry Seidel, "Really New Literature," *American Memoir*. Boston: Houghton Mifflin Company, 1947, pp. 339-349.

Engle, Paul, "Five Years of Pulitzer Poets," *English Journal*, vol. 38, February, 1949, pp. 59-66.

Gregory, Horace and Marya Zaturenska, *History of American Poetry, 1900-1940.* New York: Harcourt, Brace and Company, 1946.

Melcher, F. G., "Poet and Gallant Fighter," *Publisher's Weekly*, vol. 143, March 20, 1943, p. 1257.

Van Gelder, Robert, *Writers and Writing.* New York: Charles Scribner's Sons, 1946.

Page 152, Unit Self-Test

3.

	8
Schreiber, George, ed., *Portraits and Self-portraits.* Boston: Houghton Mifflin Company, 1936, pp. 13-16.	

Page 160, Developing Your Skill

A. 1. Subjects for creative writing should be familiar, concrete, and easily manageable within the limits set. **2.** The writer soon finds that he doesn't know enough about the subject to write easily and fluently. He must stop to check statements; he begins to question his interpretation. Anxiety about subject matter tends to make the presentation stiff and awkward. **3.** Good sources for subjects include the following: family, school, and social experiences; hobbies; incidents observed; travel experiences; recollections of persons and events.

Page 174

A. The warrior is aware of the conflict between his profession and the beauty of the earth. He sees the destructive qualities of the sword. The Japanese storyteller is aware of the conflict that disturbs the warrior. He is sympathetic toward the warrior. The Hebrew poet and the translator have placed the seal of approval on the humanity shown by the Japanese warrior and by the storyteller.

Page 175

A. Notice the greater compression in the Henderson translation. Because it it not as explicit as the Page translation, it permits broader and more varied interpretation. The speaker is not so obviously the child's mother. The use of the word *hunter* might even suggest a male speaker. In the first version of the *haiku*, the child may only have grown up and gone away; in the second version, the child has obviously died.

Page 176

D. The last line of the poem comes as a shock. The juxtaposition of the idea of tranquillity with the gore of the rest of the line points up the horror of war and its violence. The last line offers a study in contrast.

Page 177

> I watch the lake on a mid-June noon,
> When the sandpipers run and the seagulls ride,
> And the waters lap on the shore with glee.
>
> I climb with the wind to the top of the dune,
> And the blue lies before me—deep and wide—
> And my heart is no longer cribbed, but free.
>
> I sit with my book till the golden moon
> Lightens the east from the lake's far side,
> And the world disappears—but for moon and me.

Page 180, Discussion Topics

1. Awareness, use of all the senses, familiarity with self, understanding of various forms of writing. **2.** Writers draw ideas from the world around them. Familiarity with subject obviates the necessity for extensive research, dispels anxiety about accuracy, and permits the writer to concentrate on his presentation.

Page 181, Discussion Topics

3. These prose forms permit the writer to incorporate other forms, such as the jest, the anecdote, the compliment, the proverb, the pun, the caricature, and so on. **4.** The poet and the essayist are alike in their awareness of the world around them. They are different in that the poet uses fewer words, uses language more forcefully than does the essayist, and may have greater awareness of the possible interpretations of events in his world. **5.** Form in art becomes the focus of this discussion. Students will undoubtedly disagree with each other in discussing this point. For example, is a gem always more beautiful after it has been shaped and polished and mounted? Is form essential to poetic expression? A lively discussion should ensue.

Page 200

B. *Proper Nouns:* Frank Lloyd Wright, Guggenheim Museum, New York City, Solomon R. Guggenheim. *Common Nouns:* equality, abstract; ideas, abstract; people, collective; pounds, concrete; potatoes, concrete; salad, concrete; group, collective; museum, concrete; collection, collective; works, concrete; art, abstract; painters, concrete; sculptors, concrete; artists, concrete; counseling, abstract; testing, abstract; methods, abstract; field, abstract; guidance, abstract; students, concrete; problems, abstract.

Page 221

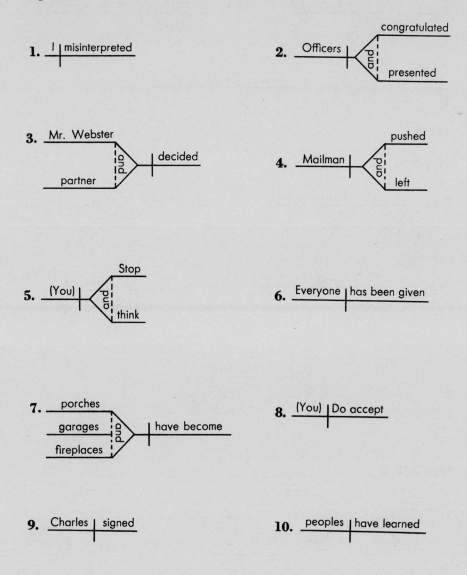

Page 225, C

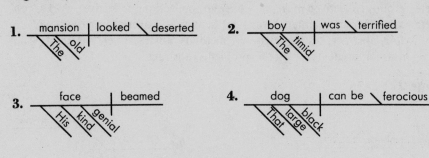

Page 230, C

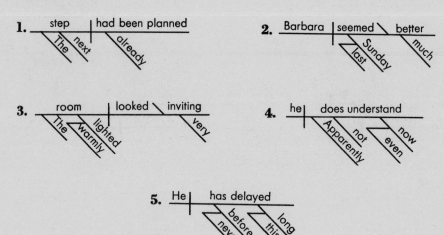

Page 235, B

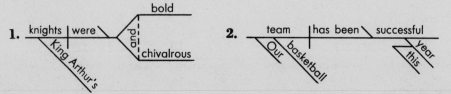

3.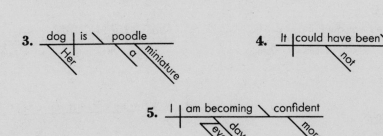

4.

5.

Page 236, B

1.

2.

3.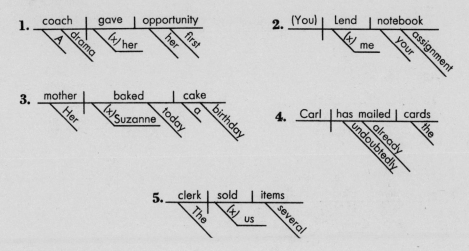

4.

5.

Page 237, B

1.

2.

3.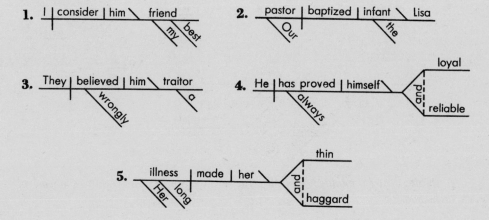

4.

5.

Page 239, C

1.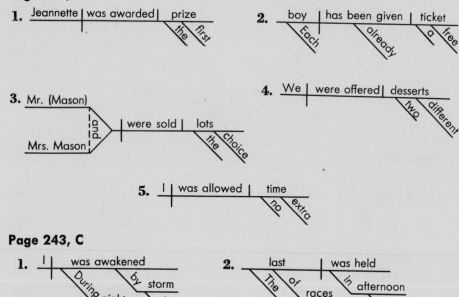

2.

3.

4.

5.

Page 243, C

1.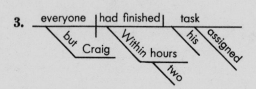

2.

3.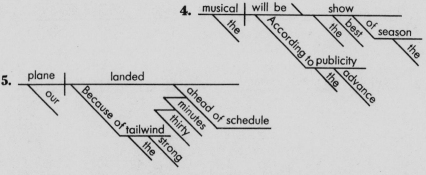

4.

5.

Note: *Thirty minutes* modifies the entire prepositional phrase *ahead of schedule.*

Page 247, C

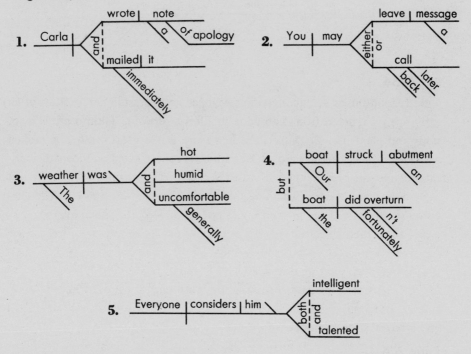

Page 249, B

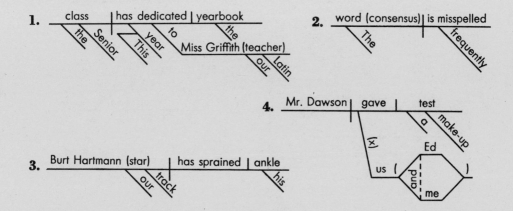

5.

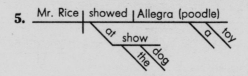

Page 256

B. 1. John James Audubon, (who developed an interest in nature study at an early age,) wandered from Labrador to Florida drawing faithful sketches of birds and plant life. **2.** Daniel Webster, (who was a great orator,) is ranked with Demosthenes and Cicero. **3.** The students concentrated on the mathematical problem (their teacher had discussed in class on the previous day.) **4.** He just came back from Mexico (where he spent his Christmas vacation.) **5.** The television set (that I ordered last week) has not yet arrived. **6.** This road, (which is a branch of the expressway,) leads directly to the expressway. **7.** The corner lot (where we used to play baseball) now houses a supermarket. **8.** The rain, (which had been pouring down for hours,) suddenly stopped. **9.** Mr. Nelson, (whom Mr. Carter recommended for this position,) has proved himself competent. **10.** Gary, (who has been practicing at least two hours each day,) will give a recital in the school auditorium.

Page 256, C

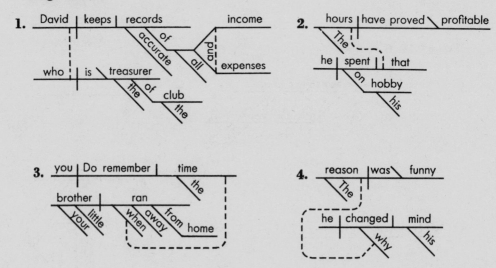

5.

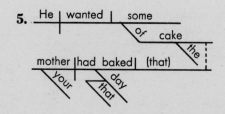

Page 259, C

1.

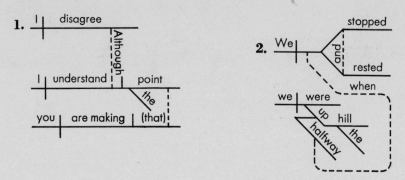

2.

3.

4.

5.

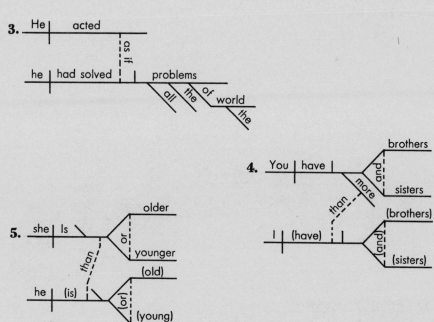

Page 262, B

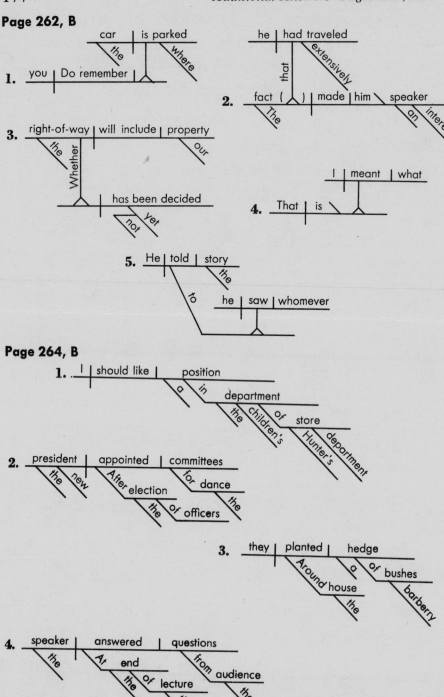

Page 264, B

5.

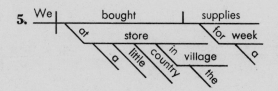

Page 273, C

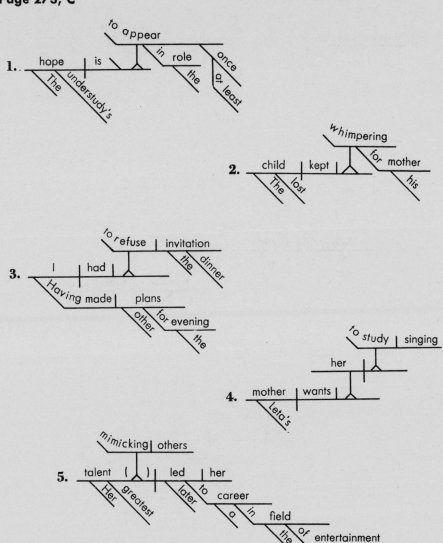

Page 277, B

1.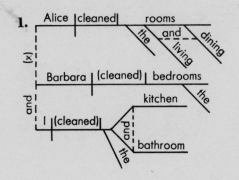

2.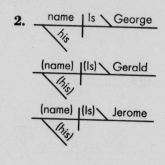

3.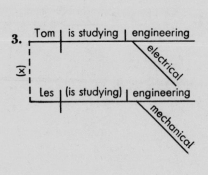

4.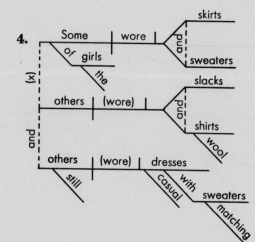

5.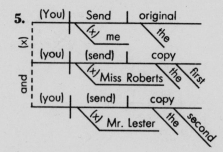

Page 281, C

1.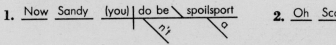

2.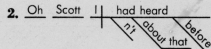

3. My Lynne You look beautiful just

4. dear cookies were made my Those for sale the goods baked

5. What Pat I can believe that hardly

Page 281, D

1.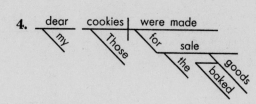
brother parents encouraged to attend school him an art My having shown flair a for designing

2.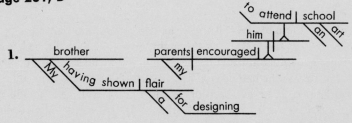

3.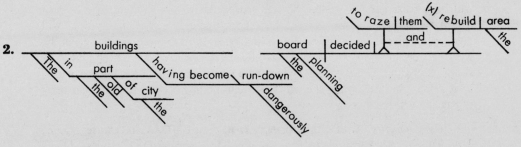

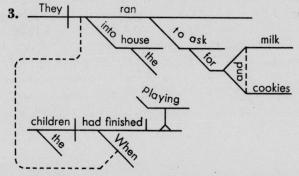

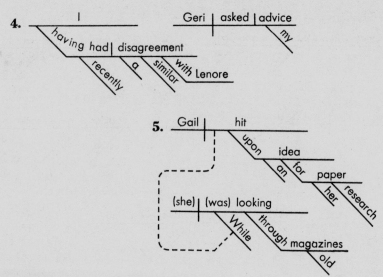

Page 282

B. He *thinks*, he thought, he will think, he has thought, he had thought, he will have thought, he is thought, he was thought, he will be thought, he has been thought, he had been thought, he will have been thought; he *drives*, he drove, he will drive, he has driven; he had driven, he will have driven, he is driven, he was driven, he will be driven, he has been driven, he had been driven, he will have been driven; he *freezes*, he froze, he will freeze, he has frozen, he had frozen, he will have frozen, he is frozen, he was frozen, he will be frozen, he has been frozen, he had been frozen, he will have been frozen; he *gives*, he gave, he will give, he has given, he had given, he will have given, he is given, he was given, he will be given, he has been given, he had been given, he will have been given; he *swings*, he swung, he will swing, he has swung, he had swung, he will have swung, he is swung, he was swung, he will be swung, he has been swung, he had been swung, he will have been swung.

E. *Complements:* **1.** effective—P.A.; **2.** n. clause—D.O., n. clause—D.O.; **3.** difficult—P.A., determined—P.A.; **4.** boy—I.O., sheet—D.O., copies—D.O.; **5.** Shelley, me—I.O., idea—D.O.; **6.** inf. phrase—D.O., toboganing—O.C.; **7.** beautiful—P.A., color—D.O., ugly—P.A., inf. phrase—D.O.; **8.** advantages —D.O.; **9.** inf. phrase—D.O., adult and adventurous—P.A.; **10.** encourage- ment—R.O., man—P.N., inf. phrase—D.O. *Parts of Speech:* **1.** adj., n., adv., adj., n.; **2.** conj., pron.; **3.** n., conj. or adv.; **4.** conj., adv., adj., adv., adj.; **5.** n., adj.; **6.** n., n.; **7.** interj., adv., n., v., pron., conj., adv., n.; **8.** prep., n., adv., prep., pron., adj.; **9.** n., adv., adv., adj., adj., adj; **10.** adj., adj., adj.

Page 316

B. 1. Laura and Ed play tennis well. **2.** Since Marilyn passed the scholarship exam with the highest grade ever received, she is sure to be granted a full tuition scholarship. **3.** Although Ed's accident will keep him from playing football this year, he plans to work for the team in any way he can. **4.** We didn't have a quorum present; therefore the meeting was postponed until next week. **5.** Unless Howard decides about the job offer today, the offer will be withdrawn.

Page 368

1. *Acquit*, acquitted, acquitting, acquittance. **2.** *Argue*, argued, arguing, arguable, argument. **3.** *Begin*, beginning. **4.** *Believe*, believed, believing, believable. **5.** *Benefit*, benefited, benefiting. **6.** *Courage*, courageous, courageously. **7.** *Debate*, debated, debating, debatable. **8.** *Desire*, desired, desiring, desirous, desirable, desirably. **9.** *Drastic*, drastically. **10.** *Endure*, endured, enduring, endurable, endurance, endurably. **11.** *Excite*, excited, exciting, excitable, excitement, excitedly, excitably. **12.** *Happen*, happened, happening. **13.** *Manage*, managed, managing, manageable, management, manageably. **14.** *Marriage*, marriageable. **15.** *Note*, noted, noting, notable, notedness, notedly, notable. **16.** *Recognize*, recognized, recognizing, recognizable, recognizably. **17.** *Rebel*, rebelled, rebelling. **18.** *Refer*, referred, referring, referable, referrible. **19.** *Silly*, silliness, sillily. **20.** *Value*, valued, valuing, valuable, valuably.

Page 414

B. "Put dots, not circles, over your *I*'s, Betty," said Miss Martin. "Two women I know use circles," said Betty, "and I think their writing is pretty." "But this is a class in business English, and it is not businesslike to make circles," replied Miss Martin. She continued, "If you're planning a business career, students, make your writing as simple and legible as possible. Nowadays, employers are too busy to waste time on fancy touches."

Page 417

A. The first paragraph of a theme is usually the introduction; the last, the conclusion. Each other paragraph indicates the discussion of a single topic. The reader can tell at a glance what the general organization of the theme is.

In an outline, Roman numerals indicate main topics; capital letters indicate first subtopics; Arabic numerals, second subtopics; lower-case letters, third subtopics; and so on. The correct use of numerals and letters, the correct indention of subtopics, and parallel structure within each category of topics and subtopics reveals the plan of the outline.

The form of a letter indicates whether it is a friendly or a business letter. Paragraphing indicates the number of topics discussed.

B. A business letter includes an *inside address*. Also, the business letter is concise and is formal in tone whereas the friendly letter may be long, rambling, and informal.

C. Such errors detract from clarity by putting stumbling blocks in the way of the reader. When a reader must stop to puzzle out misspellings, capitalization errors, and incorrect syllabication, he must interrupt the thought of the written work, with the result that he loses the meaning of what he is reading.

D. Because English is not an inflected language, it reveals its meaning largely through fixed word order and punctuation. Punctuation keeps related ideas together and separates unrelated ideas. Draw from students examples such as those included in the text on pp. 377-378.

123456789   098765432

THE Using Good English SERIES

USING

COMPOSITION and GRAMMAR

GOOD ENGLISH

JOHN E. BREWTON
Chairman, English Department
George Peabody College for Teachers
Nashville, Tennessee

R. STANLEY PETERSON
Head of the English Department
New Trier Township High School
Winnetka, Illinois

B. JO KINNICK
Teacher of Creative Writing
Oakland High School
Oakland, California

LOIS McMULLAN
Formerly Teacher of English, Laboratory School
George Peabody College for Teachers
Nashville, Tennessee

LAIDLAW BROTHERS • PUBLISHERS

River Forest, Illinois

SUMMIT, NEW JERSEY   PALO ALTO, CALIFORNIA   DALLAS, TEXAS   ATLANTA, GEORGIA

ILLUSTRATIONS BY: Dan Siculan

ACKNOWLEDGMENTS: Excerpt from the review of the movie *The Diary of Anne Frank* by Hollis Alpert: Reprinted from the *Saturday Review*, April 4, 1959. / Excerpts from *The Santa Ana* by Sanora Babb: Reprinted by Special Permission of *The Saturday Evening Post*. © 1959 by The Curtis Publishing Company. / Excerpt from *R.M.S. Titanic* by Hanson W. Baldwin: Reprinted by permission of Willis Kingsley Wing. Copyright 1934 by Hanson W. Baldwin. / *Yehoash* by Solomon Bloomgarden, translated by Marie Syrkin: Permission granted by *The Menorah Journal*. / Excerpt from *Sporting Life in America: Watching* by Robert Benchley: From *Chips Off the Old Benchley*, Harper & Brothers Publishers. / Excerpt from *Round About Parnassus* by William Rose Benét: Reprinted from *Saturday Review*, December 27, 1930. / Excerpt from a review of Jean Anouilh's *Becket* by Charles A. Brady: Reprinted from the *Buffalo Evening News*. January 28, 1961. / *Alarms and Discursions Concerning Words:* Reprinted by permission of Dodd, Mead & Company from *Alarms and Discursions* by G. K. Chesterton. Copyright 1911, 1938 by Frances Chesterton. / *Chanson Innocente:* Copyright, 1923, 1951, by E. E. Cummings. Reprinted from *Poems 1923-1954* by E. E. Cummings by permission of Harcourt, Brace & World, Inc. / Excerpt from *The Devil and Daniel Webster* by Stephen Vincent Benét: From *Selected Works of Stephen Vincent Benét*, published by Holt, Rinehart and Winston, Inc. Reprinted by permission of Brandt & Brandt. / *The Listeners* by Walter de la Mare: Permission granted by The Literary Trustees of Walter de la Mare and The Society of Authors as their representative. / Excerpt from *The Love Song of J. Alfred Prufrock* by T. S. Eliot, Harcourt, Brace & World, Inc. Reprinted by permission of the publishers. / Excerpt from *Mississippi* by William Faulkner: Reprinted by special permission from *Holiday*, copyright April, 1954, by The Curtis Publishing Company. / Excerpt from *Spotted Horses*, by William Faulkner, copyright 1931, 1940, 1958 by William Faulkner. Reprinted by permission of Random House, Inc. / Excerpt from *The Death of the Hired Man* from *Complete Poems of Robert Frost*. Copyright 1930, 1939 by Holt, Rinehart and Winston, Inc. Reprinted by permission of Holt, Rinehart and Winston, Inc. / Excerpt from *The Diary of Anne Frank* by Anne Frank: Permission to reprint granted by Doubleday and Company, Inc. and by Otto Frank. / *A Goblin Lives in Our House* from *Picture Rhymes from Foreign Lands* by Rose Fyleman. Copyright 1935 by Rose Fyleman. Published by J. B. Lippincott Company. / Excerpt from *Art* by Theophile Gautier, translated by George Santayana: Published by Charles Scribner's Sons. / Excerpt from *Old Red* from *Forest of the South* by Caroline Gordon: Published by Charles Scribner's Sons. / Excerpt from *Only They Can Really Fly* by Oskar and Katharina Heinroth: Reprinted from the *Saturday Review*, November 5, 1960. / Two haiku: From *The Bamboo Broom*, translated by Harold G. Henderson. / *The Habit of Perfection* by Gerard Manley Hopkins: From *Poems of Gerard Manley Hopkins*, Oxford University Press. / Excerpt from *The Furnished Room:* From *The Four Million* by O. Henry. Permission to reprint granted by Doubleday and Company, Inc. / Excerpts from *Araby* and *The Dead:* From *The Dubliners*, by James Joyce. Copyright 1914, the Viking Press. / Excerpt from *Albert Camus in the Sun* by Blanche Knopf: From the *Atlantic Monthly*, February, 1961. / Excerpt from *The Erie Canal*, Collected, adapted, and arranged by John A. & Alan Lomax. Copyright 1934 by John A. & Alan Lomax in the book *American Ballads and Folk Songs*. Copyright assigned 1958 to Ludlow Music, Inc., New York, New York. / Excerpt from *Science and Man's Fate* by David E. Lilienthal: From *The Nation*, July 13, 1946. / Excerpt from *On a Chinese Screen* by W. Somerset Maugham: Permission to reprint granted by Doubleday & Company, Inc., Mr. W. Somerset Maugham, and Messrs. William Heinemann Ltd. / *Protracted Tears* by John McCarten reprinted by permission; © 1959 The New Yorker Magazine, Inc. / *Two Hearts at the Edge of Doom*, a review of the movie *The Diary of Anne Frank:* From *Newsweek*, March 30, 1959. / One stanza from *Japanese Poetry*, translated by Curtis Hidden Page: Published by Houghton Mifflin Company. / Excerpt from *War* by Luigi Pirandello: From *The Medals and Other Stories*, published by E. P. Dutton & Co., Inc. / Excerpt from *In an American Factory* by Stoyan Pribichevich: By permission from *World Neighbors*, by James, Northcott & Shattuck. Copyright 1950, McGraw-Hill Book Company, Inc. / *The Sleeper of the Valley* by Arthur Rimbaud: From *The Poets of Modern France* translated by Ludwig Lewisohn. Copyright 1918 by B. W. Huebsch, 1946 by Ludwig Lewisohn. Reprinted by permission of The Viking Press, Inc. / *Buffalo Dusk:* From *Smoke and Steel* by Carl Sandburg, copyright 1920, by Harcourt, Brace & World, Inc.; renewed, 1948, by Carl Sandburg. Reprinted by permission of the publishers. / *The People Will Live On* from *The People, Yes* by Carl Sandburg, copyright, 1936, by Harcourt, Brace & World, Inc. Reprinted by permission of the publishers. / Excerpt from *Windwagon Smith* by Wilbur Schramm, from *Windwagon Smith and Other Yarns:* Permission granted by Harold Ober Associates, Inc. / Excerpts from *Jalopies I Cursed and Loved* by John Steinbeck: Reprinted by special permission from *Holiday*, copyright July, 1954, by The Curtis Publishing Company. / Excerpt from Robert Louis Stevenson letter: From *A Second Treasury of the World's Great Letters*. Copyright 1941 by Simon and Schuster, Inc. Reprinted by permission of the publishers. / Quotation from *University Days* by James Thurber reprinted by permission; copr. © 1933, 1961 The New Yorker Magazine, Inc. / Excerpt from the story *Byézhin Meadow:* From *The Novels and Stories of Ivan Turgenieff*, translated by Isabel E. Hapgood, published by Charles Scribner's Sons. / Excerpt from *The Diary of Adam and Eve* by Mark Twain: Harper & Brothers Publishers. / Excerpt from *Africa* by Laurens Van der Post: Reprinted by special permission from *Holiday*, copyright March, 1954, by the Curtis Publishing Company. / *The Ballad Tree* by Evelyn Kendrick Wells: Copyright 1950, The Ronald Press Company. / Excerpt from *Poetic Styles Old and New* by Yvor Winters: From *Four Poets on Poetry*, edited by Don Cameron Allen, 1959, published by the Johns Hopkins Press. / Excerpt from *Here in New York* by E. B. White: Reprinted by special permission from *Holiday*, copyright April, 1949, by The Curtis Publishing Company. / Excerpts from *You Can't Go Home Again* by Thomas Wolfe: Harper & Brothers Publishers. / Excerpt from *Ideas of Good and Evil* by William Butler Yeats: By permission of The Macmillan Company, The Macmillan Company Canada, Ltd., A. P. Watt and Son, and Mrs. W. B. Yeats.

PHOTOGRAPHS: J. Julius Fanta—Colorpix: x, 1, 17, 37, 61, 89, 153. / H. Armstrong Roberts: 117.

Printed in the United States of America
2 3 4 5 6 7 8 9   0 9 8 7 6 5 4 3 2

CONTENTS

Unit 1   Movies and Stage Plays   1

Unit 2   Listening   17

Unit 5 Reading for Appreciation—continued

Unit 6 The Research Paper 117

Unit 7 Creative Writing 153

Unit 1

Movies and Stage Plays

The wide appeal of the drama in all ages and among all men indicates the importance of this mode of expression in shaping men's minds.

From the time of the ancient Egyptians, man has used the drama to express his ideas and emotions or to tell a story. Throughout the centuries, the drama, or play, has served to reflect the customs, the life, and the ideals of mankind.

In the theater, for two hours or more, you may live in any part of the world in any period of history. You may see people and events so vividly portrayed that they become real. You may laugh or weep at the situations and problems that unfold before you; you may know fear as you recognize some of the problems as your own. Without exposing yourself to danger, you may take part in bold adventures. Such is the magic of the theater.

Today, because of the increased media of mass communication, plays are available to everyone. Radio and television offer a wide range of dramatic programs; most cities have theaters in which stage plays are performed; and even the smallest town usually has at least one motion-picture theater.

Unfortunately, motion pictures have not always met the high standards originally expected of them. Given unlimited settings and given budgets that allow for top talent and costly production, movie producers should have been able to give the public consistently excellent films. In their technical aspects, they have generally succeeded. Photography has been excellent; costumes and sets have been magnificently authentic; historical details have been accurate. But, in their treatment of stories and of people, the movies have often failed. Too frequently, the stories they tell repeat

Since students today are so frequently exposed to dramatic art, they should establish criteria for differentiating between superior and inferior drama.

1

Although TV drama and movies are not discussed explicitly in the unit, the criteria presented apply to TV productions, as well.

2   *Movies and Stage Plays*

the same trite boy-meets-girl or hero-foils-villain formula; and the characters are exaggerated stereotypes rather than believable human beings.

The great number of movies available to you and the varying quality of both films and stage plays make it important that you be discriminating in your choice of theater entertainment. By studying and applying critical approaches to movies and plays, you can learn to select those offerings that will be worth the time and money spent in watching them.

Selectivity is the major emphasis of the unit.

Theater attendance is not a new experience for you. You have been going to the movies and perhaps seeing stage plays since you were a child. Do you carefully select the movies and plays you see, or do you just "happen" to see them? Before you begin the study of this unit, make an inventory of your theater attendance habits and of your motion-picture and stage-play preferences by completing the Check Yourself section that follows.

Answers will vary. The discussion should give the teacher a picture of class theater preferences.

CHECK YOURSELF

Spend some time discussing these questions but do not engage in exhaustive discussions. The purpose here is to stimulate interest.

After answering the following questions, compare your answers with those of your classmates. Wherever possible, determine the class preferences and theater attendance habits by tabulating the answers given.

1. How often do you see a motion picture? A stage play?
2. Do you try to find out anything about a picture or a stage play before you see it? If so, what sources of information do you use?
3. What types of pictures or stage plays do you like most? If possible, make a master list of the class preferences. Is any one type more popular than the others? Why?
4. Has your taste in moving pictures or stage plays changed during the past few years? If so, how?
5. What, in your opinion, are the characteristics of an excellent motion picture? An excellent stage play?

1. Choosing Movies and Plays

SOME AIDS TO FINDING GOOD MOVIES AND PLAYS

Only a comparatively small number of motion pictures and stage plays produced each year are outstanding. It is these pictures and stage plays that you will want to see.

Much of the criticism directed at students' movie choices
is the result of the students' lack of selectivity.
Choosing Movies and Plays   3

There is no single way in which you can determine in advance whether
or not a film or play is worth seeing. However, there are several techniques
you may use to help you select movies and stage plays.

1. If some of your friends have already seen the performance in which
you are interested, discuss it with them. Try to get more than one opinion;
you may find that your friends' judgments will vary.

2. Certain movie and stage directors are noted for the consistent excellence of the films and plays they direct. Learn to recognize the names of
directors. If the past performances of a director have been outstanding,
it is reasonable to assume that a new effort may be worth seeing.

3. Notice the names of the actors in the production. Have the stars
established themselves as being outstanding in their field? Are the supporting actors recognized for their unusual talents? Have any of the actors won
awards? What awards have they won? The most esteemed awards in motion pictures are the "Oscars," given annually by the Academy of Motion
Picture Arts and Sciences. For stage plays, the most coveted awards are the
Antoinette Perry Awards, known as "Tonys," which are given annually by
the American Theater Wing; the Clarence Derwent Awards; the New York
Drama Critics Circle Awards; and the *Variety* Poll of New York Drama
Critics. These awards are presented for all phases of production, as well as
for acting.

Stress the
point that
no one way
is in it-
self of
sufficient
validity
for deter-
mining the
choice of
a movie or
play.

DEVELOPING YOUR SKILL

A. In the following list are items which sometimes influence a person to
   select a motion picture or stage play to see. Which of these usually
   influence you? Discuss the list in class, indicating which items you
   consider of great value and which of little, if any, value in selecting a
   motion picture or stage play. Give reasons. See p. T54.

title	nothing else to do
stars	parent recommendation
director	teacher recommendation
story	double feature
advertisement	friend

B. Using newspapers and magazines, find the most recent accounts of
   Academy Awards, Antoinette Perry Awards, Clarence Derwent
   Awards, New York Drama Critics Circle Awards, and, if possible, the
   results of the *Variety* Poll of New York Drama Critics. Your teacher

The bulletin board can be used to advantage for displaying
clippings from local papers, from news magazines, and from
movie and theater journals.

may wish to have you work in committees on this assignment. Be prepared to discuss the following questions:

1. Which actors and directors received these awards for work in movies or stage plays?
2. What films and plays received awards?
3. Why do you think are awards given in different categories? Why, for example, would it be unfair to try to judge a full length comedy and a cartoon by the same standards? See p. T54.

In carrying out this assignment, you will find the *Reader's Guide,* the *New York Times Index,* and other library aids helpful.

C. In a well-constructed paragraph, discuss a picture or stage play that has received an award of merit. Be sure to tell what qualities the picture or play has that caused it to be chosen as outstanding. See p. T54.

CRITICAL REVIEWS

It is important that several reviews be read. Distinguish carefully between reviews and advertisements

Critical reviews are the most valuable aid in helping you to select movies and plays wisely. These reviews may be found in local newspapers, in metropolitan newspapers, and in magazines. Before seeing a film or stage play, read several reviews. Be sure, especially with newspaper reviews, that they are unprejudiced; that is, be certain that they are critical reviews of, not merely advertisements for, the movie or play. Be wary, too, of reviews that are quoted in advertisements. These are usually excerpts from reviews and, taken out of context, are frequently misleading. For example, an advertisement may quote a reviewer as having said "Sensational!" Actually, the reviewer may have said, "The entire production is too sensational!"

Among the reviews that appear in magazines, those in the *Saturday Review, The New Yorker, Time,* and *Newsweek* particularly deserve your attention. Make it a point to see copies of these magazines and to compare the reviews. You will notice that each review is written in a distinctive style. The movie reviews that appear in *Time,* for example, have become noted for their coined words, as *cinemactor,* and for their caustic wit.

Read the following review of a movie which many of you may have seen.

PROTRACTED TEARS
John McCarten

George Stevens, who began his distinguished movie career as a cameraman, is responsible for the production and direction of the film version of "The Diary of Anne Frank," and he has used his lens to artful advantage in relating this sad chronicle of a Jewish girl in her early teens hiding, with some of her relatives, in an Amsterdam attic in the days when the city was swarming with Nazis. The picture is done in CinemaScope, though, and it seems to me that this was a mistake, because, when compelled to work in its yawning expanse, not even such an able man as Mr. Stevens can quite establish the sense of awful confinement that Frances Goodrich and Albert Hackett got into their play on the subject a few years back. (They wrote the screenplay for this enterprise by the way.) If I may be allowed a couple of further quibbles, I'd like to say—and maybe this isn't a quibble but a major objection—that it is much too long, stretching out over three full hours. I might also take exception to the casting of Millie Perkins, an inexperienced girl, as the heroine. Miss Perkins does her adolescent best to keep up with the adults in the company, but, after all, she is playing against the likes of Joseph Schildkraut, Shelley Winters, Ed Wynn, Gusti Huber, and quite an assortment of other good actors. Mr. Schildkraut, as he did on the stage, gives a really definitive performance as the father of young Anne, and Miss Huber, who also contributed to the success of the Broadway production, is right up there with him as his wife. But if you were to ask me, I'd say that the most endearing character to turn up in the picture is the crotchety old dentist, portrayed by Ed Wynn. Still, no matter what reservations I may have about "The Diary of Anne Frank," it excites a tear or two as it goes its lengthy way, and that, after all, is probably good for your soul.

Analyze the review. What are the reviewer's objections? Are they valid? Should the same standards be applied to all members of the cast? What does the last sentence tell the reader about the reviewer?

Notice that the reviewer has summarized the plot briefly without spoiling the story for the reader. He has commented on the direction, the photography, and the casting, as well as the acting.

Permit students to discuss the reviews at length. In addition to the content of each review, have students try to determine the tone of the writing as a reflection of the writer's personality.

Compare the following review of the same movie with the one you just read. On what points do the reviewers agree? On what matters do they disagree?

Point out
the dif-
ference in
this re-
viewer's
approach
from that
of the
previous
reviewer.

As the film "The Diary of Anne Frank" opens there is a shot of some sea gulls and clouds; a moment or two later a sound is heard that could be the cry of the gulls or it could be a girl sobbing. The moviegoer had best make up his mind right at that point that what he hears is a bright, free sound and not a tragic one. Otherwise, this filmed version of a 14-year-old girl's diary will stun and depress him more than it is meant to. Anne Frank's diary was a sensitive and impulsive account of the two years she and seven other Jews spent hiding from the Nazis in an Amsterdam garret. Like the diary itself, the movie is not a melancholy matter but a moving document about the durability of the young in spirit.

As a book, it was first published in Holland in 1947. The American edition five years later became a best seller. (It has been translated into 21 different languages.) The Albert Hackett-Frances Goodrich dramatization opened on Broadway in 1955 and ran for almost two years. It has since been put on with devastating effect in some 30 countries.

Students should
note both the
areas of
agreement and
those of dis-
agreement.

Producer-director George Stevens has translated the account of the huddled day-to-day living of eight very human people into a film that is emotionally stunning. (Of the originals, all but the father, Otto Frank, died in Hitler's prison camps.) Joseph Schildkraut as the quiet, proud father repeats the role he played on the stage for 1,087 performances. Shelley Winters is properly dowdy and peevish as the mother of Anne's young friend Peter (Richard Beymer). Ed Wynn is excellent as the old bachelor who is not quite wise but not quite a fool. As Anne, Millie Perkins, an 18-year-old fashion model with no previous acting experience, is considerably more than satisfactory; she is haunting.

Summing Up: Out of a famous diary, a moving movie.

—Newsweek

In the first review you read, you will remember that the reviewer objected to the use of CinemaScope for this film. He felt that the wide screen

Caution students about accepting everything they read as being absolute. Point out to them that numerous plays that have received poor reviews have been popular successes whereas many critical successes have closed after short runs.

made it impossible to establish the feeling of confinement that the characters suffered. The second reviewer made no direct comment about this
technique. The following paragraph is taken from a third review of the
same movie.

> George Stevens has been kind enough to provide an intermission
> during the three hour running time of "The Diary of Anne Frank."
> The respite is welcome because it provides some relief from the
> group claustrophobia that Mr. Stevens creates in his film reworking
> of the Frances Goodrich and Albert Hackett drama. The people
> huddled in those cramped attic rooms in Amsterdam are Anne, her
> parents and sister, Mr. and Mrs. Van Daan and their son, Peter, and   This re-
> old Mr. Dussel, the dentist. That makes eight, and <u>when *you* are</u>   viewer adds
> <u>watching it the total becomes nine.</u> When someone on the screen   a new note.
> moves in the close quarters, you feel like moving too, to make room.

—Hollis Alpert, *Saturday Review*

    You have seen that even professional reviewers are not always in com-   It is im-
plete accord about the movies they see. If you read reviews of stage plays,   portant
you will find the same thing to be true. This is one reason why it is impor-   that stu-
tant that you read several reviews of the same performance before you de-   dents
cide whether or not it is worth seeing. Ask yourself whether the reviewers   learn to
are being objective or whether they are permitting prejudices to influence   analyze
their writing, whether they are expressing honest opinions or are merely   reviews.
trying to be clever. Base your final decision upon the general consensus of   Objec-
opinion. Even so, you may sometimes find that you don't like a film or play   tivity—
which has received "rave" notices or that you do enjoy a performance   insofar
that has been "panned" by the critics. Remember that your personal prefer-   as one
ences and your mood of the moment may cause you to disagree with the   can be
critics.   objective—
  is es-
  sential.

 DEVELOPING YOUR SKILL   Answers will vary.

Newspapers. A. Be prepared to discuss in class any movie and drama critics whose
Magazines.   names are familiar to you. Where can you find their reviews?
     B. Read a movie or stage-play review in a newspaper or in a magazine.
        Be sure you select a critical review, not an advertisement. Using the

     Point out to students that reviewers, too, being human,
are likely to react somewhat subjectively. No one can be
absolutely objective.

8   *Movies and Stage Plays*

following questions as the basis of your discussion, write a commentary on the review you selected.

1. Is this a completely unprejudiced review? If not, what statements show the reviewer's prejudice?
2. What parts of the review show the reviewer's objectivity?
3. Does the reviewer seem to be expressing honest opinions or is he merely trying to be clever?
4. What aspects of the film are discussed other than the acting?
5. Based upon the reviewer's evaluation, would you choose to see this movie? Why or why not?

Review Exercises—Choosing Movies and Plays

The results of this first exercise may indicate that students are missing many good movies and plays by limiting their choices to a few types.

A. Assume that you will be permitted to see only three motion pictures this year. Select from the current movies and those that you know are being produced the three you would put on your "must see" list. One student may be asked to list the class preferences, arranging them by types of movies (westerns, comedies, musicals, historical costume plays, etc.). How much variety is there in the types included? Which types are most popular?

See pp. 3, 4-7.

B. Write a brief, but carefully thought out, composition on the subject of selecting movies and stage plays that you would like to see. Be sure to include the various aids available to you and your evaluation of those aids.

For superior students.

C. Select at least three reviews of a movie you have not seen. This part of the exercise may be done most easily by referring to the *Readers' Guide to Periodical Literature*. In each volume of the *Readers' Guide* you will find the following heading:

MOVING picture plays.
criticisms, plots, etc.

Under this heading you will find a subheading *single works,* under which are listed the titles of individual movies and, below each title, the names of magazines in which reviews may be found.

After you have read the reviews of the film you selected, write a paragraph in which you state, based upon the reviewers' comments, whether or not you feel that the motion picture is one you would be interested in seeing. Be specific in giving the reasons for your decision.

This exercise may be used for the selection of a stage play rather than a movie. Perhaps your teacher may want to have half the class read film reviews and the other half stage-play reviews.

2. Judging Movies and Plays

EVALUATE THE STORY

The intelligent theater audience expects a story of merit. Unless the story is intended to be unrealistic, as in a fantasy, discriminating members of the audience look for a portrayal of real life. <u>It must be remembered, however, that the importance of the story depends upon the purpose of the movie or play.</u> For example, a musical comedy whose primary purpose is to show off singing and dancing may be built around a thin, exaggeratedly simple plot. The so-called "smash hits" in this category are frequently those which offer believable plots as well as memorable music.

Stress the purpose as the determining factor in the importance of the story.

The first point which must be considered, then, is the intention of the movie or stage play: Is the story intended to be of primary importance? If it is, the questions which follow will help you to evaluate the quality of the stories in motion pictures and stage plays.

1. Is the story idea or the method of presentation original or unusual?

All too often the plots of movies and stage plays are so hackneyed that, having seen one of a given type, you feel that you have seen them all. How many westerns have you seen in which the city "dude" falls in love with the cattleman's daughter who is also being courted by a bully cattle rancher? After a series of narrow escapes, the "dude" proves that the rancher is a bully and a rustler and, that he, the "dude," is the better man. Suddenly, the city-bred man can outride, outshoot, and outfight the entire gang that threatens the well-being of the heroine.

Students may be able to give other examples of hackneyed plots.

The number of completely original plots is, of course, limited. You may wish to have students list some of the most common plots and then draw upon their viewing experiences to show how writers have avoided triteness in developing the plots.

2. Is the story easy to follow?

You may
wish to
illus-
trate the
points
made
here by
applying
them to
a cur-
rent
movie or
to one
that all
the stu-
dents have
seen in
school.

A good plot is not necessarily complicated. Even when the story requires a more complex plot, it should be so put together that the story is clear to the audience.

3. Is interest aroused early and maintained throughout by a series of conflicts or crises leading directly to a climax and a logical ending?

Although conflict—a struggle—is necessary to every plot, the conflict need not be a physical one between human beings. It may be a struggle of man against the forces of nature, as in a picture of the farmers in the dust bowl of the Great Plains. The conflict may be with poverty, dishonesty, greed, intolerance, ignorance, disease, or many other conditions or ideas. Whatever the conflict, it should be so resolved that the audience feels that the ending is reasonable and satisfying. The antagonist does not have to be another person.

4. Is the theme interesting and significant?

While it is true that a good story offers entertainment, it is also true that a good story presents in dramatic form some significant truth about man. The theme may revolve around individuals in society, or it may point up a situation which affects society as a whole.

5. Are the characters real people; that is, are they individuals rather than stereotypes?

In a good story the characters are believable, complex human beings. No person is entirely good or entirely bad. Each man has varied facets to his personality.

As the story develops, the characters should show change just as people in real life do. If the story covers a span of years, there should be gradual physical changes evident. Throughout any story there should be signs of change in the characters' attitudes, emotions, reactions, and beliefs; for human beings change daily as they respond to the things that happen to them. Compare static characters and dynamic characters.

B. Other stereotypes may include the following: male office
clerk, receptionist, typist, Shakespearean actor, gambler,
banker, foreign diplomat.

Judging Movies and Plays   11

DEVELOPING YOUR SKILL

A. Your teacher may ask you to discuss the standards suggested for See pp. 9–10. evaluating motion-picture or stage-play stories. Suggest additional standards that may occur to you.

B. The movies frequently present stereotypes: the poor little rich girl; the dedicated genius living the life of a recluse; the plain, bespectacled secretary who suddenly becomes a beauty when her glasses are removed and her hair is fluffed out. Be ready to discuss the pictures that are brought to mind as you read the following items: Students should give first picture that comes to mind. There may be some variation. See also above.

professor	manicurist
gangster	police detective
New York cab driver	private investigator
newspaper reporter	male author
woman executive	female author

Add to this list and discuss other stereotypes you have seen in movies.

C. Write a review commending or condemning a recent motion picture or stage play which you have seen. Be sure your review is concerned with how the picture or play meets or fails to meet the standards of a good motion-picture or stage-play story. Be sure this is a review, not just a summary of the plot.

EVALUATE DIRECTION, ACTING, AND PHOTOGRAPHY

The director works with the writers, the designers, the cameramen, the casting director, and the actors. From the time he first sees the script, the director must visualize and plan the entire production as it will appear on the stage or screen. He suggests changes to the writers, he plans sets and costumes with the designers; in the case of movies, the director discusses his goals with the cameramen; he interprets the characterization to the casting director in order that suitable actors may be selected; and he coaches the actors so that they may achieve the best interpretation of the story.

Good actors lose their individual identities when interpreting roles. They try to get inside the characters they are playing until, for the duration of the play or movie, they become those characters. The actor's goal is to make his interpretation natural and believable.

The cameraman plays an important part in the success of a picture. He must use his camera in such a way that the photography does not interfere with the story but, rather, helps to move it along. The cameraman may

Students will have to develop awareness of elements other than the story that contribute to the success of a movie or play.

accomplish this by shooting from various angles and by using lights, different lenses, and filters to achieve diverse effects.

He may shoot from below to get the effect of height; he may use close-ups to center attention upon certain details or to record emotions. It is the responsibility of the cameraman to blend scenes in such a way that the transitions are smooth. He may use special effects to indicate the passage of time or to establish a particular mood.

The following standards should help you evaluate direction, acting, and photography:

1. The picture or stage play is ably directed; that is, the picture or play is so put together that the story is told in the most effective way.

2. There is evidence that the members of the cast were chosen because of their fitness for the roles.

3. There is evidence that supporting members of the cast were chosen as carefully as were the stars.

4. The acting is natural and life-like.

5. The characterization is consistent throughout the picture or play.

6. The acting creates the illusion of reality.

7. The photography reveals the story rather than the cleverness of the cameraman.

8. A variety of shots—long, medium, close-up—is used to increase interest.

DEVELOPING YOUR SKILL

Good direc-
tion is evi-
dent in the
interpreta-
tion and in
the over-all
effect.

A. Your teacher may wish to have you discuss pictures or stage plays which you consider were ably directed and in which the acting was excellent.

B. Write a critical review of a motion picture. Let your review be concerned with direction, acting, and photography. Your teacher may wish to divide the class into committees of three and let each committee member contribute one part of its entire review. Reviews will vary.

EVALUATE BACKGROUND ELEMENTS

The effectiveness of a movie or a stage play depends in large measure on the degree to which such elements as settings, costumes, sound, music, and color aid in creating the illusion of reality. Details of background should never be conspicuous in themselves. Their purpose is to help develop the mood or atmosphere of the picture or stage play.

The blending of background elements can be illustrated by reading part of T. S. Eliot's "The Hollow Men" while a Chopin record is playing. Students will recognize the discord.

The following standards should help you evaluate the background elements: Discuss each of the standards in detail.

1. The background is appropriate to the story.
2. The settings create the proper mood or atmosphere.
3. The settings indicate, and are appropriate to, the cultural, social, and financial status of the characters of the story.
4. The costumes are appropriate and authentic.
5. Sound and music are used for their dramatic value as an accompaniment to the story.
6. Silence, as well as sound, is used effectively.
7. The music lends atmosphere to the story.
8. The music tempo matches accurately the tempo of the scene.
9. The color is natural.
10. The background elements create a feeling of reality.

DEVELOPING YOUR SKILL

A. Your teacher may ask you to discuss pictures or stage plays in which, in your opinion, the illusion of reality is created by the background elements. Require that specific examples be given.

B. After seeing a motion picture, write the answers to the following questions: Answers will depend upon movie seen. You may wish to have all students see the same movie.

Discuss these points beforehand so that students are aware

1. What details established the time and place of the story?
2. Did any characters live in surroundings too rich for their circumstances as described in the story?
3. Were you conscious of any studio-made sets? Did they lessen your enjoyment?

of elements that they are to evaluate. If students all see the same movie, you may wish to have them discuss their evaluations. Answers are to be fuller than just Yes or No.

4. Was there any especially effective scene or set? What was its effect on you?
5. Were the costumes appropriate and authentic?
6. Were any characters too well dressed for their parts?
7. Were there any unusual sound effects that added to your enjoyment?
8. Did the music suit the scenes?
9. Was there any unusual music? What was its effect upon you?
10. How did color add to, or detract from, the picture?

Review Exercises—Judging Movies and Plays

Story
Direction
Acting
Photography
Settings
Costumes
Music
Color

A. Be prepared to discuss in class the various elements that must be considered in evaluating movies. Be sure that you consider the importance of each element to the success of the movie. See also pp. 9-10, 11-13.

B. Using the following questions as guides, write a report on a movie you have seen which was based on a book you have read. Were any parts of the plot omitted? Were any new characters and scenes introduced into the movie? What changes, if any, were made in the plot, characterization, and sequence of scenes? Was the theme, or main idea, of the book retained in the movie? Did the movie have the same ending as the book? Evaluate the movie.

See bottom margin.

UNIT SUMMARY

Motion pictures and stage plays are rich sources of culture and entertainment. Unfortunately, however, many motion pictures and stage plays are of mediocre or low artistic or intellectual quality. It is important, therefore, that you choose wisely the motion pictures and stage plays you see.

In studying this unit and through doing the exercises, you have learned to plan your theater attendance so as to make your time spent at the theater both pleasurable and profitable. You have learned that you should vary the types of motion pictures and stage plays you see. You have learned to use aids to discover the best pictures and plays available.

Intelligent theater-goers employ certain standards as a basis for evaluating the quality of motion pictures and stage plays. You have been introduced to standards for evaluating such elements of motion pictures and stage plays as the story, direction, acting, and background elements.

Do not accept a series of answers to the questions posed. The questions are intended only to serve as guides to developing a thorough, well-organized evaluation.

UNIT REVIEW EXERCISES

DISCUSSION TOPICS

No.

A. Should motion pictures and stage plays be judged by their popularity <u>alone</u> See or should their artistic and intellectual qualities also be considered? Why? bottom

B. Discuss the following statement in the light of motion pictures and stage margin. plays you have seen. Give specific instances to prove your point. Try to include in your discussion movies and plays whose settings vary from early periods of history to the present. Discussion will depend upon movies selected as examples.

Although his environment, his attire, and other outward characteristics have changed throughout the years, man's basic emotions have remained the same. In every period, in every century, man has known love, hate, fear, envy, and greed.

WRITTEN WORK

A. Write a review of a movie or stage play you have seen. Remember that your review should contain a summary of the plot—without revealing the ending—and comments on the following: theme, acting, casting, direction, and background elements. A plot summary is not enough.

B. Write a composition in which you discuss an unusually good characterization you have seen in a film or stage play. Be specific in showing how the character was interpreted and developed. Insist upon specific references.

C. Write a comparison of two films (or stage plays) of the same type. Decide which you think is the better of the two and defend your choice using the standards you have learned in this unit. For better students.

VOCABULARY

Did you know the meaning of all the words in this unit? The following sentences use some of the words in different contexts. Write the numbers 1 to 5 on your paper. After each number, write the letter of the word or phrase that could best be substituted for the italicized word in each sentence. Before making your choice, find the word on the page indicated to see how it is used in the unit.

c
1. He made a *significant* speech. [p. 10]
    (*a*) enthusiastic; (*b*) impromptu; (*c*) important; (*d*) eloquent

a
2. He was one of the most *esteemed* citizens of the town. [p. 3]
    (*a*) highly regarded; (*b*) prosperous; (*c*) enlightened; (*d*) intelligent

c
3. The director's *caustic* comments infuriated the actors. [p. 4]
    (*a*) blunt; (*b*) critical; (*c*) stinging; (*d*) gruff

A box office "name" can make popular a movie or play of little or no merit. This is particularly true of movies. However, popularity may be an indication of worth, depending upon the reason for the popularity.

4. They made certain that the information was *authentic*. [p. 1]
b   (*a*) convincing; (*b*) reliable; (*c*) conclusive; (*d*) authorized

5. The story was weakened by the use of *hackneyed* figures of speech. [p. 9]
d   (*a*) exaggerated; (*b*) well-known; (*c*) boring; (*d*) trite

SPELLING

The following spelling words appeared in the unit or were chosen because they are commonly misspelled. Study these words so that you will be prepared to write them from dictation.

Combine spelling with vocabularly enrichment. Students should be able to use words as well as spell them.

1. significant
2. esteemed
3. caustic
4. authentic
5. hackneyed
6. discriminating
7. consensus
8. consistently
9. wary
10. stereotypes
11. media
12. revolutionary
13. immensely
14. distinctive
15. prejudices
16. absorbing
17. authoritative
18. comparatively
19. conferred
20. distinguish

UNIT SELF-TEST

See answers below.

1. What aids are available to help you choose worthwhile motion pictures and stage plays?
2. What are the characteristics of a good critical review?
3. Name three standards for evaluating motion-picture and stage-play stories.
4. Name two standards for evaluating each of the following: direction, acting, photography.
5. What are the background elements necessary to an effective motion-picture or stage production? Name one standard by which each is judged.

1. Friends' opinions; actors' and directors' reputations, if based on past performances; critical reviews.
2. Unprejudiced, objective, honest.
3. See numbered standards on pp. 9-10.
4. See p. 12.
5. See p. 13.

Unit 2

Listening

The distinction between hearing and conscious listening is an important one.

The modern world is filled with sound. Although you may hear the clamor all around you, you listen only to a small part of the total. Listening is more than hearing; you might call it "selective hearing."

Stop whatever you are doing and concentrate on the sounds you hear. Are you now aware of particular sounds that you were not conscious of earlier? Most of these sounds have probably been there, in the background; but, although you may have *heard* them, you did not *listen* to them. On the other hand, there are many times when you must listen actively, not merely hear or half-listen.

When you listen for information, you must give your full attention to what is being said. This is the kind of listening you do when you listen to assignments, directions, explanations, and announcements and when you listen to lectures and speeches.

To appreciate poetry, music, or any other form of expression intended for listening, you must not only listen actively, but must also have some understanding of the form and know what to listen for. Such understanding will increase your listening pleasure.

In this unit you will learn to develop the skills needed for informational and appreciative listening. You will learn how to listen to remember, how to take notes while listening, and how to enjoy poetry and choral speaking.

How good a listener are you now?

Students will readily accept the importance of developing informational listening skills. They must be led to understand, also, that enjoyment will increase as they develop appreciative listening skills.

18   *Listening*

| ✓ | CHECK YOURSELF

After you have answered the following questions, be prepared to discuss the questions and answers with your teacher and your classmates. Try to determine which of the listening skills mentioned you need to learn and which you already know but need to improve. The additional points listed may be raised in discussion.

Yes   1. After listening to a speaker in assembly, can you remember what he said well enough to discuss his talk? What factors made listening easy or difficult?

No   2. Do you ever find that you have missed a main idea in a speech and, therefore, cannot follow what is being said? Lack of attention or difficulty of topic?

No   3. Have you ever answered a test question incorrectly because you didn't remember the directions accurately? Comment on oral instructions as opposed to written.

No   4. Have you ever done the wrong assignment because you were only half-listening when the assignment was given? Would a notebook have helped?

No   5. Do you ever half-listen because you are not interested in the speaker's subject? The audience has an obligation to the speaker—to listen.

No   6. Have you ever tried to take notes to help you remember important ideas only to find that you missed most of what was being said?

Yes   7. Do you enjoy listening to poetry when it is well read?

Yes   8. Have you ever listened to recordings of poets reading their own work?

Yes   If so, did you enjoy this listening experience?

Yes   9. Do you enjoy listening to a speech choir?

Yes   10. Do you know what is meant by *appreciative listening?* Understanding increases appreciation.

1. Informational Listening

LISTEN ACTIVELY

The three steps that are underlined constitute a good formula for active listening.

Your success in school and, later, your success in the business world depend to a great extent upon your knowing how to listen to and remember information. Informational listening requires that you <u>make a conscious effort to follow</u> what is being said; that you <u>organize the ideas</u> as you hear them; and that, if possible, you <u>ask intelligent questions or make intelligent comments</u> to help you understand and remember the information.

Assignments

In your classes, when your teachers make assignments for class work or homework, do not put yourself in the embarrassing position of having to ask that assignments be repeated because you were not listening. When an assignment is made, listen for details. Jot down page numbers, problem numbers, exercise numbers, or any other important details. An assignment notebook or a special section in your class notebook will help you to remember important information.

Directions and Explanations

When directions are being given for a test, be sure you listen to the entire question. Think about what is being said. Listen for words such as *define, discuss, compare,* or *list* that tell you how to develop your answer. Make a mental note of the details in the directions and, if you are permitted to do so, write down the important items in the directions.

Very often you may find that you have to depend solely upon your memory when you have been given directions or explanations. In fact, remembering is an important part of all effective listening. As you listen to directions or to an explanation, note the details and their relationship to each other; try to visualize each step as it is developed. Whenever possible, ask pertinent questions about points which are not clear. Finally, repeat the instructions mentally to fix them in your memory and repeat them step by step as you carry them out.

Discuss with students differences in meaning of the directions define, discuss, compare, and list.

Announcements

The same techniques as those discussed in the preceding paragraphs will help you listen better to announcements. Know what the general topic of the announcement is and listen for details. Think through the details to be sure sufficient information has been given. If any points have been omitted or are not clear, ask about them when given the opportunity to do so.

Read the following announcement:

The Halloween meeting of the Student Council will be replaced by a record hop. As in the past, members of the Junior and Senior classes are invited to attend the dance. Refreshments will be served.

Although the announcement seems to be complete, a careful listener would quickly recognize the fact that there are three important omissions: On what day is the dance to be held? At what time will it start? Where will it be held? When listening to announcements, listen for the details that tell *Who? What? When? Where?* and, frequently, *Why?*

One way to help students develop alertness is to give an assignment, a direction, or an explanation or to make an announcement and then ask students to write a summary.

Lectures and Speeches

Recent studies have shown that the average person absorbs only about 25 per cent of what he hears. Frequently, the failure of a person to comprehend what he hears is the result of inattention. He hasn't listened to what the speaker has been saying.

Concentration can be developed through practice.

Listening to lectures and speeches <u>requires a longer period of concentration</u> than do the other listening situations discussed. Because many persons have not yet learned how to listen for a long period of time, they may find themselves confused and restless during a speech. Like most other skills, <u>listening to long talks is a skill to be learned and practiced.</u> The seven suggestions that follow will help you to listen intelligently and thoughtfully to informative lectures and speeches.

1. Be ready to listen.

Avoid physical and mental distractions.

When you enter the room in which the lecture or speech is to be given, try to find a seat that will enable you to see and hear the speaker without difficulty. Clear your mind of irrelevant matter. Whom you are taking to the next dance or what you will wear to the next dance are thoughts that will distract your attention from what the speaker has to say. Sit up in your seat and give your full attention to the speaker.

2. Listen with an open mind.

Suspend prejudices.

If you decide in advance that you are not interested in what a speaker has to say, you are likely to let your mind wander during his presentation. Any prejudices you have about either the speaker or his subject must be held in abeyance if you are to become a good listener.

3. Listen from the beginning.

Know the theme.

Most speakers state their theme, or central idea, in the opening sentences of their talks. If you do not listen at the start, you may find that the ideas expressed later are meaningless to you since you will not know the topic to which they are related.

Provide practice in listening to lectures and speeches. Present some aspect of the English curriculum by means of a lecture. If possible, invite a debater or a member of another department to give a lecture to your classes.

4. Listen for the main ideas.

Relate main ideas to the central theme.

You will find that most speakers provide signposts to help you recognize main ideas. Good speakers usually signal important ideas by transitional expressions as *first, second, another point, as a result,* and so on. Listen, too, for the speaker's summaries as he develops his ideas and as he ends his speech.

5. Listen for the supporting details.

Relate important supporting details to the main ideas.

It will not be possible for you to remember all the supporting details in a speech, but you should be able to retain the most significant ones. You will find, as you listen, that speakers frequently expand upon what they are saying and give examples in order to allow their listeners an opportunity to absorb one idea before the next is presented. Thus, a speaker may express a main idea, give the important supporting details, and then talk further about the idea or the details before going on to the next idea.

6. Summarize ideas as you listen.

Organize and summarize.

It has been determined that you can think about four times as rapidly as a person can speak. Therefore, you have ample time during a speech to organize your thoughts and relate the material to what you already know about the subject. If possible, take notes.

7. Use the material.

Evaluate and use the ideas for retention.

If you have an opportunity to discuss the information you have acquired, you are more likely to retain it. Such discussion will also involve an evaluation of the ideas presented by the speaker.

If, however, you do not have an opportunity to discuss the ideas immediately, make a written record to help you remember. Think through the information you have learned from the speech and write a summary of it. In your introductory sentence, state the speaker's general topic and theme. Then note his major ideas as he develops them.

Approximately 45 per cent of your time is spent in listening situations. Although you may listen for many reasons, much of your listening is done for the purpose of acquiring information. You will find that giving immediate attention to a speaker, developing a receptive attitude, and learning to remember and evaluate what is said will make your informational listening experiences both pleasurable and profitable.

Good listening is essential to learning. As listening skills improve so should learning increase.

DEVELOPING YOUR SKILL

A. What are the various situations in which you listen for information? In which ones are details of primary importance? In which situations are the main ideas most important? See p. T54.

B. What are the skills you must develop for informational listening? Be prepared to discuss them in class. See p. T54.

This exercise provides practice in the application of listening skills.

C. Write out a direction, an explanation, or an announcement. When you are called upon, read your paragraph to the class. When you have finished reading, call on someone to restate what you have said. Did that person listen attentively?

TAKE NOTES

Stress the point that notes are not a verbatim record of a speaker's words.

Have you ever tried to take notes only to find that you had missed several important ideas while you were writing? This generally happens when you try to put too much into your notes. Notes are not a verbatim record of what the speaker says but, rather, are a record of key words and phrases that will help you recall the important ideas expressed in the speech. Such notes can be used for study purposes and frequently provide ideas for speaking and writing assignments.

As you take notes, try to keep up with the speaker. If you miss a point, leave a space and go on. Frequently, speakers repeat their major points when they summarize, and you may be able to fill in what you missed. If, however, you spend time trying to recall the point you have forgotten, you may miss other important material.

You will have to work out for yourself short cuts and abbreviations that will enable you to record ideas rapidly and accurately. It is not necessary to write notes in sentences; in fact, you will lose too much time if you try to do so. Instead, write down only those words and phrases that will concisely summarize the main ideas and the important supporting details. To make the pattern of the talk clear, write the main ideas as headings in your notes and indent the supporting ideas as subheadings.

Go over your notes as soon as possible while the material is still fresh in your mind, and make any necessary revisions. You may find it helpful to expand your notes to make them clearer and more usable. Frequently, the abbreviations and other short cuts that you use are meaningful at the time but are undecipherable at a later date. Usable notes represent a record of information that is important to you.

Notes are valuable only if they are usuable. Emphasize the importance of revising and expanding notes while the material is still fresh in the listener's mind.

3. Leave space and go on. Listen for points missed when speaker summarizes. 4. Write main ideas as headings and indent supporting ideas as subheadings.

DEVELOPING YOUR SKILL

A. Be ready to answer the following questions in class:
   1. What is the purpose of taking notes? To help one recall important ideas.
   2. Why is it important to use key words and phrases rather than sentences in your note-taking? To record ideas rapidly and accurately
   3. If you miss a point while taking notes, what should you do? See above.
   4. How can you write notes so that the importance of the ideas is clear? See above.
   5. What can you do to make your notes understandable and usable for future reference? Revise and expand notes while ideas are still fresh.

B. Take notes on a speech that your teacher recommends. It may be a radio, television, assembly, or recorded speech; or it may be a speech given by one of your classmates or read by your teacher. Write a summary of the talk. Your teacher may wish to collect both the notes and the summaries. This exercise enables students to recognize the importance of clear, usable notes. Good summaries depend upon accurate notes here.

Review Exercises—Informational Listening

A. Listen, without taking written notes, as your teacher reads an article from a newspaper or a magazine or reads some other informative material. After the reading, write a summary of the article. Mental organization is stressed here.

B. Take notes as you listen to a speech given or read by a member of the class or to a speech from a record. After the speaker has finished, compare your main headings and subheadings with those of the other members of the class. You may wish to repeat this exercise at intervals throughout the year. Students going on to college should be able to take comprehensive, usable notes.

C. Write a well-organized composition on the importance of knowing how to listen for information. Be specific in telling how these listening skills are important to you. Compositions will vary but should all include the basic skills developed in this unit and their application to specific situations.

2. Appreciative Listening

Much of the listening you do is listening for pleasure. You may enjoy listening to stories, to plays, to poetry, to music, or to other forms of oral expression. You will find that your enjoyment of all forms of oral expression will be heightened if you learn to listen appreciatively—with understanding as well as interest.

ENJOYING POETRY

Poetry is one of the oldest of the arts. It is not known who first had the idea of telling a story or expressing an emotion in words with a rhythmic beat, but it is an idea which persists today and is likely to continue.

If the first poet had merely wanted to tell of happenings in an ordinary way, he would have told his story in the straightforward language of prose. But he wanted his listeners to be stirred as he was stirred; so he created a song in words. He may have used a drum beat to emphasize the rhythm, or he may have stamped his feet and clapped his hands against his body to stress the beat of his song. However he accompanied his chant, he was using the music of poetry to tell his story.

Although the distance from the primitive chanter to the modern, printed volume of poetry is great, the intention of the poet remains unchanged. The poet is trying to tell you in rhythmic, musical language something that will arouse your imagination, stir your emotions, and leave an imprint on your mind. He uses words for their sound, as well as for their meaning. Since this is so, poetry can be appreciated more fully when it is heard.

When you hear poetry read aloud and respond to the rhythms, you may also begin to discover the other qualities that are necessary to understanding and appreciation. Listen for the *melody* of a poem—the flow of vowels and consonants. The melody, together with the *tempo* of the lines, can help to establish the mood. Notice, as you read the first lines of Edgar Allan Poe's "The Raven," how the sounds of the words and the slowness of the rhythm combine to create a mood of gloom and mystery.

> Once upon a midnight dreary, while I pondered, weak and weary,
> Over many a quaint and curious volume of forgotten lore—

The *mood* changes slightly in the next line as the narrator is roused from his half-sleep.

> While I nodded, nearly napping, suddenly there came a tapping,

Here the poet has used sharp, clipped sounds to create the effect of suddenness. Also, the repetition of the *n* sound, speeds up the tempo of the line. The next line brings the listener back to the mood of the first lines.

> As of someone gently rapping, rapping at my chamber door.

Through discussion, students should be led to recognize the various elements in poetry that combine to produce the desired effects.

Marginal notes:

This is a good definition of poetry.

Discuss rhythm, melody, and tempo.

As you listen to poetry, notice the severity of one poem, the restlessness Tone. of another, the sadness of a third, the gaiety of a fourth. Notice, too, how the music of the poem frequently provides clues to the meaning of the lines. You may have had the experience of not understanding a poem when reading it silently, only to have the meaning become evident when the poem was read aloud to you.

The poet uses his imagination to transform the usual into the unusual. He can take simple, commonplace objects and events and change them to memorable images and experiences. The poet appeals to the senses and to the emotions in his use of *imagery*. The word pictures he paints strike responsive chords in his readers and listeners. Consider the following lines from Robert Frost's "The Death of the Hired Man." Imagery. Discuss the purpose and the effect of the imagery in the excerpt.

> Part of a moon was falling down the west,
> Dragging the whole sky with it to the hills.
> Its light poured softly in her lap. She saw
> And spread her apron to it. She put out her hand
> Among the harp-like morning-glory strings,
> Taut with the dew from garden bed to eaves,
> As if she played unheard some tenderness
> That wrought on him beside her in the night.

Frost's imagery has translated moonlight, a woman's apron, and the morning-glory strings into a setting of quiet beauty and a mood of tenderness and compassion.

As you respond to the music, the mood, and the imagery in poetry, you will find that your understanding of poetry increases. And as your understanding increases, your enjoyment of poetry will be heightened.

Introduce other poems for discussion. Encourage students to bring in poems that illustrate the effects of rhythm, melody, tempo, sounds, and imagery.

Students frequently have difficulty with this poem
when they read it silently, but find it delightful when
26   they hear it read.

Listening

DEVELOPING YOUR SKILL

A. Read the following poem silently. Then listen as your teacher reads
the poem aloud. Did your reactions to the poem differ when you read
it silently and when you heard it? If so, what was the difference? See
above.

CHANSON INNOCENTE

in Just-

spring   when the world is mud-

luscious the little The balloonman

lame balloonman personifies spring.

whistles   far   and wee The line
stretches out to a piping note.
and eddieandbill come The lines

running from marbles and race to a

piracies and it's   climax.

spring

when the world is puddle-wonderful

the queer The balloonman appears

old balloonman whistles again with

far   and   wee   his faint cry.

and bettyandisbel come dancing The
                poem hastens on
from hop-scotch and jump-rope and and

it's   reaches another

spring   climax...

and   Then it slows

     the   meditatively...

        goat-footed and suddenly
                the truth
balloonMan   whistles dawns that

far   it was Pan all

and   the time, dressed
               up like a balloon-
wee   man.

—E. E. CUMMINGS

B. Your teacher may wish to set aside time for listening to recordings of poetry read either by the poets themselves or by actors. Be prepared to discuss one of the poems in terms of melody and tempo, mood, and imagery. How do these elements contribute to the effectiveness of the poem? See p. T54.

C. Write a paragraph in which you discuss the following statement: Poetry can be appreciated more fully when it is heard. The important point here is that poetry depends upon rhythmic, musical language for its effect. Word sounds are often as important as word meanings. You may wish to have students apply the discussion to a specific poem of their own choosing.

ENJOYING CHORAL SPEAKING

Choral speaking is the interpretation of poetry by a speaking choir. When you participate in choral speaking, you share a poem with others. You become a co-operative part of a group which is communicating to listeners the thoughts and feelings expressed by a poem or story. And, as a participant in, or as a listener to, choral speaking, you may acquire a better understanding of poetry and sense a new delight in the melody and movement of this form.

A speaking choir is usually divided into groups according to the pitch of the voices. Just as a singing choir may be grouped according to soprano, alto, tenor, and bass, so a speaking choir is divided according to high-pitched voices and low-pitched voices. Depending upon the range of voices and the selections offered, a speaking choir may have from two to six groups. It may be divided into two groups, girls and boys. Each of these groups may be further divided into light (high-pitched) voices and dark (low-pitched) voices or into light, medium, and dark voices. It is important to group voices according to the pitch of the speaking voice, not the singing voice. A girl, for example, may sing soprano but may have a low-pitched speaking voice.

The conductor of a verse-speaking choir holds a position of importance. The success of a presentation depends largely upon his skill. He conducts the speaking just as a music director conducts the singing of a chorus or the playing of an orchestra. The conductor signals with his hands to indicate rhythm, tempo, beginnings, pauses, and endings.

Arrangements for choral speaking vary as to type, the arrangement used depending principally upon the kind of selection being spoken. Among the types of arrangements are the refrain, antiphonal speaking, sequential speaking, part speaking, and unison.

Even if you have had no training or experience in directing choral speaking, do not hesitate to experiment with this way of teaching poetry. The experimentation is part of the learning situation for students.

Refrain

The simplest and easiest form of choral speaking is the refrain. In this arrangement, a soloist or a small group may carry the story, with the entire choir responding in unison on the refrain. Ballads and folk songs lend themselves well to refrain interpretation. The first stanza of "The Erie Canal" illustrates this arrangement.

You may wish to have several students do some background research for this ballad. Have them determine whether this is a bright, noisy ballad. If so—and it is—the reading should be appropriately vigorous.

THE ERIE CANAL

Type: Refrain

Solo: I've got a mule, her name is Sal,

Unison: Fifteen miles on the Erie Canal;

Solo: She's a good old worker and a good old pal,

Unison: Fifteen miles on the Erie Canal.

Solo: We've hauled some barges in our day,

Filled with lumber, coal, and hay,

And we know ev'ry inch of the way

From Albany to Buffalo.

Refrain:

Unison: Low bridge, ev'rybody down!

Low bridge, for we're going through a town;

And you'll always know your neighbor,

You'll always know your pal,

If you've ever navigated on the Erie Canal.

Antiphonal

Antiphonal or two-part speaking is the same as responsive reading. The group is divided into two sections, light voices and dark voices, or girls and boys.

Question-and-answer poems lend themselves readily to this type of arrangement, as in the first stanza of "Up Hill" by Christina Rossetti.

UP HILL

Type: Antiphonal

Girls:	Does the road wind up hill all the way?
Boys:	Yes to the very end.
Girls:	Will the day's journey take the whole long day?
Boys:	From morn to night, my friend.

Have students search for other poems that will lend themselves to antiphonal reading.

Sequential Speaking

Poems that present a series of ideas, images, or experiences lend themselves to sequential arrangement. Such a poem is Robert Browning's "Pippa's Song." Note how the unison reading of the last two lines gives a climactic effect.

PIPPA'S SONG

Type: Sequential Speaking, with Unison Ending

Solo 1:	The year's at the spring,
Solo 2:	And the day's at the morn;
Solo 3:	Morning's at seven;
Solo 4:	The hillside's dew-pearled;
Solo 5:	The lark's on the wing;
Solo 6:	The snail's on the thorn;
Unison:	God's in His heaven—
	All's right with the world.

The reading of this selection should be light and joyous.

Part Speaking

From the point of view of arrangement, part speaking is the most difficult and the most interesting of the various types of choral speaking. Voices

With practice, students will learn to listen to the voices around them and to adapt their own speaking to that of the group.

If there is a recording of <u>John</u> <u>Brown</u>'s <u>Body</u> available,
you may wish to play some of the parts that include passages
that are spoken chorally.

30

Listening

are classified and grouped into light, medium, and dark (soprano, second
soprano, alto; first tenor, second tenor, baritone-bass). Interpretation of
a poem or prose selection is comparable to an orchestral arrangement. The
voices are the instruments, and the arranger and the director strive for the
most effective blending, to interpret the rhythm, the melody, the mood,
and the meaning of the selection.

An amusing traditional verse from the French illustrates how effective
this type of arrangement can be.

A GOBLIN LIVES IN OUR HOUSE

Type: Part Speaking

Build gradually in speed and volume and then gradually decrease in the last four lines.	*Second Soprano*:	A goblin lives in *our* house,
	Soprano:	in *our* house,
	Alto:	in *our* house,
	Unison:	A goblin lives in our house all the year round.
	Solo 1:	He bumps
	Solo 2:	And he jumps
	Solo 3:	And he thumps
	Solo 4:	And he stumps,
	Alto:	He knocks
	Second Soprano:	And he rocks
	Soprano:	And he rattles at the locks.
	Second Soprano:	A goblin lives in *our* house,
	Alto:	in *our* house,
	Soprano:	in *our* house,
	Unison:	A goblin lives in our house all the year round.

Unison Speaking

Since in unison speaking all the words are spoken by the entire choral
group, no arrangement is necessary. A difficulty in unison speaking is the
requirement that many voices speak as one with the same rate of speech,
timing of pauses, and uniformity of inflection, phrasing, pronunciation,
and emphasis.

It is helpful to develop some system of notation to indicate pitch. Usually the human voice makes use of four
levels of pitch that can be designated <u>4</u>, <u>3</u>, <u>2</u>, <u>1</u>, with <u>4</u>
representing the highest pitch.

The pitches marked in "Buffalo Dusk" represent the four
pitch points of the human voice and are designated 4, 3, 2, 1
from high to low.
Appreciative Listening   31

The choral speaking of Carl Sandburg's poem, "Buffalo Dusk," in unison will demonstrate to you how effective this type of choral speaking can be once you have mastered the difficulties inherent in unison speaking.

BUFFALO DUSK

Type: Unison Speaking

Students may wish to change the suggested notations to achieve a different tonal effect.

Unison: The buffalo are gone.
And those who saw the buffaloes are gone.
Those who saw the buffaloes by thousands and how
they pawed the prairie sod into dust with their
hoofs, their great heads down, pawing on in a
great pageant of dusk,
Those who saw the buffaloes are gone.
And the buffaloes are gone.

> DEVELOPING YOUR SKILL

A. Your teacher may wish to have you practice speaking the following selections. Before you try speaking them chorally, discuss each of the selections. What is the mood of the poem? What words or ideas should be emphasized? Does the arrangement suggested bring out the best interpretation of the poem? If you think not, what arrangement would you suggest? If new arrangements are suggested, try them chorally and compare them with the ones suggested in your text. Using the arrangements you and your teacher choose, practice the selections until you can speak them effectively as a speaking choir.

MOLLY MALONE

Type: Refrain

Solo: In Dublin's fair city where the girls are so pretty
I first set my eyes on sweet Molly Malone
As she wheeled her wheelbarrow through the streets
    broad and narrow,

Unison: Cryin', "Cockles and mussels, alive, alive, oh!"

Solo: She was a fishmonger, and sure! 'twas no wonder,
For so were her father and mother before.

Discussion beforehand is essential to effective choral interpretation. Stress the importance of following the director once the arrangement and interpretation have been decided upon.

The arrangements
suggested
here are
only that—
suggestions.
Make any changes
that you and your
students feel
will better
express the
poetry. Compare
various inter-
pretations.

And they wheeled their wheelbarrow through the
   streets broad and narrow,

Unison: Cryin', "Cockles and mussels, alive, alive, oh!"

Solo: She was a fishmonger, and sure! 'twas no wonder,

Sure! and that was the end of sweet Molly Malone.

Now her ghost wheels her barrow through the streets
   broad and narrow,

Unison: Cryin', "Cockles and mussels, alive, alive, oh!

Alive, alive, oh! Alive, alive, oh!"

Cryin', "Cockles and mussels, alive, alive, oh!"

I HEAR AMERICA SINGING

Type: Sequential Speaking

Unison:	I hear America singing, the varied carols I hear;
Boys:	Those of mechanics—each one singing his, as it should be, blithe and strong;
Solo 1:	The carpenter singing his, as he measures his plank or beam,
Solo 2:	The mason singing his, as he makes ready for work, or leaves off work;
Solo 3:	The boatman singing what belongs to him in his boat—
Solo 4:	The deck-hand singing on the steam-boat deck.
Solo 5:	The shoemaker singing as he sits at his bench,
Solo 6:	The hatter singing as he stands;
Solo 7:	The wood-cutter's song—
Solo 8:	The ploughboy's on his way in the morning or at the noon intermission, or at sundown;
Solo 9:	The delicious singing of the mother—or the young wife at work—or the girl sewing or washing—
Solo 10:	Each singing what belongs to her, and to none else;
Unison:	The day what belongs to the day—at night, the party of young fellows, robust, friendly,

Singing with open mouths, their strong melodious songs.

—WALT WHITMAN

The rhythm of the Whitman selection is unlike that of
the ballad that precedes it. You may wish to compare it
with the rhythms found in the Bible.

B. Stress the point that interpretations may differ somewhat and still be equally good so long as they do not violate the poet's intention.

B. Select one of your favorite poems and arrange it for choral speaking. Your teacher may wish to have various students act as director and lead the class, or part of the class, in speaking their arrangements. Be prepared to comment upon the various presentations. See above.

C. Write a paragraph in which you discuss the ways in which listening to choral speaking and participating in a speech choir contribute to your enjoyment of poetry. Paragraphs will vary. An important point, however, is the increased appreciation of the music of poetry and awareness of rhythm, mood and imagery.

Review Exercises—Appreciative Listening

A. Be prepared to tell how an awareness of <u>melody</u>, <u>tempo</u>, <u>mood</u>, and <u>imagery</u> in poetry helps you to listen more appreciatively. See p. T55.

B. Write a paragraph in which you show the relationship between choral speaking and appreciative listening. How does the choral interpretation of a poem help you to be a more appreciative listener? See p. T55.

C. The Irish poet, William Butler Yeats, once wrote:

> I have just heard a poem spoken with so delicate a sense of
> its rhythm, with so perfect a respect for its meaning, that if
> I were a wise man and could persuade a few people to learn
> the art I would never open a book of verse again.

Write a composition in which you discuss Yeats's statement. What does he mean? Do you agree or disagree? Why? See p. T55. See also below.

UNIT SUMMARY

In this unit you have worked to improve your listening skills when listening for information and when listening for appreciation. You have learned that both kinds of listening require that you take an active part in the experience. In your study of informational listening, you learned to recognize main ideas and supporting details. You also learned to organize ideas as you heard them and to take notes.

Your study of appreciative listening gave you a broader appreciation of poetry. By learning more about the particular qualities of poetry, you learned to listen with closer attention and deeper understanding. Participation in choral speaking experiences taught you to hear the music of poetry while interpreting it.

You may wish to have some of the compositions written for Exercise C above read aloud in class. Discuss both Yeats's statement and the students' interpretations.

UNIT REVIEW EXERCISES

DISCUSSION TOPICS

A. What are the values to be gained, both now and later, from improving your informational and appreciative listening skills? See p. T55.

B. Listening to remember is an important feature of listening for information. What are the various techniques you may use to help you remember information? Why is remembering so important? See p. T55.

C. Read the following poem several times. Then listen as your teacher, or a chosen student, reads the poem aloud. Discuss the melody, tempo, mood, and imagery of the poem. How would you arrange it for choral speaking? Decide upon the best arrangement and then interpret the poem chorally. Your teacher may wish to divide the class into two speaking choirs so that each group may listen to the others interpret "The Listeners."

One possible arrangement is suggested.

THE LISTENERS

Solo:	"Is there anybody there?" said the Traveler, Medium Voices
Medium Voices:	Knocking on the moonlit door;
	And his horse in the silence champed the grasses
	Of the forest's ferny floor.
Light Voices:	And a bird flew up out of the turret,
	Above the Traveler's head:
Medium Voices:	And he smote upon the door again a second time;
Solo:	"Is there anybody there?" he said. Medium Voices
Dark Voices:	But no one descended to the Traveler;
	No head from the leaf-fringed sill
	Leaned over and looked into his gray eyes,
	Where he stood perplexed and still.
Light Voices:	But only a host of phantom listeners
	That dwelt in the lone house then
	Stood listening in the quiet of the moonlight
	To that voice from the world of men:
	Stood thronging the faint moonbeams on the dark stair
	That goes down to the empty hall,
	Hearkening in an air stirred and shaken
	By the lonely Traveler's call.

Discuss thoroughly the poet's use of sound, tempo, rhyme, and imagery to create the mood. Consider any changes in mood. Students with art ability may wish to draw the scene as they picture it.

Dark Voices: And he felt in his heart their strangeness,

        Their stillness answering his cry,

        While his horse moved, cropping the dark turf,

        'Neath the starred and leafy sky;

All Voices: For he suddenly smote on the door, even

        Louder, and lifted his head:—

Solo: "Tell them I came, and no one answered,

Medium Voices: That I kept my word," he said.

Dark Voices: Never the least stir made the listeners,

        Though every word he spake

        Fell echoing through the shadowiness of the still house

        From the one man left awake:

Light Voices: Aye, they heard his foot upon the stirrup,

Medium Voices: And the sound of iron on stone,

Dark Voices: And how the silence surged softly backward,

        When the plunging hoofs were gone.

—WALTER DE LA MARE

WRITTEN WORK Provide as many opportunities as possible for note-taking activities.

1. Your teacher may wish to read a speech or some other informative selection to the class. Take notes as you listen. Write a summary based on your notes.
2. Write a short, but carefully thought-out, composition on one of the following topics.

> Poetry Is Meant to Be Heard
> Choral Speaking Helped Me Appreciate Poetry.

VOCABULARY

Did you know the meaning of every word in this unit? In the following sentences, some of the words are used in different contexts. Write the numbers 1 to 5 on your paper. After each number, write the letter of the word or phrase that could best be substituted for the italicized word in each sentence. Before making your choice, find the word on the page indicated to see how the word is used in this unit.

1. The art dealer spent hours writing an *evaluation* of the paintings.   [p. 21]
    (*a*) criticism; (*b*) discussion; (*c*) appraisal; (*d*) validation

c

Words in the vocabulary study should be employed whenever natural to the classroom situation.

2. We shall keep the matter in *abeyance* until we have additional
   information.   [p. 20]
a   (*a*) waiting; (*b*) expectation; (*c*) observance; (*d*) consideration
3. A reverent mood was created throughout the church by the *antiphonal*
   chant.   [p. 29]
c   (*a*) deep-toned; (*b*) solemn; (*c*) responsive; (*d*) musical
4. The *sequential* placement of the letters was from *z* to *a* rather than from
   a to *z*.   [p. 29]
a   (*a*) successive; (*b*) unusual; (*c*) reverse; (*d*) ridiculous
5. Despite the teasing, she kept her *inherent* good temper.   [p. 31]
b   (*a*) cheerful; (*b*) characteristic; (*c*) inherited; (*d*) well-developed

SPELLING

The following spelling words appeared in the unit or were chosen because
they are commonly misspelled. Study these words so that you will be prepared
to write them from dictation.

Point out the
trouble spots
in spelling words.
Help students to
create mnemonic
devices whenever
possible.

1. evaluating	11. apparatus
2. abeyance	12. intellectual
3. antiphonal	13. repetition
4. sequential	14. inevitable
5. inherent	15. initiative
6. techniques	16. questionnaire
7. climactic	17. specimen
8. comparable	18. invariably
9. irrelevant	19. acquired
10. narrator	20. acquaintance

UNIT SELF-TEST

1. Name four situations in which you listen for information. See p. T55.
2. Name five important guides to listening to informative speeches. See pp.20-21
3. What is the purpose of taking notes? To help one retain information.
4. What techniques must you practice in order to take usable notes? See p.
5. How can notes be utilized? See p. T55.   T55.
6. Name three qualities of poetry. Rhythm, melody, tempo, mood, imagery.
7. How does the poet appeal to the senses and the emotions? Through imagery.
8. How is a speech choir divided? According to pitch of voices.
9. Why is the conductor of a verse-speaking choir so important? See p. T55.
10. Name and define three kinds of arrangements for choral speaking. Refrain
    (p. 28), Antiphonal and sequential (p. 29), Part
    (pp. 29-30), Unison (pp. 30-31).

Unit 3

Discussion and Debate

Discussion is a way of thinking together through purposeful conversation. The form of a discussion varies with the topic to be considered and the nature of the group. Some topics are better handled by a committee, others in an informal class discussion, and still others by means of formal debate. Regardless of the form a discussion takes, its main purpose is the exploration of a subject or problem from all angles.

Definition of discussion.

If you are to take part in making decisions, you must be able to discuss issues and problems and to organize and present an argument convincingly. In addition, you should be able to distinguish sound reasoning from unsound reasoning and valid argument from invalid argument.

Skills to be developed.

In the pages that follow, you will learn how to become more effective in discussion and in debate. First, however, determine how much you already know about discussion and debate by answering the following questions.

CHECK YOURSELF

Number a sheet of paper from 1 to 20. Read each of the following statements and write *Yes* or *No* after the corresponding number on your paper.

1. Do you know what is meant by a round-table discussion? A panel discussion? A forum? A symposium? A debate?
2. Do you keep an open mind when discussing a problem?

The ideal is twenty Yes answers. It is unlikely, however, that students will know this much about discussion and debate. It is also unusual that anyone should meet all the high personal standards included.

37

Questions
2-13 and
15-16 provide
a basis for
diagnostic
self-analysis
of students'
attitudes as
participants
in discus-
sion.

3. Do you contribute to discussions by volunteering opinions or facts and by answering or asking questions?
4. Do you practice good manners in discussion?
5. Do you talk only when you have a contribution to make?
6. Do you argue against ideas rather than against people?
7. Do you disagree in an inquiring mood, not just to contradict?
8. Do you avoid being the kind of person who agrees just to be agreeable?
9. Do you avoid an all-knowing attitude?
10. Are you careful to control emotion with reason?
11. Are you careful to stay on the subject?
12. Do you back up your statements with ample evidence?
13. Do you try to analyze all sides of questions presented?
14. Do you know how to preside during a discussion?
15. Do you wait for evidence before you reject the broad statements of others?
16. Do you avoid interpreting difference of opinion as a personal attack?
17. Can you detect fallacies in reasoning?
18. Can you analyze a debating proposition?
19. Can you construct a brief?
20. Can you expand a brief into a constructive speech?

If you answered *Yes* to most of the 20 questions, you already have an excellent background for studying this unit. If most of your answers were *No,* this unit will be of particular value in helping you to improve your skills in discussion and debate.

Use questions 2-13 and 15-16 as a guide for setting up standards for participating in discussions.

1. Discussion

SELECTING AND ANALYZING A DISCUSSION SUBJECT

Questions like "Which is the greatest influence for good: motion pictures, radio, or television?" or ideas like "Where everybody thinks alike, nobody thinks much," or problems like "How can we make our school grounds more attractive?" are thought-provoking subjects for discussion. Personal experience, school problems, subjects you want to learn more about, and controversial subjects of local or national concern are good sources for discussion topics.

The word thought-provoking is the key to the selection of topics for discussion.

A question which requires a single, direct, factual reply is not suitable for discussion. For example, "Do any teachers at our school conduct examinations on the honor system?" would not be a good question for discussion. On the other hand, "Should examinations be conducted on the honor system?" is a question which should arouse a difference of opinion and result in a lively discussion.

After you have selected a subject for discussion, you will need to analyze it. What is the meaning and significance of the subject? How can the subject be divided so that it may be discussed from all sides? What examples, illustrations, and facts are available to help develop the discussion subject? What significance does the discussion have for the group?

When the purpose of a discussion is the solution of a problem, the discussion should follow the process of reflective thinking; that is, it should follow the six steps required to define, explore, and solve the problem:

1. Define the exact nature of the problem with which the group is concerned.

2. Review why the problem exists or what caused it.

3. Explore possible solutions. Avoid an either-or solution; try to present at least three choices.

4. Consider the advantages and disadvantages of each solution.

5. Decide upon the best solution.

6. Consider how the solution may best be put into operation.

> DEVELOPING YOUR SKILL

A. Bring to class a list of four subjects that you think would be suitable for discussion and that would be interesting to your classmates. Include the following types of subjects: (1) a subject that you know about through personal experience; (2) a school problem you feel strongly about; (3) a subject of general interest that you feel your classmates would like to learn more about; and (4) a question of local or national interest. One student may list on the board the topics which are of greatest interest to the entire group. Be sure the master list includes all four types of topics. Copy the master list and keep it for reference throughout your study of group discussions.

B. Choose one of the questions or ideas from the master list prepared for Exercise A as a subject for discussion, and analyze and outline the topic, using the six steps suggested in the text. Keep your outline for possible use in a later exercise. Six steps are listed on this page. The exercise requires a problem-type topic.

Topics should be multi-faceted or allow for differences of opinion.

The order is important in the process of reflective thinking.

Be sure that subjects are of the types suggested. Variety and interest are important.

PARTICIPATING IN DISCUSSION

In order that a discussion be effective, it is necessary for each member of the group to take an active part. This requires knowledge of the subject under discussion. Sometimes you may be thoroughly familiar with the subject from your own personal experience; at other times you may have to investigate the subject further. Your value to your discussion group will be in direct proportion to the amount and quality of advance preparation you are willing to make. When you know what the discussion topic is to be, follow these procedures:

1. Think over what you know about the subject or problem. Make a brief outline of the information and ideas you have. Follow the procedure of the man who said: "I first examine my own mind, searching to find what I already know about the subject, and then I read to learn what I don't know about it."

2. Make a systematic study of the subject or problem. Consult encyclopedias, dictionaries, yearbooks, books of quotations, and reference books in special fields, such as biography, history, literature, or science. Consult articles in newspapers and magazines. Although you can often find articles on a subject by consulting the magazines themselves, you can save time in locating articles by using the *Readers' Guide to Periodical Literature*.

3. Discuss the subject with your family and friends. If an authority on the subject lives in your neighborhood, try to arrange for an interview with him.

4. Organize your information on cards, one idea or point to a card. By using cards in this way, you can easily rearrange them as the need arises.

Effective participation in discussion requires that you recognize discussion to be a co-operative undertaking rather than a competitive one. Discussion is not argument. It is neither a contest nor a debate. It is a co-operative effort to explore all phases of a subject in order to understand it. Or, when a problem is being considered, it is a co-operative effort to examine all aspects of, and possible solutions to, the problem in an effort to arrive at the best solution.

Be ready to <u>make your contributions at the right time.</u> To do this will require that you <u>listen attentively</u> and follow closely the development of the discussion. When you agree with a speaker, listen carefully to add to what you already know. When you disagree with a speaker, listen to accept or refute what he says, depending upon the evidence offered. If you refute his stand, be <u>sure your reasoning is logical and based upon evidence.</u> Feel free to <u>ask questions.</u>

The points made here are important. Discuss them in detail.

Clear thinking is one of the chief requisites of effective discussion. How clearly can you think? Read the following four reasons why you may not wish to have someone as a friend. Then decide which reasons you consider poor ones.

1. She lives in a poor neighborhood.
2. She cheats on examinations.
3. She is often untidy in appearance.
4. She cannot dance well.

The second and third reasons were logical ones to have selected. Cheating is evidence of a weak character; a slovenly appearance indicates carelessness. The first and fourth reasons have nothing to do with her character or with qualities of friendship.

In discussion, clear thinkers stay on the subject. They make pertinent, timely contributions. Too often careless thinkers stray away from the subject into devious bypaths. They are like drivers who wander in and out of traffic, changing their minds as they please and confusing everyone.

Clear thinkers seldom draw wrong or illogical conclusions from statements or facts. Careless thinkers often jump at conclusions which are unjustified. For example, a careless thinker was once cheated by a stranger from another state. Ever after, he was prejudiced against all persons from that state, wrongly believing them to be dishonest.

Logical reasoning can be discussed at a general level here without your becoming involved in specific kinds of reasoning and fallacies.

It is important that you take time to think before coming to conclusions. Avoid the kind of poor reasoning indicated in the conclusions drawn from each of the following statements:

1. *Statement:* George failed the geometry test.
   Invalid conclusion: George is a dull student.
2. *Statement:* Marie wore a different dress three days in succession.
   Invalid conclusion: Marie thinks more of clothes than of anything else.

The compulsive talker and the too reticent student always present problems in discussion groups. Each must be helped to become a part of the group.

✓ indicates statements rejected.
See pp. T55-T56 for reasons.

Imagine that you are to discuss the subject "The best place to live is in the suburbs of a city." Read the following statements and decide which ones have little or no bearing on the subject. List the numbers of the statements you rejected and give your reasons for rejecting them.

✓ 1. I live in the suburbs.
✓ 2. Suburban neighborhoods are friendly.
  3. There is less traffic and noise in the suburbs than in the city.
✓ 4. I like to live in a suburban neighborhood.
✓ 5. My friends live in the suburbs of the city.
  6. There is more room for outdoor activities in the suburbs.
  7. Suburbs are generally cleaner than the city.
✓ 8. I have many pets.
✓ 9. The schools in the suburbs are just as good as those in the city.
✓ 10. Nearly everyone in the suburbs has a television set and two cars.

LEADING A DISCUSSION

If you are selected to be the chairman of the discussion group, you have a particularly important job. It is up to you to start the discussion, to keep it going smoothly, and to summarize the main points at the conclusion of the discussion.

As discussion leader, you will have to assume certain responsibilities:

1. If possible, confer in advance with the participants. Plan together an outline, or agenda, for the discussion.

2. Get the discussion off to a good start. Indicate briefly and clearly the nature and importance of the subject or problem. Introduce the speakers. Call on a participant to begin the discussion. Make what you say short and to the point.

You may wish to have students list responsibilities of a leader in their notebooks.

Not every student will be a good leader, but every student should have the opportunity to develop the skill to the best of his ability. If the classroom atmosphere is right, even the most awkward and reticent student will be willing to try.

3. <u>Keep the discussion moving and on course</u>. See that the talk never lags, veers off the subject, or trails off into nothingness. <u>Be tactful</u> in seeing that the backward and shy are drawn into the discussion, and that the over-eager discussants kindly but firmly are held to their fair share of time.

4. <u>Make brief and impartial summaries</u> from time to time. By summarizing what has been said, you will be giving the participants a chance to take stock of the points that have been sufficiently emphasized and to see what points need developing.

5. Insist that <u>all phases of a subject or all sides of a problem</u> be brought out. <u>Invite</u> and <u>encourage</u> participants to express <u>opposing points of view</u>.

6. Bring the discussion to a conclusion with <u>a summary statement</u> indicating the thinking of the group on the subject or problem discussed.

Students can observe or hear these points in practice by watching or listening to a TV or radio discussion.

DEVELOPING YOUR SKILL

A. At your teacher's direction, choose a member of the class to act as leader for a class discussion. The discussion may be based on one of the subjects you analyzed and outlined in the previous lesson or on a new subject that the class selects. Discussion will depend upon subject and upon time available.

B. Write a composition in which you discuss this statement: "Discussion is a co-operative undertaking, not a competitive one." Be specific in your comments. Show why the statement is true. See p. T56.

SPECIAL TYPES OF DISCUSSION

Types of discussion vary from informal group discussion to formal debate. In between these extremes are four special types of discussion: the round-table discussion, the panel discussion, the forum, and the symposium.

A round-table discussion is conducted in a manner similar to a class discussion. Seated around a table, the group participates in a discussion, the purpose of which is to clarify all phases of the subject. This type of discussion is especially suited to committees or other small groups. As in a classroom discussion, a capable leader or chairman is needed to guide the discussion so that all participants have the opportunity to express varying opinions. The chairman also must summarize the ideas and opinions of the group. A round-table discussion does not require an audience, but it may be presented before one.

If time is limited you may wish to confine the study to round-table and panel discussions. Practice in speaking with and before small groups is an invaluable experience for the student.

A panel
discus-
sion re-
quires
an audi-
ence,
whereas
a round
table
discussion
does not.

A panel discussion is conducted for an audience. Its purpose is to bring out all sides of a subject in free discussion by a group of well-informed people. From four to ten chosen participants, seated in an informal manner before the audience, are led in discussion by a chairman. The participants present their ideas informally. They never make long or formal speeches. Under the guidance of the chairman, the panel members try to present a well-rounded, thorough, but not formal, discussion of a subject. The participants address all their remarks to the other members of the panel but keep in mind the audience in front of them. At the conclusion of the discussion by the panel, the chairman asks the audience to raise questions or make pertinent comments. Participants on the panel respond to questions from the audience as the questions are directed to them or when the chairman calls upon them.

A forum is also conducted for an audience. A speaker, chosen for his over-all knowledge of a subject, addresses an audience. Following this direct address the audience engages in an open discussion. The forum is becoming increasingly popular because it affords a way of working out community, state, and national problems and of becoming informed on controversial issues.

A symposium is similar to a forum. In both, the speakers directly address the audience, and the audience is allowed a period for discussion. In the symposium, however, special effort is made to secure several speakers, each of whom is an authority on a particular phase of the subject.

Students should understand the format and purpose of the forum and the symposium even if they do not participate in either type of discussion in class.

➤ DEVELOPING YOUR SKILL

A. Working with your teacher and classmates, plan and present a series These
of panel discussions on school problems of current interest or on prob- exer-
lems of general interest. The master list you compiled in an earlier cises
exercise may be helpful to you.   provide

B. A group of students may be selected to organize and conduct a sym- practice
posium on a question of local or national interest. The chairman in re-
will have to meet with the group to discuss the various phases of the search,
topic, to decide who is to speak on each phase, and to determine the in or-
order of presentation. Each speaker will have to do research in order ganiza-
to present his phase of the question.   tion, in

C. Write an evaluation of the discussions suggested in *A* and *B* above. speaking,
Use the following questions as the basis for your evaluation: in listen-

1. Did the participants indicate knowledge of their subject?   ing, and
2. Did the participants support statements with evidence?   in eval-
3. Was the discussion courteous?   uation.
4. Did the chairman guide the discussion well? Did he summarize?
5. Did the audience ask relevant questions? Did the speakers answer
   questions without evading issues?

Review Exercises—Discussion

A. List in class the various pitfalls to watch for when carrying on discussions.
The following may help you to start your list: See p. T56.

> Speaking too long and too often
> Interrupting other speakers
> Making statements of fact without supporting evidence

B. Select a problem that is suitable for discussion and write an analysis of it.
Be sure that the following questions are answered in your analysis. Analyses will

1. What is the exact nature of the problem?   vary according to the prob-
2. Why does the problem exist? What caused it? lems selected. Insist
3. What are the possible solutions?   that all six steps be
4. What are the advantages and disadvantages of each solution? followed.
5. What do you feel is the best solution?
6. How can the solution best be put into operation?

The questions suggested in Exercise C above may be used as
a basis for evaluating all discussions.

2. Debate

THE FORM OF A DEBATE

Definition
of
debate.
A debate is a contest in which formal arguments are presented for and against a proposal. In formal debate, there are two teams, each having the same number of speakers. The team supporting the proposal is called the *affirmative;* the opposing team is called the *negative.*

A debate is presented in two parts: *constructive* speeches, in which both teams present their arguments for and against the proposal; and *rebuttal* speeches, in which both sides attempt to refute or disprove the arguments of their opponents. In the traditional form of debate, each speaker makes a constructive speech and a rebuttal speech. The order of speaking, with two speakers on a side, is as follows:

Constructive Speeches	Rebuttal speeches
1. First affirmative	1. First negative
2. First negative	2. First affirmative
3. Second affirmative	3. Second negative
4. Second negative	4. Second affirmative

Notice that the affirmative team begins and ends the debate, that the order of speaking reverses in the second part of the contest. Each of the speakers on both sides is given an opportunity to present his arguments and to reply directly to his opponents. Affirmative and negative speakers alternate in presenting their arguments and all speeches must be kept within the given time limit.

DEVELOPING YOUR SKILL

A. Be prepared to answer the following questions in class: See p. T56.
   1. What is meant by the term *debate?*
   2. What is the name given to the team that favors the proposal?
   3. What is the team opposed to the proposal called?
   4. What is meant by *constructive speeches?*
   5. What is meant by *rebuttal speeches?*

B. In a brief, but carefully thought out composition, discuss the chief differences between group discussion and formal debate. See p. T56.

The depth of the study of debate will depend upon the abilities of your students. Even slower classes can absorb and profit from studying the introductory material and the general terminology and procedures of debate.

SELECTING AND ANALYZING THE PROPOSITION

The subject chosen for a debate should be timely and should be of interest both to the debaters and to the audience. There is no point in debating an obsolete issue or one that does not lend itself to informative, stimulating debate. Questions for debate may be chosen from the subject fields you study, from problems of school policy, and from questions of public importance.

The choice of a debate subject is important.

A debate question must be debatable; that is, it must have two sides. The question of whether athletics is an important part of the school program is too one-sided to be debatable. However, the question of whether athletics is overemphasized in your school is debatable; it is a subject about which a definite difference of opinion exists, and each point of view may be supported with argument.

After you have selected a subject for a debate, you must state the question in the form of a *proposition*. A proposition is a carefully worded, formal statement of the question. The statement of a proposition should meet the following tests:

1. It should be stated in the form of a resolution and should propose a change from present practice or policy or present an idea to be accepted.

These tests should be discussed at length and in detail.

2. It should be stated in the affirmative.
3. It should be so worded that neither side has an unfair advantage.
4. It should be confined to one subject or proposition.
5. It should be free from ambiguous terms. (*Freedom*, for example, has different meanings for different people.)
6. It should place the burden of proof on the affirmative side.

As you read the following resolutions, notice how they conform with the requirements for the statement of a proposition:

1. Resolved: That some form of censorship should be instituted by the comic-book industry.
2. Resolved: That limits should be placed on the time a student is allowed to spend on extracurricular activities.
3. Resolved: That the hydrogen bomb should be outlawed by all nations.
4. Resolved: That the national government should appropriate as much money for atomic development of industrial possibilities as it does for military uses.

Apply the tests for a debatable proposition to the four resolutions at the bottom of the page. Show that each proposition meets all the requirements.

Stress the importance of understanding both sides of
a question. A debater must be able to anticipate his
48 opponents' arguments.
                                        Discussion and Debate

After you have selected a subject and have stated the proposition correctly, you are ready to analyze the proposition. You must first study the question thoroughly so that you understand both sides. After you have a general understanding of the question, study it further to select the arguments which are relevant to each side of the question and to discard those which are not. In analyzing the proposition you should answer the following questions:

1. Why is the proposition of interest at the present time?
2. What is the history of the question?
3. What terms need to be defined and limited by mutual agreement in order that the debate may center around issues and not upon disputed meanings of terms?
4. What are the main points at issue?

Clash of opinion should be upon issues; therefore, the main points at issue should form the framework of your argument. The issues are the important questions around which a debate is developed.

You may
wish to
illus-
trate
this
tech-
nique
at the
chalk-
board.
To find the main issues, it is helpful to list in parallel columns the reasons why the proposition is true and the reasons why it is not true. By examining these reasons—these pros and cons—you should be able to find three or four controversial points. These controversial points should be stated in the form of questions or issues and the most important issues should form the framework of the debate. The affirmative must be able to answer *Yes* to the questions; the negative, *No*. As an aid to finding the main issues, consider the following questions in your analysis of the proposition:

1. Is a change in the present policy necessary or desirable?
2. Is the proposed solution practicable; that is, would it improve conditions or make them worse?
3. Is there some other solution that would be better than the one proposed?

RESOLVED: THAT OUR SCHOOL SHOULD PUBLISH A YEARBOOK

Debate   49

DEVELOPING YOUR SKILL

A. Discuss reasons why each of the following propositions is or is not debatable. See p. T56.
    1. Resolved: That our school should publish a yearbook.
    2. Resolved: That advertising over radio and television should be reduced to a minimum.
    3. Resolved: That high-school seniors should not be granted special privileges.
    4. Resolved: That high-school credits should be given for participation in extracurricular activities; however, a student should be allowed to participate in only one extracurricular activity.
    5. Resolved: That all criminals should be punished.

B. Be prepared to state one original proposition for debate. Your teacher may wish to have you discuss reasons why the propositions suggested by members of the class are or are not debatable. A master list of the debatable propositions may be compiled.
C. Choose one of the propositions stated in answering Exercise B, and list in parallel columns five arguments for and five arguments against the proposition. Save your paper for use in a later lesson.
D. Compare the arguments listed in Exercise C. Try to discover which arguments are controversial points. Select three of the issues and write each in the form of a question. The affirmative must be able to answer *Yes* to the questions; the negative, *No*. You will need this paper later in the unit.

The exercises are part of a cumulative plan leading to actual participation in a debate.

COLLECTING AND ORGANIZING DEBATE MATERIAL

Once you have determined the main issues of a proposition, you are ready to begin collecting material that will prove or disprove them. Argument, to be sound, must be supported by evidence. No amount of shouting " 'Tis!" and " 'Tisn't!" ever proved anything. If you would persuade others to act according to your wishes or to accept your ideas or opinions, you must convince them that there are valid reasons why they should.

Proof is sufficient evidence for accepting a proposition. Sufficient evidence is produced by the collection, arrangement, and presentation of important considerations that will help establish the truth or falsity of the proposition being considered. Pertinent, authentic, significant, and up-to-date facts are the best evidence. Opinions of experts, while impressive, should be relied upon to lend validity to your argument, not prove it.

Students must realize that the collecting of sufficient proof requires extensive research. Stress the importance of documented, authoritative evidence. For help in doing research, refer to Unit 6.

It is
essen-
tial
that a
clear,
logical
system
of rec-
ords be
insti-
tuted.

In order to be a successful debater, you must do extensive research to find as much pertinent material as possible. If you will classify and record debate material as you collect it, organization of the debate will be facilitated. You will find it particularly helpful to use 3- by 5-inch or 4- by 6-inch cards and file them under such headings as *History of the Question, Definition of Terms, Issues, Affirmative Arguments, Negative Arguments,* and *Rebuttal Arguments.* Each card should have only one item of information on it so that it may be moved in your file of cards without misplacing other items. Each card, regardless of the type of item recorded, should have on it the name of the authority and the source of the item. If you will place a key word or topic heading in the upper right-hand corner of each card, you will be able to keep your cards properly filed so that they will always be readily accessible.

Cards of different colors may be used to help you assemble information quickly for a definite purpose. For example, white cards may be used for recording material useful in preparing your constructive speech; blue cards may be used for recording material which you think your opponent may use; and yellow cards may be used to record material useful in refutation. Such a system will be particularly helpful during an actual debate, when you will have to find and organize material quickly.

 DEVELOPING YOUR SKILL

A. Be ready to discuss the meaning of "sufficient evidence for accepting a proposition." See pp. T56-T57.
B. <u>Collect and organize debate material</u> on the affirmative or negative side of the proposition chosen for analysis in Exercises C and D on page 49. Follow the suggestions made for using the card file system. <u>This material will be used in a later lesson.</u> This is another step in the cumulative plan leading to a debate.

CONSTRUCTING THE BRIEF

After you have assembled your evidence, you are ready to make a logical sentence outline of all the arguments and evidence on your side of the debate question. Such an outline is called a *brief* and consists of three parts: the *introduction,* the *body* or *proof,* and the *conclusion.* The members of each team usually work together to brief one complete side of the debate.

Because of its rigid organization, the brief is somewhat different from sentence outlines to which students may be accustomed.

Statement of the Proposition

Resolved: That .Be .sure .the .proposition .can .meet .all .the.
tests .listed .on .page .47 . . . .

Introduction

The introduction to the brief includes all the preliminary matter neces- Emphasize
sary to an understanding of the question. Since it presents no argument, the point
the introduction is the <u>same for both teams</u>. that the
introduc-
tion to

I. The immediate cause for discussion: the brief
Why is the question important at this time? contains
no argu-

II. The origin and history of the question: ment.
When and how did the problem arise? Why did it become important? Has anything been done about it? If so, how successful has
the program been?

III. Definition of terms:
Are there any doubtful terms in the proposition? If so, state explicitly the meaning to be used throughout the debate.

IV. Restatement of the resolution in the light of the newly defined
terms:
If any of the terms have been defined, restate the resolution so that
its meaning is clear. You may wish to begin the restatement by
saying, "What the proposition really means, then, is: *Resolved:
That . . . .*"

V. Exclusion of extraneous matter:
If the proposition suggests matters which are related, but which
have no direct bearing on the question, include a statement of these
matters in the brief.
If there are points on which both sides agree, state them in the introduction and exclude them from the debate proper. Sometimes the
weight of evidence is so strong that to dispute these facts would be
to weaken your case. Admitting them gives the impression of fair-
ness and permits you to debate the major issues.

Use this outline for constant reference during the preparation of any briefs the class will prepare. Since there is
a logical sequence to the material presented, students should
be required to know the exact order of presentation.

This step- VI. The contentions of both sides:
by-step   Here you have left only the matter relevant to the debate, the points
develop-   on which there is a clash of opinion. The opinions of both sides
ment leads   should be listed in the brief.
directly   A. The affirmative contends . . . .
to the   B. The negative contends . . . .
statement
of issues. VII. The resulting issues:
                 The issues are the controversial points in the contentions. State the
                 main issues in interrogative form. These become the bases for
                 your main arguments. Letter the issues *A, B, C.*

Body or Proof

The body of the brief contains all the arguments and evidence presented
in logical order. Each heading contains one main argument in direct support of your side of the proposition; each subheading offers direct support
of the heading immediately above it. Notice that the word *for* is used to
indicate that supporting evidence is to follow.

I. The first main argument . . . , for

   *This is a statement, in declarative form, of the first issue ex-
   pressed in the introduction (VII). The wording of your argument
   will depend upon which side of the question you are debating. In
   either case, it is based directly upon the statement of the issue.*

   A. Evidence to support first main argument . . . , for

      1. Evidence to support A
      2. Further evidence to support A

   B. Further evidence to prove first main argument . . . , for

      1. Evidence to support B
      2. Further evidence to support B . . . , for
         a. Evidence to support 2
         b. Further evidence to support 2

II. The second main argument . . . , for

   *This point would be developed in a manner similar to the devel-
   opment of the first main argument, as would be all other issues.*

Each main argument in the body of the brief must correspond to one of the issues raised in part VII of the
introduction.

Conclusion

The conclusion of the brief is a summary of the main points proved, followed by a restatement of the proposition in the affirmative or negative.

I. Since (first main argument stated exactly as in the body);

II. Since (second main argument);

III. Since (third main argument);

IV. Since (fourth main argument);

Therefore, (restatement of proposition in the affirmative or negative).

DEVELOPING YOUR SKILL

These exercises are part of the cumulative plan.

A. After your teacher has separated the class into two groups, affirmative and negative, select a chairman for each group. Work together, to prepare a brief on the proposition you have been developing in this unit. As you work together, discuss each step of the brief. Save the briefs for use in later exercises.

B. Your teacher may wish to divide each group into teams of two or three speakers each, depending on the amount of material to be covered in the debate. Every person on each team will write a constructive speech based on part of the brief. One possible division follows:

> First speaker: Introduction and first main argument
> Second speaker: Second main argument
> Third speaker: Third main argument and conclusion

Your teacher may have each team read its speeches for the entire class. Be ready to discuss the speeches. Is the proposition clearly defined? Are the issues relevant? Does the evidence support the arguments? Is the evidence based on fact, not opinion?

The last part of Exercise B simulates a first run-through of constructive speeches in a debate.

LOGICAL REASONING

Logical reasoning is necessary for argument. When you have collected your evidence, you must know how to apply it if you are to support the position you have taken. The two kinds of reasoning that involve moving from the data given to a conclusion are *inductive* and *deductive* reasoning.

Inductive reasoning involves moving from specific instances to a generalization, from *some* to *all*. If, for example, you caught a bus at your corner at 8:10 every morning during the first week of school, you undoubtedly arrived at the conclusion that the bus reaches your corner every morning at 8:10. Notice that the conclusion is a probability rather than a certainty.

The material presented here is basic to an understanding of logical reasoning. If you plan to develop the debate techniques in depth, you may wish to expand upon this section.

You may
wish to
illus-
trate
syllo-
gisms
by using
Euler
circles
or Venn
diagrams

It is possible that some unforeseen circumstance—a storm, motor trouble, an accident—might cause the bus to be late or not to arrive at all. Since this negative instance can be explained reasonably, you may continue to accept the conclusion you reached. For inductive reasoning to be valid, you must investigate a fair number of typical examples and you must be able to explain any negative instances.

Deductive reasoning moves from a generalization to a specific instance, from *all* to *some*. The conclusion reached in deductive reasoning is a certainty rather than a probability. Deductive reasoning frequently takes the form of a *syllogism,* an argument or form of reasoning in which two statements, or premises, are made and a logical conclusion drawn from them.

> All mammals are warm-blooded.   (major premise)
> Whales are mammals.   (minor premise)
> Therefore, whales are warm-blooded. (conclusion)

Sometimes illogical reasoning may be expressed in the form of a syllogism and therefore *appear* to be logical. What is the fallacy in the following example?

> Language experts are needed as interpreters.
> David earns high grades in French.
> Therefore, David should plan to become an interpreter.

Obviously, the fallacy here lies in the fact that insufficient investigation has been made. It has been assumed that David's high grades in French are sufficient qualification for a career as interpreter. David's interests and other aptitudes have not been considered.

Among the common fallacies a successful debater must avoid in his reasoning and detect in the reasoning of his opponents are the following:

1. The *hasty generalization* or general statement based on too few observations; as, *Politicians cannot be trusted, for I know several who are dishonest.*

2. The *post hoc* fallacy, which consists of a conclusion reached by reasoning that because one occurrence (*B*) follows another occurrence (*A*), *B* is caused by *A*. Terms such as *after this, therefore,* and *because of this* are used to imply a cause-effect relationship when none actually exists; as, *The miners struck after war was declared; therefore, war causes strikes.*

An understanding of fallacies will enable the student not only to avoid them in his own reasoning but also to recognize them in his opponents' reasoning.

3. The *faulty dilemma,* which places one in a position of having to make one of two possible choices when in reality other choices are possible; as, *You are at the crossroads; you must go to the right or to the left.* (One could go forward or return the way he came.)

4. The *mistaken causal relationship,* which is similar to the *post hoc* fallacy and results from reasoning incorrectly from cause to effect and from effect to cause, thereby relating wrong causes or effects; as, *Miss Jones is beautiful because she uses — soap.*

5. The *faulty analogy,* which assumes a greater similarity between two situations than actually exists; as, *Jack and I make high grades in science. Jack plans to be a physician. Therefore, I should plan to be a physician.*

Discuss each type of faulty reasoning in detail. Draw additional examples from students.

The successful debater must be able to reason clearly. Not only must he use logic to support his own arguments, but he must also be able to recognize any illogical reasoning in his opponents' arguments.

DEVELOPING YOUR SKILL

A. Read the following pairs of statements. Decide whether or not you consider the second statement, or conclusion, in each pair justified by the fact stated in the first statement. Be ready to discuss your decisions with your classmates. See also p. T57.

1. James is a constant reader of good books.
   James is a well-informed person.   Not justified
2. Mary learned to knit in an hour.
   Knitting is easily learned.   Not justified
3. Sara always avoids walking under a ladder.
   Sara is a superstitious person.   Not justified

You may wish to have students bring in examples of faulty reasoning that they find in advertisements.

See p. T57.4. John is always ill after he eats rhubarb.
Rhubarb is an unhealthful food. Not justified

5. The science teacher punished Harry.
The science teacher does not like Harry. Not justified

B. Write the numbers 1 to 10 on a sheet of paper. Find the fallacy in each of the following statements and indicate its type after the appropriate number.

1. Fraternities have contributed much to college life; therefore, they should be encouraged in high schools.   Post hoc

Mistaken causal 2. Eat — breakfast food and you will have a happy, contented life.
relationship

3. It is bad luck to break a mirror. John broke one yesterday and is in the hospital today. Mistaken causal relationship

4. Roses cannot be grown in my garden. I planted two this year and both of them died.   Hasty generalization

Faulty dilemma 5. Examinations encourage dishonesty by forcing a student to choose between cheating and failing. The student will usually cheat.

Faulty dilemma 6. My opponent must disprove this scientific fact or forfeit the debate.

7. This system has worked in Chicago; therefore, it should work in our town.   Post hoc

8. The cashier at the market is dishonest. She short-changed me yesterday.   Hasty generalization

9. Dr. Smith's prescription has done wonders for me. I took the medicine all the time I was on vacation and now I feel like a new person. Mistaken causal relationship

10. You should eat clams if you want to live a long life. I know six men who are ninety and they have all eaten clams since they were young men. Faulty analogy or mistaken causal relationship

REFUTING YOUR OPPONENT'S ARGUMENTS

The point
that no
new argu-
ment may
be intro-
duced in
rebuttal
should be
stressed.

It is *refutation*—the act of answering, of attacking an opponent's arguments for the purpose of disproving them—that makes debating difficult and at the same time challenging. Refutation often occurs in the second speech of each debater, which is referred to as a *rebuttal*. In these rebuttal speeches, the debater may refute an opponent's argument or may reconstruct any of his own arguments which have been weakened by an opponent. New arguments may not, however, be introduced in rebuttal speeches.

Refutation may be introduced in debate at any time and may be accomplished in any one of a number of ways. You may expose some faulty

Rebuttal is often the most challenging part of a debate.
Material must be organized and arguments countered on the
spot. Several skills are involved—reasoning, organization,
and speaking.

reasoning on the part of your opponent. You may produce evidence contradicting a fundamental statement or cite a more recent contradictory opinion given by the authority quoted by your opponent. You may refute by using an analogy or a humorous absurdity. You may admit a point your opponent has proved only to turn the tables on him by showing that the point strengthens rather than weakens your case.

The techniques of rebuttal are varied.

You should not attempt to refute all an opponent says. Some arguments are too unimportant to refute; others are too true to be refuted. A skillful debater weighs the value of arguments and selects to refute important arguments which can be attacked successfully. Since material cannot be gathered while a debate is in progress, you must anticipate an opponent's arguments and prepare beforehand to refute them. Rebuttal should be planned while you are gathering material and preparing your case.

Read this paragraph aloud and stress the points made.

➤ DEVELOPING YOUR SKILL

This represents one of the final steps in debate preparation.

Select the two most important arguments on the opposite side of the proposition that you chose to uphold in the previous exercises and brief a refutation of them, using the following form as a guide.

Introduction

Two major arguments have been offered by the opposition: (1)_____

_____

(2)_____

_____

Refutation

I. The argument that_____

_____ is _____, because

   A. _____, because

      1. _____

      2. _____

   B. _____

II. The second argument that_____

_____ is _____, because

   A. _____

   B. _____

Each step in the refutation brief is important again. Logic is essential—both in the counterarguments offered and in the order of presentation.

Since the affirmative team always begins and ends a debate, the negative must try not to leave itself in a vulnerable position at the end of its final rebuttal speech.

Conclusion

I. Since _____

_____

II. Since _____

_____

Therefore, we believe _____

_____

Review Exercises—Debate

This is the culminating activity in the series of cumulative exercises on debate.

Your teacher may wish to divide the class into groups of four. Each group will select a question for debate. You may use the master list that you made, the list that follows, or a question decided upon by the group. Be sure your question is debatable. Each group will then prepare a debate according to what has been learned about debating in the study of this unit. On scheduled days, each group will present its debate.

Debate Questions

1. Resolved: That small high schools offer better opportunities than do large high schools.
2. Resolved: That giving prizes in school contests is harmful.
3. Resolved: That eighteen-year-olds should be permitted to vote.
4. Resolved: That the President of the United States should be elected by a direct vote of the people.
5. Resolved: That our school should adopt the honor system for examinations.

UNIT SUMMARY

In school and out, you spend considerable time discussing subjects of common interest or problems of common concern. You are living in a democracy where discussion and debate influence decisions and choices. Therefore, it is important that you should be able to discuss issues and problems intelligently and that you should be able to organize and present an argument convincingly. Likewise, it is important that you should be able to distinguish sound reasoning from unsound reasoning, and valid argument from invalid argument.

Re-emphasize the importance of the skills developed in discussion and debate. They are skills that have value for one's entire lifetime.

UNIT REVIEW EXERCISES

DISCUSSION TOPICS

To analyze a topic or problem; to disseminate information;

A. What are the purposes of discussion? to solve a problem.

B. How has the ability to participate in group discussions helped you in school and out of school? Awareness and ability to communicate should be major points.

C. What is the purpose of debate? To present both sides of a question.

D. What are the skills needed by a successful debater? See p. T57.

E. What are some common fallacies in reasoning? Post hoc, hasty generalization, faulty dilemma, mistaken causal relationship, faulty analogy.

WRITTEN WORK

A. Write a paragraph explaining why discussion is of great importance in a democratic society. See p. T57.

B. Write a paragraph discussing the values to be derived from engaging in formal argument. See p. T57.

C. Select a newspaper or magazine editorial whose subject would be a good topic for discussion or debate. Write a paragraph telling why the subject is important, what phases of it need to be explored, and whether the subject is more suited to discussion (indicate type) or debate, and why. Pargaraphs will vary according to editorials selected.

VOCABULARY

Did you know the meaning of all the words in this unit? The following sentences use some of the words in different contexts. Write the numbers 1 to 5 on your paper. After each number, write the letter of the word that could best be substituted for the italicized word in each sentence. Before making your choice, find the word on the page indicated to see how the word is used in the unit.

c
1. She assumed a *reflective* attitude. [p. 39]
   (*a*) listless; (*b*) resolute; (*c*) thoughtful; (*d*) restrained

b
2. They decided to *investigate* the matter further. [p. 40]
   (*a*) discuss; (*b*) explore; (*c*) review; (*d*) explain

a
3. An *extensive* tract of land was needed for the housing project. [p. 50]
   (*a*) sizable; (*b*) expanded; (*c*) limited; (*d*) expensive

d
4. Campaign speeches usually center about *controversial* issues. [p. 44]
   (*a*) authentic; (*b*) positive; (*c*) conclusive; (*d*) disputed

b
5. His comments on the subject were not *pertinent*. [p. 41]
   (*a*) admissible; (*b*) relevant; (*c*) persuasive; (*d*) authoritative

SPELLING

The following spelling words appeared in this unit or were chosen because they are commonly misspelled. Study the words carefully and be prepared to write them from dictation.

1.	reflective	11.	fallacy
2.	investigate	12.	systematic
3.	extensive	13.	constructive
4.	controversial	14.	rebuttal
5.	pertinent	15.	proposition
6.	aptitude	16.	affirmative
7.	competitive	17.	negative
8.	analogy	18.	brief
9.	probability	19.	syllogism
10.	anticipate	20.	dilemma

See below for 1-4. *UNIT SELF-TEST*

1. List three important characteristics of a discussion topic.
2. List three helpful suggestions for preparing to discuss a subject or problem.
3. Name three qualities which a discussion leader should have.
4. Name and define three special types of group discussion.
5. Write on a sheet of paper the letters *a* through *h*. Read the following statements and write either *True* or *False* after each corresponding letter.

False

True

    a. You should attempt to refute all the points an opponent makes.

    b. Reasoning from particular facts to a general conclusion is inductive

False   reasoning.

False   c. The brief is the written speech for the debate.

True   d. A clever debater needs to study only one side of a question.

    e. Reasoning from a general principle to an individual case is deductive

True   reasoning.

True   f. Facts constitute evidence.

False   g. A proposition for debate should be stated as a resolution.

    h. New constructive argument is permitted in a rebuttal.

1. Thought-provoking, stimulating multi-faceted, timely.
2. See numbered suggestions on p. 40.
3. Ability to plan, ability to organize, tact, ability to summarize, impartiality, ability to keep discussion moving.
4. Round-table discussion (p.43), panel (p.44) forum (p.44), symposium (p.44).

Unit 4

Words and Meanings

Studies have shown that one characteristic common to successful people is the ability to use words appropriately and precisely. Within your school, as in society in general, the persons who achieve the most and who hold positions of responsibility and leadership are usually those who have both an understanding of language and the ability to use language effectively.

Understanding of language involves knowing what words are, what they mean, and how they develop meaning. Since language is constantly changing, it is necessary to know how these changes affect word forms and meanings. Some words may fall into disrepute; words that were formerly disreputable may become reputable. Other words may vary in appropriateness according to the situations in which they are used.

Another characteristic of English is that it contains many terms and expressions that are peculiar to the English language; that is, they have no corresponding terms or expressions in other languages. These usages usually have a fixed pattern and must be memorized if you are to use them correctly.

This unit is intended to help you increase your knowledge of language and develop selectivity and accuracy in the use of words. The following Check Yourself exercises will help you determine how much you already know about language. After you have completed the exercises, your teacher will give you the correct answers.

CHECK YOURSELF

A. Write on a sheet of paper the headings *Abstract Words* and *Concrete Words*. List each of the following words under the appropriate heading.

Concrete	actress	sportsmanship	Abstract
Abstract	loyalty	school spirit	Abstract
Abstract	success	swimming	Abstract
Concrete	teacup	weapons	Concrete
Concrete	strawberry	superstitions	Abstract

B. Write the answers to the following questions:

Context

1. What is the name given to the surrounding words or the situations through which words reveal their meaning?

Denotation

2. What term is used to refer to the literal meaning of a word?

Connotation

3. What term is used to refer to the emotional or associative meaning of a word?

Idiom

4. In the sentence *He split his sides laughing,* what is the expression *split his sides* called?

C. Rewrite the following sentences, choosing from the words in parentheses the word that best expresses the meaning of each sentence.

1. That may be true, but I doubt (whether, if) it is.
2. They could not agree (to, on, with) a solution.
3. Your coat is different (than, to, from) mine.
4. Her choice was identical (with, to) his.
5. There was nobody (at, to) home when we arrived.
6. She differed (from, with) us on a matter of principle.
7. If we have to wait (on, for) her much longer, we shall be late.
8. Her hair, which is dark brown, looks black as compared (with, to) mine, which is blond.
9. You never listen (to, at) what I am saying.
10. The patient died (of, with) cancer.

The aim of the Check Yourself exercises is to stimulate interest in the various aspects of language study. Discuss the answers only briefly, leaving more detailed discussion for later study of specific areas.

1. Increasing Your Knowledge of Words

WORDS AS SYMBOLS

> 'Twas brillig and the slithy toves
>> Did gyre and gimble in the wabe;
> All mimsy were the borogroves,
>> And the mome raths outgrabe.

The sheer nonsense of Lewis Carroll's "Jabberwocky" has delighted people for years. At some time you may have tried to substitute words for the nonsense syllables in an attempt to give the lines meaning. In doing so, you recognized *brillig, slithy, toves,* and the other nonsense sounds as having no meaning because they do not represent any known things. In order for a group of sounds or a combination of letters to be a meaningful word, it must have a *referent;* that is, it must stand for something.

A baby just learning to talk frequently produces sounds intended to symbolize known referents; for example, *loke* and *fim-fim.* Although his family learns to understand the baby's meaning, these sounds cannot be called words; their intended referents are represented by accepted words in the language—*milk* and *fish.* Imagine the consternation of a clerk if you were to ask him for a quart of "loke" or for two tropical "fim-fims!"

A word, then, is more than just a combination of sounds or a group of letters. It is a symbol that enables men to communicate with each other It must be remembered, however, that symbols differ according to the various cultures in which men live. The English symbol, "I am hungry," becomes *"J'ai faim"* in French and *"Es hungert mich"* in German. The letters *p-a-i-n* in English suggest suffering, whereas the same combination of letters in French spells the word for *bread.*

Although there are no records to indicate how man began to use words, it is reasonable to assume that as his experiences grew he found it necessary to create symbols in order that he might communicate with others. He could no longer rely solely on gestures. As a result, he began to use sounds to represent the things around him. With the general acceptance of each of the sounds as a symbol for the thing it named, man began to build a vocabulary.

Students will undoubtedly be able to offer additional examples of nonsense syllables that have become part of their families' vocabularies.

You may wish to have several students do research and report on some of the theories that have been offered as to language origin and growth.

If your dictionary has a new words section, you may
wish to have students look up the origin of words that
have recently entered the language.

64   *Words and Meanings*

Stress the
point that
a word
is a
symbol
for some-
thing; it
is not
the thing
itself.

Today, new words come into use in much the same way. Every new concept, discovery, or invention must be given a convenient symbol in order for men to communicate about it. When people begin to use the same symbol to represent the same referent, the word becomes a part of the language. An example of this, in the field of mathematics, is the word *googol.* Dr. Edward Kasner, an American mathematician, once asked his nine-year-old nephew to suggest a name for the number 10^{100}, or 1 followed by 100 zeros. The youngster decided to call the number a *googol,* a term that is now in common use in mathematical writings.

 DEVELOPING YOUR SKILL

A. Be prepared to answer the following questions. See p. T57.

1. Why are *gimble* and *wabe* not words?
2. What is meant by the term *referent?*
3. What is the major reason for the creation of new words?
4. How does a new word become part of the language?
5. If no new words were to be added to the English language, what might this indicate about the English-speaking world?

B. Each of the following words or phrases has a meaning of recent origin. Look up the word in your dictionary and write its meaning. If you are unable to find the word or phrase in your dictionary, try to define it yourself. See pp. T57–T58.

picture window	exurbanite	ballistic missile
cold war	brainwash	tranquilizer
carport	fluoridate	fallout
sound barrier	egghead	nuclear fission
freeway	split-level	sputnik

LANGUAGE CHANGES AND GROWTH

English is a living language, subject to change and growth. New words are coined to represent new ideas, discoveries, and inventions; old words become obsolete as they fall into disuse. In addition to these easily recognizable processes of change, there are changes in word meaning that take place so gradually that they are not immediately apparent. Some of the most common processes by which words change meaning are known as *generalization, specialization, elevation, degeneration,* and *transference.*

A comparison of a work of modern literature with a literary work of an earlier period will point up the fact that changes in the language are frequent.

Generalization is the process by which words that had limited, specialized meanings have acquired broader, more general meanings. The word *bonfire,* for example, originally meant *a fire of bones (bone-fire).* It was the term used to refer to the fires in which the bodies of heretics were consumed. Today a bonfire is any large fire built in the open air. By the same process, *citizen* has acquired a broader meaning. As originally used, *citizen* was a term used to refer to persons who lived in the city.

Word meanings that change by the process of specialization move from broad, general meanings to narrow, specialized meanings. In the original meaning of the word, *wife* meant *woman.* Today the term *wife* is used to refer to a *married* woman. *Girl* at one time meant any *young person;* today the meaning has been narrowed to apply to a young *female. Starve* originally meant *to die* (compare the German *sterben).* Today, to starve is to perish from lack of food or to suffer extreme hunger. Notice that in the most specialized meaning, *to suffer extreme hunger,* the original meaning of *to die* has completely disappeared.

Elevation is the process by which word meanings change for the better; that is, they acquire more favorable meanings. At one time *nice* meant *ignorant;* later it meant *foolish* or *silly. Pretty,* which today has such a favorable meaning, once meant *sly.* A *constable* was once the *count of the stable,* an attendant who was good at jumping onto the back of a horse to chase culprits.

By the process of degeneration, words that were once considered to have favorable or inoffensive meanings have acquired less favorable or even offensive meanings. An *idiot* was originally *a private person,* probably one who kept to himself and kept things to himself. Later the word came to refer to an ignorant person and, finally, to a person who was mentally defective. *Sly,* which now carries the unpleasant idea of craftiness or roguishness, once meant *wise, shrewd,* or *skillful. Silly* once meant *happy;* a *boor,* now an ill-bred person, was once a *farmer.*

Discuss each of the examples in detail to be sure that students understand not only the change in meaning but also the process by which the change took place.

65

Words that change meaning by <u>transference</u> go through a series of changes that result in additional meanings, some of which are far different from the original meanings. *Journey* first meant *a day's work or travel,* then *a day's travel* (estimated at 20 miles in the Middle Ages), and, finally, *a trip of any duration.* Other words whose meanings have changed by the process of transference include *quick* and *thrill. Quick* meant *not dead,* then *lifelike,* and now means *rapid, swift,* or *speedy. Thrill* first meant *to pierce.* Some words that were originally used only as nouns have acquired meanings as verbs. This is particularly true of words that name parts of the body: *to head* the committee, *to shoulder* responsibility, *to toe* the mark, and so on.

It is interesting, too, that language sometimes changes because of errors and misunderstandings. Many of the words you use today are the results of such confusions. The word *sneeze,* for example, comes from the Middle English *fnesen.* Someone, mistaking the letter *f* for the Old English *s,* spelled the word *snesen.* The word was widely circulated in this form and later became *sneeze.* Two other words that are the results of misunderstandings are *apron* and *umpire. Apron* should be *napron,* and *umpire* should be *numpire.* Can you see how the confusion might have happened? It is easy to understand if you realize that *a napron,* said rapidly, sounds like *an apron,* and *a numpire* sounds like *an umpire.* In the case of the word *nickname,* the error was just the reverse. *Nickname* should be *eke-name* or *ickname.* However, *an eke-name* sounded so much like *a neke-name* that through usage the word became *neke-name* and then *nickname.*

Modern English owes much of its variety to the many sources upon which it has drawn. Numerous words have been borrowed directly from other languages. French has contributed such terms as *ballet, avalanche,* and *rendezvous.* Notice that the language from which the word was drawn is not necessarily the same as the origin of the word. *Ballet,* for example, came into English from the French. Its origin, however, is the Italian *balletto.* Spanish has contributed such terms as *tango, mosquito, embargo;* German, such words as *kindergarten, semester, sauerkraut;* Italian, such words as *piano, motto, miniature.* From North American Indian, English has taken *raccoon, moccasin, moose;* from Chinese, *tea, pongee, pekoe;* and from Malay, *bamboo* and *ketchup.* Many other words that have been borrowed from other tongues are now part of your language.

> DEVELOPING YOUR SKILL

A. Be ready to discuss the following quotation. Look up the derivation of each of the italicized words in order to understand fully the point being made. See p. T58.

I am in favor of *alarums* and against *alarms*. It is vain to tell me that these two words were the same once and came from a common derivation. The people who trust to derivations are always wrong: for they ignore the life and adventures of a word, and all that it has done since it was born. People of that sort would say that every man who lives in a *villa* is a *villain*. They would say that being *chivalrous* is the same as being *horsy*.

Perhaps some of your students can be motivated to write a similar paragraph using other pairs of words.

—G. K. CHESTERTON, *Alarms and Discursions*

B. Write each of the italicized words in the following sentences. Use the dictionary to find the original meaning of each word in order to compare the original meaning with the meaning of the word as it is used in the sentence. After each word write the name of the process of change in meaning that has taken place—*generalization, specialization, elevation, degeneration,* or *transference.* Be prepared to discuss your answers in class. See also p. T58.

Example: Please *hand* me that hammer.
hand—*transference*

1. He could eat *meat* three times a day. Specialization
2. He has shown himself to be a *hypocrite.* Degeneration
3. They had to *shoulder* their way through the crowd. Transference
4. John plans to work as a *steward* on a liner next summer. Elevation
5. She discussed the problem with her *pastor.* Elevation
6. The life of the American *pioneer* was a hard one. Elevation
7. The *manuscript* had been carefully typed. Generalization
8. Arthur played the part of the *villain* in the melodrama. Degeneration
9. Mr. Smith is in the *prime* of life. Transference
10. May I please use your *pen?* Generalization

C. Each of the following groups of three words came into the English language from the same language. Write each group of words on your paper. Then, using your dictionary, identify the source of each group.

Chinese 1. kowtow, tea, typhoon
Latin 2. altitude, nasal, consul
Spanish 3. fiesta, siesta, patio
Dutch 4. sloop, reef, hoist
Italian 5. balcony, stanza, allegro

6. thyroid, pediatrics, biography Greek
7. kind, strength, lane Anglo-Saxon
8. tycoon, ju-jitsu, kimono Japanese
9. skunk, persimmon, hominy Algonquian
10. vogue, ravine, restaurant French

CONCRETE AND ABSTRACT WORDS

Be sure that stu-dents un-derstand the dis-tinction between concrete and abstract.

Words whose referents can be seen or touched—words whose refer-ents exist in the physical world—are called *concrete words*. Such terms as *boy, man, girl, woman, chair,* and *table* have the same general mean-ings for all users of language. The symbol *man,* for example, brings to mind an adult male human being. People may disagree, however, about the meanings of words such as *success, happiness, truth, honesty,* and *loyalty.* Since the referents of these words do not exist in the physical world, their meanings depend upon the individual's experience with them. Words that symbolize ideas, actions, or qualities are known as *abstract words.*

Both concrete and abstract words vary in degree of exactness. The most general concrete words are those that stand for any one of a large group of similar referents: *musician, city, animal, memorial.* Less spe-cific are words that symbolize any one of a limited group of similar refer-ents: *composer, capital, canine, monument.* The most exact concrete words are those that refer to persons, places, animals, or things, each of which is the only one of its kind: *Jerome Kern, Washington, D. C., Lassie, Statue of Liberty.* Notice the progression of the examples used. They move from the general to the specific, although they are all concrete words.

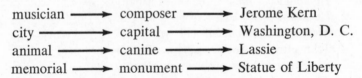

Often the degrees of variation are even finer than in the preceding exam-ples. The general concrete word *literature* might progress to the specific as follows.

literature ➜ prose ➜ fiction ➜ novel ➜ romance ➜ *Jane Eyre*

Although abstract words differ in exactness, the variation is less ap-parent than in concrete words. Since one cannot point to the referent of an abstract word, the meaning of the word may depend upon individual interpretation. Some abstract words, however, symbolize generally known activities and are, therefore, the most specific in meaning: *skiing, skating, manufacturing, sight.* Less exact, but still rather specific in meaning, are

Impress upon students the point that both concrete and abstract words are essential to full expression of ideas. Concrete words alone are limiting; abstract words alone are often vague or ambiguous.

abstract words that refer to relationships and to certain qualities: *owner-ship, leadership, friendship, politeness, length.* It is important that you realize that the examples given are still abstract words. While the broad concepts they suggest are the same for most people, the exact meaning of each abstraction may depend upon the experience of the individual.

Abstract words that express complex ideas are the least specific in meaning: *freedom, democracy, equality, patriotism, Americanism, cour-age, success.* As with all abstractions, misunderstandings may arise be-cause these words do not mean the same thing to all people. When using an abstract word, be sure your listeners know what you mean. Start with your definition of the word and then expand your definition by giving concrete examples that make your meaning clear. What, for instance, do you mean by *Americanism?* Is it the right to vote, the right to attend school, the right to say what you mean, or does *Americanism* mean some-thing else to you? When using abstractions, develop your idea fully so that no misunderstandings will arise.

In the following excerpt, the author defines *freedom,* as he is using it, as *absolute personal freedom* and, then, goes on to explain fully what he means.

In this country [the United States] I experienced for the first time the magnificent feeling of absolute personal freedom. No po-liceman could stop me in the street or in a restaurant and ask me to show my papers. I could walk about without carrying an identity card in my pocket, change my address without reporting to the po-lice, and slap a cop on the shoulder just because I was feeling fine. Only a European can appreciate the personal freedom a man enjoys in this country.

—Stoyan Pribichevich, "In an American Factory"

Context
often
deter-
mines
whether
a word
is concrete or abstract.

Many words·may be concrete or abstract depending upon their use in sentences. Notice the use of the world *culture* in the following sentences: Dr. Harper prepared a *culture* for microscopic examination. The Aztecs had a highly developed *culture*. In the first sentence, *culture* has a specific referent; in the second, it does not. *Culture* is, therefore, concrete in the first sentence but abstract in the second.

  DEVELOPING YOUR SKILL

A. Divide your paper into two columns. Label the first column *Concrete Words* and the second, *Abstract Words*. Write the words from the · following list in the appropriate columns.

book	C	window	C	home	C	flannel	C
loyalty	A	attitude	A	economy	A	persistence	A
honor	A	desk	C	truth	A	education	A
drill	C	chair	C	ladder	C	automobile	C
knife	C	shopping	A	calendar	C	happiness	A

Follow
alphabetical
order.

B. Rewrite the following groups of words, arranging them so they progress from the most general to the most specific.

1. science, drugs, progress, Salk vaccine, medicine
2. food, nourishment, ham and eggs, breakfast, meals
3. human being, biped, male, Roy Watson, animal
4. publishing, magazine, publication, *Atlantic*, enterprise
5. culture, *Mona Lisa*, art, civilization, painting

C. Write the italicized words from the following sentences and label each *concrete* or *abstract,* depending upon its use in the sentence.

Abstract   1. He was already ambitious in his *youth.*
Abstract   2. They took the city by *force.*
Concrete   3. The *youth* stood gazing at the scene.
Concrete   4. He entered his *painting* in the art competition.
Concrete   5. The dentist deadened the *nerve* before drilling.
Concrete   6. A large *force* entered the town.
Abstract   7. Of all the arts I prefer *painting.*
Abstract   8. *Sprinkling* the lawn can be almost effortless today.
Abstract   9. It took *nerve* for her to say that.
Concrete   10. Put a *sprinkling* of nuts on that sundae, please.

Compare the pairs of words used in different contexts
in Exercise C. Be sure students recognize why each word
is concrete or abstract.

Effective writing and good reading depend also upon recognition of the fringe meanings that are attached to words.

CONNOTATION AND DENOTATION

If someone were to say to you, "Ann's work in school is generally average, but her recitations are only fair and her notebooks are mediocre," you would undoubtedly assume the following:

1. Ann's recitations and notebooks are below the level of the rest of her school work.
2. Ann's notebooks are below the level of her recitations.

Actually, if you were to check in a dictionary, you would find that the *denotation*—the literal, dictionary meaning—of *average, fair,* and *mediocre* is the same; in fact, the three words are listed as synonyms. The differences, then, lie in the *connations* of the words—the emotional or associative meanings.

The meanings of synonyms may vary according to their connotative associations.

Connotative meanings are not limited to abstractions such as those given above. Concrete words, too, may have various associations for different people, depending upon the individual's experience with the word. A spider, for example, may be a fascinating many-legged engineer to one person and a source of horror to another. Even a word that usually has a pleasant association for you might, under certain circumstances, have an unpleasant connotation. If you were just recovering from an attack of food poisoning after having eaten your favorite food, it is doubtful whether the name of that food would hold a pleasant connotation for you. Your experience with the word, or with its referent, makes the difference.

Emphasize the part played by personal experience in word connotations.

The *complete* meaning of a word depends both on its denotation and its connotation. Too often, people are misled because they react only to the connotative meanings of words. Words such as *mother, church, Americanism,* and *politician* are *loaded words;* that is, their connotative meanings are so strong that people tend to react to such words emotionally rather than intellectually. *Democracy, monarchy,* and *communism* merely denote types of governmental organization, but, even more, they arouse emotions of loyalty or hate. The simplest words can be used to "load" sentences. Consider again the suggested sentence at the beginning of this section: "Ann's work in school is generally average, but her recitations are only fair and her notebooks are mediocre." Notice how the use of *but* and *only* helps to strengthen the derogatory connotations of *fair* and *mediocre.*

Reading of poetry or personal essays is improved when students are aware of the connotative values of words. In straightforward expository and scientific and technical prose, the denotative values of words are most important.

The preceding discussion is not intended to suggest that connotative meanings are always used to mislead. Actually, language would be dull and uninteresting if it had to rely solely on the denotative meanings of words. The creative writer, particularly the writer of fiction and poetry, uses the associations words may have to carry the reader beyond the literal meanings of the words. By using language that has suggestive power, the writer helps his readers to experience the emotion the writer has intended and to accept the situations, characters, and events he has created. The following passage from Stephen Vincent Benét's "The Devil and Daniel Webster" illustrates the author's use of ordinary words to achieve an effect beyond the literal meaning of the words.

Reading this excerpt aloud will help demonstrate the emotional effect of words.

The fire began to die on the hearth and the wind before morning to blow. The light was getting gray in the room when Dan'l Webster finished. And his words came back at the end to New Hampshire ground, and the one spot of land that each man loves and clings to. He painted a picture of that, and to each one of the jury he spoke of things long forgotten. For his voice could search the heart, and that was his gift and his strength. And to one, his voice was like the forest and its secrecy, and to another like the sea and the storms of the sea; and one heard the cry of his lost nation in it, and another saw a little harmless scene he hadn't remembered for years. But each saw something. And when Dan'l Webster finished, he didn't know whether or not he'd saved Jabez Stone. But he knew he'd done a miracle. For the glitter was gone from the eyes of judge and jury, and, for the moment, they were men again and knew they were men.

Many words carry connotations that are appropriate only in particular circumstances. You would not say, "I was punished because I was *naughty*," but you might say to a very young child, "You were punished because you were *naughty*." Some words, then, are suited to conversations with children, others to conversations with your contemporaries, still others to conversations with adults. Some words are suited to formal situations, others to informal situations. Using words well requires not only knowledge of a word's denotation but also a feeling for its connotation.

Words achieve their standing as a result of maintaining or changing their denotative and connotative values. Language is a vital, living thing; consequently there are changes.

Illustrate the effect of using the words in Exercise A in
sentences. Students will readily note the increase in emotional
tone when loaded words are used.

Increasing Your Knowledge of Words 73

▶ DEVELOPING YOUR SKILL

A. Be prepared to discuss the following pairs of terms. One term in each
pair is a neutral, factual term; the other is intended to arouse strong
feelings. Distinguish between the neutral term and the loaded term
in each pair. Be ready to 'tell whether the loaded term has pleasant
or unpleasant connotations.

Neutral	intellectual	egghead	Loaded-unpleasant
Neutral	hairdo	coiffure	Loaded-pleasant
Loaded-pleasant	antique	old-fashioned	Neutral
Loaded-unpleasant	newshawk	journalist	Neutral
Neutral	horse	steed	Loaded-pleasant
Loaded-unpleasant	skinny	slender	Neutral
Loaded-unpleasant	grease monkey	mechanic	Neutral
Loaded-unpleasant	spies	intelligence officers	Neutral
Neutral	well-dressed	chic	Loaded-pleasant
Loaded-unpleasant	bureaucrat	public official	Neutral

B. From newspaper and magazine advertisements, select five examples
of the use of loaded words. Write these examples on your paper (use
the full statement, not just the words). After each, tell what the
advertising device is intended to convey to the reader.

C. Look through your newspaper to find an article that should be a factual report, but actually contains loaded words. Court cases and reports of domestic and foreign disturbances are usually good sources.
Do not select an editorial. Rewrite one paragraph of the article, omitting all heavily connotative words. In other words, make the paragraph factual and objective. Clip the original article to your paper
before you hand it in.

Examples
and in-
terpre-
tations
will vary.
Feature
articles—
particu-
larly
human
interest
stories—
are rich
in such
material.

WORDS IN CONTEXT

Although English offers a vast number of words with which to express
ideas, man's expression is so varied that he has found it either convenient
or necessary to give many meanings to individual words. The following
passage illustrates this point.

It was the *second* time that day that Arthur and Bob had spoken
at almost the same *second*. This time, each of them had been eager
to *second* the motion that the Fencing Club sponsor a mock duel.
After the motion had been carried, plans were laid. When Arthur
was selected as one of the "duelists," Bob immediately volunteered
to act as his *second*.

You may wish to have students write paragraphs similar
to the one above in which a single word is used in different contexts.

The role
of con-
text in
reveal-
ing word
meanings
is im-
portant.

Each time the word *second* appears in the preceding illustration, it is used in a different sense. Yet, the various meanings of the word are not confusing to you because the rest of the passage helps to make clear, in each case, which meaning is intended. If, however, you were to be asked to define *second* without knowing how it is to be used, you would find it difficult to give a single, clear definition. Since the word *second* has more than one referent, you must know which referent is intended before you can know which meaning is intended. Words reveal their meaning through *context,* the words that surround them or the situations in which they are used.

Context is often a matter of situation—time, place, circumstances. There was a time when a fifty-cent dinner was considered an *expensive* dinner. *"It's a hit!"* means one thing at the ball park and another on Broadway. *"Help!"* shouted by someone hanging from a fifth-story window of a burning building needs no other words to give it meaning; the circumstances provide the context.

The meaning of a word or idea can be completely changed by lifting the word or idea out of its context. Read the following passage.

> The book is cleverly written but has no depth. The characters are brilliantly conceived, but never really come to life. This young author has a promising career ahead of him if he will stop "grinding out" this kind of inferior novel.

Having read the foregoing paragraph, what would be your reaction if you were to see the review quoted in an advertisement for the book as follows?

> John Boone says: "Cleverly written . . . characters brilliantly conceived . . . author has a promising career ahead of him."

Notice that the advertisement does not misquote John Boone; it quotes him out of context. The result, of course, is that the meaning of the ideas is radically changed.

74

Misreading often results from the failure to recognize
the possibilities of multiple meanings and the failure
to choose the right meaning to fit the specific context.

In speaking situations, context is often a matter of tone and gesture. A particular voice inflection and/or facial expression can make a word mean the exact opposite of its apparent meaning. In the expression *"You're so good to me,"* *good* can mean *bad* or *nasty,* for example, if the words are spoken in a biting, saracastic tone. A wink of the speaker's eye often says, "Pay no attention to this. I don't mean it."

Context is a combination of many elements; the word in a sentence, the idea within a given discourse, the time, the place, the circumstances, tone of voice, and gesture. Words enable men to express ideas; context enables men to understand words. Context allows the reader to be more sure of interpreting words as the writer intended. Students should recognize too, however, that, at best, language is imperfect and misunderstandings will arise.

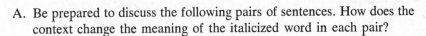

DEVELOPING YOUR SKILL

A. Be prepared to discuss the following pairs of sentences. How does the context change the meaning of the italicized word in each pair?

1. I plan to have a *key* made for that lock. Device for unlocking doors
   The music was off *key*. Out of harmony
2. We plan to *book* passage early. To arrange
   His new *book* will be published in the spring. A volume
3. The actors in the *play* were excellent. A drama
   She was learning to *play* the piano. To perform
4. The *batter* stood ready at home plate. Baseball position
   That *batter* is too thin for a cake. A semiliquid mixture
5. He had to appear in *court* to pay his traffic fine. Place of justice
   Some people deliberately *court* danger. Invite, tempt
6. They see each other many times in the *course* of a year. Passage of time
   Our school is offering a new *course* in advanced Spanish conversation. Unit of instruction
7. They were *limp* with exhaustion. Without strength, drooping
   The injury to his leg caused him to *limp*. To walk lamely
8. She has made a *name* for herself as an artist. Reputation
   He did it in the *name* of friendship. For the sake of
9. The architect sketched a rough *draft* of the plans. Drawing
   There is a *draft* coming from that window. Current of air
10. It seemed doubtful that the badly beaten boxer would *survive* the eighth round. Last through
    The normal expectancy is that young persons will *survive* older persons. Outlive

B. Write a paragraph that is out of context in terms of time. For example, if George Washington's orders to his troops were to be given to members of today's army, the orders would not mean today exactly what they did then. You may prefer to go ahead in time rather than back. Develop your paragraph as though the experiences you are discussing were happening. Write from the point of view of the period about which you are talking. Paragraphs will vary according to subject matter and approach taken.

Review Exercises—Increasing Your Knowledge of Words

Nonsense words have no known referents.

A. Write five sentences in which you substitute a nonsense syllable for one word in each sentence; for example, I am going to a *gloop* on Saturday. Be ready to read your sentences in class. Ask your classmates to try to guess what word you intended. Are the suggestions varied? Why?

B. Write the following words on your paper. After each, write the name of the language from which the word came into English. Then write the process by which the meaning of each of the words changed. Use your dictionary to help you do this exercise. Refer to pp. 64–67.

AS	1. cupboard Generalization		OF	6. slave Degeneration
AS	2. barn Generalization		OF	7. bachelor Specialization
AS	3. knight Elevation		AS	8. deer Specialization
ME	4. fast Transference		ONF	9. cattle Specialization
OF	5. minister Elevation		L	10. precocious Elevation

C. Write a one sentence definition of *democracy*. Your definition should explain what you mean by *democracy*. Develop your definition into a paragraph in which you make the abstraction concrete by giving specific examples. Paragraphs will vary according to definitions and examples.

D. Find a paragraph in an essay, a short story, or a novel in which the author uses connotative words to achieve a particular effect. Write a paragraph in which you discuss the author's use of connotation. Give specific examples of the words he uses and the effects he achieves. Paragraphs will vary.

E. Your teacher may wish to have a committee do this exercise and report to the class. Look through the theater section of a newspaper to find reviewer's comments in the advertisements for plays or movies. Make a list of five such quotations. Using the *Readers' Guide to Periodical Literature* find the source of each of the reviews. Read the reviews to determine whether the words quoted out of context mean what they did in the original reviews. For students of superior ability.

Vocabulary growth should be one of the outcomes of students' increased understanding of language.

2. Using Language Selectively

WORDS THAT FIT THE OCCASION

Mature use of language requires that you be able to communicate your ideas in words that are suited to the situation. In writing a paper on Albert Einstein, you would not say, "That cat was somethin' else. He sure had some way-out ideas." Neither would you say, in greeting a friend, "Good morning, William. Is this not a salubrious day?" The question here is not so much one of correct usage as it is one of appropriate usage.

There are three generally recognized levels of usages—*formal* and *informal* (often grouped under the single heading *standard*) and *substandard*. You will find, as you study these ways of using language, that they are not three distinctly separate classifications of language, but, rather, that they overlap. Formal English, as its name implies, is the kind of language used by educated people in formal situations. It is used more frequently in writing than in speaking, especially in writing of a technical or scholarly nature. Formal English is also employed in essays, biographies, fiction, and poetry intended to appeal to those whose interests are intellectual. The tone of formal English is dignified and literary. Words not normally used in everyday conversation appear, and frequently, literary, Biblical, and historical allusions (references) are incorporated. The langugage of formal English is exact in nature and adheres rigidly to the rules of grammar. No short cuts in sentence structure are permitted; no contractions are used. Read the following excerpt from a book review.

> To the English or American ear, French historical plays have a way of sounding like the Epilogue to Shaw's "St. Joan." If other historical playwrights seem oriel windows blazing with shattered color, French ones tend to resemble tall shafts of gray stone set off in plain glass.
>
> —CHARLES A. BRADY, *Buffalo Evening News*

You probably found that you had to read the foregoing passage carefully and thoughtfully to understand its meaning. Undoubtedly, you had to look up the meaning of *oriel*. Notice the allusion to the Epilogue to

Despite the levity behind this presentation, the point being made is an important one.

Students must understand that recognizing the three levels of language is not opening the doors to license in language usage. Emphasize the concept of appropriateness.

George Bernard Shaw's play "St. Joan." If you are familiar with the Epilogue, the point Dr. Brady is making was undoubtedly clear to you immediately. However—and this is often true of allusions—even if you do not understand the specific literary reference, its use within the entire context of the paragraph suggests the idea the reviewer has tried to convey: the contrast between the French and other historical plays. Notice, too, the formal, literary tone and the use of imagery: "oriel windows blazing with shattered color" contrasted with "tall shafts of gray stone set off in plain glass."

One of the errors frequently made by students is to assume that formal English is stilted and pompous. It is not. Formal English is completely natural to the situation for which it is intended. Were you to write a research paper, take part in a formal debate, or make a formal presentation of a class gift, for example, the level of language appropriate to each of these situations would be formal English. The only time that formal English sounds pompous and ridiculous is when it is used in an inappropriate situation, as in the greeting included in the first paragraph of this section.

Informal English is the kind of language used by educated people in informal speaking and writing situations. It is the language of the classroom and the business office; it is the language of most plays and novels; it is the language of magazines and newspapers. Informal English is the language of everyday living. It is most easily recognized by its conversational tone. Sentences are relatively uncomplicated and the vocabulary is easy to understand.

Here, again, the emphasis is on what is suitable to a particular situation.

The primary aim should be for students to attain the level of language used by educated persons in informal speaking and writing situations.

The range of informal English is wide. It may vary from the serious to the nonsensical. At its most precise, informal English is the language used by professional people to make their technical fields understandable to laymen. The language in this usage is closer to formal English, but does away with the highly specialized vocabulary of the particular field and is more informal in tone. The following is an example of the use of informal English in an excerpt from a book on birds. Notice particularly the non-technical language.

Read and discuss this material in detail. Students should be aware of the wide range within the informal level of language.

All the many kinds of bird flight rely on the principle familiar to every little boy who has put his hand out of the window of a moving car; that a flat surface inclined slightly upward to a current of air will be pushed upwards, or, in other words, is able to support a weight. The slower the speed of the air relative to the wing, the less weight can be supported. For a bird to support itself in the air, it is not enough that it spread its wings sideways; it must also arrange to pass through the air fast enough to get the necessary lift to balance its weight. If it does not move fast enough, the wing will not give any lift, and we say that it "stalls."

—OSKAR AND KATHARINA HEINROTH, *The Birds*

In its lightest vein, informal English follows the patterns of everyday speech. Like conversation, it often makes use of the personal pronouns and even includes an occasional slang expression for effect. In a humorous, even nonsensical vein, is the following excerpt from an essay by Robert Benchley.

Excavation watchers, as a class, are very conscientious sportsmen. You very seldom catch them watching anything else when they are on an excavation job. Fire engines may go by in the street behind their backs, old ladies may faint over their very heels, and even a man with a sidewalk stand of bouncing dolls may take up his position on the curb across the street, but the cellar-hole boys stick to their post without ever so much as batting an eyelash. In fact, the eyelash-batting average of some of the old-timers has gone as low as .005 in a season.

Discussion of the excerpts as they evidence the points made in the developmental material should help students better to understand the variations of usage within a given level.

You may wish to have students list slang expressions that were popular recently but that have already been discarded.

Conversational English, sometimes called *colloquial English,* often contains some slang. Slang, when used selectively and cleverly, adds color and freshness to speech. It is also appropriate to certain kinds of informal writing—articles intended for current reading only, such as articles about teenagers, sports activities, and similar subjects. Generally, however, except to reproduce familiar conversation, you should avoid slang when you write. One reason for this is the rapid death of most slang expressions. Although a few slang expressions may eventually become an accepted part of the language, most of them do not last after their novelty has worn off. Expressions that were once fresh and novel now sound worn out and ridiculous: *twenty-three skidoo, dumb Dora, the cat's pajamas, horn-swoggle.*

Although some slang is appropriately used in informal standard English, slang is generally considered *substandard* English. The constant use of slang falls into the same category as illiterate usage, the language of the uneducated: *I could of went, That ain't gonna do nobody no good, Youse better watch yer step, Ah reckon ah'll mosey along.* The vocabulary is limited to the expression of only the most simple ideas; the usage is ungrammatical. Incorrect verb forms, double negatives, incorrect pronoun usage, dialect, and localisms abound in substandard speech.

Substandard speech is not to be criticized or ridiculed as it is used by people who have had little or no educational opportunities or by people whose speech patterns are those of a particular national or regional background. On the other hand, educated people avoid using this level of language, except as a deliberate device for achieving a particular effect. A good writer, for example, will use substandard English in reproducing the dialogue of uneducated characters in his book. The validity of this use of substandard English is obvious: no reader could believe in an illiterate character who sounded like an intellectual.

To develop the ability to use language effectively, you must know the standing of a word, as well as its meaning, in order that you may use it in appropriate situations. *Impecunious, penniless,* and *broke* are all synonyms, but are not all suited to the same situations. Also just as a word may have several meanings, so may the various meanings have different degrees of dignity. For example, when *dead* is used to express the meaning "deprived of life," as opposed to *alive,* it is a standard word; when it

The concept of varying degrees of dignity within the meanings of a word should be developed in detail.

is used to mean "very tired," it is colloquial. When *break* is used to mean "a gap or a breach," it is standard; when it is used in the sense of "a good or a bad chance; as, a lucky or a bad *break*," it is slang. Notice also the examples below.

His vicious attack left me *dumb* and astonished. (Standard)
Don't be *dumb!* Of course I want you to be there. (Colloquial)

He suffered a broken *jaw* in the accident. (Standard)
Don't just *jaw* at me; do something. (Slang)

DEVELOPING YOUR SKILL

A. Be prepared to discuss the following statement: The level of language that a person should use depends upon what is appropriate to the situation. See p. T58.

B. Divide your paper into three columns headed *Slang, Informal, Formal.* In the first column list at least five current slang terms. After each, write one synonym that is appropriate to informal usage and one that is appropriate to formal usage. You may find that you have to use phrases instead of single-word synonyms. In some cases there may be only one standard term that is used in both informal and formal situations.

You may wish to extend this exercise beyond the five-word minimum suggested.

	SLANG	INFORMAL	FORMAL
Examples:	pad	house	domicile
	gig	job	employment

IDIOMS

An *idiom* is a form of expression that is peculiar to the language in which it is used. Idioms frequently cannot be analyzed grammatically; their meanings develop through usage rather than through the relationship of the words to each other. Think, for a moment of the literal meanings of the italicized idioms in the following sentences.

Mr. Baxter paced *back and forth.*
Look up that word in your dictionary.

Taken literally, the first idiom presents a picture of Mr. Baxter backing across a room and then going forward. A literal interpretation of the words in the second idiom would require your holding the dictionary overhead. Yet, both these usages, and numerous others, are an accepted part of your speech patterns.

Some of your students may be able to give literal translations of idioms from other languages to illustrate the loss of meaning that results.

Each language has its own idioms. Because there are no rules governing their patterns, idioms lose meaning when translated into other languages. Under what circumstances do you think someone might say to you, "Chop me not a teapot" or "In the mouth of the wolf"? The first is a literal translation of an idiom from another language and has the general meaning of "Don't pester me!"; the second means "Good luck!"

Draw from
students
examples
of other
common
idioms—
up in the
air, odds
and ends,
etc.

English, similarly, uses idiomatic expressions that would make no sense if translated into other languages. Some of these idioms are used in the following passage:

The *field* of applicants *had been narrowed* to four. Each of the other three had been interviewed a second time. It was now my turn.

"I have only one question to ask you, young man. Why do you want to work for this company?"

My tongue was suddenly *tied in knots*. Apparently, his decision *hung* only *by a thread*. What I said now could *make or break me*. "Please *bear with me*. . . ," I began.

"You have three minutes in which to answer that question!" he snapped.

So, I was *to talk against time?* I took a deep breath and began again. As I spoke, my *tongue loosened* and the words came easily. When I had stopped talking, Mr. Stratton said, "You'll do. You ought to *make good* in this business."

It is unlikely that anyone would pepper his speech or writing with as many idioms as are used in the example. The purpose here was to illustrate the ease with which idioms fit into the language and to indicate the untranslatability of idioms. If you consider the idioms individually and literally, you will readily see why they cannot be translated into other languages.

Sometimes idiomatic language depends upon the use of particular kinds of words in combination with specific words. Certain words are always followed by infinitives; others, by gerunds.

INFINITIVES	GERUNDS
I *plan to go*.	I *could not help hearing*.
He is *able to work*.	He is *capable of working*.
I shall show you the *way to cut this*.	We use this *method of cutting*.

Some words combine with specific prepositions to express their meaning.

> die *of* (not *with*) a disease
>
> comply *with* (not *to*) instructions
>
> different *from* (not *than*) yours
>
> graduated *from* (not *graduated*) high school
>
> identical *with* (not *to*) his
>
> *at* home (not *to*) home
>
> wait *for* (not *wait on* when the meaning is *await*) someone
>
> absorbed *in* (not *by*) an activity

Other words involve the use of different prepositions to express different meanings. For example, you adapt yourself *to* a situation; a story may
be adapted *for* the movies; the story may have been adapted *from* a TV
play. Other examples of idiomatic uses of prepositions are listed below.

> I do not *agree with* you.
>
> I cannot *agree to* such a proposal.
>
> They could not *agree on* a plan of action.

> I was very *angry about* that incident.
>
> Don't be *angry with* him.

> The poet *compares* her hair *to* sunlight.
>
> As *compared with* him, I am tall.

> His ideas *differ from* mine.
>
> I must *differ with you.* I don't agree, at all.
>
> They *differed over* the proposal.

> They always find it hard to *part from* their friends.
>
> I hate to *part with* this book.

When using two idiomatic expressions that have different prepositions
but are followed by a single object, be sure to express both prepositions.
See the example below.

> She was aware *of* his interest and flattered *by* it.
>
> (Not *She was aware and flattered by his interest.*)

On the other hand, if both idioms use the same preposition, the preposition need be expressed only once.

> She was pleased and flattered *by* his attention.

The correct use of these idiomatic prepositional expressions is essential to good formal and informal writing and speaking.

The use of lively idioms will add spice to a student's
writing and will improve his style by giving it naturalness.
Caution against the use of trite idioms.

DEVELOPING YOUR SKILL

A. Be ready to explain why the italicized idioms in the following sentences have meaning only in English. Translations into other languages would have to be literal, unless the idiom existed in the other languages.
   1. We laughed so hard we nearly *split our sides*.
   2. *Carry out* the directions carefully.
   3. They are *living on a shoestring*.
   4. He found himself *at loose ends* in a strange city.
   5. We'll have to *look into* the matter thoroughly.

B. Number on your paper from 1 to 10. After each number write the expression from the parentheses that will make the sentence idiomatically correct.
   1. Please show me the way (of cutting, to cut) this pattern.
   2. Ray is planning (on going, to go) to New York.
   3. When we arrived, there was nobody (to home, at home).
   4. If you hurry, I'll (wait for, wait on) you.
   5. Your dress is identical (with, to) mine.
   6. He was completely absorbed (by, in) what he was doing.
   7. His proposal is different (than, from) mine.
   8. Andrea always hates to part (from, with) her parents.
   9. Both the union and the management representatives agreed (with, to) the proposal.
   10. He is capable (to do, of doing) that assignment.

Sentences will vary.

C. List at least five idioms, other than those presented in this lesson, and use them correctly in sentences. You may wish to use newspaper and magazine articles to help you find vivid idioms. Listen to the speech of others and be aware of your own speech.

Review Exercises—Using Language Selectively

A. Different situations call for different levels of language. Write what you would say in each of the following situations.
   1. You are thanking your closest friend for a gift you have wanted for a long time. Informal-colloquial

Informal
Formal
   2. You are thanking a guidance counselor for helping you to find a job.
   3. You are accepting a gift from the senior class in behalf of the school.

B. Write each of the following sentences, correcting any errors.
   1. The color of your gloves is similar to that of your purse but is not identical to it. with
   2. Mark's brother will graduate college in June. from

3. The stage manager did not agree ~~with~~ my plan for lighting the play. to
4. As compared ~~to~~ others with the same years of training, she is unusually gifted. with
5. This year's work in Spanish is very different ~~than~~ last year's. from
6. Many people in this country die ~~with~~ heart diseases. of
7. Jack hates to part ~~from~~ any of his belongings. with
8. It is always difficult to part ~~with~~ one's friends. from
9. There was nobody ~~to~~ home when we arrived. at
10. If you hurry, I'll wait ~~on~~ you. for

UNIT SUMMARY

Words are the symbols of language. They are the means by which men communicate with each other. As the need for new symbols arises, men create new words that, through use, become part of the language.

The English language is a living language; that is, it is constantly growing and changing. New words are added; old words take on new meanings or modified meanings; other words fall into disuse. The words that remain in use vary in definiteness of meaning. The most definite words are called *concrete;* the least definite, *abstract.* Within each classification there are variations in exactness from the general—*culture,* for example—to the specific—the *Mona Lisa.* Word meanings vary, too, according to the denotations and connotations of the words and the contexts in which they are used.

Mature use of language depends upon an understanding of words and the selective use of them. Language must be appropriate to the situation in which it is used. Some situations require formal, literary English; others, informal English. In very informal conversational situations, some slang may be used to achieve a particular effect. In writing, however, all substandard usage should be avoided except to reproduce the conversation of illiterate characters in a story.

English, as other languages, includes many idiomatic expressions. Since idioms do not follow rules of grammar, they must be memorized. Most idioms are used correctly through habit and familiarity. The most difficult are those used in combination with specific prepositions. Practice in using these expressions will result in accuracy.

Successful completion of this unit should make students aware of the importance of selectivity in language—both in the choice of words and in the level of language used.

UNIT REVIEW EXERCISES

DISCUSSION TOPICS

See p. A. Discuss the statement "English is a living language." In your discussion in-
T59.   clude the ways in which the English language changes and grows. Give
        specific examples wherever possible.

See p. B. How can the use of abstract words generate misunderstanding? What can
T59.   be done to avoid such misunderstanding?

See p. C. In what ways are connotative meanings used to mislead readers and lis-
T59.   teners? How else may connotative meanings be used?

See p. D. What is meant by *context?* How does context affect the meaning of a word?
T59.   Give examples to support your discussion.

See p. E. Discuss the statement "Mature use of language depends not only upon an
T59.   understanding of language but also upon the selective use of language."
        Develop your ideas fully in the discussion.

WRITTEN WORK

A. Divide your paper into five columns headed *Generalization, Specialization,*
See also *Elevation, Degeneration,* and *Transference.* Look up each of the following
p. T59. words in your dictionary to determine by which process the meaning has
        changed and list the word in the appropriate column. After each word,
        write the name of the language from which the word came into English.

Transference	1. manufacture F		OF 6. disease	Specialization
Degeneration	2. saloon F		L 7. nervous	Degeneration
Elevation	3. bank F	F & It 8. carnival	Transference
Degeneration	4. undertaker AS		Gr 9. enthusiasm	Degeneration
Degeneration	5. menial ME		AS 10. thimble	Generalization

B. Each of the following words may have different meanings depending upon
   the context in which the word is used. Write sentences in which you use
   each word in at least two different contexts. Sentences will vary.

1. date	6. edge
2. bridge	7. hamper
3. fence	8. mark
4. direct	9. muscle
5. figure	10. particular

C. Write a composition in which you discuss the following statement: Propa-
   gandists use loaded words to arouse the emotions of their listeners and
   readers. Insist that students cite specific examples to
   establish their points.

VOCABULARY

Did you know the meaning of every word in this unit? In the following sentences, some of the words are used in different contexts. Write the numbers 1 to 5 on your paper. After each number, write the letter of the word or phrase that could best be substituted for the italicized word in each sentence. Before making your choice, find the word on the page indicated to see how the word is used in this unit.

1. His expression showed *consternation* when he realized the error
   he had made. [p. 63]
c   (*a*) anger; (*b*) annoyance; (*c*) dismay; (*d*) panic
2. What *interpretation* would you place on that incident? [p. 68]
b   (*a*) criticism; (*b*) explanation; (*c*) illustration; (*d*) translation
3. The court recognized the *validity* of the pedestrian's claims for
   the injuries he had sustained. [p. 80]
b   (*a*) strength; (*b*) soundness; (*c*) value; (*d*) defense
4. He acted the role of a *pompous* old man convincingly. [p. 78]
a   (*a*) showy; (*b*) insincere; (*c*) majestic; (*d*) formal
5. As they learned to understand her, they *modified* their opinion
   of her. [p. 85]
d   (*a*) improved; (*b*) softened; (*c*) lessened; (*d*) changed

SPELLING

The following spelling words appeared in the unit or were chosen because they are commonly misspelled. Study these words so that you will be prepared to write them from dictation.

1. consternation	11. elevation
2. interpretation	12. degeneration
3. validity	13. transference
4. pompous	14. factual
5. modified	15. mimicking
6. symbolize	16. bureau
7. generalization	17. economically
8. specialization	18. superstitious
9. abstraction	19. thorough
10. associative	20. notoriety

Encourage students to use both Vocabulary and Spelling
words in speaking and writing.

UNIT SELF-TEST

A. Name and define three processes by which words change meaning. See below.

B. Arrange the following groups of words so they progress from the most abstract to the most specific. Follow alphabetical order.

1. actress(c), Doris Day(e), human being(a), movie star(d), female(b)
2. orange juice(e), fluid(c), beverage(d), juice(b), liquid(a)
3. Guernsey(e), mammal(b), vertebrate(a), Bossie(f), bovine(c), cow(d)
4. plant(b), pine(e), vegetation(a), evergreen(c), Georgia pine(d), tree(c)
5. mathematics(b), science(a), engineering(d), applied mathematics(c), civil engineering(e)

C. Name and define the three generally recognized levels of language usage. See below.

D. Some of the following sentences are correct; some are incorrect. If the sentence is correct, write the word *Correct* after the appropriate number; if the sentence is incorrect, rewrite it correctly.

1. They scoured the woods all night in search for the lost child. of
2. Jerry waited on the customers in the first two booths. Correct
3. Your new purse is identical with mine. Correct
4. What kind of a book do you need? Omit a
5. I am sure that they are planning on going to the movies tonight. to go
6. Jim ran in the house to ask his father to leave him use the car. into let
7. I am interested to know if she suspicions anything. in knowing, whether, suspects
8. Agnes has a real interest and feeling for poetry. in
9. When my family moved, the principal complied to my request to let me with remain at Easton so I could graduate school with my friends. from
10. I can't decide nothing until I know if he is planning on speaking before or after dinner. anything, whether, to speak

A. Generalization (p. 65), specialization (p. 65), elevation (p. 65), degeneration (p. 65), transference (p. 66)

C. Formal (p. 77), informal (p. 78), substandard (p. 80)

Unit 5

Reading for Appreciation

Appreciative reading requires that students recognize
authors' devices and that they master a technique of analysis

"But I already know how to read!" you protest. Perhaps. If by *reading* you mean the ability to recognize and understand words, phrases, sentences, and paragraphs, then you can read. Whether or not you read appreciatively is another matter. Appreciative reading involves the ability to understand the full meaning of a work of literature, the meaning that frequently lies below the surface. It requires that the reader be able to read between the lines; to relate ideas and events from the past to those of the present; to recognize and interpret human behavior in the light of the behavior of literary characters. Unless you get more than the surface meaning from a work of literature, you miss the full pleasure to be found in reading.

An understanding of the writer's craft will lead you to a greater appreciation of the literature you read. An author uses many devices and techniques to create the effects he wishes to produce on the reader. In this unit you will study some of the devices and techniques used by writers, particularly as they apply to poetry and to the short story.

Discuss the ideas developed in the introduction, particularly those that relate to the requirements for comprehending the full meaning of a work of literature.

Before you begin the study of this unit, determine how much you already know about authors' devices and techniques by doing the Check Yourself exercises.

 CHECK YOURSELF

After you have completed the following exercises, your teacher will read the correct answers to you.

1. Identify the figures of speech in each of the following quotations as *simile, metaphor, personification, metonymy,* or *hyperbole.*

Metaphor   In came Mrs. Fezziwig, <u>one vast substantial smile.</u>

—CHARLES DICKENS, *A Christmas Carol*

Metaphor   At one extremity of an open space, <u>hemmed in</u> by the <u>dark wall of</u>
Metaphor   <u>forest,</u> arose a rock. . . surrounded by four <u>blazing</u> pines, their tops
Simile   aflame, their stems untouched, <u>like candles at an evening meeting.</u>

—NATHANIEL HAWTHORNE, "Young Goodman Brown"

Irony   2. What literary device involves a deliberate twisting of facts, events, or
                 meanings?
Sarcasm   3. What form of irony is usually intentionally cruel? What form of irony
Satire   ridicules mankind's vices and follies?
Climax   4. What term refers to the decisive moment in the action of a story?
Conflict   5. What is the struggle, or problem, in a work of fiction called? What is
Denouement   the solution of the problem called?

Since all the terms in the Check Yourself answers are discussed in detail in the development of the event, do not engage in exhaustive discussion at this point.

1. Recognizing the Author's Devices

FIGURATIVE LANGUAGE

Because language is adaptable and lends itself to imaginative usage, man can express the same idea in different ways. He may make a direct, informative statement of fact—*Everyone in the room was excited;* or he may use figurative language, language that has an emotional appeal—*A tremor of excitement ran through the room.* <u>Figurative language goes beyond the literal meanings of words to achieve a particular effect.</u>

Students who do not recognize an author's use of figurative language often lose not only the primary meanings of sentences but also the overtones of suggestion.

Professional writers use figures of speech to make their writing more colorful, more expressive, and more forceful. This statement is not intended to suggest that figurative language is something that an author decides to add to or omit from his writing, depending upon his whim of the moment. Often, it is the best means, or even the only means, by which a writer can convey an experience to his readers. Compare the literal language of *The passengers were thrown back and forth; Camus was born in the south and always yearned to be in the sun;* and *The sky is bright* with the figurative language of the following.

. . . The passengers bounced around like popcorn.

The familiar makes the unknown more vivid.

—WILBUR SCHRAMM, "Windwagon Smith"

Camus was born of the sun and always had a yearning to be in it.

There is more than just a compass direction here.

—BLANCHE KNOPF, "Albert Camus in the Sun"

The steel mill sky is alive.

—CARL SANDBURG, "The People, Yes"

There is movement as well as light.

Simile, metaphor, and personification

Authors frequently use figurative language to make comparisons between things or qualities that are unlike in most respects but strikingly similar in at least one respect. The three figures of speech most commonly used for making comparisons are the *simile,* the *metaphor,* and *personification.*

A simile is a direct comparison that is introduced by *like* or *as.* In order to be effective, the comparison expressed in a simile must make the idea clearer to the reader or must have a stronger appeal to the imagination than a literal statement would. The similes in the following examples are italicized.

There must always be one point of similarity between the unlike things being compared.

When he looked directly at anyone, his eyes became *like two pieces of flint turned suddenly up in dug earth.*

—WILLIAM FAULKNER, "Spotted Horses"

The thin upper edges of the outstretched cloudlet begin to flash *like darting serpents. . . .*

—IVAN TURGENIEFF, "Byézhin Meadow"

Point out to students that trite or strained figures of speech may destroy rather than enhance the writing.

Illustrate
by drawing
a square
and a
triangle
on the
chalk-
board.
Include
in each
a small
circle.
The cir-
cle is
the point
of simi-
larity.

All night the fog rolled up the hills from the sea and filled the garden, and in the morning lay cushioned against the door *like an amiable dissolute ghost left over from the night.*

—SANORA BABB, "The Santa Ana"

Unless the comparison made is between two essentially unlike things, there is no use of figurative language involved. *John's haircut is like Roy's* is an ordinary comparison, not a figure of speech.

A metaphor is an implied comparison between unlike things. When using a metaphor, an author does not say that one thing is *like* another, but, rather, that one thing *is* another. To say *"He is an ostrich"* is to suggest that the person being discussed has some characteristic in common with the ostrich. Note the italicized metaphors in the following examples.

... *time was a banner* that whipped before him always in the wind.

—CAROLINE GORDON, "Old Red"

The great *snake* that you see there *is the Mississippi River.*

—THOMAS WOLFE, *You Can't Go Home Again*

The man was playing with this town; *it was a toy* for him.

—STEPHEN CRANE, "The Bride Comes to Yellow Sky"

Personification is a particular type of metaphor. It is a figure of speech that attributes the qualities or characteristics of a human being to an abstract idea or to an inanimate object, as in the following examples.

The yellow fog that rubs its back upon the window-panes.

—T. S. ELIOT, "The Love Song of J. Alfred Prufrock"

I remember how it used to shudder and sigh when I cranked it and how its crank would kick back viciously. It was a mean car. It loved no one. . . .

—JOHN STEINBECK, "Jalopies I Cursed and Loved"

Figures of speech, to be effective, should astonish the reader but at the same time should illuminate the idea. They should not be used merely for adornment.

Metonymy

A more difficult form of figurative speech involves the substitution of one word for another. *Metonymy* is the device of letting one word stand for another closely associated word. This may involve such usage as *capital* when employers are meant and *labor* for workmen. It may mean the substitution of the name *Chaucer* for the writings of Chaucer; the use of *sword* to suggest *death; shouting* for *victory; blade* for *dagger; nation* for *the people.* The last two examples given are, strictly speaking, examples of *synecdoche,* the use of the name of a part when the whole thing is meant or of the whole for the part. However, synecdoche is considered one type of metonymy. The following example illustrates the use of metonymy in context.

It is not necessary to make the distinction between metonymy and synecdoche; however, if you wish to illustrate synecdoche further, use examples such as <u>sail</u> for <u>ship</u> and <u>motor</u> for <u>automobile</u>.

> Recently I drove from Garrison-on-Hudson to New York on a
> Sunday afternoon, one unit in a *creeping parade of metal, miles and*
> *miles of shiny paint and chrome* inching along bumper to bumper.
>
> —JOHN STEINBECK, "Jalopies I Cursed and Loved"

Metonymy is so common a figure of speech, both in writing and in speech, that it frequently contributes to language change. Figures such as *heart* for *courage* and *throne* for *king* or *queen* have become so much a part of language that these meanings are listed in dictionaries as accepted usage.

Hyperbole

Hyperbole is deliberate exaggeration, not to deceive, but to emphasize a point or situation or to create humor. Exaggeration may be achieved through the use of words whose meanings are broader or more intense than the literal meaning of the situation requires: *starved* for *hungry; thousands of times* for *many times; perfect* for *excellent.* Notice the naturalness of the use of hyperbole in the following examples.

> One evening after dark a young man prowled among these *crumbling red mansions,* ringing their bells.
>
> —O. HENRY, "The Furnished Room"

> Lily, the caretaker's daughter, was *literally run off her feet* [answering the door and helping the gentlemen remove their overcoats].
>
> —JAMES JOYCE, "The Dead"

Hyperbole is so common in speech that unless the author chooses a striking example the effect is sometimes lost.

DEVELOPING YOUR SKILL

See p. T59.

A. Name and define the five figures of speech studied in the lesson.

B. Number from 1 to 10 on your paper. After each number, write the figure of speech that appears in the corresponding quotation and label the figure.

Personification 1. He sat staring at the yellow, <u>singing</u> gaslight.

—O. HENRY, "The Furnished Room"

Metonymy 2. Costly thy habit as thy <u>purse</u> can buy, But not express'd in fancy; rich, not gaudy; For the apparel oft proclaims the man.

—WILLIAM SHAKESPEARE, *Hamlet*

Simile 3. . . . roll after roll of thunder crashed <u>like the drum of a great orchestra</u> performing a symphony of defied and defeated fate.

—LAURENS VAN DER POST, "Africa"

Hyperbole 4. Tomorrow night I appear for the first time before a Boston audience—<u>4000 critics</u>.

—MARK TWAIN, letter to Pamela Clemens Moffet

Personification 5. The great Pullman was whirling onward with such <u>dignity of motion</u> that a glance from the window seemed simply to prove

Metaphor that the <u>plains of Texas were pouring</u> eastward.

—STEPHEN CRANE, "The Bride Comes to Yellow Sky"

Personification 6. Like no other morning, <u>this one sang</u> with the pristine mystery of the first morning of time.

—SANORA BABB, "The Santa Ana"

Personification 7. It [New York City] carries on its <u>lapel</u> the unexpungeable odor of the long past . . . .

—E. B. WHITE, "Here is New York"

Metonymy 8. This word "love," which <u>greybeards</u> call divine.

—WILLIAM SHAKESPEARE, *King Henry VI, Part III*

Hyperbole 9. Ready <u>to split his sides</u> with laughing.

—MIGUEL DE CERVANTES, *Don Quixote*

Simile 10. There were deer to drift in herds <u>alarmless as smoke</u>. . . .

—WILLIAM FAULKNER, "Mississippi"

IRONY

Closely related to figurative language is the device known as *irony.* Irony may
The essential characteristic of irony is the <u>deliberate twisting of facts,</u> be evi-
<u>events, or meanings</u> to imply something different from, sometimes even denced in
the opposite of, what is actually said. The force of irony lies in the con- words or
trast between the actual words and the implied meaning. The tone may in ac-
range from gentle humor to bitter invective. While there are no specific tions—
names by which to identify all the gradations between the extremes of irony or
irony, they may be recognized by the tone of the writing: light and mock- dramatic
ing, gay, whimsical, quiet, sneering, and so on. irony.

Sometimes a writer chooses to present an ironical situation rather than
make ironical statements. Here the contrast is between the apparent situation with its anticipated outcome and the actual outcome. For example,
in an account of the sinking of the *Titanic,* the author presents the following description of the passengers' activities less than two hours before the
disaster:

> Dinner that night in the Jacobean dining room was gay. It was
> bitter on deck, but the night was calm and fine; the sky was moon-
> less but studded with stars twinkling coldly in the clear air.
>
> After dinner some of the second-class passengers gathered in the
> saloon, where the Reverend Mr. Carter conducted a "hymn sing-
> song." It was almost ten o'clock and the stewards were waiting with
> biscuits and coffee as the group sang:
>
> > *O, hear us when we cry to Thee*
> > *For those in peril on the sea.*
>
> —HANSON BALDWIN, "R. M. S. *Titanic*"

In an ironic situation, the reader or the audience usually
knows more about what fate is in store for the characters involved than do the characters themselves.

Discuss
the ele-
ments
that con-
tribute
to the
irony of the situation.
The irony in this situation is pointed up by the gaiety of the passengers' mood, the brightness of the stars' "twinkling," the clear air, and the general atmosphere of well-being. The force of the irony lies in the picture of the passengers, who in a very short time may, themselves, perish, praying in song for " . . . those in peril on the sea."

Sarcasm and satire

Point out
to stu-
dents
that
sarcasm
and
satire
may over-
lap.
Sarcasm and *satire* are forms of irony. Sarcasm is intentionally cruel. It involves the making of stinging remarks for the express purpose of wounding someone's feelings. Sarcasm is not always ironical; it is sometimes direct and depends upon tone of voice rather than the reversed meaning of the words. When Macbeth greets Duncan, whose murder Macbeth has been planning, with the words "O worthiest cousin!" the sarcasm is ironical.

Satire is intended to criticize or ridicule mankind for his vices and his follies. It may be gentle, moderate, or bitter and may be directed against an individual, an idea, a custom, or an institution. Satire may be intended as a bitter attack against someone or something that the author wants to brand. The subject matter of satire may range from the trifling to the momentous, from women's telephone conversations to national or world politics. Dickens's calling the guillotine "National Razor!" is one kind of satire. Another may be seen in the lines called "On a Magazine Sonnet" by Russell Hilliard Loines.

Thank goodness
that the author
wrote fourteen
lines. He might
otherwise have
gone on and bored the reader for a hundred lines.
"Scorn not the sonnet," though its strength be sapped,
    Nor say malignant its inventor blundered;
The corpse that here in fourteen lines is wrapped
    Had otherwise been covered with a hundred.

The satirist frequently directs his barbs at women.

The satire lies
in the sudden
shift in the
last line—the
deliberate twist-
ing for humorous
and, perhaps, somewhat malicious effect.
All honour to woman, the sweetheart, the wife,
    The delight of our firesides by night and by day,
Who never does anything wrong in her life,
    Except when permitted to have her own way.

                    —FITZ-GREENE HALLECK, "Woman"

The cause of women does not go unsupported, however.

Students may enjoy hearing the entire poem if a copy is available.

> They're always abusing the women,
>   As a terrible plague to men;
> They say we're the root of all evil,
>   And repeat it again and again—
> Of war, and quarrels, and bloodshed,
>   All mischief, be what it may.
> And pray, then, why do you marry us,
>   If we're all the plagues you say?
>
> —ARISTOPHANES, "Chorus of Women"

Paradox

Sometimes, in order to jolt his reader into paying close attention, an author will employ an ironical device known as *paradox*. On the surface, a paradox appears to be a contradiction; however, the careful reader will see that there is an underlying truth in what the author has said. Read the following excerpt.

> "A father gives *all* his love to each one of his children without discrimination whether it be one or ten, and if I am suffering now for my two sons, I am not suffering half for each of them but double . . ."
>
> —LUIGI PIRANDELLO, "War"

Develop the concept of paradox carefully. This is usually the most difficult of the devices for students.

Your initial reaction may have been: "How is it possible for a father to give *all* his love to each of his children?" As you think about this, however, you must realize that a parent does not divide and subdivide his love as his family grows; he loves each child to his full capacity for loving. As a result, the death of two sons in war will cause a father to suffer doubly—fully for each one.

A well-known paradox exists in the artistic philosophy that life succeeds in that it seems to fail.

▸ DEVELOPING YOUR SKILL

See p. T60. A. Be prepared to discuss the following questions.

    1. What is meant by *irony*?
    2. When is sarcasm ironical?
    3. What is meant by *satire*?
    4. What is the scope of satire?
    5. What is the irony involved in paradox?

See p. T60. B. Write an explanation of the irony in the following situation.

"Do you remember that diamond necklace which you lent me to wear at the ministerial ball?"

"Yes. Well?"

"Well, I lost it."

"What do you mean? You brought it back."

"I brought you back another just like it. And for this we have been ten years paying. You can understand that it was not easy for us, us who had nothing. At last it is ended, and I am very glad."

Mme. Forestier had stopped.

"You say that you bought a necklace of diamonds to replace mine?"

"Yes. You never noticed it, then! They were very like."

And she smiled with a joy which was proud and naïve at once.

Mme. Forestier, strongly moved, took her two hands.

"Oh, my poor Mathilde! Why my necklace was paste. It was worth at most five hundred francs!"

—GUY DE MAUPASSANT, "The Necklace"

See p. T60. C. Write an explanation of the satire in each of the following.

    Men, dying, make their wills, but wives
        Escape a work so sad;
      Why should they make what all their lives
    The gentle dames have had?

—JOHN GODFREY SAXE, "Woman's Will"

    The man recover'd of the bite,
      The dog it was that died.

—OLIVER GOLDSMITH, "An Elegy on the Death of a Mad Dog"

Students who can complete these exercises successfully have gained a basic understanding of irony.

D. Write an explanation of the paradox involved in each of the following situations. You may have to refer to the plays in order to understand the situations more fully. See p. T60.

1. "Parting is such sweet sorrow." *(Romeo and Juliet)* II:2, line 184
2. "I must be cruel in order to be kind." *(Hamlet)* III: 4, line 178

Review Exercises—Recognizing the Author's Devices

Read each of the following selections and identify the various devices the authors have used to achieve their effects. More than one device may be evident in a selection. In every case, show that you not only recognize the device but also understand it. For example, if you are identifying a figure of speech, write the figure on your paper and label it; if satire is involved, explain who or what is being satirized; and so on.

1. This record will forever stand,   Satire on women's promises

   "Woman, thy vows are trac'd in sand."

   —LORD BYRON, "To Woman"

2. A polychromatic rug like some brilliant-flowered rectangular, trop-   Simile
   ical islet lay surrounded by a billowy sea of soiled matting.   Metaphor

   —O. HENRY, "The Furnished Room"

3. Elected Silence, sing to me. . . .   Personification

   —GERARD MANLEY HOPKINS, "The Habit of Perfection"

4. His eyes blazed with light, and his throat worked like a pump. Simile
   Metaphor   —STEPHEN CRANE, "The Bride Comes to Yellow Sky"

5. The guest reclined, inert, upon a chair, while the room, confused in Personifi-
   speech as though it were an apartment in Babel, tried to discourse to cation
   him of its divers tenantry.

   —O. HENRY, "The Furnished Room"

6. That spreading constellation to the north is called Chicago, and that Metaphor
   giant wink that blazes in the moon is the pendant lake that it is built Metaphor
   upon.

   —THOMAS WOLFE, *You Can't Go Home Again*

Once again, impress upon students the effectiveness of the somewhat startling, yet appropriate, figure of speech.

Metonymy 7. The other houses of the street, conscious of decent lives within them,
             gazed at one another with brown imperturbable faces. Personification

—JAMES JOYCE, "Araby"

8.   A man said to the universe,
Satire on the   "Sir, I exist!"
"world owes me   "However," replied the universe,
a living" theme.   "The fact has not created in me
                           A sense of obligation."

—STEPHEN CRANE, "Lines"

2. Reading Critically

ASPECTS OF STYLE

Style is   Style is everything about a piece of writing that makes the writing dis-
not a   tinctive. It is the author's choice of subject matter. It is the melody and
single   rhythm of his characteristic pattern of language. It is the reflection of
defin-   the author's tastes, habits, attitudes, and emotions. In short, style *is* the
able ele- author.
ment of   A writer's style may vary with the kind of writing he is doing and with
writing. the characters and situations he is portraying. However, despite the pos-
          sible variations in his style, close study of the body of an author's work
          will usually reveal recognizable elements of attitude, theme, and language
          that make the writing characteristically his. Sinclair Lewis's style is satir-
          ical; Jonathan Swift's is bitterly so. Thomas Wolfe writes with a love of
          the sound of language. Walt Whitman and Carl Sandburg write as though
          the great books of the Bible had sunk deep into their consciousness—and
          the rhythms sing out in their prose and in their poetry. Longfellow loves
          a moral; this, too, is a man's style.

 DEVELOPING YOUR SKILL

Select a story or essay in your literature text as the basis for a written discussion of the author's style. Discuss the subject matter, the theme, the language
patterns, the writing as a reflection of the author's personality, and any other
relevant elements of style. Organize your material. Make specific reference to
the text to support your statements. You may wish to have students
all read the same story for this exercise—perhaps a
story by Ring Lardner, Mark Twain, Edgar Allan Poe, or
Ernest Hemingway, all of whom write in a distinctive
style.

A METHOD OF ANALYSIS

Students often protest that critical reading of a work of literature destroys their enjoyment of literature. "Picking it apart destroys the freshness," they say. This need not be true. How does the mechanic learn about engines? Doesn't he remove every screw and bolt, every gasket, every valve—in fact, every item in the entire engine—so that he will know the engine from the inside? Does the doctor expect to know surgery by instinct, without studying anatomy and surgical techniques? Does the lawyer learn law without studying cases? The student of literature learns to read appreciatively by studying the word, the sentence, the paragraph, and the techniques that develop the whole composition. When he has learned to read critically, all other reading seems spiritless and vague.

When reading fiction, you must first give yourself over completely to the story. Cultivate an attitude of *suspension of disbelief*. Fiction is a product of the author's imagination, although it may be true to life in many respects. You must be willing to accept the fanciful and see what the author does with it. At the same time you must be ready to recognize true aspects of life that may be presented and realistic character traits that may appear. With this mental attitude you are ready to analyze the piece of literature.

The following ten questions will help you develop the ability to read critically and appreciatively. In actual analysis the order will vary and many of the questions will overlap or be considered simultaneously.

Impress upon students that an understanding of an author's techniques will increase their appreciation of literature.

The teen-age sophistication of the eleventh-grader sometimes makes suspension of disbelief difficult. Discuss the point that the reader must be willing to accept the fanciful along with the realistic.

What is the point of view of the story?

When an author writes a story, he must decide who is to tell the story. His decision depends upon the point of view from which the story will be most credible. There are two basic points of view from which the story may be narrated: first person and third person. A story narrated in the first person may have the narrator as the main character telling his own story or as an observer-participant, a minor character telling another character's story. A story narrated in the third person may be told by the author as an observer or by the omniscient author. The latter can report not only the physical aspects of characters and events but also what passes through the minds of the characters. The omniscient author may investigate and interpret the motives and feelings of the characters. The point of view from which a story is narrated is often referred to as the *focus of narration.*

Has the author established sufficient background for his story?

Every writer must decide at what point to begin his story. Although his characters obviously must have histories that extend back before the time of the story, the author must begin his narration at a point from which it can move rapidly and logically to its decisive moment. Still, some background is necessary to make the story clear—the characters must be introduced, the setting must be established, and the situation must be defined. The amount of background, or *exposition,* will depend upon what is necessary for an understanding of the particular story.

How does the setting contribute to the story?

Impress upon students the importance of description. Too many readers skip descriptive passages.

The description of a story's setting should be judged not only in terms of the accuracy of the picture but also in terms of what it contributes to the story. Does it increase the believability of the story? If the setting can be accepted as real, the characters and events gain in credibility. Does the setting contribute to the atmosphere of the story? Sometimes an author presents certain details of setting that add to the feeling the author is trying to convey. The description of certain details of furnishings in a room, for example, can convey the feeling of loneliness or of warmth and companionship. Does the setting help to define character? Sometimes the descriptive material is an index to the personality of the character. This is particularly true when the character describes his surroundings or when the author describes the character's reactions to his surroundings.

You may wish to have students draw a comparison between the methods of revealing background in a short story and in a play.

What is the mood of the story?

The mood, or *atmosphere,* of the story is built up through setting, characterization, plot, and the style of writing. Sometimes the mood can be described as cheerful, mysterious, depressing, and so on; at other times it defies description and is purely a matter of "feeling."

The list of adjectives can be extended—cynical, satirical philosophical.

How does the author provide clues to the characters, events, and situations?

When reading a story, watch for hints that will tell you more about the characters, events, and situations than the author tells you directly. Certain gestures, patterns of speech, or style of dress may give you important information about a character. Bits of dialogue, description, or action may foreshadow coming events or situations. Be alert to such clues.

Foreshadowing

How is character developed?

Characters may be dynamic and grow, or they may be static and remain little-changed at the end of the story.

Character development is an essential ingredient of a good story. Whatever a character becomes, the development must be such that the reader is ready to accept the final personality in the story. If there is an apparent reversal of personality—good to bad or bad to good—the reader must be made to realize that the potential for both was present and that the result was logical and inevitable. The good writer achieves this through action, primarily—and action includes movement, speech, and thought—and through physical description and analysis of the character's motives.

If the plot is most important, the characters may change little. Otherwise, the essence of good characterization is change—for good or bad.

What is the conflict?

In every work of fiction there is a conflict, or struggle—a problem to be solved. There are many kinds of conflict. Conflict may exist between man and man, between man and society, between man and nature. The conflict may be one of ideas. The conflict may exist within a man's own mind—he may be in conflict with himself. There may be elements of several kinds of conflict within a story, but, usually, there is one major conflict. The short-story form is built around a basic conflict. Without a conflict, there is usually no story.

What is the decisive moment in the action?

The decisive moment in the action is usually referred to as the *climax.* The climax is the point at which the story reaches its moment of greatest tension, when it turns toward its solution. Another way of looking at the idea of climax is to think of that point at which there must be a decision at which something occurs to drive the solution in one specific direction.

How does the author build to the key moment?

The key moment, or *moment of illumination,* is the event that contains the key to the entire story, the moment when all previous events are brought into focus and their meanings become clear. Sometimes the climax and the key moment are the same; often, they are not.

The author builds to the climax and key moment through a series of *complications,* moments of tension, that usually increase in intensity until the high point is reached. Sometimes, however, the complications are of equal intensity. Also, it is possible that an author may begin his story at its climax and then, using a flashback technique, go back to present the events leading up to the climax. The pattern of a story depends upon the effect the author is trying to achieve.

Has the story been satisfactorily resolved?

The pattern of the story descends from the climax to the *denouement,* the moment when the problem has been solved, when the fate of the main character, or protagonist, is clear; that is, the moment when the protagonist finally sees the outcome of the conflict or when the reader sees the outcome. The descending action may lead to the moment of illumination, which may coincide with the denouement, just as it may coincide with the moment of decision.

If the outcome of the story is logical, the story has been satisfactorily resolved. In judging the resolution, analyze the total story as the author

has written it, not as you wish he had written it. Ask yourself whether, in
the light of character development and preceding events, the outcome is
logical and reasonable.

Remember, too, that the denouement provides the solution only to the
problem that forms the conflict of the story; the author does not suggest
that the resolution will provide a settlement of all conflict.

Impress
upon
students
that a
short
story
is nec-
essarily
limited
in scope.

> DEVELOPING YOUR SKILL

A. Be prepared to discuss the meanings of the following terms. How is
   each of the terms important to an analysis of a work of fiction?

   1. focus of narration See p. 102   6. conflict See p. 103
   2. exposition See p. 102   7. climax See p. 103
   3. setting See p. 102   8. complication See p. 104
   4. atmosphere See p. 103   9. moment of illumination See p. 104
   5. character development See p. 103 10. denouement See pp. 104-105

B. Your teacher may wish to assign a story in your literature text as the
   basis for this exercise. Read the story and then write a composition
   in which you answer the following questions.   Insist upon a well-
                                                  organized, unified
   1. From what point of view is the story told? composition, not just
   2. What is the setting of the story?   a series of
   3. What information does the author give in the exposition? answers to the
   4. How would you describe the mood of the story?   questions.
   5. How does the author develop the character of the protagonist?
   6. What is the conflict?
   7. Where does the story reach its climax?
   8. What are the complications that lead to the climax?
   9. At what point does the moment of illumination occur?
   10. Is the denouement logical?

AN ANALYSIS

The following is a story by Hans Christian Andersen, the Danish story
teller and author of numerous "fairy tales" for children. You are to be
the judge as to whether this particular story is for little children or for
older boys and girls—or, perhaps, for adults.

You will notice that the story is printed only on the left-hand side of
the page. Pay no attention to the notes and comments on the right-hand
side; save them for a second reading of the story.

In the discussion that follows the reading of the story,
refer to the question raised above. While it is true that
the story can be accepted purely at the "fairy tale" level,
students should also be aware of the adult satire in the
story.

THE EMPEROR'S NEW CLOTHES

1 Many years ago there lived an Emperor who was so exceedingly fond of fine clothes that he spent all his money on being elaborately 5 dressed. He took no interest in his soldiers, no interest in the theater, nor did he care to drive about in his state coach, unless it were to show off his new clothes. He had differ- 10 ent robes for every hour of the day, and just as one says of a King that he is in his Council Chamber, people always said of him, "The Emperor is in his wardrobe!"

15 The great city in which he lived was full of gaiety. Strangers were always coming and going. One day two swindlers arrived; they made themselves out to be weavers, and 20 said they knew how to weave the most magnificent fabric that one could imagine. Not only were the colors and patterns unusually beautiful, but the clothes that were made 25 of this material had the extraordinary quality of becoming invisible to everyone who was either unfit for his post, or inexcusably stupid.

"What useful clothes to have!" 30 thought the Emperor. "If I had some like that, I might find out which of the people in my Empire are unfit for their posts. I should also be able to distinguish the wise from the fools.

Enjoyment of a story such as "The Emperor's New Clothes" demands that the reader adopt an attitude of suspension of disbelief. Notice how the exposition helps: the time is vague; the Emperor rules over no particular empire; the reader knows immediately that this ruler is not wise.

Why is the omniscient observer the best focus of narration for this story?

The humorous tone of the story has been established. The Emperor is proud, vain, foolish, and you begin to visualize him frantically pawing through racks of his costumes, trying on this one, then that one, and meanwhile strutting up and down before the mirror. Your creative imagination begins to help your reading.

Does the mention of the two swindlers and the fact that they are weavers make you recall the fact that the Emperor loved clothes? Here you have the first complication. Is it possible that his vanity has made the Emperor foolish enough to accept the idea of invisible clothes?

Do you see the possibilities of the story theme? Just suppose that there were such a method of discovering unfitness and stupidity!

The Emperor's logic is not very good, you say. What is to prevent his officials from pretending to see the cloth in order to keep their posts? Is this a clue to future events?

The first reading of the story should be a silent reading. Insist that students ignore the notes during the first reading.

35　Yes, that material must be woven
for me immediately!" Then he gave
the swindlers large sums of money
so that they could start work at once.

Quickly they set up two looms and
40　pretended to weave, but there was
not a trace of anything on the frames.
They made no bones about demand-
ing the finest silk and the purest gold
thread. They stuffed everything into
45　their bags, and continued to work at
the empty looms until late into the
night.

"I'm rather anxious to know how
much of the material is finished,"
50　thought the Emperor, but to tell the
truth, he felt a bit uneasy, remembering that anyone who was either
a fool or unfit for his post would
never be able to see it. He rather
55　imagined that he need not have any
fear for himself, yet he thought it
wise to send someone else first to see
how things were going. Everyone in
the town knew about the exceptional
60　powers of the material, and all were
eager to know how incompetent or
how stupid their neighbors might be.

"I will send my honest old Chamberlain to the weavers," thought the
65　Emperor. "He will be able to judge
the fabric better than anyone else,
for he has brains, and nobody fills
his post better than he does."

So the nice old Chamberlain went
70　into the hall where the two swindlers

There is no doubt now as to what the
major conflict is. Do you begin to get the
impression that the author is poking fun at
everyone—even at you, the reader? Notice that the complications are building.
The Emperor is committed to the project;
the swindlers must keep him convinced of
the marvelous qualities of the cloth.

The humor here lies in the absurdity
of the picture of the "weavers" stuffing
the silk and gold thread into their bags
and then pantomiming feverishly at the
empty looms.

The suspense hasn't been built up sufficiently for the Emperor himself to go
to the weavers' room. Then, too, the Emperor's attitude is the basis for the satire
introduced here. Isn't his behavior at this
point characteristic of the behavior of
mankind?

Notice that the author first speaks of
the Chamberlain as "honest old Chamberlain." In the next paragraph he becomes "nice old Chamberlain." What does
he become in line 81? Do you think this
progression is intentional? What kind of
person does the Chamberlain become in
your mind? What other details does the
author use to make you see the Chamberlain as a humorous character?

You may wish to remind students of an earlier meaning of
nice—foolish (see p. 65). The use of the word in line 69
may or may not be a deliberate play on the two meanings,
but it is an interesting consideration.

were sitting working at the empty looms.

"Upon my life!" he thought, opening his eyes very wide, "I can't see
75 anything at all!" But he didn't say so.

Both the swindlers begged him to be good enough to come nearer, and asked how he liked the unusual design and the splendid colors. They
80 pointed to the empty looms, and the poor old Chamberlain opened his eyes wider and wider, but he could see nothing, for there was nothing. "Heavens above!" he thought, "could
85 it possibly be that I am stupid? I have never thought that of myself, and not a soul must know it. Could it be that I am not fit for my post? It will never do for me to admit that I can't
90 see the material!"

"Well, you don't say what you think of it," said one of the weavers.

"Oh, it's delightful—most exquisite!" said the old Chamberlain, look-
95 ing through his spectacles. "What a wonderful design and what wonderful colors! I shall certainly tell the Emperor that I am enchanted with it."

100 "We're very pleased to hear that," said the two weavers, and they started describing the colors and the curious pattern. The old Chamberlain listened carefully in order to re-
105 peat, when he came home to the

The reader is conditioned by this time to expect a double meaning to almost everything that happens in the story. The satiric situation has been completely established. The reader recognizes the absurdity of the story, but he also recognizes the application to men in general.

How often men speak in just this kind of generality when they can make no specific comment!

Of course. The weavers must describe the colors and the pattern in detail. You, the reader, know the truth; the swindlers know the truth; but no one else does.

Remind students that irony frequently lies in the reader's knowing more about a situation than do the characters involved.

Emperor, exactly what he had heard,
and he did so.

   The swindlers now demanded
more money, as well as more silk and
110 gold thread, saying that they needed
it for weaving. They put everything
into their pockets and not a thread
appeared upon the looms, but they
kept on working at the empty frames
115 as before.

   Soon after this, the Emperor sent
another <u>nice</u> official to see how the
weaving was getting on, and to en-
quire whether the stuff would soon
120 be ready. Exactly the same thing
happened to him as to the Chamberlain. He looked and looked, but as
there was nothing to be seen except
the empty looms, he could see noth-
125 ing.

   "Isn't it a beautiful piece of material?" said the swindlers, showing
and describing the pattern that did
not exist at all.

130 "Stupid I certainly am not,"
thought the official; "then I must be
unfit for my excellent post, I suppose. That seems rather funny—but
I'll take great care that nobody gets
135 wind of it." Then he praised the material he could not see, and assured
them of his enthusiasm for the gorgeous colors and the beautiful pattern. "It's simply enchanting!" he
140 said to the Emperor.

Once again the swindlers have fattened
their purses by playing upon the folly of
mankind. Notice that they are now even
surer of themselves. They demand more
money as well as costly thread.

Here the author leaves an entire scene
to the imagination of the reader. Too
much detail could destroy the effect of
the story. Visualize the scene in which
the old Chamberlain reports to the Emperor! Can you imagine the Chamberlain's discomfiture?

Again the author adds to the complications by sending another official. What is
your reaction to the word *nice* here?
Notice the brevity with which the scene
is covered. The details are left to the imagination of the reader. Picture the scene
as it would be presented before an audience. Would it be as successful as the
scene in which the old Chamberlain visited the weavers?

Point out the use of <u>nice</u> in line 117. Its use here seems
to substantiate the theory proposed in the note at the bottom
of p. 107. Notice that the word is repeated again in lines
148 and 155.

The whole town was talking about the splendid material.

And now the Emperor was curious to see it for himself while it was still

145 upon the looms.

Accompanied by a great number of selected people, among whom were the two <u>nice</u> old officials who had already been there, the Emperor

150 went forth to visit the two wily swindlers. They were now weaving madly, yet without a single thread upon the looms.

"Isn't it magnificent?" said the two

155 <u>nice</u> officials. "Will your Imperial Majesty deign to look at this splendid pattern and these glorious colors?" Then they pointed to the empty looms, for each thought that the oth-

160 ers could probably see the material.

"What on earth can this mean?" thought the Emperor. "I don't see anything! This is terrible. Am I stupid? Am I unfit to be the Emperor?

165 That would be the most disastrous thing that could possibly befall me— Oh, it's perfectly wonderful!" he said. "It quite meets with my Imperial approval." And he nodded appre-

170 ciatively and stared at the empty looms—he would not admit that he saw nothing. His whole suite looked and looked, but with as little result as the others; nevertheless, they all

175 said, like the Emperor, "It's perfectly wonderful!" They advised him to

Now the excitement has spread to the whole town. The tension builds.

At last, the Emperor can contain his curiosity no longer. The Emperor is the third to visit the weavers. Of what significance is the number three in fairy tales, legends, and folklore?

Just who could the "selected" people be? From the looks of things, everybody in the empire is silly (except the two swindlers!). The Emperor begins to look more and more like a comic strip character and the court like a group of vain, pompous fools. You are almost inclined to applaud the swindlers (but not quite!). You can see that the satire is beginning to work on you when you discover that you are joining forces with the evil doers and wishing harm to the supposedly good people. But this is just what the satirist wants you to do. He wants you to laugh at mankind—at least at their foolish traits. If it so happens that everyone in this story is greedy, suspicious, vain, and fearful, then so much the worse for mankind. They had better reform or the swindlers and the thieves will take over the world.

Alas! the Emperor has fallen. He is no better than his subjects. Can't you just see the puzzled looks on the faces of the court? Who was the brave one (or was he the most fawning of the courtiers?) who first suggested that the Emperor have some new clothes made from this "splendid stuff"?

Emphasize the elements of satire that causes the reader to laugh at the foibles of mankind.

have some new clothes made from
this splendid stuff and to wear them
for the first time in the next great
180 procession.

"Magnificent!" "Excellent!" "Pro-
digious!" went from mouth to mouth,
and everyone there was exceedingly
pleased. The Emperor gave each of
185 the swindlers a decoration to wear
in his button-hole, and the title of
"Knight of the Loom."

Americans might not find this detail so
funny as Englishmen would. The practice of wearing ribbons, medals, and other
insignia is more a part of monarchies than
of democracies.

Before the procession they worked
all night, burning more than sixteen
190 candles. People could see how busy
they were finishing the Emperor's
new clothes. They pretended to take
the material from the looms, they
slashed the air with great scissors,
195 they sewed with needles without any
thread, and finally they said, "The
Emperor's clothes are ready!"

The pantomime goes on. Is there anything about this scene that is funnier than
the first time you saw the weavers pretending to be busy at their weaving?

Then the Emperor himself arrived with his most distinguished
200 courtiers, and each swindler raised
an arm as if he were holding something, and said, "These are Your
Imperial Majesty's knee-breeches.
This is Your Imperial Majesty's
205 mantle," and so forth. "It is as light
as a spider's web, one might fancy
one had nothing on, but that is just
the beauty of it!"

Does the humor gain or lose by the
pointing out of specific articles of wearing apparel? Is there irony in the idea
expressed that "one might fancy one had
nothing on, but that is just the beauty
of it"?

"Yes, indeed," said all the cour-
210 tiers, but they could see nothing, for
there was nothing to be seen.

In answer to the question in the note opposite line 192,
student reactions may vary; however, the humor is, for most
readers, increased by the fact that so many people have now
been duped by the weavers.

"If Your Imperial Majesty would graciously consent to take off your clothes," said the swindlers, "we
215 could fit on the new ones in front of the long glass."

So the Emperor laid aside his clothes, and the swindlers pretended to hand him, piece by piece, the new
220 ones they were supposed to have made, and they fitted him around the waist, and acted as if they were fastening something on—it was the train; and the Emperor turned round
225 and round in front of the long glass.

"How well the new robes suit Your Imperial Majesty! How well they fit!" they all said. "What a splendid design! What gorgeous colors!
230 It's all magnificently regal!"

"The canopy which is to be held over Your Imperial Majesty in the procession is waiting outside," announced the Lord High Chamber-
235 lain.

"Well, I suppose I'm ready," said the Emperor. "Don't you think they are a nice fit?" And he looked at himself again in the glass, first on one
240 side and then the other, as if he really were carefully examining his handsome attire.

The courtiers who were to carry the train groped about on the floor
245 with fumbling fingers, and pretended to lift it; they walked on holding

The pantomime grows more and more elaborate. Does the comical situation grow accordingly, or have you just about reached the height of your amusement? One of the artistic principles at work here is that an emotion, whether of humor or of tragedy, cannot be maintained for a long period of time. It is sometimes necessary to let the reader rest for a while while before making him laugh again (or cry!).

Which is funnier, the King looking around at his train or the courtiers trying to pick it up off the floor?

Point out the speed with which the story is now building to the climax.

their hands up in the air; nothing
would have induced them to admit
that they could not see anything.

250 And so the Emperor set off in
the procession under the beautiful
canopy, and everybody in the streets
and at the windows said, "Oh! how
superb the Emperor's new clothes
255 are! What a gorgeous train! What a
perfect fit!" No one would acknowledge that he didn't see anything, so
proving that he was not fit for his
post, or that he was very stupid.

260 None of the Emperor's clothes had
ever met with such a success.

"But he hasn't got any clothes on!"
gasped out a little child.

"Good heavens! Hark at the little
265 innocent!" said the father, and people whispered to one another what
the child had said. "But he hasn't got
any clothes on! There's a little child
saying he hasn't got any clothes on!"

270 "But he hasn't got any clothes on!"
shouted the whole town at last. The
Emperor had a creepy feeling down
his spine, because it began to dawn
upon him that the people were right.
275 "All the same," he thought to himself, "I've got to go through with it
as long as the procession lasts."

So he drew himself up and held
his head higher than before, and the
280 courtiers held on to the train that
wasn't there at all.

Can it be that all the townspeople are
duped? The tension has built rapidly to
this point.

Suddenly, the voice of innocence
speaks and the climax is reached. The
story could take one of at least two directions from this point. What are the possibilities?

Now everybody knows. The key moment has been reached.

Why is the resolution a good one? Do
you feel that it is the best possible ending? Why?

Did you notice that in this story the
climax, key moment, and denouement
follow so closely upon each other as almost to coincide? Why do you think this
was necessary? What would have been the
effect if the descending action had taken
longer?

After the story and notes have been discussed, you may wish
to have students read the story again in the light of their
new awareness.

DEVELOPING YOUR SKILL

Analyses
will depend
upon
stories
selected.

A. Your teacher may wish to assign a short story from your literature text for this exercise. Working as a group, analyze the story to determine why it is a successful short story.

B. Select a short story from your literature text. Write a composition in which you show how the author builds the story to its climax or how he develops the character of the protagonist. Do not retell the story except where necessary to your analysis. You are concerned in this essay with the writer's technique.

Review Exercises—Reading Critically

Insist upon specific reference being made to the text.

A. Write an analysis of the style of your favorite author. Include in your discussion a consideration of all the important elements of style. Cite examples from the writings of the author you have selected.

B. Write an analysis of a short story you have enjoyed. Point out the techniques the author has used to make the story successful. Tell only enough of the story to make your analysis clear.   Analyses will vary.

UNIT SUMMARY

A writer's aim is to convey a particular idea, emotion, or experience to his reader. To accomplish his aim, the writer uses various devices and techniques. He may use figurative language to lend color and force to his words. He may use ironical language or present ironical situations. Depending upon the effect he wants to achieve, an author's use of irony may range from the very gentle to the bitter.

Appreciative reading involves the ability to read critically. This requires an awareness of the author's style of writing and an understanding of the techniques an author uses in introducing, developing, and resolving a story. The greater a reader's understanding becomes, the more heightened his enjoyment and appreciation of literature will be.

Insist that students' analyses be true analyses and not merely plot summaries.

UNIT REVIEW EXERCISES

DISCUSSION TOPICS

A. How may the use of figurative language increase the effectiveness of an author's work? Can you think of any times when the use of figurative language might destroy the effectiveness of the writing? See p. T60.

B. Discuss the meaning of *irony*. How are sarcasm, satire, and paradox forms of irony? See p. T60.

C. What is meant by an author's style? How does his style reflect the personality of the author? See p. T60.

D. Discuss the author's techniques that must be considered if you are to develop the habit of reading critically. How does critical reading increase your appreciation of literature? See p. T60.

WRITTEN WORK   Answers will vary. You may wish to assign specific selections.

A. Select a poem, short story, or essay in which the author has used figurative language. Write the figures of speech on your paper and label them.

B. Write a critical analysis of a short story. Analyze the author's style as well as the form and content of the story. Tell only enough of the plot to make your analysis clear. Quote from the story, whenever necessary, to illustrate the points you make. Analyses will vary.

C. Write a composition in which you discuss the following statement: When one has learned to read critically, all other reading seems spiritless and vague. See below.

VOCABULARY

Did you know the meaning of all the words in this unit? The following sentences use some of the words in different contexts. Write the numbers 1 to 5 on your paper. After each number, write the letter of the word or phrase that could best be substituted for the italicized word in each sentence. Before making your choice, find the word on the page indicated to see how it is used in the unit.

1. His criticism of his opponent's proposals was filled with *invective*. [p. 95]
a   (*a*) condemnation; (*b*) anger; (*c*) insults; (*d*) annoyance
2. Synonyms have various *gradations* of meaning.   [p. 95]
c   (*a*) levels; (*b*) standings; (*c*) degrees; (*d*) inequalities
3. Gloria's version of the story was the most *credible*.   [p. 102]
b   (*a*) exaggerated; (*b*) believable; (*c*) unbelievable; (*d*) humorous

C. The major point in this discussion should be the increased perceptiveness and appreciation that result from critical reading—the awareness of subtle nuances that escape the non-critical reader.

4. His *discomfiture* was apparent to everyone who knew him.   [p. 109]
d   (*a*) surprise; (*b*) annoyance; (*c*) pain; (*d*) embarrassment
5. Ralph's use of slang in his story was *intentional*.   [p. 107]
d   (*a*) effective; (*b*) casual; (*c*) incidental; (*d*) deliberate

SPELLING

The following spelling words appeared in the unit or were chosen because they are commonly misspelled. Study these words so that you will be prepared to write them from dictation.

Work on pro-
nunciation as
well as meaning
and spelling.

1. invective	11. illumination
2. gradations	12. suspension
3. credible	13. denouement
4. intentional	14. complication
5. discomfiture	15. exhilarate
6. momentous	16. perseverance
7. simultaneously	17. mischievous
8. characteristic	18. monotonous
9. metonymy	19. vengeance
10. hyperbole	20. ridiculous

UNIT SELF-TEST

See answers below.
Follow the directions given in each of the following exercises:
1. Name and define three figures of speech.
2. Name and define two forms of irony.
3. What is the essential characteristic of irony?
4. List three elements that influence an author's style.
5. List the ten questions that must be considered if you are to read critically.

1. Simile (p. 91), metaphor (p.92), personification (p. 92), metonymy (p. 93), hyperbole (p.93)
2. Sarcasm (p. 96), satire (p. 96), paradox (p. 97)
3. The deliberate twisting of facts, events, or meanings to imply something different from, or even the opposite of, what is actually said.
4. Subject matter, characteristic patterns of language, tastes, habits, attitudes, emotions—all may be summarized as theme, language, and attitude.
5. See italicized questions on pp. 102-104.

Unit 6

The Research Paper

Ther nys no werkman, whatsoevere he be,

That may bothe werke wel and hastily; . . .

—GEOFFREY CHAUCER, "The Merchant's Tale"

A research paper is based on thoughtful planning, thorough investigation, and careful sequential organization. It is a project that requires time
and effort; it cannot be done well if it is done hastily and haphazardly.
Usually, the students who complain most loudly about writing research
papers are those who have left the entire project for the last minute and
are, as a result, totally disorganized in their work. Those who plan ahead
and work systematically find the experience to be a rewarding one.

Knowing how to carry out a research project will give you invaluable
experience for later life. The techniques you will learn in this unit are the
same as those you will use in preparing reports in college, in business and
professions, and for the various organizations with which you may be
associated. As you use the skills you learn, you will find that many of
them will become automatic and will help you to achieve the goals you
have set for yourself.

In this unit the emphasis will be laid on the learning of the mechanics of doing research: choosing a research topic, using library resources, developing research techniques, and organizing material for a unified paper. Before you begin your study of the research paper, do the following Check Yourself exercise to determine how much you already know about the terminology and techniques of research.

CHECK YOURSELF   See p. T61

After you have completed the following inventory, your teacher will read the correct answers so that you may check what you have written.

1. Which of the following topics would be best for a research paper? Why?

>The Entertainment World
>Vaudeville Comedy
>My Favorite Comedians

2. Name five resources the library offers for research.
3. What information belongs on a bibliography card for a book?
4. What is meant by a note card? What information belongs on such a card?
5. What two kinds of notes may be taken for a research paper?
6. What is meant by an *ellipsis?* How is it shown?
7. When is the term *sic* used?
8. What device is used to insert explanatory material into a direct quotation?
9. When are *ibid.* and *op. cit.* used?
10. What is the purpose of the final bibliography?

1. The Research Topic

SELECTING A TOPIC

The topic you select for a research paper should be, first of all, one in which you are interested. You may wish to select a subject that will help you learn more about the business or profession you plan to engage in; a subject related to a hobby you pursue; or a subject you would like to learn more about. You will find that a well-chosen subject can make the research project an absorbing undertaking.

Topics selected for research should be within the scope of the eleventh-grade student's interests and capabilities. Avoid highly technical subjects, except in unusual cases.

When you choose a subject for investigation, be sure it is one that requires research. A topic such as "Life at Our House" is too personal for a project based on developing research techniques.

DEVELOPING YOUR SKILL   R = requires research   N = too narrow

Be ready to discuss the following subjects. Which topics would require research? Which topics are too personal or too narrow for research?

N	1. My favorite TV program	R	6. Customizing a car
R	2. Making a hobby pay	R	7. Slum clearance
R	3. Sculpture in architecture	N	8. Learning to dance
N	4. The duties of a camp counselor	N	9. Listening to music
R	5. Child labor laws	R	10. The Greek and Roman gods

LIMITING THE TOPIC

Many students make the mistake of thinking that the broader a topic is, the easier it will be to handle since there will be more material available on the subject. Actually, the great volume of material makes the broad topic unwieldy for what will be a limited research project. Suppose, for example, that you were to decide to write a paper on the history of music. You would be faced with tracing the development of all kinds of music from the time of primitive man to the present, including a discussion of instrumental development and representative composers of each period. *Too broad a topic is not only unwieldy but is also discouraging to the beginner in research.*

When you decide upon a general area in which you want to work, you must then limit your topic to what will be manageable in the length paper assigned. Taking the subject of the history of music again, you might limit the scope to "The History of Music in the United States." You would now have a subject that could be handled more readily. However, in carrying out your investigation, you would find that the coverage of this topic is still rather broad: folk music, jazz, popular music, light classical, classical, and so on. The topic must be limited further, perhaps to "The Development of Jazz in the United States" or, even more specifically, to "The Beginnings of Dixieland Jazz." Notice that in establishing the subject for a research problem you move from the general to the specific— from the broad subject to a specific topic that can be satisfactorily discussed within the limits of your paper.

You will probably wish to limit the extent of the research to what could be covered in a paper of 1000 to 1500 words.

Caution
students
that en-
cyclopedic
material
is often
not up
to date,
especially
in scien-
tific
subjects.
The en-
cyclope-
dia
should be
used as
a lead to
other ma-
terials
and for
an over-
view of a
subject.

The History of Music
  The History of Music in the United States
     The Development of Jazz
        The Beginnings of Dixieland Jazz

In working with a subject that is new to you, you may find that you don't know how to proceed with limiting the subject. An encyclopedia can be a valuable aid in such a case. Read one or two general articles about the subject and note the various divisions of the article. Note, too, the cross references to related articles that deal with more specific aspects of the broad subject. For example, the references that follow the general article on painting in the *World Book Encyclopedia* include: "Cubism," "Expressionism," "Impressionism," "Surrealism," "Caricature," "Cyclorama," "Illustration," "Mosaic," "Mural Painting," and many other articles. Scanning several of these articles should lead you to a single aspect of painting that can be discussed thoroughly in a research paper.

One of the pitfalls to avoid in choosing a topic for research is the selection of a subject that is too technical. Many topics that sound interesting can be discussed intelligently only by specialists in the various fields. A layman's attempt to write on such subjects might result in a very superficial discussion or even in distortion. On the other hand, do not avoid all technical subjects. Your interest, your comprehension, and your ability to present the material should be the determining factors.

 DEVELOPING YOUR SKILL

A. Make a list of at least three topics that you feel would be suitable for a research paper. Be ready to discuss the various topics proposed by the class in terms of what you have learned about selecting and limiting a topic for research. The following list of broad subjects may suggest more limited topics to you.

Atomic Power	Jet Power
Boating	Legendary Heroes
Ceramics	Magic
Designing	National Parks
Engineering	Outlaws
Fishing	Political Parties
Folklore	Recreation
Glassmaking	Superstitions
Homemaking	Theater

Search for aspects of the broad subject matter that will interest students and that will be workable within the prescribed limits.

2. Because of the great volume of material that must be explored, a broad topic becomes too unwieldy for a research paper.

B. Select a topic to be used as the basis for the research you will do in the rest of this unit. You may wish to use one of the topics you suggested for Exercise A or one that was suggested by another member of the class. If you decide to use a topic proposed by a classmate, check with that person to be sure he is not planning to use the topic for his research. This exercise begins a series of cumulative exercises leading to the writing of a research paper.

Review Exercises—The Research Topic

Write the answers to the following questions.

Carefully planned, well-organized, thorough.
See top margin.

1. What are the characteristics of a good research paper?
2. Why is a broad subject more difficult to handle than a limited topic?
3. Where can you find help in limiting a subject about which you know very little? An encyclopedia.
4. What is the danger in trying to write on a highly technical specialized subject? The discussion might be superficial or even distorted.
5. What are the values of doing a research project? Develop skills that are valuable in college, in business, in professions— techniques of research, planning, organizing, writing.

2. Doing Research

If possible, arrange a library period during **LIBRARY RESOURCES** which students will have an opportunity to examine reference books with which they are unfamiliar and to look through the vertical files.

After you have selected and limited your subject, you will have to determine how much material is available on the topic you have chosen. Your initial investigation can be accomplished more easily if you know the various kinds of resources a library offers.

The *card catalog* lists all the books available in the library by author, title, and subject. If the library is small, most of the books will be found on open shelves where they are easily available. In a large library, where it is often necessary to store books in *stacks* in an area apart from the main reading room, *call slips,* or *request slips,* must be filled out and presented to the librarian, who will get the books for you.

The *vertical file,* sometimes called the *clipping file,* contains pictures, charts, pamphlets, circulars, bulletins, and newspaper clippings of articles of current interest. The vertical file is often the source of the most recent information on a current topic, particularly one in which changes are taking place.

Reference books, such as encyclopedias, atlases, yearbooks, and indexes are usually kept where they are readily accessible. These books fall into two categories—general reference books and reference books on special subjects. For a complete list of reference books see the *Guide to Reference Books* and its supplements by Constance M. Winchell. The *Guide* was the source used for the information presented in the following annotated bibliography, which describes some of the most helpful reference books available.

General Reference Books

Emphasize the point that the coverage of general reference books is broad and is suited to overviews of subjects.

General reference books—encyclopedias, yearbooks, and dictionaries—are especially useful for summaries and surveys since they cover broad areas of information. For topics on which current information is necessary, always check the date of publication of the reference you are using to be sure the data is the most recent available.

ENCYCLOPEDIAS

Compton's Pictured Encyclopedia. Broad, general coverage of the major fields of knowledge is presented in clear, simple language. An abundance of illustrations supplements the text.

Encyclopedia Americana. The **Americana** is especially strong in its coverage of material about American towns and cities and in its articles on scientific and technical subjects.

Encyclopaedia Britannica. **Britannica** is the most famous encyclopedia in English and, for broad coverage of scholarly subjects, is considered the best. Current editions contain more short articles on small subjects than do earlier editions.

Permit students to explore as many reference books as possible.

World Book Encyclopedia. World Book offers broad coverage of the major fields of knowledge in easy-to-understand language. Special features are the cross references to related articles in the encyclopedia and the reading and study guide.

YEARBOOKS

Americana Annual. This volume is published as a supplement to the **Encyclopedia Americana** and as a record of progress and events in given subjects. Each volume contains many biographies.

Britannica Book of the Year. Published as a supplement to the **Encyclopaedia Britannica,** this yearbook includes many short articles and numerous cross references. It contains some biography.

Information Please Almanac. Each volume contains miscellaneous information including special timely articles, statistical and historical descriptions of the various countries of the world, sports information, and many kinds of general information.

Statesman's Year-book. This almanac contains concise and reliable descriptive and statistical information about the governments of the world. The data for each country includes information about its constitution and government, industries, finance, and population.

World Almanac. This useful handbook is a comprehensive almanac of miscellaneous information. It contains statistics on social, political, financial, industrial, educational, and other subjects, as well as historical lists of famous events and other kinds of information.

Encyclopedia yearbooks serve to keep encyclopedic information up to date.

LANGUAGE DICTIONARIES

Evans, Bergen and Cornelia Evans, **A Dictionary of Contemporary American Usage.** This is an informally written, and often witty, dictionary of contemporary American usage. The informality in no way detracts from the scholarship of the work.

Funk and Wagnalls' New Standard Dictionary of the English Language. The special feature of this one volume work is its emphasis upon current information; that is, present-day meaning, pronunciation, and spelling.

Mencken, Henry Louis, **The American Language.** Although this work is not, strictly speaking, a dictionary, it is frequently included in this category. The basic volume, with its two supplements, contains a historical treatment of the English language in the United States. It covers such subjects as the two streams of English; the beginning and growth of the American language; pronunciation and spelling; proper names in America; American slang, etc.

Students will find this bibliography an invaluable reference for any research they do.

Nicholson, Margaret, ed., **A Dictionary of American-English Usage.** This volume is based on Fowler's **Modern English Usage.** Some of the articles have been shortened, others omitted, and new entries have been added to bring the dictionary up to date.

Oxford English Dictionary (formerly **A New English Dictionary).** This is the great dictionary of the English language. Its plan is different from that of other dictionaries in that its purpose is to show the history of every word included from the date of its introduction. It shows differences in meaning, spelling, pronunciation, usage, etc., at different periods and supports the information with numerous quotes from the works of authors of all periods.

Roget's International Thesaurus. In this book of synonyms and antonyms in American and British usage, the words are grouped according to the ideas they express—abstract relations, space, matter, etc.—and are indexed alphabetically.

Webster's Dictionary of Synonyms. For many purposes, this is the most useful of the dictionaries of synonyms. Shades of meaning are carefully discriminated. The volume is thumb-indexed.

Webster's New International Dictionary. The oldest and best-known American dictionary, the **New International** is reliable and is noted for the clarity of its definitions. It is the most used and, for general purposes, the most useful of the one-volume dictionaries.

Special Reference Books

Since their coverage is limited to one area, reference books in special fields offer more specific information than general reference books can. The following will be helpful to you in doing research in various fields.

BIOGRAPHY

Current Biography, 1940—. Published monthly, this is a cumulative index of biographical sketches of persons of various nationalities. Each biography averages three to four columns and includes references to sources for further information.

Dictionary of American Biography. This outstanding scholarly American biographical dictionary is planned along the lines of the English **Dictionary of National Biography.** It does not include living persons. See also the supplements.

Dictionary of National Biography. This work constitutes the most important reference work for English biography. It includes all noteworthy inhabitants of the British Isles and the colonies, exclusive of living persons. Also included are noteworthy Americans of the Colonial period. Supplements bring the record to 1940.

Special reference books contain more detailed information than do general reference books.

(Margin notes: If possible, all students should have an opportunity to examine the Oxford English Dictionary.)

Webster's Biographical Dictionary. This volume contains brief biographical sketches of persons of all periods, nationalities, races, religions, and occupations. It includes living persons.

Who's Who, 1844—. This is principally British biography but it also includes biographical sketches of a few prominent persons of other nationalities. The biographies are reliable and are fairly detailed.

Who's Who in America, 1899—. An excellent dictionary of contemporary biography, this work contains concise biographical data with addresses and, in the case of authors, lists of works. Beginning with volume 23, a few selected names from Canada and Latin America are included. See also the supplements which contain current biographical sketches and a supplement to **Who Was Who.**

Who Was Who in America, 1897—1940/1941. This companion volume to **Who's Who in America** includes sketches removed from twenty-one volumes of **Who's Who in America** because of the death of the subjects of the sketches.

BUSINESS

Statistical Abstract of the United States, 1878—. This reference contains statistics on the political, social, industrial, and economic organization of the United States. See also the various supplements for cities, counties, historical statistics, vital statistics, etc.

GEOGRAPHY

Hammond New World Atlas. In addition to historical, economic, political, and physical maps of the entire world, this work also contains the races of mankind, an illustrated gazeteer of the world, and an illustrated gazeteer of the United States and its territories.

Encourage students to find out about other reference books in specific areas of study.

Rand McNally-Cosmopolitan World Atlas. The maps in this atlas are based on regional divisions of the world. A major country or a significant grouping of countries is the focal point for each map. Supplementary materials include tables of areas and population, climatic and economic information, historical data, transportation, and highway distances.

HISTORY

Dictionary of American History. This work contains clear, concise articles, each dealing with a particular aspect of American history. The coverage includes political, economic, social, industrial, and cultural history.

LITERATURE

A. L. A. Index. . . to General Literature. The basic volume of this reference, published by the American Language Association, covers material io January 1, 1900; the supplement, to 1910. It is a subject index to articles in collections and miscellaneous works.

Baker's Guide to the Best Fiction. This is a comprehensive index of authors, titles, subjects, historical names, allusions, places, characters, etc.

Baker's Guide to Historical Fiction. This lists about 5000 novels which, in any way, portray the life of the past. Arrangement is by country and then chronologically by the historical period. It contains a full index of authors, titles, etc.

Bartlett, John, **Familiar Quotations.** This is a comprehensive collection of passages, phrases, and proverbs traced to their sources in ancient and modern literature. The material is arranged chronologically by authors and is indexed by key words.

Cambridge History of American Literature. This is often considered the most important history of American literature. Coverage of the early period is particularly thorough. Each chapter is written by a specialist.

Cambridge History of English Literature. This is a comprehensive history of English literature from earliest times to the end of the nineteenth century. Each chapter is written by a specialist.

Essay and General Literature Index. A continuation of the **A. L. A. Index,** this index begins with 1900. It lists essays by a given author; authorship of an essay when only the title is known; criticisms of individual books; different places or collections in which an essay is printed; and other important information for finding essays.

Firkins' **Index of Plays, 1800-1926.** This comprehensive index shows where the text of each of 7872 plays can be found in collections or other publications. It indexes plays in English, including translations of foreign plays. See also the supplement.

The Essay and General Literature Index is a particularly valuable research aid.

Granger's Index to Poetry and Recitations. Standard and popular collections of poetry, recitations, selections from drama, etc., are indexed in this work by title, author, and first line. See also the supplements.

Literary History of the United States. This is the first comprehensive history since the **Cambridge History of American Literature.** Volumes 1 and 2 present a survey from colonial times to the middle of the twentieth century. Volume 3 is bibliography and contains a guide to resources, literature and culture, movements and influences, and individual authors.

Oxford Companion to American Literature. This contains an alphabetical arrangement of short biographies and bibliographies of American authors. Brief essays contain information about the authors' style and subject matter.

Oxford Companion to English Literature. This work contains brief articles on authors, literary works, characters in fiction, drama, etc., and literary allusions commonly met in English literature.

Stevenson's Home Book of Quotations. This is a comprehensive collection of more than 50,000 quotations arranged alphabetically by subject. The volume contains an index of authors and a key word index.

U. S. Catalog with **Cumulative Book Index,** 1898—. Together, these references offer a comprehensive record of books in print in English. The **U. S. Catalog** contains books published by American publishers. The **Index,** a continuation of the **Catalog,** contains listings of all English language books. Both are indexed by author, title, and subject.

MUSIC

Grove's Dictionary of Music and Musicians. This work includes biographies of musicians and individual articles on compositions, music history, theory and practice, terminology, etc.

MAGAZINE, NEWSPAPER, AND DOCUMENT INDEXES

The most recent information about a subject frequently appears in newspaper and magazine articles. The indexes that are listed in this section are guides to finding such articles. The list also includes indexes to pamphlets, bulletins, and other documents in various subject areas. Before using any index always read the first few pages that explain the use of the reference work.

Agricultural Index, 1916—. This contains a detailed alphabetical subject index to agricultural and related periodicals and bulletins. A record of new books and book reviews is included.

All students should be familiar with the U. S. Catalog and Cumulative Book Index. You may wish to introduce them also to the Library of Congress Catalog.

Art Index, January, 1929—. This work is a cumulative subject index to a selected list of fine arts periodicals and museum bulletins. It indexes American and foreign periodicals, museum bulletins, annuals, etc. in the fields of archaeology, architecture, arts and crafts, ceramics, painting, sculpture, and others.

Dramatic Index, 1909-1949. This was an annual subject index covering articles about the stage and the players in American and British periodicals.

Education Index, January 1929—. This is a cumulative author and subject index to a selected list of educational books, periodicals, and pamphlets. It is published monthly and cumulates to annual and triennial volumes.

Engineering Index, 1884—. This is an index to technical and engineering periodicals in English and other languages. It gives the title, author, and a brief digest or description of each article, the length in number of words, the periodical, and the exact date. From 1906-1934 the title varies. A weekly card service keeps the annual up to date.

Facts on File, 1940—. This is a weekly world news digest including world, national, and foreign affairs in finance and economics, arts and science, education and religion, sports, and other miscellany.

Industrial Arts Index, 1913—. This is a cumulative subject index which is issued monthly. It indexes a selected list of engineering, trade, and business periodicals, books, and pamphlets. This index has a wider range of subjects than the **Engineering Index** and contains less foreign material.

Music Index, 1949—. This is a monthly cumulating index of periodicals representing various aspects of the music field. It gives complete indexing for music periodicals and indexes articles pertinent to music in some more general periodicals.

New York Times Index, 1913—. This is a cumulative index giving exact references to date, page, and column of each article (section given for Sunday papers). It contains brief synopses of the articles and gives plentiful cross references to related subjects and to names. It also serves as a guide to articles of current interest in other newspapers since all newpapers publish reports of any event of general interest at about the same time.

Public Affairs Information Service. This is a cumulative index to current books, pamphlets, periodicals, government documents, and other materials in the fields of political science, government, legislation, economics, sociology, etc.

Readers' Guide to Periodical Literature, 1900—. This is a cumulative index with issues published every two weeks to be used as supplements to the cumulative volumes. Articles are catalogued by author, subject, and, occasionally, title. It indexes general and popular magazines, as well as some scientific and scholarly periodicals.

Impress upon students the value of the New York Times Index as a guide to articles in other newspapers, as well.

Familiarizing yourself with the various resources your library has to offer will expedite your research and will make it more rewarding. Learn to know where to find information and how to use the many references available to you.

DEVELOPING YOUR SKILL Card catalog, vertical file, stacks, general reference books, special reference books.

A. Be ready to discuss the different kinds of resources a library may offer. How can knowing how to use these resources facilitate research?

B. Write the answers to the following questions.

1. How are cards arranged in the card catalog? Author, title, subject
2. How does the information on the three types of cards differ? See below.
3. What is meant by the *call number?* Identification number of a book
4. When is a *call slip* necessary? When books are not on open shelves
5. What kinds of material are kept in the vertical file? Pictures, charts, pamphlets, circulars, bulletins, newspaper clippings

C. Write the numbers from 1 to 10 on a sheet of paper. After each number write the name of a reference book in which you could find the information asked for. See p. T61.

1. The capacity of Yankee Stadium in New York City.
2. The name of the governor of British Honduras.
3. The history of the name *Smith* in the United States.
4. The date of birth of an important American now in the news.
5. A recent essay on conservation.
6. What books have been published recently on the subject of electronics.
7. An article about the English theater in the 1920's.
8. An article about a recent agricultural development.
9. A quotation about straw votes.
10. The membership of the leading labor unions for a given year.

B. 2. The information is the same. However, the subject and title cards include an additional line at the top giving the subject and the title, respectively.

The working bibliography is important as an indication
to the student whether or not there is sufficient material
available for a research project.

THE WORKING BIBLIOGRAPHY

You are now ready to determine how much material is available on the subject you have chosen for research. In making the survey you will be concerned with any books, articles, pamphlets, or other sources that have bearing on your topic. There is no need to do any reading of the material, except, perhaps, for an encyclopedia article. You are to make a list of sources known as a *working bibliography*. You may, later, discard some of the references if you find, through reading, that they are not suited to your approach to the topic. At the start, however, you should include any references that seem pertinent.

Insist upon a consistent form for the bibliography card.

The most useful method of procedure for your survey is to prepare bibliography cards, using a separate index card for each entry. Each card should contain a *source number,* the number you will use throughout your work to identify the source listed on the card. Start with the number *1* and number the cards consecutively as you prepare them. The rest of the information on a bibliography card will vary somewhat with the kind of reference being recorded. The following sample bibliography cards show some of the types of entries you may have to make. Notice particularly the form and punctuation of the entries. This is one of several possible forms. Use consistently whatever form your teacher decides upon throughout your work. Using the appropriate form at the start will eliminate the need for changes later.

A BOOK BY ONE AUTHOR

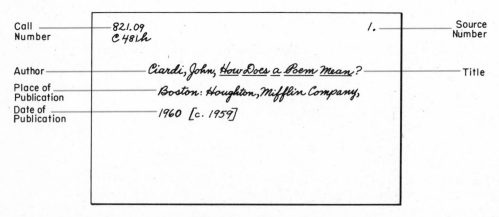

Discuss each of the sample bibliography cards, pointing
out similarities and differences.

A Book by More Than One Author

> 821.09
> 486
>
> 2.
>
> Hubbell, Jay Broadus and John O. Beaty,
> *An Introduction to Poetry*, Rev. ed.
> New York: The Macmillan Company,
> 1950.

A Book by an Author and an Editor

> B
> B 435b
>
> 3.
>
> Benét, Stephen Vincent, *Selected Letters*,
> Charles A. Fenton, ed. New Haven:
> Yale University Press, 1960.

A Book Compiled by an Editor

> 808.81
> Un 8 mod
>
> 4.
>
> Untermeyer, Louis, ed., *Modern American
> and Modern British Poetry*. New York:
> Harcourt, Brace and Company, 1955.

The call numbers shown on these cards are Dewey Decimal numbers. Caution students that some libraries use other systems.

A TRANSLATION

861
G165yb   5.

Barea, Arturo, *Lorca, The Poet and His People*,
trans. Ilsa Barea. New York: Harcourt,
Brace and Company, 1949.

ARTICLE FROM A COLLECTION (ESSAYS, STORIES, ONE CHAPTER)

821.09
AL 53f   6.

Winters, Yvor, "Poetic Styles, Old and New,"
ed. Don Cameron Allen, *Four Poets on Poetry*.
Baltimore: The John Hopkins Press, 1959.
pp. 44-75.

MAGAZINE ARTICLE

                                                              7.

Clements, R. J., "Poets, Painters, and the
Paragon," *Saturday Review*, vol. 43,
October 8, 1960, pp. 23+.

On cards for magazine, newspaper, and encyclopedia
articles, the publication data is unnecessary since it
is implicit in the name of the publication.

NEWSPAPER ARTICLE

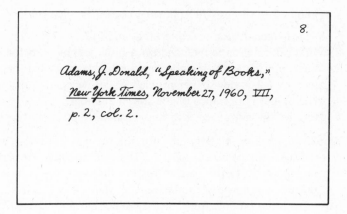

The Roman numeral refers to the section of the paper. This information is usually given only for the Sunday edition of the *New York Times*.

ENCYCLOPEDIA ARTICLE

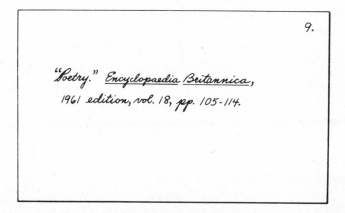

When making bibliography cards for magazine and newspaper articles whose authors are not named, begin with the title of the article. In the case of a newspaper article that has neither title nor author's name, record the information beginning with the name of the newspaper. Signed encyclopedia articles are recorded beginning with the author's name. Encyclopedias that contain initialed articles include a list of the full names of the contributors, usually in the front of each volume.

If your school has an encyclopedia that contains initialed articles, point out to students the list of the contributors' names.

A. Be prepared to discuss the following questions. See p. T61.

1. What is meant by a *working bibliography?*
2. What information is included on a bibliography card for a book?
3. What information is included on a bibliography card for a magazine article? A newspaper article? An encyclopedia article?
4. What is the importance of the source number?
5. How would you proceed in making a working bibliography?

This is the
second of
the cumu-
lative
exercises.

B. Prepare a working bibliography for the topic you have selected for research. Are there enough sources (books, magazines, etc.) available at your library to enable you to write a thorough research paper? If not, decide on a new topic to be used for the rest of this unit and prepare a working bibliography for that topic. Do not expect to be able to do this research in one night. Thorough research takes time.

READING AND TAKING NOTES

Provide
opportu-
nities
for
practice
in
skim-
ming.

The next step in carrying out your research is reading and taking notes for use in your paper. Examine each of the sources you have listed on your bibliography cards. Look through the table of contents of books to determine what chapters seem to apply to your topic. Then skim those chapters to see whether they are really applicable. If so, list on the bibliography card the actual pages you will use. If you use the entire book, you need not list the pages unless your teacher wishes to have you do so. Follow the same general procedure for other sources.

When your skimming indicates to you that the material has a bearing on your topic, go back and reread the subject matter carefully, taking notes. You will find that 3-inch by 5-inch or 4-inch by 6-inch lined index cards are best suited to taking notes. Since you will have to sort and shuffle your note cards as you continue working on the research project, use a different card for each note you record. This procedure will enable you to organize your material more efficiently later.

Every note card should contain the *source number,* which will correspond to the number on the bibliography card; a *heading,* which tells the topic to which the note is related; the *page reference,* which gives the exact page or pages from which the note was drawn; and the *body* of the note. Using the source number does away with your having to record bibliographical data on each card, although this method is equally correct and is

Warn students against trying to take notes before they
have determined the applicability of the material.

frequently used. The heading will be of use when you sort your cards. Page references enable you to verify facts if you find you have to do so later in your work. You will also use the page references in any footnotes you may include.

The body of the note may be in either of two forms—the summary or the direct quotation. Most of your notes will be summaries of paragraphs or even longer passages. Sometimes an entire page can be reduced to a sentence or two. Skim the material, noting topic sentences and key words. Then read carefully to fill in the details. On your note card summarize in your own words that matter which is relevant to your topic. Such summaries, when written in complete sentences, are called *précis*.

Use textbooks for practice in writing precis.

Notes are often recorded in abbreviated form; that is, in key words and phrases. Unimportant words are omitted and abbreviations are used for words that appear frequently. It is a good policy to write each word in full, the first time you use it, as a key to the abbreviation. Be sure you do not abbreviate to the point where the notes are unintelligible to you when you read them later.

When you find a statement that imparts the exact idea you wish to convey, you may want to quote it verbatim. In such a case, be sure you enclose the statement in quotation marks on your note card so that you will recognize it as another writer's material and not a paraphrase.

Textbooks may also be used for practice in taking abbreviated notes.

Stress the importance of marking all verbatim notes with quotation marks. You may wish to introduce a discussion of plagiarism.

The following are sample note cards.

SUMMARY

Distinguish
between
this kind
of summary
and a précis.

> 6
>
> *Style in early poetry*
>
> pp. 44-45: Poetry of late middle ages through
> early 17th century rational in
> structure. Within rational frame, two
> schools in 16th cent. and earlier: plain
> style and ornate. Wyatt, Gascoigne,
> Raleigh, Greville, and Jonson examples
> of former; Sidney and Spenser of latter.

QUOTATION

> 6
>
> *The poet's art*
>
> p. 75: "There is more to the art of poetry than a
> kind of imagery or the lack of imagery.... We must
> have an important theme, an understanding of the
> theme which is in some measure defensible, and a
> command of syntax, meter, rhythm, and diction;
> and one will not come by these simple-sounding
> acquisitions without both genius and education."

Notice the four dots in the direct quotation. They indicate an *ellipsis,* an omission of part of the material. An ellipsis is indicated by the use of three dots. When it occurs at the end of a sentence, as in the example above, the period is added, making a total of four dots.

When quoting directly, you must always be sure that you have copied the author's wording, punctuation, and spelling exactly. If you find an error, do not correct it; copy it just as it is written and then, to indicate your awareness of the error, write *sic* in brackets: [*sic*]. *Sic* means *thus* and is used to indicate that the wording, spelling, or the like, exactly reproduces the original.

Be sure students understand the use of the mechanical devices used in direct quotations.

Sometimes it is necessary to insert explanatory material in a direct quotation. If, for example, the quotation you select begins with a personal pronoun that has no antecedent, put the antecedent in brackets immediately following the pronoun: "It [New York City] ...."; "They [17th century poets] ...."; "He [Ben Jonson] ...."; and so on.

In taking notes you must work for accuracy and honesty. Check all facts and statistics to be sure you have recorded them accurately. Be certain that your summaries of a writer's ideas in no way distort those ideas. Credit opinions and the information on which they are based to the persons from whom you have borrowed the opinions and the facts.

These points constitute a code of honor for writers.

> DEVELOPING YOUR SKILL

A. Be ready to discuss the following questions. See p. T62.

1. What procedure should be followed in reading in sources for your research project?
2. What information should appear on a note card?
3. What are the two kinds of notes you will take and how do they differ?
4. How do abbreviated notes differ from the précis?
5. What is an ellipsis? When is *sic* used? How is explanatory material treated in a direct quotation?

B. Your teacher may wish to assign a page in one of your textbooks for practice in taking notes. First skim the page and then read for details. Prepare three note cards: a précis, an abbreviated summary, and a direct quotation. Students should develop skill in taking all

C. Read the sources you have selected for your research project and take notes. Your teacher may wish to see your note cards from time to time to be sure you are proceeding correctly. This is the third of the cumulative exercises in the preparation of a research paper.

three kinds of notes.

Review Exercises—Doing Research

A. What kinds of information can be found in each of the following library resources? See p. T62.

1. card catalog	6. *Readers' Guide to Periodical Literature*
2. vertical file	7. *New York Times Index*
3. encyclopedias	8. *Essay and General Literature Index*
4. atlases	9. *Statistical Abstract of the United States*
5. *World Almanac*	10. *U.S. Catalog with Cumulative Book Index*

All students should know at least the reference sources listed in Exercise A of the Review Exercises.

B. Using three of your textbooks, prepare complete bibliography cards.
C. Prepare a bibliography card for an article in a local newspaper. Write a summary note card on the article. Clip the original article to the cards before handing them in.

3. Writing the Paper

PREPARING AN OUTLINE

When you have completed your research, you will have a stack of note cards, each of which has a topic written at the head of the card. These headings will help you work out an outline for your paper.

Sort your note cards into groups, putting all the cards that have the same heading in one group. Then read your notes carefully to get an overview of your subject and to determine the central theme of your paper. When you have decided what direction your paper is to take, write an opening statement of theme. Having such a statement for reference will help you on the topic while you are working out your outline and writing your paper. In the written paper, this statement will serve as a statement of intention to let the reader know at what point you are starting and where you are going. Study the following example. Notice that the writer's theme and intention are clearly stated, without being so obvious as to insult the intelligence of his readers.

> The dominant fact of our time is the towering place of the machine, of applied science in the lives of mankind. And the great issue of our time, with which the peoples of the whole world will be at grips day in and day out for the rest of our lives, is simply this: Are machines and science to be used to degrade man and destroy him, or to augment the dignity and nobility of humankind? How can man use and direct science and the machine so as to further the well-being of all men?
>
> —DAVID E. LILIENTHAL, "Science and Man's Fate"

Permit time for the outline to be made in a leisurely fashion, thoughtfully and carefully. The success of a research paper depends largely upon the development of a good plan.

Writing the Paper 139

Keeping your theme in mind at all times, look through the headings on your cards and select the ones that will develop the main topics of your theme. These will be the major divisions of your outline. Be sure the topics you have selected cover the subject of your research paper, and decide on the most logical order of presentation. Write the headings opposite Roman numerals, leaving space below each one for subtopics. Many students have found that it is a good idea to list each major topic on a separate sheet of paper. In this way there is no danger of having to crowd any part of the outline.

The procedure developed here should be discussed in detail.

Go through your cards again, sorting them into as many piles as you have main topics. Be sure that all the cards you include in one group are related to the topic. You will probably find that you will have to set aside some note cards because they do not apply to your development of the subject. The cards that remain will constitute subtopics of your outline. Study the cards in each pile and jot down on scratch paper any ideas for subheadings that the notes suggest to you. Organize the subheadings into subdivisions of the major headings, narrower divisions of those subheadings, and so on. These subheadings may then be written into your outline in logical order and in order of importance. On each note card mark the number(s) and letter(s) of the outline to which the notes apply; for example, I. A., I. A. 1., I. A. 1. a., II., and so on.

The following illustrates the form of an outline:

Subject

I. Major topic
   A. Subtopic of I
      1. Subdivision of A
      2. Subdivision of A
         a. Subdivision of 2
         b. Subdivision of 2
   B. Subtopic of I
II. Major topic

The outline enables you to see the relationship of ideas. Roman numerals signal the major divisions of the general subject; capital letters indicate subdivisions of the major topics; Arabic numerals label the third order of subtopics; and lower-case letters mark the fourth order of subtopics. Notice that every topic that is divided is broken into at least two parts. If you will remember that *outlining* involves dividing large ideas into smaller parts, and that *division* means separating something into two or more parts, you will not make the mistake of writing single subheadings under a topic.

When you have completed your outline, check to see that each division labeled with a Roman numeral develops a single, important topic and does not overlap any other such division. Check, too, to make certain that all the subdivisions marked with capital letters are of equal importance, and so on through the subdivisions indicated by Arabic numerals and lower-case letters.

DEVELOPING YOUR SKILL

A. Your teacher may wish to assign a number of pages in one of your textbooks for practice in using the outline form. Skim the material and note the major topics. Then read to determine the subtopics. Prepare an outline of the pages assigned. Check to be certain the form of your outline is correct.

B. Sort your note cards and write a statement of theme and purpose. Prepare the outline for your research paper. Your teacher may wish to check your outline for form and organization before you begin writing your paper.

WRITING A FIRST DRAFT

Your major objective in writing the first draft of your paper is to get your ideas down on paper. You have read widely in your field of study, have taken notes, have thought about your subject and formulated a statement of purpose, and have organized your material into an outline. By the time you are ready to write, then, you should know your subject thoroughly.

You may wish to start by developing your statement of theme and purpose into an introductory paragraph. Some students prefer to write both the introduction and the conclusion after they have completed the body of the paper. Use whichever approach works better for you.

As you write, refer to your statement of purpose and your outline as often as necessary to keep your ideas within the limits you have set and in logical order. Do not feel that you must adhere rigidly to the plan of your outline. If, as you write, you find that another organization of details or a different approach will be better, feel free to reorganize your plan, add details, or make other changes. Be sure you adjust your outline accordingly.

Once you have started writing, try to complete the first draft of your paper without interruption. Concentrate on the content of your paper, on expressing your ideas accurately, vividly, and interestingly. If a part you have written does not satisfy you, mark it for revision and go on with the rest of the paper until you have completed the first draft. Mechanics, such as spelling, punctuation, and grammar, can be polished when you make revisions. Write on one side of the paper only, leaving room between the lines for corrections and revisions.

Caution students against slavish imitation of the styles of authors whose books and articles they have used.

For the most part, the ideas expressed in your paper should be in your own words. Do not, however, take credit for facts and opinions that you borrow from your sources. Whenever you quote directly, be sure you enclose the material in quotation marks. Direct quotations and facts and opinions that are not the result of your own thinking should be footnoted in the final draft of your paper. In you first draft, mark such places so you will know where footnotes are needed. One system is to write the source number and page reference in parentheses immediately following the material to be footnoted (6, p. 75).

When you have finished the body of your first draft, write the introduction, if you have not yet done so, and the conclusion. The introduction should lead naturally into your subject; the conclusion should leave your readers with a clear impression of the theme you have developed.

> DEVELOPING YOUR SKILL

A. Your teacher may wish to have you discuss the following questions.

1. What should be your major objective when writing the first draft of your research paper? To get ideas down on paper.
2. Why, do you think, do some writers prefer to write the introduction to a paper after they have completed the body? See p. T62.
3. Why, do you think, is it recommended that the first draft of your paper be written without interruption? See p. T62.
4. What is the purpose of marking material that will require footnotes? Why can't this be left for the final draft? See p. T62.
5. Why is it usually necessary to footnote facts and opinions borrowed from your sources, even though they are not direct quotations? When is it necessary to footnote such material? See p. T62.

Emphasize again the importance of crediting sources and of marking material to be footnoted in the first draft. Exceptions to the rule of footnoting are facts that are general knowledge.

This is the
fifth of the
cumulative exercises that develop a research project.

B. Write the first draft of your research paper. Be certain to mark all material for which footnotes will be needed. Leave room for revisions.

MAKING REVISIONS

Impress
upon
students
the im-
portance
of sev-
eral
readings
when they
are mak-
ing re-
visions,
each
reading
to be
done for
a dif-
ferent
purpose.

When you have completed the first draft of your research paper, put it aside for a day or two. This time lapse is necessary to allow you to develop a degree of objectivity about your work. Were you to attempt to revise your first draft immediately after writing it, you would be too close to the work to recognize all errors and weaknesses. It might seem to you that you had said what you intended exactly as you intended it.

After a day or two, reread what you have written. First of all, read for content. Have you said what you meant to say? Do there have to be any changes made in the order of presentation? Are there any gaps in the ideas presented? Should any of the ideas be omitted? Any major changes in order can best be made by cutting and pasting. Cut your material apart, reorganize it, and paste it onto sheets of paper in the new order. Additional paragraphs can be written and fitted into the paper when you are cutting and pasting. One-word and one-sentence changes can be made in the spaces you left between the lines of writing.

Now read your paper again, this time for mechanics of style and usage. Are there any confused or awkward sentences? Is there any unnecessary repetition? Is there variety in sentence structure? Have you written any fragments or run-on sentences? Are there any punctuation or spelling problems? Would changing any verbs from the passive to the active voice make your writing more forceful? Check your writing for trite, overworked expressions and for jargon. Be certain of such matters as subject-verb and pronoun-antecedent agreement, as well as reference of pronouns, verb tenses, and idiomatic usages. Many of these errors will be more evident to you if you read your paper aloud. Underline, circle, or check any areas that seem doubtful to you and make a marginal note of the kind of error you have found—a pencil with colored lead is useful for this purpose. Then go back and make the revisions.

The last step in reworking the first draft of your paper is the final editing. This time you are looking for details of style that can be improved. Have you used any unnecessary words? For example, have you said things such as "a towering, eighty-six-floor building"? Decide what you want

You may wish to prepare a revision check list based on the material included in this section of the unit.

to emphasize and change the expression to "a towering building" or "an eighty-six-floor building." Have you overstated your case; that is, have you made any absolute statements that should be qualified by words such as *probably, usually, often,* and *some?* Have you worded each sentence so that the emphasis falls where you intended it to or have you tacked on a phrase at the end of a sentence when it would be better at the beginning? These corrections can be made easily, usually without rewriting.

Illus-
trate
the tech-
niques of
revision
and final
editing.

DEVELOPING YOUR SKILL

A. Be ready to discuss the procedures and techniques of making revisions. In your discussion consider the following questions.

1. Why is it wise to put your first draft aside for a time before revising it? To allow time to develop a degree of objectivity.
2. How would you handle major changes in content? See bottom margin.
3. What errors in mechanics should you look for? See bottom margin.
4. What procedure may be followed in correcting mechanics of style and usage? Mark with colored pencil, change in spaces above lines.
5. What effect do you think the final editing will have on the style of the paper? It will make the style smooth, polished, mature.

B. Revise the first draft of your paper. Continue working on revisions until you are certain the paper represents your best effort. This is the sixth of the cumulative exercises.

PREPARING THE FINAL DRAFT

The final draft of your paper should be typed or written in ink on one side of a good grade of unlined paper. Leave margins of 1 to 1½ inches at the top, bottom, and sides of your paper. If the paper is to be fastened into a folder, leave a wider margin at the left to allow for the fastenings. Indent paragraphs seven spaces or about ¾ inch. Double-space between lines in the text (leave extra space in the handwritten papers) except for direct quotations of more than three lines. Such quotations may be indented four spaces from the margin (or about ½ inch) and single-spaced. When quotations are indented and single-spaced, the quotation marks are omitted. Number all pages, except the first, in the upper right-hand corner. Place the title of your paper on the first page about 2 inches down.

As you prepare the final draft, insert superior numbers at all places that you have marked for footnotes. Superior numbers are numerals that are raised slightly above the line of writing. You will have to allow room

A. 2. Cutting and pasting and fitting in new paragraphs. 3. Confused or awkward sentences, unnecessary repetition, lack of variety in sentence structure, fragments, run-on sentences, punctuation, spelling, voice of verbs, triteness, overworked expressions, jargon, agreement.

In
larger
papers
foot-
notes
are
some-
times
num-
bered
by page
or by
chapter
rather
than
consecu-
tively
through-
out the
entire
paper.

at the bottom of the page for the footnotes. Footnotes are single-spaced within each note and double-spaced between notes. In a paper of the length you are writing, number your footnotes consecutively throughout the paper. Separate the footnotes from the text by a short line.

The first time you refer to a source, use a complete entry. Study the following sample entries for books, periodicals, and encyclopedia articles. Notice that in a footnote, the author's name is written in natural order.

[1] John Masefield, *King Cole* (London: William Heinemann, 1921), p. 52.

[2] George Schreiber, ed., *Portraits and Self-portraits* (Boston: Houghton Mifflin Company, 1936), pp. 14-15.

[3] H. S. Commager, "Poet of America's Heroic History," *Scholastic,* vol. 43, September 20, 1943, pp. 22-23.

[4] Charles W. Cooper "Poetry," *World Book Encyclopedia,* 1961 ed., vol. 14, pp. 528-529.

Subsequent entries may be shortened by using *ibid.* (from the Latin *ibidem* meaning "in the same place") and *op. cit.* (from *opere citato* meaning "in the work cited"). *Ibid.* is used to refer to a source in the footnote immediately preceding. Used alone, it means that the reference is exactly the same as the one before it. If the work is the same, but the page reference is different, *ibid.* is followed by the page number.

[5] Robert Frost, *Collected Poems* (New York: Henry Holt and Company, 1939), p. 236.

[6] *Ibid.*

[7] *Ibid.,* p. 147.

If other sources intervene, use the last name of the author, *op. cit.,* and the page reference. *Op. cit.* may be used only if a single work by the author has been used.

[8] Masefield, *op. cit.,* p. 34.

[9] Frost, *op. cit.,* p. 166.

If more than one source by the same author has been cited, the title of the work must be given.

[10] Frost, *Hard Not to Be King,* p. 5.

[11] Frost, *Collected Poems,* p. 92.

Review with students the use of underlining for italics. You may wish to correlate this material with the teaching of the use of italics (see pp. 409-410).

When you have finished the final draft of your paper, there are still a few details to be completed. You will need a title page, which contains the title of the paper, the writer's name, the course title, the teacher's name, and the date on which the paper is submitted.

The outline is usually included with the research paper and may serve as a table of contents. After checking to be certain you have made all necessary revisions in your outline, retype it and, after each main heading, insert the page number on which that section begins.

Next, arrange the bibliography cards for the sources you actually used in writing your paper in alphabetical order according to the last names of the authors. If no author's name is given, alphabetize by the first word of the entry, except for *a, an,* or *the.* Bibliographies are sometimes divided by types of sources—books, magazines, newspapers, and so on. Since yours will not be a long bibliography, include all types of materials used in one list. Type the final bibliography on a separate sheet of paper headed BIBLIOGRAPHY. If several sources by the same author are included, the author's name need be given once only. Subsequent entires use a seven-space line in place of the author's name. Single-space within each entry; double-space between entries.

Your paper is now almost ready to be submitted. Proofread your final draft to catch any errors you may have made in typing or copying. These errors can usually be corrected neatly in ink. Draw a single line through any words or letters that should have been omitted. Use a caret ($\wedge$) to indicate insertions. If a page requires too many corrections to look neat, retype or rewrite it.

The final step in your research project is assembling and submitting your paper. The order of the parts is as follows:

1. Title page
2. A blank page (usually left after the title page)
3. Table of contents (outline)
4. The body of the paper
5. Bibliography

Enclose your paper in a plain folder. On the outside of the folder, type or write the same information that appears on the title page.

The following illustrations show a sample title page, table of contents, first page, and bibliography for a research paper.

A check list of the final steps in compiling the research paper will prove valuable.

The final proofreading is important.

Insist upon neat, unadorned folders for research papers. Only in exceptional cases is art work relevant and appropriate.

FOLKLORE AND LEGEND IN THE WORK OF STEPHEN VINCENT BENÉT

Robert F. Drew
English 3
Miss Bishop
April 27, 19—

The information on the title page should be arranged so
as to make the page look balanced.

FOLKLORE AND LEGEND IN THE WORK OF STEPHEN VINCENT BENÉT

Page references must be accurate and must be so placed that they clearly apply to specific topics.

FOLKLORE AND LEGEND IN THE WORK OF STEPHEN VINCENT BENÉT

William Rose Benét wrote about his brother
Stephen, "There has always been in my brother's work
delight in legend, . . ."[1] The truth of this
statement becomes increasingly evident to the reader
of the younger Benét's work. Stephen Vincent Benét's
poems and stories, devoted to American themes, contain
frequent allusions to the legends and folklore of the
United States. His poetic cadences repeatedly pick up
the rhythms of American folk songs and folk dances.
Where no legend exists, he selects an American figure
about whom many stories have been woven and creates a
new legend. This paper will make no attempt to explore
the many paths into which Benét's folklore references
lead the reader; it will, instead, concern itself only
with the folk songs and legends created by the poet.

BALLADS

> Benét is unusually sensitive to the power
> of the ballad. He uses its devices with judgment
> . . . , respecting its form and style as worthy
> of straight narrative, and working freely in
> its medium.[2]

---

[1]William Rose Benét, "Round About Parnassus,"
Saturday Review of Literature, vol. 7, December 27,
1930, p. 491.

[2]Evelyn Kendrick Wells, The Ballad Tree (New
York: The Ronald Press Company, 1950), p. 324.

Point out to students the various forms that are included on this page: form of text, short direct quotation, long direct quotation set off, footnote references
within text, footnotes at bottom of page, ellipses.

BIBLIOGRAPHY

Adams, J. Donald, "Speaking of Books," <u>New</u> <u>York</u> <u>Times</u>,
July 11, 1943, VII, p. 2, col. 2.

Benét, Stephen Vincent, <u>Ballads</u> <u>and</u> <u>Poems,</u> <u>1915-1930.</u>
Garden City, New York: Doubleday, Doran and
Company, Inc., 1931.

————, <u>John</u> <u>Brown's</u> <u>Body</u>. Garden City, New York:
Doubleday, Doran and Company, Inc., 1928.

————, <u>Selected</u> <u>Works</u> <u>of</u> <u>Stephen</u> <u>Vincent</u> <u>Benét</u>, Volume
One: Poetry, Volume Two: Prose. New York:
Farrar and Rinehart, Inc., 1942.

————, <u>Western</u> <u>Star</u>. New York, Toronto: Farrar and
Rinehart, Inc., 1943, pp. 152-156.

————, <u>Young</u> <u>Adventure</u>. New Haven: Yale University
Press, 1918, pp. 59-65.

Benét, William Rose, "Round About Parnassus," <u>Saturday</u>
<u>Review</u> <u>of</u> <u>Literature</u>, vol. 7, December 27, 1930,
p. 491.

La Farge, C., "Narrative Poetry of Stephen Vincent
Benét," <u>Saturday</u> <u>Review</u> <u>of</u> <u>Literature</u>, vol. 27,
August 5, 1944, p. 106+.

Wells, Evelyn Kendrick, <u>The</u> <u>Ballad</u> <u>Tree</u>. New York:
The Ronald Press Company, 1950.

In a short bibliography all references are compiled into a single list. In long bibliographies references are sometimes separated according to type.

DEVELOPING YOUR SKILL

A. Be ready to discuss the steps involved in preparing the final draft of a research paper. In your discussion, name the various parts of the paper and the final arrangement of the parts. See pp. 143-145.

B. Type or write the final draft of your paper. Proofread your paper for typographical errors or errors in copying. Assemble the paper and submit it to your teacher. This exercise represents the final step in the series of cumulative exercises.

Review Exercises—Writing the Paper

A. Write an outline showing the steps to be followed in writing the research paper. Use each step as a major topic, and list the steps within each major topic as subtopics. See pp. T62-T64.

B. Write a composition based on the outline you prepared for Exercise A. Details should be added to the basic outline material.

UNIT SUMMARY

Students who have difficulty with the research paper are usually those who do not follow the step-by-step procedure but try to complete a paper in a sudden burst of energy at the last minute.

Carrying out a research project requires that you develop specific skills: selecting and limiting a topic; doing research; reading and taking notes; organizing material; and writing and assembling the paper that shows the results of your research.

The topic that you select for research should be one that is interesting to you, that is narrow enough for the limits of your paper, and that requires research rather than personal experience for its development. Investigation to your topic is made easier if you know what resources the library offers and how to use them.

Careful organization of procedures and techniques when doing the research and writing the paper enable you to progress logically. The first step in this phase of the research project is the preparation of a working bibliography, which indicates how much material is available on the subject. The next step involves reading and taking notes. Only material that proves to be relevant to the specific topic you are investigating should be recorded. Note cards should be limited to one note or group of related facts on each card. The note cards are used in the next step—the preparation of the outline. With the outline as a guide, the first draft of the paper is written and then set aside for a day or two. Next, revisions are made, the final draft is prepared, the title page, table of contents, footnotes and a bibliography are added, the final proofreading is done, and the completed paper is assembled.

UNIT REVIEW EXERCISES

DISCUSSION TOPICS
See p. T64.

A. Discuss the step-by-step procedure involved in preparing a research paper.

B. What factors enter into the selection of a research topic? Discuss each factor fully. See p. T64.

C. How can the skills learned in doing research be related to subjects other than English and to your future business or professional life? Cite specific examples. See p. T64.

WRITTEN WORK

A. Arrange the following information in the correct order for a bibliography. Be sure each entry is in correct order and then arrange the entire bibliography. Use the form learned in doing this unit. See pp. T64-T65 for form of entries.

4   1. Horace Gregory and Marya Zaturenska, *History of American Poetry, 1900-1940,* New York, Harcourt, Brace and Company, 1946.

1   2. Blair Walter and Chandler, W. K. Approaches to Poetry. New York, London: 1935, D. Appleton-Century Company, Inc., pp. 9-77.

2   3. "Really New Literature," Henry Seidel Canby, *American Memoir.* Houghton Mifflin Company, 1947, pp. 339-349, Boston.

6   4. Van Gelder, Robert, *Writers and Writing.* Charles Scribner's Sons: New York, 1946.

3   5. Engle, Paul, *English Journal,* "Five Years of Pulitzer Poets." vol. 38, pp. 59-66, February, 1949.

5   6. F. G. Melcher, "Poet and Gallant Fighter," *Publisher's Weekly,* vol. 143, March 20, 1943, p. 1257.

B. Write a composition in which you discuss the values to be gained from doing a research paper. Make specific reference to the research project you developed in this unit. You may wish to approach the subject from the point of view of the personal values, the educational values, the career values, or a combination of these. Compositions will vary.

VOCABULARY

Did you know the meaning of all the words in this unit? The following sentences use some of the words in different contexts. Write the numbers 1 to 5 on your paper. After each number write the letter of the word or phrase that could best be substituted for the italicized word in each sentence. Before making your choice, find the word on the page indicated to see how it is used in the unit.

1. We have a valuable *annotated* edition of that book.   [p. 122]
a   (*a*) with notes; (*b*) illustrated; (*c*) early; (*d*) annual
2. Her comments show how *superficial* her thinking is.   [p. 120]
c   (*a*) critical; (*b*) superior; (*c*) shallow; (*d*) superfluous
3. Anger tends to *distort* one's thinking.   [p. 137]
b   (*a*) color; (*b*) twist; (*c*) aggravate; (*d*) disturb

The completion of a research project can be a satisfying experience for students. The teacher will find the final reading less difficult if he has checked students' progress at each step.

4. Your assistance will *expedite* the survey.   [p. 129]

c
   (*a*) improve; (*b*) rush; (*c*) facilitate; (*d*) shorten

5. Be sure those papers are arranged *consecutively*.   [p. 144]

d
   (*a*) alphabetically; (*b*) numerically; (*c*) logically; (*d*) sequentially

SPELLING

Point
out
trou-
ble
.spots
in the
spelling
words.

The following spelling words appeared in this unit or were chosen because they are commonly misspelled. Study these words so that you will be prepared to write them from dictation.

1.	annotated	11.	terminology
2.	superficial	12.	initial
3.	distort	13.	supplements
4.	expedite	14.	familiarize
5.	consecutively	15.	interpolate
6.	haphazardly	16.	summarize
7.	applicable	17.	competent
8.	unwieldy	18.	abbreviate
9.	verbatim	19.	imminent
10.	cumulative	20.	prevalent

UNIT SELF-TEST

Choices will vary for 1. and 2. (See pp. 122-123, 125-126)

1. Name three encyclopedias, one yearbook, and one atlas.
2. Write the names of five special reference books and tell the purpose of each.
3. Draw the outline of a bibliography card and arrange the following information within the outline. See p. T65.

   Source number 8
   George Schreiber, editor
   Portraits and Self-portraits
   Published in Boston by the Houghton Mifflin Company in 1936
   Pages 13-16 were used

4. Using the same information given you in Exercise 3, write the first footnote for material quoted from the book. Assume that the quotation was drawn from page 15. See bottom margin.
5. In a direct quotation how do you mark an error to indicate that you have reproduced the original exactly and that the error is not yours? [sic]
6. How is explanatory material inserted into a direct quotation? Brackets
7. When do you use the abbreviation *ibid*.? Same as preceding entry.
8. When is *op. cit.* used? When other entries intervene
9. What is the caret (∧) used for? To insert omitted words or letters
10. List in order the parts of a research paper. See bottom margin.

4. [1]George Schreiber, ed., Portraits and Self-portraits
        (Boston: Houghton Mifflin Company, 1936), p. 15.

10. Title page, a blank page, table of contents, body,
    bibliography

Unit 7

Creative Writing

Writing is a basic skill that everyone can develop through application and practice. Not all of you will become great short-story writers, novelists, or poets. Many of you may never publish an essay or an article. But all of you will, at some time in your lives, have to express yourselves in writing.

The written word imposes limitations. You have no gestures, no facial expressions, no voice inflections to help you convey meaning. You must, then, find the words and the ways of using them that will make up for your physical absence. Style takes the place of the man; rhythm replaces the gesture; a large and flexible vocabulary gives the words the significance and color that is achieved by voice inflection.

The main cause of failure to write interestingly and effectively is a lack of industry and self-discipline. Others may make suggestions and may guide you in your writing, but for the most part, creative writing is self-taught. You must develop alertness and you must practice. When you read, be alert to the techniques writers have used to create certain moods and to achieve particular effects. When you study the world around you,

Constant
practice
is the
key to
achieving
a smooth,
flowing
style of
writing.

use all your senses. Write as much as you can as often as you can. Fluency
will result from constant practice.

   This unit is intended as a guide to help you with original writing. Forms
of writing are suggested, models are included, and opportunities for practice are provided. Your own interest and determination to write well
should lead you to investigate other forms of writing and to discover ideas
for writing practice.

 CHECK YOURSELF

   The following questions and exercises will help you determine how
   much you already know about creative writing. Your teacher may wish
   to discuss some of the questions after you have checked your answers.

   A. Write the answers to the following questions.

No   1. Is it true that a writer must shut himself off from associations
        with other people so that he will have time for his writing?

Made   2. Are writers "born" or are they "made"?

       3. Where do writers get their ideas?   The world around them

Yes   4. Do poets and novelists have anything in common?   Awareness

       5. What is a couplet? A quatrain?   Two successive lines of
   poetry that rhyme. Four-line stanza, usually abab or abcb

   B. Write the numbers from 1 to 5 on your paper. In each of the follow-
      ing statements one word is less specific than the others. Find the
      word and write its letter after the corresponding number.

d   1. The flavor was (*a*) peppery (*b*) sharp (*c*) tangy (*d*) unpleasant.

c   2. He moved down the street at a (*a*) shuffle (*b*) hobble (*c*) walk
       (*d*) sprint.

a   3. Dorothy's singing voice was (*a*) disagreeable (*b*) sharp (*c*) shrill
       (*d*) raucous.

a   4. Then in the darkness of the closet she touched something (*a*) soft
       (*b*) furry (*c*) bristly (*d*) spongy.

c   5. The scent which drifted up to him was (*a*) acrid (*b*) musty
       (*c*) fragrant (*d*) spicy.

   C. Write the numbers from 1 to 5 on your paper. In each of the follow-
      ing statements one word is more specific than the others. Find the
      word and write its letter after the corresponding number.

c   1. The man's face was (*a*) ugly (*b*) repulsive (*c*) pock-marked
       (*d*) unattractive.

c   2. The old house on the hill was (*a*) big (*b*) huge (*c*) tomb-like
       (*d*) immense.

b   3. His new car was (*a*) keen (*b*) low-slung (*c*) beautiful (*d*) shiny.
b   4. The drums (*a*) pounded (*b*) throbbed (*c*) beat (*d*) sounded.
c   5. The polished surface was (*a*) glassy (*b*) smooth (*c*) satin-like
       (*d*) glowing.

1. The World Around You

WAKE UP YOUR SENSES

All creative writing starts from the same first principle—*know yourself
that you may know others*. Everything you have experienced, everything
you have seen, heard, touched, smelled, and tasted—all these things are
part of you and are sources of material for writing. The degree to which
you can bring these experiences to life in your writing depends upon the
extent to which they live for you. The person who is aware of and sensitive
to the world around him and who reacts vigorously to it can usually learn
to write with a vitality that will communicate itself to his readers.

You have at some time probably said something like, "I can still see it,"
or "I can hear it yet," or "I still shiver when I remember how cold it was,"
or "I get hungry thinking about the smell of a steak sizzling over char-
coal," or "My mouth puckers when I think about the taste of a fresh
lemon." Such sensations are memorable and are still alive in your con-
sciousness. You have received many equally vivid sense impressions,
some of which you have permitted to slip into the area of forgotten, or
half-forgotten, experiences. On the other hand, you have probably missed
recording some impressions because your senses were not awake. Draw from students memorable sense impressions they have had.

One way to stimulate your senses is to make lists of some of the sights,
sounds, tactile sensations, smells, and tastes that you have experienced. For
example, you might list persons and places you can recall having seen.
Then you might add to this list objects associated with farming, with
science, with manufacturing, with the sea, and so on. Do the same for the
other senses: the sounds of human voices, musical instruments, machines,
animals; the varieties of touch—smooth, slimy—and specific tactile sensations; the varieties of taste—sweet, sour—and specific taste experiences;
the varieties of smell—smoky, spicy—and specific olfactory impressions.

Create in the classroom as many opportunities as possible
for training the sensory faculties of your students. Concentrate on their translating sensory experiences into vivid
verbal experiences.

Go through your lists item by item. Close your eyes and try to relive each experience. Can you *see* the old lady you used to think was a witch? Do you *hear* the creaking of the steps on the first night you were left alone in the house? Can you *feel* the icy lemonade on your lips and tongue and in your throat on a hot summer day? Can you *taste* the freshly-baked, warm cookies and the cold milk? Can you *smell* the field of clover you whizzed by on the highway?

Most people go through life missing stimulating sensory experiences, unobservant of what is going on around them. It is possible, through practice, to wake up the senses to new experiences and to bring to life again forgotten experiences so they will be in your mind ready for use in your writing. As you work to revitalize old sense impressions, you will find that your senses will become more alert to new impressions. You will see the world around you with greater awareness and understanding.

DEVELOPING YOUR SKILL

A. Describe two persons who have played important roles in your life. Limit yourself to visual impressions: appearance, dress, mannerisms, unusual features, and so on. Before you write, close your eyes and see the person. Include all the details you can recall.

B. Write a paragraph in which you describe a memorable sound experience. Be sure you can hear the sounds you plan to describe before you attempt to make others hear them.

C. Write a paragraph, using as your first sentence *I can taste it yet.*

D. Write a paragraph in which you recall touch sensations you have experienced. Do not just list; describe your reactions to the touches you mention.

E. Write a paragraph that might be entitled "The Adventures of My Nose." Take your nose on an imaginative tour of remembered scents and odors.

WRITE ABOUT THE FAMILIAR

The subjects you select for creative writing should be familiar to you. Often, beginning writers mistakenly feel that they can write best about a subject that is new and fresh and that, therefore, arouses their enthusiasm.

The problem here is that the writer soon finds that he doesn't know enough about the subject to write easily and fluently. He finds himself bogged down by having to stop to check statements; he wonders whether he is interpreting the subject correctly. His anxiety about his knowledge of the subject frequently makes his presentation stiff and awkward. The writer who has mastered a subject can devote his energies to an attractive presentation.

Think about possible subjects for writing. Think back over your life and the people and events in it. What subjects are you interested in? What subjects could you write about without having to do research? Start out by making a list of subjects that are familiar to you. Draw your subjects from family, school, and social experiences, from incidents that you have observed, from travel experiences, from hobbies, and from recollections of persons you have known. As ideas for writing occur to you, add them to your list.

Keep your subjects concrete and within easily handled limits. Unless you are writing a completely factual paper, do not hesitate to combine elements of different situations or characteristics of different individuals and assign them to the situation or the character you are writing about. The primary requisite at the outset is that you use material that you know and can write about easily.

Perhaps one of the subjects on your list refers to a time when you were punished for having broken something valuable—an heirloom vase, for example. You were sent to bed without supper, and your father made you give up your allowance for a month to help pay for repairing the vase. You couldn't understand why everyone made such a fuss over one vase; after all, your mother had lots of other vases. You smoldered with resentment every time you thought of the incident until you were old enough to understand why the heirloom meant so much to your parents. You decide to use this incident as the central theme for a short narrative, but you would like to give it a little more interest.

Another subject on your list is the incident in which the five-year-old daughter of one of your neighbors decided that her father's new contact lenses would make pretty little houses for ants. She took the box containing the lenses and, while playing with "the little pieces of glass," lost one of them in the grass in a nearby lot. You decide to combine parts of the two incidents into one story.

Having to stop to check tends to discourage the neophyte writer.

New situations may be created by combining difficult elements of familiar situations.

Point out to students that the subject matter of most stories, essays, and poems is often quite ordinary. It is the writer's presentation that makes the material different or unusual.

Next, since you know her better, you decide to use your little sister as the central character. Your sister is in the first grade, is a little chatterbox, and loves to take part in the "show and tell" period. No matter what happens at home, it is sure to be reported to the first-grade class at the elementary school. Your narrative might be developed as follows:

Discuss with students the ways in which the elements of the various situations have been combined.

It was "show and tell" time in the first grade. Mary Elliot bounced up to tell her story.

"Last night I got a spanking and had to go to bed right after supper just 'cause I lost a tiny piece of glass. I was going out to play in the lot at the corner 'cause there are lots of ants there, and I like to play with ants. Anyway, I was looking for something to put the ants in and I saw a pretty little box on Daddy's dresser. I opened the box and found two tiny upside-down glass saucers and I thought they would make beautiful houses for two ants. I tried to ask Mommy. Really I did. But she was washing clothes in the basement and didn't hear me.

"So I went out to play, and I caught an ant and put him in his house. He looked so pretty with the sun shining on him in his glass house. Then I caught another ant, and while I was trying to put him in his glass house, the other house and ant fell out of the box. I looked and looked for the piece of glass, but it was so tiny and the grass was so long that I couldn't find it. Pretty soon it got late and I got hungry. So I went home.

"Daddy was home when I got there and looked all funny and red in the face. Mommy was running around pulling out drawers and looking on things and under things and all over. When I said 'Hello,' nobody answered me or kissed me or anything. Daddy just said, 'Mary, have you seen the little box that was on my dresser?' I felt funny inside, but I gave him the box. When Daddy opened it, he got redder and shouted, 'Where's the other one?' and I told him. We went back to the lot and looked and looked some more, but we couldn't find the tiny glass anywhere.

"Then when we got home Daddy spanked me and made me go to bed right after supper. Mommy told me that the pieces of glass fit over Daddy's eyeballs so he can see. I think it's kind of silly. Why does he need glasses for his eyeballs when he has glasses that cover his whole eyes?

"And that's not all. This morning Daddy said his eyeball glasses cost a lot of money and I have to help pay for them out of my allowance.

"Miss Blake, how many five centses are there in a dollar?"

In everyone's memory are certain buildings, certain scenes that are held on to; and in the passage of time they gather about themselves a glow or mist of charm (what the poets might call a romantic aura). Perhaps you have some recollection of a place in the woods, a particular stretch of beach, a long road that winds over a hill, a brook hidden away from the main road where the trout lie watchful. This picture is one you can call up at will and see in all its detail. Somerset Maugham must have had a vivid recollection of seeing the Great Wall of China. It is obvious that the sight was familiar to him—that he had actually seen it and had absorbed it with all his senses. Notice with what detail and with what feeling he describes it for his readers in *On A Chinese Screen*.

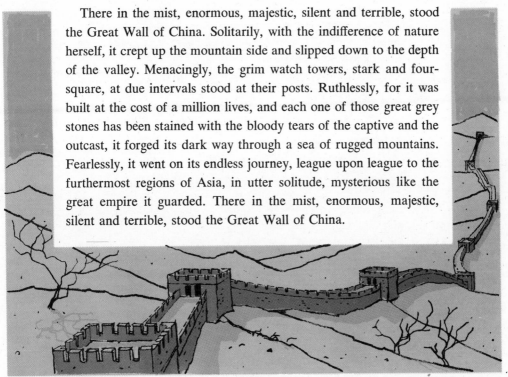

There in the mist, enormous, majestic, silent and terrible, stood the Great Wall of China. Solitarily, with the indifference of nature herself, it crept up the mountain side and slipped down to the depth of the valley. Menacingly, the grim watch towers, stark and four-square, at due intervals stood at their posts. Ruthlessly, for it was built at the cost of a million lives, and each one of those great grey stones has been stained with the bloody tears of the captive and the outcast, it forged its dark way through a sea of rugged mountains. Fearlessly, it went on its endless journey, league upon league to the furthermost regions of Asia, in utter solitude, mysterious like the great empire it guarded. There in the mist, enormous, majestic, silent and terrible, stood the Great Wall of China.

Suppose that Maugham had not seen the Great Wall. Could he have acquired so much experience from looking at a picture? Introduce the idea of vicarious experience.

A. Be ready to discuss the following questions. See p. T65.

    1. What are the characteristics of a good subject for creative writing?
    2. Why is it a mistake to choose a subject that is new to you?
    3. What sources should you draw upon for subjects?

Stress
appeals
to the
senses
in these
exercises.

B. Everyone remembers an incident about the kitchen: licking the beater after the frosting has been whipped; scraping the paddles after making homemade ice cream; sticking a finger into something hot; opening the refrigerator and sniffing the contents. Recall such an incident and recount it, emphasizing the sense impressions you experienced. You may wish to make someone other than yourself the central character.

C. Think back to a time when you were punished, either justly or unjustly. Assign this incident to a fictitious character and recount the details. Your account should be as vivid for your readers as the experience was to you.

D. Out of your memory bring back the picture of someone who left a deep impression on you. Assume that you are the center of your story and that one part of the story deals with a person who played an important role in your life—a teacher, a grandparent, a neighbor, anyone who was important to you. Start your character sketch with a sentence such as *I remember Miss C. best of all.* Make your reader see and know your character.

E. Select one of the moments when an impressive sight or a simple scene has appealed to your emotions. Recount what happened and describe what you saw and what you felt. You may wish to shift the focus to the third person rather than use the first person. Direct your appeal to your readers' senses.

Review Exercises—The World Around You

Write a composition based on a familiar subject. Direct your appeal to the senses. The following titles may suggest ideas to you. Use one of these titles or an idea of your own.

Composi-
tions will
vary.

Ant Hills in the Sun	Baking Day
Swishing Tails	For Idle Hands
Open Road	Sun and Sea
Uncle Joe	By a Stream in the Woods
The Flower Shop	Night Music

You may wish to discuss some of the subjects suggested by the titles. Some students may need such discussion in order to get started.

2. Informal Prose

The informal prose forms are the ones students will use most during their adult years.

The best forms for a beginning writer to use are the somewhat free forms of prose such as the letter, the diary, reminiscences, and the essay. These forms may be spoontaneous and impromptu, as the letter; they may be rambling, as the reminiscence. Whatever their individual characteristics, all the forms mentioned are informal and personal and lend themselves to varied effects. They permit the writer to include other forms of prose, as the jest, the anecdote, the compliment, the proverb, the pun, the parody, the caricature, and so on.

THE LETTER WRITER   The aim here is to bring into the students' writing an informal and personal tone without

One of the best exercises for the beginning writer is the writing of sacrificing friendly letters. The letter writer has the advantage of knowing his audience. He knows the thoughts, interests, tastes, and peculiarities of the good person to whom his letter is directed. Since there is a kind of personal manners rapport between letter writers, the author can express himself freely. The and letter can achieve the personal touch, limit itself to a few main topics, and good make its point indirectly and effectively. The only limitation placed upon diction. the letter writer is that he not become a bore.

Reading models of good letters can help you improve your own letters. Do not attempt to imitate the models you read; rather, study them for their varied subject matter and for their style. Numerous examples may be found in two volumes called *A Treasury of the World's Great Letters,* edited by M. Lincoln Schuster and *A Second Treasury of the World's Great Letters,* edited by Wallace Brockway and Bart Keith Winer. Although some of the letters included were written many years ago, they

Some imitation on the part of the student is inevitable, at least until the student finds his own style. Insofar as possible, however, discourage imitation.

still provide interesting and pleasurable reading. The following excerpts are taken from a letter written by Robert Louis Stevenson in 1881. *The Sea Cook* was the original title of *Treasure Island*.

The humor in this letter is literary and adult.

And now look here—this is next day—and three chapters are written and read. (Chapter I. The Old Sea-dog at the Admiral Ben-bow. Chapter II. Black Dog appears and disappears. Chapter III. The Black Spot.) All now heard by Lloyd, F., and my father and mother, with high approval. It's quite silly and horrid fun, and what I want is the best book about the Buccaneers that can be had—the latter B's above all, Blackbeard and sich, and get Nutt or Bain to send it skimming by the fastest post. And now I know you'll write to me, for the Sea Cook's sake . . . .

A chapter a day I mean to do; they are short; and perhaps in a month the "Sea Cook" may to Routledge go, yo-ho-ho and a bottle of rum! My Trelawney has a strong dash of Landor, as I see him from here. No women in the story, Lloyd's orders; and who so blithe to obey? It's awful fun, boys' stories; you just indulge the pleasure of your heart, that's all; no trouble, no strain. The only stiff thing is to get it ended—that I don't see, but I look to a volcano. O sweet, O generous, O human toils. You would like my blind beggar in Chapter III, I believe; no writing, just drive along as the words come and the pen will scratch!

R. L. S.
Author of Boys' Stories

Sometimes the letter form is used as a literary device. A writer who wants to make his material seem more personal may present it in the form of a letter. Biographies and autobiographies may be written in the letter form. Articles commenting on the behavior of individuals or on political and social situations sometimes take the form of letters. Public debates are often carried on in the form of letters.

The letter form—whether used to communicate with a friend or used as a literary device—permits you a wide range of roles and topics. You can be, for example, a narrator, a gossip, a recorder of impressions, a humorist, or a jester. Almost any topic that lends itself to conversation may be adapted to the letter.

Discuss with students the broad range of roles and topics permitted by the letter form. Illustrate also the incorporation of other shorter forms into the letter.

> DEVELOPING YOUR SKILL

A. Write a letter to a friend. You may wish to make a single topic the theme of your letter, or you may wish to write a chatty letter covering a variety of topics. In either case, make your letter lively and conversational in tone. Letters will vary.

B. Using the letter form, develop one of the following ideas:

1. A famous man or woman writes to tell you, a high school student, about one of his achievements.

2. A person who has just regained his eyesight writes a letter telling a friend what it is like to see again.

3. An idea of your own. You may wish to make a list of possible ideas on the chalkboard. Draw suggestions from students.

THE DIARIST

The diary form is closely related to letter writing, though it may tend to become more introspective—more personal and more secretive. The advantage of the diary form is that it releases the imagination of the writer by establishing a kind of bond between the writer and the abstract being who becomes known as "Diary." The danger of using this device for creative work is that the writing sometimes becomes over-emotional, effusions gush forth, and the writing lacks form and discipline. In the hands of a sensitive, restrained individual, the diary can be an effective literary device. Point up both the advantage of and the danger in the diary form.

Occasionally, in Anne Frank's *The Diary of a Young Girl,* the author achieves a fortunate blending of personal narrative, emotional utterance, and dignity of bearing. No one entry can do justice to the entire book, but the entry for Saturday, January 30, 1943, is interesting.

> I'm boiling with rage, and yet I mustn't show it. I'd like to stamp my feet, scream, give Mummy a good shaking, cry, and I don't know what else, because of the horrible words, mocking looks, and accusations which are leveled at me repeatedly every day, and find their mark, like shafts from a tightly strung bow, and which are just as hard to draw from my body.
>
> I would like to shout to Margot, Van Daan, Dussel—and Daddy, too—"leave me in peace, let me sleep one night at least without my pillow being wet with tears, my eyes burning and my head throbbing. Let me get away from it all, preferably away from the world!"

You may wish to read to the class other excerpts from Anne Frank's diary to illustrate the effectiveness of the diary form.

This is
a com-
pletely
personal
diary.
The next
example
offers
a con-
trast
with
this
excerpt.

but I can't do that, they mustn't know my despair, I can't let them see the wounds which they have caused, I couldn't bear their sympathy and their kindhearted jokes, it would only make me want to scream all the more. If I talk, everyone thinks I'm showing off; when I'm silent they think I'm ridiculous; rude if I answer, sly if I get a good idea, lazy if I'm tired, selfish if I eat a mouthful more than I should, stupid, cowardly, crafty, etc., etc. The whole day long I hear nothing else but that I am an insufferable baby, and although I laugh about it and pretend not to take any notice, I *do* mind. I would like to ask God to give me a different nature, so that I didn't put everyone's back up. But that can't be done. I've got the nature that has been given to me and I'm sure it can't be bad. I do my very best to please everybody, far more than they'd ever guess. . . .

ANNE FRANK, *The Diary of a Young Girl*

The diary form may also be used for writing that is humorous and inventive, writing whose obvious intent is to entertain. Notice that in Mark Twain's hands it becomes impersonal in outward form, but underlying Adam's utterances are many of the attitudes and prejudices of the author.

THE DIARY OF ADAM AND EVE

PART I—EXTRACTS FROM ADAM'S DIARY

Monday   This new creature with the long hair is a good deal in the way. It is always hanging around and following me about. I don't like this; I am not used to company. I wish it would stay with the other animals. . . Cloudy today, wind in the east; think we shall have rain. . . . *We?* Where did I get that word?—I remember now—the new creature uses it.

Tuesday   Been examining the great waterfall. It is the finest thing on the estate, I think. The new creature calls it Niagara Falls—why, I am sure I do not know. Says it *looks* like Niagara Falls. That is not a reason; it is mere waywardness and imbecility. I get no chance to name anything myself. The new creature names everything that comes along, before I can get in a protest. And always that same pretext is offered—it *looks* like the thing. There is the dodo, for instance. Says

Do not permit your students' appreciation of the
humor in the Mark Twain excerpt totally to eclipse
their awareness of the form.

the moment one looks at it one sees at a glance that it "looks like a dodo." It will have to keep that name, no doubt. It wearies me to fret about it, and it does no good anyway. Dodo! It looks no more like a dodo than I do.

Wednesday   Built me a shelter against the rain, but could not have it to myself in peace. The new creature intruded. When I tried to put it out, it shed water out of the holes it looks with, and wiped it away with the back of its paws, and made a noise such as some of the other animals make when they are in distress. I wish it would not talk; it is always talking. That sounds like a cheap fling at the poor creature, a slur; but I do not mean it so. I have never heard the human voice before, and any new and strange sound intruding itself here upon the solemn hush of these dreaming solitudes offends my ear and seems a false note. And this new sound is so close to me; it is right at my shoulder, right at my ear, first on one side and then on the other, and I am used only to sounds that are more or less distant from me.

Friday   The naming goes recklessly on, in spite of anything I can do. I had a very good name for the estate, and it was musical and pretty—GARDEN OF EDEN. Privately, I continue to call it that, but not any longer publicly. The new creature says it is all woods and rocks and scenery, and therefore has no resemblance to a garden. Says it *looks* like a park, and does not look like anything *but* a park. Consequently, without consulting me, it has been new-named —Niagara Falls Park. This is sufficiently high-handed, it seems to me. And already there is a sign up:

KEEP OFF
THE GRASS

My life is not as happy as it was.

You may wish to have students analyze the selection for evidence of satire.

Point out the effect of understatement in the last sentence of the Mark Twain selection.

166

DEVELOPING YOUR SKILL

Creative Writing

Entries will vary.

A. Using the diary form and drawing upon some incident of your past, record two or three entries in which you (1) tell a personal incident, (2) express your feelings about the incident, and (3) draw some conclusion about what that experience has meant to you in the past or what it means to you now.

Students will have to look at the familiar with new awareness.

B. Keep a diary for one week, recounting the happenings around your school but seeing them through the eyes of a fictitious character. Assume that you are a foreign student coming to this country for the first time and living in your new American town and going to your new school. You need not record everything that happens each day; include only those happenings or comments that would strike the new student as being worth recording.

THE ESSAYIST

The study of the essay will introduce form into the students' writing.

The essay is a form of writing that cannot be easily defined. The early definition of the word was "an effort to do something; attempt; trial." As a literary composition an essay is an attempt to present an analytical or interpretive treatment of a subject from a personal point of view. The essay reveals the personality of the writer, either directly or indirectly.

Essays are classed as *formal* and *informal* according to the method of presentation and the intention of the author. Formal essays are usually developed accoording to a unified, logical plan: the opening statement, which establishes the mood; the body of the essay with its smooth transitions and its unexpected turns; and the conclusion, which frequently reveals the larger significance of the subject.

Formal essays are serious in tone and attempt to instruct or influence the thinking of the reader. Informal essays, on the other hand, allow for greater freedom of form. However, even here the essayist proceeds in an orderly manner. It is only his apparent spontaneity that leads the reader to believe that no plan was followed. The tone of the informal essay may range from the light and whimsical to the reflective and philosophical.

In this section you will study two kinds of informal essay—the personal narrative and the reflective essay.

The personal narrative

The personal narrative may be a reminiscence about people the author has known or it may be based on incidents in the writer's life. In the process of describing Grandmother or Father or Miss Purdy's school for girls, the author expresses his own points of view and reveals his own character traits.

Often, the personal narrative is written in a humorous vein with characters and situations being somewhat exaggerated for effect. As you read the following excerpt from "University Days," notice that the author's humor, while often uproarious, is never harsh or cruel.

From "UNIVERSITY DAYS" by JAMES THURBER

I PASSED all the other courses that I took at my University, but I could never pass botany. This was because all botany students had to spend several hours a week in a laboratory looking through a microscope at plant cells, and I could never see through a microscope. I never once saw a cell through a microscope. This used to enrage my instructor. He would wander around the laboratory pleased with the progress all the students were making in drawing the involved and, so I am told, interesting structure of flower cells, until he came to me. I would just be standing there. "I can't see anything," I would say. He would begin patiently enough, explaining how anybody can see through a microscope, but he would always end up in a fury, claiming that I could *too* see through a microscope but just pretended that I couldn't. "It takes away from the beauty of flowers anyway," I used to tell him. "We are not concerned with beauty in this course," he would say. "We are concerned solely with what I may call the *mechanics* of flars." "Well," I'd say, "I can't see anything." "Try it just once again," he'd say, and I would put my eye to the microscope and see nothing at all, except now and again a nebulous milky substance—a phenomenon of maladjustment. You were supposed to see a vivid, restless clockwork of sharply defined plant cells. "I see what looks like a lot of milk," I would tell him. This, he claimed, was the result of my not having adjusted the microscope properly, so he would readjust it for me, or rather, for himself. And I would look again and see milk.

I finally took a deferred pass, as they called it, and waited a year and tried again. (You had to pass one of the biological sciences or

You may wish to have students read other Thurber essays and some of E. B. White's as examples of humor in prose.

Point
out to
students
that the
incident
is not
extra-
ordinary;
it is the
writer's
treat-
ment of
the inci-
dent
that
makes
it seem
unusual.

you couldn't graduate.) The professor had come back from vacation brown as a berry, bright-eyed, and eager to explain cell-structure again to his classes. "Well," he said to me, cheerily, when we met in the first laboratory hour of the semester, "we're going to see cells this time, aren't we?" "Yes, sir," I said. Students to right of me and to left of me and in front of me were seeing cells; what's more, they were quietly drawing pictures of them in their notebooks. Of course, I didn't see anything.

"We'll try it," the professor said to me, grimly, "with every adjustment of the microscope known to man. As God is my witness, I'll arrange this glass so that you see cells through it or I'll give up teaching. In twenty-two years of botany, I—" He cut off abruptly for he was beginning to quiver all over, like Lionel Barrymore, and he genuinely wished to hold onto his temper; his scenes with me had taken a great deal out of him.

So we tried it with every adjustment of the microscope known to man. With only one of them did I see anything but blackness or the familiar lacteal opacity, and that time I saw, to my pleasure and amazement, a variegated constellation of flecks, specks, and dots. These I hastily drew. The instructor, noting my activity, came back from an adjoining desk, a smile on his lips and his eyebrows high in hope. He looked at my cell drawing. "What's that?" he demanded, with a hint of a squeal in his voice. "That's what I saw," I said. "You didn't, you didn't, you *did*n't!" he screamed, losing control of his temper instantly, and he bent over and squinted into the microscope. His head snapped up. "That's your eye!" he shouted. "You've fixed the lens so that it reflects! You've drawn your eye!"

Stress the importance of naturalness in humor. Humor
that is strained is not effective.

Informal Prose

DEVELOPING YOUR SKILL

In your family there must be one incident as funny as this one. Give
the incident a good setting; then tell it in as easy a manner as that used
by Thurber. Strive for humor in your writing. Use your imagination.
You may even exaggerate or bend the truth just a little, for exaggeration
is often an important element in humor. Incidents will vary.

The reflective essay

The reflective essay is a serious essay in which the author focuses his
attention on some aspect of life and treats it in a philosophical manner.
The author of a reflective essay may raise questions, or he may answer
questions. He wants to understand what is going on in the world. He wants
to know what makes people act as they do. He wants to learn the answers
so that he may pass them on to his readers. In short, he is something of a
reformer. He becomes interested in the world because he has learned to
react to it. People make him stop and listen. Nature makes him open his
eyes. Events must have causes, and causes must have effects. Therefore
the serious writer is a camera; he is a tape recorder; and he is a loud
speaker.

Discuss
the role
of the
serious
writer.

The following student theme catches the spirit of the writer with a
philosophical turn of mind. Notice how the choice of detail affects the
tone of the essay.

THE SO-CALLED CROSS SECTION

Very often, when I have nothing better to do (and, unfortunately,
I all too frequently have nothing better to do), I think about casual
acquaintances—people whom I have met or seen only for a brief
period of time and who have passed out of my life altogether. I
wonder what they are doing now. Is Hank Larsen, the excellent soul
who drove a bus in which I rode for four hours, still in the employ
of the same bus line? At this moment, as I sit at my desk, is he
spreading butter on a roll, or sleeping, or seeing a movie, or playing badminton?

When I think about it, a wonderful, heterogeneous stream of
characters passes in review. Once I gazed from a train window in
Lawrence, Michigan, at an aged rustic, placidly sitting on a bench,
who suddenly rose and violently slapped an obese woman who was

Permit
students
to read
the essay
silently.

You may wish to initiate a discussion in which you compare
the roles of the humorist and the writer of serious essays.
Raise the question of whether the humorist's intention is
always solely to entertain.

Follow the silent reading of the essay with a discussion of techniques used and ideas presented.
170   *Creative Writing*

passing. She did nothing, but walked right on. The train pulled out
and ended a one-minute drama more mysterious to me than anything I had read in Arthur Conan Doyle or S. S. Van Dine. What
has become of the urchin who darted in front of me one day on State
Street and squeaked what sounded like either "Here's mud in your
eye" or "Watch the Fords go by"? And then there was the liquor-
steeped oldster who came to the door, sold me some shoe polish, told
me about his nephew on the Indianapolis ball team, and abruptly
departed. Are these folk dead and gone or do they baffle other innocent observers to this day? What has happened to a boy who showed
up in my adviser room the first morning of a school year a while
back and was affable and eager but who never returned?

And if I were granted the power to see these people as they are
today, I should like to deal justly with the filling station attendant,
somewhere in the wilds of Wisconsin, who, although he passed the
time of day in a pleasant manner, neglected to replace the cap on
the gas tank. Yes, I should like to meet also the wayside confectioner
who sold me six apparently lovely candy bars which later displayed
an unmistakably wormy interior. But let us hope I never come face
to face with the good wife whose name I picked from the phone book
at random, and after calling her, casually asked if she were "the
woman who washed."

A motley crowd, indeed! I am quite sure the benign old priest
who sat next to me on the train would not hit it off very well with
the vulgar bookie who happened to call at the barber shop when I
was getting a haircut. Nor would that strait-laced acquaintance of
my grandmother's, whose name I never did quite catch, relish the
companionship of the enthusiastic, if somewhat untutored and definitely malodorous, gent with whom I became friendly for a half hour
at the prize fights. But I am glad that I have met them. They are the
so-called cross section. They each represent a minute adventure, and
if the seeker after adventure will keep his eyes open to the poten-
tialities of each insignificant encounter, he will find in them all a
small but thoroughly satisfactory element of mystery, pathos, humor,
and romance.

In discussing the essay, lead students to an
awareness of the number of commonplace incidents
that have been combined to achieve an effective
picture.

Sometimes the writer chooses to interpret an incident or event. Read the following essay—also a student theme—with the meaning of the incident in mind.

A HANDFUL OF CLAY

I was idle that morning, so I walked out into the sparkling sunlight of the early spring day and unconsciously headed uptown. My eyes took in every new bud, now bursting with life; my ears thrilled to the sound of the birds singing again in the tree-tops; I remembered how long I had waited for life to return to the city. I felt good inside, but I recalled too how I had felt so dismal during the last endless months of winter. I remembered how I had walked dejectedly along the very avenue that I was now traveling; I remembered how lonely and useless I had felt then and how a seemingly plain old man had given me a new look at life.

Point out the writer's awareness of the world as evidenced by his descriptions.

I was lonely then, and as I was passing the site where the new building was being constructed, I noticed him sitting on a log, turning something over and over in his hand. I must have been staring at him, for suddenly he looked up at me and, a twinkle in his eye, cheerily said "Hello." He began talking to me and I, grateful for his company, sat down beside him. Then, curious, I asked him what it was that he had in his hand.

He turned it over again and said, "Well, could be a lot of things, but some people might say it's just a piece of clay. Could be a beautiful vase for some Fifth Avenue place—could be a plate on someone's dinner table—could be something simple like a brick—or could be just a piece of clay, a hunk of mud. All depends on what you do with it. If you want to be fancy, you can model the vase—if you want something plain, you can make a brick—if you don't want to make anything at all, you can leave it be. Could be a person's life."

I was beginning to understand.

DEVELOPING YOUR SKILL

A. What are some of the happenings that have not been significant in your life but have left you curious about their outcome? Recall several and recount them in a reflective essay. Essays will vary.

You may wish to discuss the use of symbolism in writing.

B. Write an essay in which you use one of the following as a symbol:
gold, brass, iron, stone, straw, sand, earth, air, fire, water. See
bottom margin for suggestions.

Review Exercises—Informal Prose

A. Write a theme in which you discuss the various forms of informal prose
   that a beginning writer may use. Discuss the merits of each of the forms.
B. Select one of the forms of prose you have studied for an original composition. Let your subject matter and your purpose determine the form
   you use and the tone of your writing.

You may find the following suggestions helpful in deciding on subjects for
original compositions.

THE WORLD OF THE SENSES

Storm Warnings
Nerve Endings
Quiet Zone
Night Sounds
Street Noises

A STRANGE WORLD OF CONTRADICTIONS

Uncertain Yesterdays
Cleansed in Mud
Beauty in Ugliness
The Worm and the Rose
Soft Anger

THE WORLD OF MAKE-BELIEVE

My Name is. . . . .
Midsummer Fantasy
The Night the Stop Light Died
Green Cheese After All
Machine Take All

A FIGURATIVE WORLD

Do Sheep Dream Too?
Sparks from the Anvil
Fog and Mist
Built-In Reactor
Gravel in My Shoe

THE ETHICAL WORLD

Who Believes What?
Duty Free
Tomorrow, Maybe
Who, Me?
But, Officer—

MISCELLANEOUS

On Safety Valves
Shadow and Substance
Perchance to Dream
To the Future!
Illusions

THE WORLD OF LAUGHTER

Pad That Bench!
It Happens to All of Us
I've Heard So Much About You
Have You Seen Our Colored Slides?
The Service Charge Is Moderate

For example: gold is precious; brass is lasting; iron
is strong; stone is hard; straw bends; sand shifts; earth
is common; air is free; fire is a test of courage; water
is teeming with life. Find these qualities in persons one
knows.

Continue to emphasize the importance of awareness of
the world and of appeals to the senses.

Poetry
173

3. Poetry

AWARENESS

The poet may use fewer words than the essayist; perhaps he uses language more forcefully; he may even be more aware of interpretations—but essentially the poet and the essayist are alike in their awareness of the world.

The Japanese writer of *haikus,* the old Hebrew singer, the Greek, the English, and the modern American poet have a close kinship. They are all deeply sensitive to life, their world, their loves, their fears, their dreams. The following is an old song translated from the Yiddish.

AN OLD SONG

In the blossom-land Japan
Somewhere thus an old song ran:

Said a warrior to a smith
"Hammer me a sword forthwith.
Make the blade
Light as wind on water laid.
Make it long
As the wheat at Harvest song.
Supple, swift
As a snake, without rift,
Full of lightnings, thousand-eyed!
Smooth as silken cloth and thin
As the web that spiders spin.
And merciless as pain, and cold."

"On the hilt what shall be told?"

"On the sword's hilt, my good man,"
Said the warrior of Japan,
"Trace for me
A running lake, a flock of sheep
And one who sings her child to sleep."

—SOLOMON BLOOMGARDEN, "Yehoash"

Discuss the appeals to sight, sound, and touch.

As the study of poetry progresses, students should recognize
the differences in language and interpretation that distinguish
poetry from prose.

DEVELOPING YOUR SKILL

See p. T65.

A. Discuss "An Old Song" from the point of view of awareness. What is the warrior aware of? What is the Japanese storyteller aware of? What is the Hebrew poet aware of? The translator, Marie Syrkin?

Descriptions
will vary.

B. Describe as simply as you can, not worrying about the form of your "poetry," a number of things that you are aware of. Confine your attention to the various aspects and qualities of one thing, as the ocean, the prairie, the lake, the road.

COMPRESSION

In the seventeenth century the Japanese developed an intricate little poetic form called the *haiku,* which are models of compression. *Haiku* suffer, of course, by translation, but they can still be very effective in English. Notice these two translations of the same little poem, the first a fairly literal translation.

Discuss at
length the
effect of
under<u>state</u>-
ment in
poetry.

> The dragon fly hunter—
> today, what place has he
> got to, I wonder . . .
>
> —*Translation by* HAROLD G. HENDERSON

> I wonder in what fields today
> He chases dragonflies in play,
> My little boy—who ran away
>
> —*Translation by* CURTIS HIDDEN PAGE

The poet is at his best when he suggests rather than states. Many a fine poem has been destroyed when the poet thought he had to be explicit and tell the reader what he wanted understood. As you read the following poem keep the principle of compression or understatement in mind. Notice the use of connotative words. This poem is a translation from the French poet Arthur Rimbaud.

THE SLEEPER OF THE VALLEY

> There's a green hollow where a river sings
> Silvering the torn grass in its glittering flight,
> And where the sun from the proud mountain flings
> Fire—and the little valley brims with light.

When discussing <u>haiku</u> you may wish to use Carl Sandburg's "Fog" which was inspired by his reading of the Japanese lyrics.

A soldier young, with open mouth, bare head,
Sleeps with his neck in dewy water cress,
Under the sky and on the grass his bed,
Pale in the deep green and the light's excess.

He sleeps amid the iris and his smile
Is like a sick child's slumbering for a while.
Nature, in thy warm lap his chilled limbs hide!

The perfume does not thrill him from his rest.
He sleeps in sunshine, hand upon his breast,
Tranquil—*with two red holes in his right side.*

—*Translation by* LUDWIG LEWISOHN

Here again
the force
of the
poem lies
in its un-
derstatement.

DEVELOPING YOUR SKILL

A. Discuss the two versions of the original Japanese poem. After you See p.
have decided what feeling the poems have tried to capture, compare T65.
them. Do you like "dragon fly hunter" better than "He chases
dragonflies in play"? Does the translator need to say "My little boy"?
Would you know that it is the mother speaking in the first version?
Why or why not? How did you interpret the phrase "ran away"?

Do not limit the discussion in Exercise A to the questions
suggested. The questions are intended only to initiate discussion.

B. What can you make of this compressed little poem?

The title of this
haiku should give
students the clue
they may need in
order to interpret
the poem.

A one-foot waterfall—
it too makes noises,
and at night is cool.

Small things
also afford
pleasure.

—*Translation by* HAROLD G. HENDERSON

The title of this *haiku* is "Contentment in Poverty."

C. In one line or two, try to capture some little experience and give it a personal application. You brush away a fly. You destroy a spider's web. The water runs cool. The wind rises. The owl hoots. The fox barks. The peacock spreads his tail. Impressions will vary.

See p.T66.

D. Discuss the effect of the last line of "The Sleeper of the Valley." What has the poet said in this one line?

Lines will
vary.

E. The rhyme scheme in "The Sleeper of the Valley" calls for a final word like *side,* but you could perhaps find another rhyming word that would suggest a different way of saying that the soldier is dead. Each member of the class should try to write another final line.

FORM

Not all poets are content with a free utterance, even though it may show a keen awareness of the world and compress its truth within a few lines. Some poets contend that there must be discipline, there must be form to the poem or there is no real art.

Form in poetry involves meter, length of lines, and rhyme patterns. *Meter* refers to the rhythmical arrangement of words in a line of poetry. Each metrical line is divided into groups of syllables called *feet,* each of which contains two or three syllables. The most common metrical feet in English verse are the following:

Iamb (iambic foot)—an unaccented syllable followed by an accented syllable— ◡◦

Trochee (trochaic foot)—an accented syllable followed by an unaccented syllable— ◦◡

Dactyl (dactylic foot)—an accented syllable followed by two unaccented syllables— ◦◡◡

Anapest (anapestic foot)—two unaccented syllables followed by an accented syllable— ◡◡◦

The length of lines is designated by the number of metrical feet in a line.

The study of meter, rhyme, and stanzas bring the concept of form to the writing of poetry.

The following terms are used to indicate the number of feet in a line:

Dimeter—two feet
Trimeter—three feet
Tetrameter—four feet
Pentameter—five feet
Hexameter—six feet

Rhyme patterns, or *rhyme schemes* as they are called, are designated by letters of the alphabet. A poem in which the first and third lines and the second and fourth lines rhyme would have the rhyme scheme abab. In the following pattern, with each word representing the end of a line, the rhyme scheme would be ababbcc.

a here
b beach
a clear
b speech
b teach
c sea
c free

> DEVELOPING YOUR SKILL

See p. T66 for lines incorporating these words into a three-stanza poem.

Practice rhyming and fitting the rhyme to lines of verse. You may wish to start with simple patterns and then progress to more complicated ones. For example, you might start with a three-stanza pattern of abc abc abc such as the following. Then go back and try to fill in the lines.

noon
ride
glee
dune
wide
free
moon
side
me

The four-line stanza

The simplest form of poetry other than free verse is the four-line stanza, the *quatrain*. The lines may rhyme alternately (abab) or only the second

With some classes you may wish to amplify the study of form by introducing more complex elements of prosody.

and fourth lines may rhyme (abcb). Occasionally you may find other variations (aaba) or (aaab) or (aabb).

THE MESSAGE

In your discussion of this poem, point out to students the underlined words in the last two stanzas. Students often expect rhyme always to be full rhyme. In this case, of course, the translator may have had to change the rhyme because of the change in language.

Up, boy! arise, and saddle quick,
And mount your swiftest steed,
And to King Duncan's castle ride
O'er bush and brake with speed.

There slip into the stable soft,
Till one shall see you hide,
Then ask him: which of Duncan's girls
Is she that is a bride?

And if he say, The dark-haired one,
Then give your mare the spur;
But if he say, The fair-haired one,
You need not hurry here.

You only need, if that's the case,
Buy me a hempen cord,
Ride slowly back and give it me
But never speak a word.

—HEINRICH HEINE, *Translation by*
KATE FREILIGRATH KROEKER

 DEVELOPING YOUR SKILL

Try writing a four-line stanza about the fallen snow, the mackerel sky, the flooded fields, the hunter's cry, the white ski slope, the yellow line. . . . At the bottom of your paper, indicate the rhyme scheme you used. Stanzas will vary.

The couplet

A *couplet* consists of two successive lines of poetry that rhyme with each other. The couplet form is interesting to use, particularly for narrative. In the hands of a skillful poet it can result in effective poetry. The

Point out to students that there may be some variation in rhyme scheme within a single poem.

following student poem, for example, maintains variety and creates a well-planned effect.

EXALTATION

Snow and sky and white ski run,
And mountain and God and I are one.
Dipping and soaring toward that curve,
Then around it—swing, glide, swerve.
Danger rides with me in my flight,
Sharpens my wit and strengthens my sight.
Bank and lean and don't dare breathe;
Hope and ecstasy in me seethe.
Then down-engulfed in a spray of snow,
Roll over—leap up—and on I go.
Man, money, and strife—what matter they?
I'm wild and free and above the fray.
I know now how my life should be—
Fearless and true, keen and free.

There are many other poetic forms, but they are largely variations of the four-line stanza and the couplet. As your interest in writing verse grows, you will want to investigate all the types and perhaps experiment occasionally with some of the more unusual forms.

Encourage students who show ability in writing poetry to experiment with the various forms of poetry that are within their capabilities.

DEVELOPING YOUR SKILL

A. Practice writing rhyming couplets. Couplets will vary.

Poems
will
vary.

B. Write a poem composed entirely of couplets. You may wish to start with a quatrain, whose rhyme scheme will be aabb, and then go on to longer poems.

Review Exercises—Poetry

Analy-
ses will
vary.

A. Your teacher may wish to assign a poem for this exercise. Read the poem carefully and then write an analysis of it in which you discuss the poet's awareness, his use of compression, and the form of the poem.

Poems
will
vary.

B. Using free verse or a disciplined form, if it is better suited to your purpose, write a poem on a subject that appeals to you. Strive for imagery that shows your awareness of the world around you and for compression of language.

UNIT SUMMARY

As a beginning writer you should work in the free forms of prose and poetry at the start—the letter, the diary, the informal essay, and free verse. As you sharpen your senses and learn to know yourself and to know and interpret your world, you will find yourself writing more easily and fluently.

The suggestions for creative writing given in this unit are just a beginning. Your own sharpness of observation will determine whether you go on to write better compositions. Your reading, too, will help. Cultivate the practice of asking yourself what techniques the writer used to achieve the desired effects. Then practice. There is no other way to become a good writer.

UNIT REVIEW EXERCISES

DISCUSSION TOPICS   See p. T66.

1. What qualities of a good writer can be developed through personal effort?
2. How do writers get ideas for their poems or stories or essays? How does writing about familiar subjects increase the writer's fluency?

3. How can using forms such as letters, diaries, and essays lead you to use other prose forms?

4. How are the poet and the essayist alike? In what ways are they different?

See p. T66.

5. Discuss the following stanza from Theophile Gautier's "Art." Do you agree or disagree? Why?

> All things are doubly fair
> If patience fashion them
>   And care—
> Verse, enamel, marble, gem.
>
> —*Translation by* GEORGE SANTAYANA

WRITTEN WORK

1. Write an original prose composition. Use one of the forms you studied in this unit or one you investigated as a result of this unit.

2. Write an original poem. You may select the form that you feel would be best suited to your idea and your purpose.

Creative work will vary.

3. Write an essay in which you discuss what you consider to be the best piece of creative writing you have done. Be sure to tell what you feel made it your best. Attach a copy of the original work to your essay.

VOCABULARY

Did you know the meaning of every word in this unit? In the following sentences, some of the words are used in different contexts. Write the numbers 1 to 5 on your paper. After each number write the letter of the word or phrase that could best be substituted for the italicized word in each sentence. Before making your choice, find the word on the page indicated to see how the word is used in this unit.

1. Her eyes *smoldered* with anger. [p. 157]

   b   (*a*) sparkled; (*b*) burned; (*c*) glazed; (*d*) glared

2. Formless ramblings and *reminiscences* are often uninteresting. [p. 161]

   a   (*a*) recollections; (*b*) wanderings; (*c*) mementos; (*d*) memorials

3. There was no *rapport* between the actors and the audience. [p. 161]

   a   (*a*) harmonious relation; (*b*) dramatic relation; (*c*) sincere relation; (*d*) unpleasant relation

4. The more he learns, the more *introspective* Jack seems to become. [p. 163]

   c   (*a*) self-contained; (*b*) assured; (*c*) self-searching; (*d*) prejudiced

5. The author's treatment of the theme was *whimsical*. [p. 166].

   d   (*a*) amusing; (*b*) unusual; (*c*) imagery; (*d*) fanciful

The study of creative writing and the mastery of some of the techniques of writing both prose and poetry will increase the student's awareness of and sensitivity to language and literature.

SPELLING

The following spelling words appeared in the unit or were chosen because they are commonly misspelled. Study these words so that you will be prepared to write them from dictation.

A periodic review of spelling words from previous lessons helps students to retain words studied.

1. smoldered
2. reminiscences
3. rapport
4. introspective
5. whimsical
6. tactile
7. olfactory
8. effusions
9. analytical
10. spontaneity
11. conceived
12. valiant
13. coincidence
14. contemptuous
15. deteriorate
16. incredulous
17. liquefy
18. reconciliation
19. rescind
20. tyrannically

UNIT SELF-TEST

1. Why is it necessary for a writer to "know" himself?
2. List two characteristics of a good subject for creative writing from the author's point of view.
3. Name two advantages of the letter form.
4. What are two disadvantages of the diary form?
5. What is the difference between *seeing* and *interpreting?*
6. How does poetry differ from prose? Rhythm, imagery, compression
7. What is the major characteristic of the *haiku?* Compression
8. What is meant by *compression* in poetry? Understatement
9. What is a quatrain? Four-line stanza
10. Define a couplet. Two successive rhyming lines of poetry

1. One must know himself before he can understand others.
2. Familiar, concrete, manageable.
3. Personal, directed to a known reader, may be limited to a few main topics.
4. May become over-emotional; writing may lack form and discipline.
5. Seeing is perceiving with the eyes; interpreting is perceiving with the mind and explaining in the light of one's judgment and experience.

HANDBOOK

FOR

STUDY AND REFERENCE

KEY TO HANDBOOK

185

The page number following each rule refers not only to the rule but also to the page on which examples may be found. Exercises follow the rules and examples.

Agreement

Capitalization

187

An error marked 46a indicates that students should review agreement of singular pronouns with their antecedents. The Key refers the student to page 308.

188

189

Teachers will find that, with use, the rule numbers will be learned quickly.

Form in Writing

Style in Writing

The same numbers are used to refer to rules found in all the books in Grades 9-12. As new numbers are added for new rules, beginning with Grade 10, those numbers are used consistently in the later texts.

Unit 8

MOUND HIGH SCHOOL WINS

Sentence Skill

The aim in this unit is to present a solid body of information about the English language—its structure and its use—and to create a solid background upon which later studies of linguistics can be based.

As you become more mature, your use of language must also become more mature in order that you may express increasingly complex ideas and relationships. Facility in the use of the tools of language—words, phrases, clauses, and sentences—will enable you to communicate your ideas clearly and effectively.

Effectiveness in the use of spoken and written language depends largely upon your understanding of sentences and upon your skill in building good sentences. In this unit you will study the sentence as a complete single structure and as the sum of its parts. You will study the relationships of the parts of the sentence to each other and to the entire sentence. Through study and practice you will acquire greater skill in using sentences.

Before you begin the study of this unit, take an inventory of your knowledge of sentences by completing the following Check Yourself exercises. Do not look ahead to any of the material in the unit before completing the Check Yourself section.

The nomenclature and the fundamental outline of traditional grammar have been preserved in this unit. At the same time, some of the principles of the new approaches to grammar have been recognized wherever possible.

A. Write the following sentences. Draw one line under each independent clause; enclose each dependent clause in parentheses. Classify each sentence according to its underline{structure} and its underline{function}.

1. underline{Students planning to take scholarship examinations must register their names with the guidance counselor before the end of the week}. Simple, declarative

2. underline{Is it true} (that there are several new scholarships available this year?) Complex, interrogative

Compound-complex, exclamatory
3. underline{How gratifying it is to see the number of students} (who are interested in going to college,) and underline{how good it is to know} (that scholarships will help them to achieve their goals!)

Complex, imperative
4. underline{Plan to get a good night's rest} (before you take the examinations.)

5. underline{Students} (who are successful in the scholarship examinations) underline{can win up to four years' full tuition}. Complex, declarative

B. Write on your paper the simple and compound subjects and predicate verbs and the complements from the following sentences. Underline the subjects once and the predicate verbs twice. Enclose the complements in parentheses. Write whether the verb is transitive (T), complete intransitive (CI), or linking intransitive (LI). Label each complement according to whether it is a direct object (DO), an indirect object (IO), a predicate noun (PN), a predicate pronoun (PP), a predicate adjective (PA), an objective complement (OC), or a retained object (RO).

6. In the Elizabethan theater all the underline{action} of the plays underline{occurred} on an open stage. CI

7. underline{Payment} of a general admission fee underline{gave} (patrons) the (right) to stand in the courtyard around the stage. T, IO, DO

8. The underline{Elizabethans} underline{called} these (spectators) ("groundlings.") T, DO, OC

T, RO
9. Wealthier underline{patrons} underline{were sold} (seats) in the balcony and on the stage.

10. In Shakespeare's plays, underline{ghosts}, underline{witches}, and other supernatural underline{elements} underline{are} (common.) LI, PA

11. Unlike modern audiences, the underline{Elizabethans} underline{accepted} the (idea) of supernatural happenings. T, DO

12. Despite their superstitious beliefs, the underline{Elizabethans} underline{were} cultured (people.) LI, PN

13. Their underline{interest} in and underline{enthusiasm} for poetry and music underline{have} rarely underline{been equaled}. CI

The Check Yourself exercises should be used to discover
how much your students already know about the structure and
the function of sentences. Use them as a guide to the planning of your course and as an incentive in your classes to
master materials that follow.

14. <u>Shakespeare</u> <u>included</u> more than fifty songs in his plays and <u>wrote</u> numerous stage directions requiring musical effects. T, DO, T, DO

15. Of Shakespeare's plays, <u>*The Comedy of Errors*</u> <u>is</u> the only one written without music. LI, PP

C. Write in a column the italicized words in the following sentences. After each word write its part of speech.

16-18. Connie *felt that she* should apologize to Jeanne.
              v. conj. pron.

19-21. During the *week before* examinations, he studied even harder
                  n. prep.
than *before*.
    adv.

22-25. *Well,* I *am* not *certain;* but I think *that* is correct.
    interj. v. adj. pron.

Check your paper as your teacher reads the correct answers. Determine your strengths and weaknesses in the areas of sentence study covered.

1. Structure in Sentences

Sentences are made up of words, each of which has a particular function to perform in the sentence. In some sentences the function of a single word plays a major part in the entire structure; in others the function of the individual word is less important than that of the word group of which it is a part. Sometimes a group of words in one sentence performs the same function as that of a single word.

<u>The basic structure in a sentence is the subject and the predicate.</u> Other important elements are modifiers, complements, connectives, independent elements, and appositives. As you study and learn the various elements of sentences, the functions of words in sentences, and the relationships among the parts of sentences, you will better understand the entire structure of sentences.

A sentence is a word or a group of words conveying a completed thought and, normally, containing a subject and a predicate. [1]

SUBJECTS AND PREDICATES

The simple subject of a sentence is a word or a group of words that names whom or what the sentence is about. [1a]

Eleanor invited us to her party.
Mr. J. Robert Osborne was our guest speaker.

Most English sentences are built around the structure of a noun tied to a verb—the subject-predicate pattern.

The subject-predicate pattern may be inverted, it may be expanded, or part of it may be understood; but the basic structure of English sentences remains the same.

The complete subject of a sentence is the word group that tells whom or what the sentence is about. The most important word in the complete subject is the simple subject.   [1c]

The final decision of the contest judges surprised us.

Impress
upon stu-
dents the
fact that
all the
parts of
a com-
pound sub-
ject re-
late to
the same
verb or
verbs.
In the preceding sentence *decision* is the simple subject. *The final decision of the contest judges* is the complete subject.

When reference is made to the subject of a sentence, the simple subject is usually meant.

A simple sentence or an independent clause may contain a single noun or pronoun used as the subject, or it may contain two or more nouns or pronouns used as parts of the subject. When two or more subjects are used in a sentence and relate to all the verbs in the predicate, the sentence is said to contain a compound subject.

A compound subject contains two or more nouns or pronouns as subjects of a predicate verb. The parts of a compound subject are usually connected by *and, but,* or *or.*   [1e]

Eloise and *he* work on the yearbook and sing in the chorus. (Both Eloise and he work and sing; therefore *Eloise* and *he* are the two parts of the compound subject.)

In imperative sentences the subject frequently is not expressed. The subject of an imperative sentence is *you,* understood.

The subject is understood in a sentence which gives a command or makes a request.   [1i]

Consider all aspects of the problem. [(You) consider]
Leave a number where you can be reached. [(You) leave]

In some sentences the subject is separated from the predicate by a modifying phrase. It is important that you remember that the subject is never a part of such a phrase. If you always ask yourself what or whom the sentence is about, you should have no difficulty in identifying subjects.

Emphasize
this
point.
A phrase may come between the subject and the verb. The subject is never within the phrase.   [1j]

Several *of the team members* were issued new uniforms.
Two *of our athletes* made All-American.

Approach subject recognition from the point of view
of logical meaning.

The predicate verb is probably the most important element in a sentence. The principal idea of almost every sentence is built around the predicate verb. Together, the simple subject of a sentence and the predicate verb make up the basic framework of sentence structure. As you continue your study of this unit, you will find that one line under a word denotes a simple subject, and two lines under a word denotes a predicate verb, unless otherwise indicated.

The predicate verb in a sentence is a word or a group of words that tells what is said about the simple subject.   [1b]

An alert <u>driver</u> usually <u>avoids</u> accidents.

Every <u>organization</u> <u>contributed</u> its quota to the drive.

The complete predicate of a sentence is the word group that tells what is said about the subject of a sentence. The most important word in the complete predicate is the predicate verb.   [1d]

The complete predicate in the following sentence is in italics.

The police <u>authorities</u> *held the suspect for questioning.*

Since more than one assertion may be made about the subject of a sentence, a sentence may contain a compound predicate.

A compound predicate contains two or more predicate verbs.   [1f]

An intelligent <u>listener</u> <u>respects</u> the opinions of others and <u>considers</u> their ideas thoughtfully.

Some sentences contain both compound subjects and compound predicates.

<u>Mr. Larraby</u> and his <u>wife</u> <u>write</u> and <u>produce</u> puppet shows and <u>present</u> them for school audiences.

Students sometimes find it easier to determine the predicate of the sentence and then find the related subject.

The verbs in a compound predicate relate to all parts of the subject.

Since, except for independent elements, all parts of a sentence are directly or indirectly related to the basic framework of the sentence, subject-predicate recognition is particularly important.

DEVELOPING YOUR SKILL

A. Write the following sentences on your paper. Enclose the complete subject of each sentence in parentheses. Underline the simple and compound subjects once.

1. (All <u>books</u> in the library, except reference books) may be borrowed for use at home or in class.
2. (<u>Stuart</u>, <u>Harold</u>, and <u>I</u>) are planning to go to the same university.
3. (The <u>plans</u> of the rest of our friends) are still uncertain.
4. After listening to the speaker, (my <u>friends</u> and <u>I</u>) discussed the problem at length.

(You) 5. Always try to determine a question's exact meaning before giving your answer.

6. (The youngest <u>child</u> in our family) is three years old.
7. (<u>Molasses</u>, in spite of its supposed beneficial effects,) has done nothing to improve his health.
8. (Both the star and her <u>understudy</u>) knew the role perfectly.
9. (<u>You</u>, <u>Bud</u>, and <u>he</u>) are expected to usher at the concert.
10. (The <u>boys</u> on our team and <u>those</u> on the twelfth-grade team) are playing against each other.

Some of your students may be able to complete these exercises after a brief review of the preceding rules. Others will need more intensive study.

B. Copy the following sentences. Draw a vertical line between the complete subject and the complete predicate. Underline the simple and compound subjects once and the predicate verbs twice.

Example: The huge <u>crowd</u> | <u>applauded</u> and <u>cheered</u> the contestants.

1. The <u>directions</u> for the test | <u>were</u> clear and explicit.
2. The traffic <u>policeman</u> | <u>threatened</u> to revoke the careless driver's license.
3. The fireman's insulated <u>suit</u> | <u>protected</u> him from the intense heat.
4. John Philip <u>Sousa</u> | <u>composed</u> many stirring marches.
5. Almost every New England <u>hillside</u> | <u>is</u> ablaze with color in the fall.
6. Remembering our previous experience, <u>we</u> | <u>took</u> a map of the area with us and <u>consulted</u> it frequently.

7. The <u>chairman</u> of the discussion and <u>one</u> of the participants |<u><u>were</u></u> late.
8. <u>One</u> of our assembly speakers |<u><u>lectured</u></u> and <u><u>drew</u></u> charts at the same time.
9. <u>Mr. Henderson</u> |<u>is</u> not in his office today.
10. Bravely concealing her disappointment, my little <u>sister</u> |<u><u>returned</u></u> to her seat after missing the word *aegis*.

Nouns and pronouns   Stress the point made that the subject of a sentence is always a noun or a pronoun.

Only two parts of speech are ever used as subjects in sentences—nouns and pronouns. Remember that <u>if a word is used as the subject of a sentence, it must be either a noun or a pronoun.</u>

Concentrate now on the characteristics and classifications of nouns and pronouns.

A noun is a word that names a person, place, or thing.   [3]

Her *father* is *president* of the largest aircraft *plant* in the *state*.

A pronoun is a word that is used in place of a noun. The noun for which a pronoun is used is the antecedent of the pronoun.   [4]

I received a letter from Alex yesterday. *He* enclosed a snapshot.

In the preceding example sentences, the antecedent of *I* is the name of the speaker; the antecedent of *He* is *Alex*.

The pronoun takes on meaning only as the reader understands who or what the antecedent is.

PERSON, NUMBER, GENDER, AND CASE Since nouns do not change form except to show number and possession, the

Both nouns and pronouns have qualities known as *person, number, gender,* and *case*. These qualities are particularly important to the study of pronouns.

Person is the quality of a noun or a pronoun that indicates the speaker (first person), the person spoken to (second person), or the person or thing spoken about (third person).   [32]

study of person, gender, and case is important primarily to the study of pronouns.

Nouns do not change their form to show person and, except for nouns in direct address, are always third person. Pronouns, however, do change form to show person.

Number is the form of a noun or a pronoun that indicates whether it refers to one person, place, or thing (singular) or to more than one person, place, or thing (plural).   [33]

Nouns and pronouns and related subtopics are presented as topics related to the study of subjects in sentences.

Gender is the quality of a noun or pronoun that indicates whether the noun or pronoun is *masculine, feminine, neuter,* or *common*.   [34]

Students should memorize the personal pronouns in all their forms.

The following table shows the person, number, and gender of the most commonly used pronouns.

	SINGULAR	PLURAL
First Person	I, me, my, mine	we, us, our, ours
Second Person	you, your, yours	you, your, yours
Third Person		
masculine	he, him, his	they, them, their, theirs
feminine	she, her, hers	they, them, their, theirs
neuter	it, its	they, them, their, theirs

Common gender nouns and pronouns are those that may be either masculine or feminine, as *they, them, their, theirs, teacher,* and *friend*.

Case refers to the form a noun or a pronoun takes to show its relationship to other elements in a sentence. There are three cases in English: *nominative, possessive,* and *objective*. (See below.)

DEVELOPING YOUR SKILL   m.=masculine; f.=feminine; n.=neuter; c.=common

Write the following nouns and pronouns on a sheet of paper. Following each, write its person, number, and gender.

3rd; sing.; m.   1. he   6. princesses 3rd; pl.; f.
3rd; sing.; m.,f.,c. 2. cousin   7. mine 1st; sing.; m.,f.
3rd; sing.; n.   3. book   8. lawyer 3rd; sing.; m.,f.,c.
3rd; pl.; m.,f.,c. 4. their   9. stewardess 3rd; sing.; f.
3rd; sing.; f.   5. her   10. yours 2nd; sing., pl.;
                                                          m.,f.,c.

NOMINATIVE CASE   [35]

Nouns and pronouns that are used as subjects are said to be in the nominative case. There are no distinctions in the forms of nominative case nouns; however, personal pronouns, which are direct substitutes for nouns, do have specific nominative case forms.

	SINGULAR	PLURAL
First Person	I	we
Second Person	you	you
Third Person	he, she, it	they

Except for the possessive case, case distinctions in nouns need not be emphasized. However, students should be aware that such distinctions exist.

A noun or a pronoun that is the subject of a verb is in the nominative case. [35a]

> This *sweater* is a beautiful shade of blue.
> *She* has already left for home.
> *Lorraine* and *I* are on the same committee.

Each of the italicized words— nouns and pronouns— is in the nominative case.

DEVELOPING YOUR SKILL

List on a sheet of paper the nouns and pronouns used as subjects in the following sentences. After each word write its person, number, gender, and case. Be prepared to give the reasons for your answers.

1. The old car held up surprisingly well. 3rd, sing., n.
2. Nancy and her sister took turns driving. 3rd, sing., f.; 3rd, sing., f.
3. Mr. Smith and he are both running for the same office. 3rd, sing., m. (both)
4. During last month's cold wave, Stan and I earned money by shoveling driveways. 3rd, sing., m.; 1st, sing., m. or f.
5. Of all my friends, you have proved yourself to be the most loyal. 2nd, sing., m. or f.

All nominative case— subjects.

KINDS OF NOUNS

Nouns fall into two general classifications: *proper nouns* and *common nouns*.

A proper noun is a word that names a particular person, place, or thing. A proper noun is always capitalized. [3a]

> A statue of *Lincoln* done by *Daniel Chester French* dominates the *Lincoln Memorial* in *Washington, D.C.*

A common noun is a word that names any one of a class of persons, places, or things. A common noun is not capitalized. [3b]

> A famous *sculptor* did the *statue* that dominates the *monument* in that *city*.

Nouns are further divided into three classifications: *abstract, concrete,* and *collective* nouns.

An abstract noun names an idea, a quality, or an action. [3c]

> *Freedom* and *equality* are the bases on which a *democracy* is built.
> Their *friendship* had begun in grammar school.
> *Skiing* is my favorite sport.

The referent of an abstract noun does not exist in the physical world.

The refer-
ent of a
concrete
noun ex-
ists in
the physi-
cal world.

A concrete noun names an object.   [3d]

The term *concrete* applies to nouns whose referents exist in the physical world.

The *jars* of *fruit* and *vegetables* were stored in the *cupboard*.

The completed *manuscript* was left on the *desk*.

A collective noun names a group, or a collection, of persons or things that is regarded as a single unit.   [3e]

The *crowd* surged through the streets.

The *fleet* weighed anchor yesterday.

 DEVELOPING YOUR SKILL

A. Head three columns on your paper *Abstract, Concrete,* and *Collective.*
List the following nouns in the appropriate columns.

Concrete	1. doctor	11. rug	Concrete
Concrete	2. merry-go-round	12. friendship	Abstract
Abstract	3. evil	13. sandals	Concrete
Collective	4. committee	14. crew	Collective
Abstract	5. anger	15. coconut	Concrete
Abstract	6. manufacturing	16. culture	Abstract
Abstract	7. life	17. poodle	Concrete
Abstract	8. responsibility	18. enmity	Abstract
Collective	9. majority	19. salt	Concrete
Abstract	10. wealth	20. troops	Collective

B. Head two columns on your paper *Proper Nouns* and *Common Nouns.*
See pp. T66-T67. List each noun in the following sentences under the appropriate heading and label each common noun *abstract, concrete,* or *collective.*

1. *Equality* suggests different ideas to different people.
2. We shall need ten pounds of potatoes if we are to have enough
   salad for the entire group.
3. Frank Lloyd Wright designed the Guggenheim Museum in New
   York City.
4. The museum, which was founded by Solomon R. Guggenheim,
   houses an outstanding collection of works of art by modern painters, sculptors, and other artists.
5. Counseling and testing are the two primary methods used in the
   field of guidance to help students solve problems.

KINDS OF PRONOUNS [38]

Pronouns are classified according to their form and function as *personal, relative, interrogative, demonstrative, intensive, reflexive, indefinite,* and *reciprocal.* Although not all pronouns are used as subjects, the various kinds and forms of pronouns are discussed together in this part of the unit.

A personal pronoun is a direct substitute for a noun. The form of a personal pronoun usually indicates its person, number, gender, and case.

[38a]

Study the following table, which contains all the forms of the personal pronouns:

You may wish to have students include this table in their notebooks.

PERSON	NOMINATIVE	POSSESSIVE	OBJECTIVE
		SINGULAR	
First	I	my, mine	me
Second	you	your, yours	you
Third	he, she, it	his, her, hers, its	him, her, it
		PLURAL	
First	we	our, ours	us
Second	you	your, yours	you
Third	they	their, theirs	them

A relative pronoun is a pronoun that introduces a dependent clause.

[38b]

A relative pronoun connects or relates a dependent clause to the antecedent of the pronoun. The most common relative pronouns are *who, which,* and *that.* Other relative pronouns include *whoever, whichever,* and *whatever. Who* is used to refer to persons only. *Which* is used to refer to inanimate objects and animals (things) and to persons considered as a group. *That* may be used to refer either to persons or to things.

The man *who* spoke to us was a colonel in World War II.
The other route, *which* we should have taken, is much shorter.
Our debate team, *which* formed only last year, won the city championship.
The sweaters *that* we chose will be here on Friday.
She is the pianist *that* I told you about.

The tendency in current usage is to use <u>which</u> to introduce nonrestrictive clauses and <u>that</u> to introduce restrictive clauses.

Emphasize the difference between who and which
as relative pronouns and as interrogative pronouns.
202   *Sentence Skill*

An interrogative pronoun is a pronoun that introduces a question. [38c]

The most common interrogative pronouns are *who, which,* and *what. Whoever, whichever,* and *whatever* are occasionally used as interrogative pronouns.

> *Who* answered the telephone when you called?
> *Which* of these designs do you prefer?
> *What* is the purpose of the meeting?

A demonstrative pronoun is a pronoun that points out and identifies.
[38d]

Distin-
guish
between
the de-
monstra-
tives as
pronouns
and as
modifiers.

The demonstrative pronouns are *this, that, these,* and *those.* Demonstrative pronouns have number but do not have gender or case. *This, that, these,* and *those* may also be used as modifiers. Do not confuse the two uses of these words. If they are used as subjects or have any of the other functions of nouns, *this, that, these,* and *those* are pronouns; if they modify nouns or pronouns, they are adjectives.

> *This* is my book. (*This* is the subject; therefore it is a pronoun.)
> *This* book is mine. (*This* modifies the noun *book;* therefore it is an adjective.)
> *These* are our new neighbors. (Pronoun)
> *These* people have just moved in. (Adjective)

An intensive pronoun is a pronoun that is used for emphasis.   [38e]

A reflexive pronoun is a pronoun that is used to refer to the subject of the sentence.   [38f]

Both intensive and reflexive pronouns have the same form. They are composed of the personal pronouns plus *self* or *selves: myself, yourself, himself, herself, itself, ourselves, yourselves, themselves.* Intensive and reflexive pronouns are sometimes called *compound personal pronouns.*

> He *himself* decided to do the job. (Intensive)
> She made *herself* think clearly. (Reflexive)

An indefinite pronoun is a pronoun that refers to a person, place, or thing generally rather than specifically. Indefinite pronouns are less exact in meaning than are the other pronouns.   [38g]

You may wish to correlate the teaching of rules 38e
and 38f with the teaching of rules 39e and 39f on page
311.

Among the most commonly used indefinite pronouns are the following: Stress

all	both	few	one
another	each	many	several
any	either	neither	some
anybody	everybody	nobody	somebody
anyone	everyone	none	someone
anything	everything	nothing	something

function as being the fac- tor that deter- mines the part of speech of a word.

Many of the indefinite pronouns may also be used as adjectives. Be sure you determine the function of the word in the sentence before you decide what part of speech it is.

Several of us are planning a trip to Washington. (Pronoun)

The trip will take *several* days. (Adjective)

A reciprocal pronoun is a pronoun that indicates persons, places, or things mutually affected by the action suggested by the verb. There are only two reciprocal pronouns in English: *each other* and *one another*.   [38h]

In formal writing some writers use *each other* to refer to two persons, places, or things and *one another* to refer to more than two. In general usage the tendency is to use *each other* for all situations.

Richard and Tom have known *each other* all their lives.

All the members of our family are considerate of *one another*.

> DEVELOPING YOUR SKILL

List the pronouns in the following sentences. After each, indicate its classification by using the numbers from the following key:

1. personal   5. intensive
2. relative   6. reflexive
3. interrogative   7. indefinite
4. demonstrative   8. reciprocal

1. Unless everyone[7] agrees to the plan that[1] we[1] have presented, we[1] can do nothing[7].
2. Our[1] club is the only one[7] in the area that[2] is affiliated with the national organization.
3. Jerry himself[5] could not believe what[2] that[4] might mean to him[1].
4. What[3], if anything[7], can they[1] do to help themselves[6]?
5. The team members shouted encouragement to one another[8] as they[1] fought for what[2] was to be the decisive point for their[1] side.
6. Several[2] of my[1] teachers have announced that they[1] will give us[1] tests on Friday.

7. Chopin himself could not have played the waltz better than you did.
8. What nobody anticipated was that she would develop laryngitis on the night of her recital.
9. What prompted you to leave these here where someone might trip over them?
10. Steve convinced himself that he could do it if he made the effort.

Verbs and verb phrases

Only one part of speech is ever used as the predicate of a sentence— a verb.

A verb is a word that expresses action or state of being.   [2]

Carole *mailed* her application last month. (Action)
She *is* anxious to complete her plans. (Being)

A predicate verb may be composed of more than one verb. *Auxiliary verbs* are often used with other verbs to express various shades of meaning. The most common auxiliary verbs are *shall, should, will, would, may, might, can, must, do, did,* and all forms of *be* and *have.* When auxiliary verbs are used in combination with other verbs, the two or more verbs used together are called a *verb phrase.*

Stress the
point
that a
phrase
functions
as a single
part of
speech.

A phrase is a group of related words that does not have a subject and a predicate. A phrase performs the function of a single part of speech. [13]

A verb phrase is a phrase that contains a main verb and one or more auxiliary verbs.   [14]

The verb phrases in the following sentences are in italics.

Mr. Howard *has developed* a new research technique.
This book *was written* by a young American author.
Your trip *must have seemed* endless.

In many sentences the parts of a verb phrase are separated by another word.

The subject frequently separates parts of the verb phrase in a question.
[1h]

Is he planning to attend the conference?
How many tickets shall we need for the dance?

Verb phrases are sometimes split by words such as *not, never, ever, seldom,* and *often.* Remember, particularly, that *not* is never a part of a

When teaching verb phrases, demonstrate the loss of
meaning when part of the phrase is omitted.

Structure in Sentences   205

verb phrase, even when it is written as a contraction *(n't)*. The verb phrases in the following sentences are in italics.

>June *has* not yet *completed* the assignment.
>
>A black stallion *was* often *seen* at the head of the wild herd.
>
>That plan *does*n't *seem* feasible to me, and I *shall* not *vote* for it.

 DEVELOPING YOUR SKILL

List on your paper the verbs and verb phrases in the following sentences. Label each according to whether it shows *action* or *being*.

Action   1. The Raymonds <u>toured</u> Europe last summer.
Action   2. They <u>found</u> life there very different from life in the United States.
Action   3. They <u>enjoyed</u> their trip but <u>were</u> happy to return home. Being
Action   4. Arlene <u>said</u> that she <u>thinks</u> the Swiss Alps <u>are</u> the most beautiful sight she <u>has</u> ever <u>seen</u>. Action, Being, Action
Action   5. My parents <u>have promised</u> me a trip to Europe when I <u>am</u> twenty-one. Being
Action   6. <u>Have</u> you ever <u>considered</u> taking a bicycle tour?
Being   7. Such tours <u>are becoming</u> increasingly popular.
Action   8. How <u>did</u> you <u>travel</u> when you <u>went</u> to the West Coast last year?
Action   9. Why <u>don</u>'t you <u>apply</u> for a summer job on one of the cruise ships?
Being   10. Jerry <u>was</u> a cabin boy on a ship that <u>cruised</u> around the Mediterranean area last summer. Action

PRINCIPAL PARTS OF VERBS

The principal parts of a verb are the *present*, the *past*, and the *past participle*.   [26]

Another important part of a verb is the *present participle*. The present participle is the *-ing* form of the verb, as *seeing*.

The principal parts of a regular verb are formed by adding *d* or *ed* to the first principal part to form the past and the past participle forms.   [26a]

PRESENT	PAST	PAST PARTICIPLE
plant	planted	planted
clean	cleaned	cleaned

The principal parts of irregular verbs are formed in different ways. The pronunciation of a vowel sound may be changed, or the spelling of the second and third principal parts may be different from the spelling of the first principal part.   [26b]

Present	Past	Past Participle	Present	Past	Past Participle
arise	arose	arisen	lend	lent	lent
awake	awoke	awaked	let	let	let
be	was	been	lie	lay	lain
bear	bore	borne	lose	lost	lost
begin	began	begun	mean	meant	meant
bend	bent	bent	raise	raised	raised
bid	bade	bidden	ride	rode	ridden
bite	bit	bitten	ring	rang	rung
blow	blew	blown	rise	rose	risen
bring	brought	brought	run	ran	run
burst	burst	burst	say	said	said
buy	bought	bought	set	set	set
catch	caught	caught	shake	shook	shaken
choose	chose	chosen	shoot	shot	shot
cling	clung	clung	show	showed	shown
come	came	come	shrink	shrank	shrunk
creep	crept	crept	sing	sang	sung
dig	dug	dug	sink	sank	sunk
do	did	done	sit	sat	sat
draw	drew	drawn	slay	slew	slain
drink	drank	drunk	speak	spoke	spoken
drive	drove	driven	spin	spun	spun
eat	ate	eaten	steal	stole	stolen
fall	fell	fallen	sting	stung	stung
fight	fought	fought	strew	strewed	strewed
forget	forgot	forgotten	strive	strove	striven
forsake	forsook	forsaken	swear	swore	sworn
freeze	froze	frozen	swim	swam	swum
get	got	got, gotten	swing	swung	swung
give	gave	given	take	took	taken
go	went	gone	teach	taught	taught
grow	grew	grown	tear	tore	torn
hang	hanged	hanged	throw	threw	thrown
hang	hung	hung	tread	trod	trodden
hide	hid	hidden	wake	waked	waked
know	knew	known	wear	wore	worn
lay	laid	laid	weave	wove	woven
learn	learned	learned	wring	wrung	wrung
leave	left	left	write	wrote	written

Oral practice will prove helpful. Students must hear, as well as see, the correct forms. You may wish to have your students practice giving sentences orally in which the verb forms listed above are used.

DEVELOPING YOUR SKILL

A. Divide a sheet of paper into three columns headed *Present, Past,* and *Past Participle.* As each student, in turn, gives one form of a verb, write that form in the appropriate column and then fill in the other two principal parts. For example, if a student says *went,* write *went* under the heading *Past* and then write *go* and *gone* under *Present* and *Past Participle,* respectively. Answers will depend upon verbs chosen.

B. Select two of the verbs on your list and write three sentences for each verb, using a different principal part in each sentence. Sentences will vary.

Exercise A may also be used for oral practice.

TENSE

Tense is the time expressed by a verb. [27]

There are six verb tenses in English: *present, past, future, present perfect, past perfect,* and *future perfect.* The principal parts of a verb are used as the basis for the formation of tenses. The present form is the basis for the present and future tenses; the past, for the past tense; and the past participle, for the three perfect tenses. The following table shows how the six verb tenses are formed:

Present tense = Present
Past tense = Past
Future tense = Present + *shall* or *will*
Present perfect tense = Past participle + *have* or *has*
Past perfect tense = Past participle + *had*
Future perfect tense = Past participle + *shall have* or *will have*

You may wish to have students include this table in their notebooks.

Actually, there are only a few points you must remember to help you overcome some common problems with verb tenses. The names of the tenses give you clues to their forms if you will remember the following:

1. The present tense always adds *s* to the third person singular.

2. The word *future* in the name of a tense means that you must use the auxiliary *shall* or *will.*

3. The word *perfect* in the name of a tense means that you must use some form of the auxiliary *have* with the past participle of the main verb. If, for example, you are asked for the future perfect tense of *go* in the third person singular, masculine gender, work out the form step by step, starting with the last items given. *Third person* must be *he, she, it,* or *they; singular* narrows the choice to *he, she,* or *it; masculine gender*

You may have to distinguish between *s* added to a noun to form a plural and *s* added to a verb to form the third person singular, present tense.

Emphasize the fact that the present, past, and future
forms of <u>have</u> are used in the formation of the perfect
tenses.
208   *Sentence Skill*

limits it to *he. Perfect* tells you to use *gone* with a form of *have*. The
future form of *have* in the third person is *will have*. Therefore, the form
you want is *he will have gone.*

The following explanation will help you understand the meaning and
use of each of the tenses:

The *present* tense expresses an action going on at the present time
or a habitual action.

He *hears* me now.
I always *eat* lunch in the cafeteria.

The *past* tense expresses an action completed in the past.

We *heard* his lecture last night.

You may
wish to
teach rule
27a when
you teach
the future
tense.

The *future* tense expresses an action that will occur at some time
in the future.

I *shall hear* the radio broadcast of the concert tomorrow.

The *present perfect* tense expresses (1) an action begun in the past
and extending to the present, (2) an action begun in the past and
completed at the time of speaking, or (3) a habitual or repeated action
carried out at no definite time in the past.

We *have lived* here for three years.
I *have heard* him perform.
I *have read* that book three times.

The *past perfect* tense expresses a past action completed before another indicated time in the past.

By the time we arrived, I *had heard* the entire story.

The *future perfect* tense expresses an action that will have been
completed before an indicated time in the future.

By the end of the year, we *shall have read* three novels and two
full-length plays.

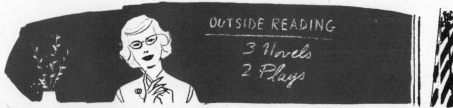

Impress upon students the fact that the past participle
must always be used with an auxiliary when the participle
is used as a verb.

A complete list of all the forms of a verb in all its tenses is called a *conjugation*. See the conjugation of the verb *see* on pages 216 to 219. An abbreviated method of conjugating a verb is to give a *synopsis* of the verb. A synopsis is a listing of a verb in one particular person and number for each of the six tenses. The following is a synopsis of *drive* in the third person singular, masculine gender.

Present	He drives
Past	He drove
Future	He will drive
Present Perfect	He has driven
Past Perfect	He had driven
Future Perfect	He will have driven

In addition to the six simple forms illustrated, English uses two expanded verb forms: *progressive* and *emphatic*. The progressive forms in all tenses show continuing action. They are formed with the auxiliary *be* and the present participle of the main verb. The emphatic forms, used for emphasis, in negative statements, and in questions, are made by using *do, does,* or *did* with the first principal part of the main verb. Emphatic forms are used only in the present and past tenses.

Stress this point.

Progressive	I *am working* very hard.
Emphatic	I *do think* that is important.
	He *does* not *think* he can attend.

> DEVELOPING YOUR SKILL

A. Write the numbers 1 to 10 on a sheet of paper. After each number write the correct form of the verb in parentheses.

1. By the time I (seen, saw) him I (forgot, had forgotten) the message.
2. The books have (laid, lain) on the desk for several weeks.
3. Has the bell (rung, rang) yet?
4. She said that he had (chose, chosen) wisely.
5. By next June I shall have (began, begun) my summer project.
6. He has (swum, swam) eight lengths of the pool.
7. Have the children (drank, drunk) all their milk?
8. He (run, ran) the motor for a few minutes before driving off.
9. Harold has (broke, broken) his arm.
10. They sat around the campfire and (sung, sang) songs.

If students can give synopses of both regular and irregular verbs, they will have demonstrated their mastery of tense forms.

B. Write sentences using the verb forms indicated in the following list.

See
bottom
margin.

1. *do*—past tense, third person, singular, feminine
2. *buy*—past tense, second person, plural, emphatic form
3. *show*—future perfect tense, first person, plural
4. *catch*—present tense, third person plural, progressive form
5. *grow*—future tense, third person singular, neuter
6. *wear*—present perfect tense, first person, singular, progressive form
7. *fall*—past perfect tense, third person, singular, neuter
8. *go*—present tense, third person, singular, masculine
9. *forget*—past perfect tense, second person, singular
10. *swing*—past tense, first person, singular

KINDS OF VERBS

The use of an arrow to indicate the passing of an action to a noun or pronoun often makes the idea of the transitive verb clearer to students.

Verbs are classified as *transitive* or *intransitive*.

A transitive verb is a verb that passes an action to a noun or a pronoun.

Subject + verb ———→ object *or* subject ←—— verb   [28]

A transitive verb must be an action verb that passes its action to a receiver. It is usually followed by a direct object, a noun or pronoun that completes a verb and receives the action of the verb. Transitive verbs may pass their action to the subject of the sentence rather than to a direct object.

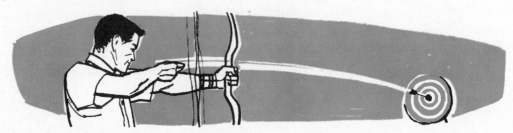

His shot *hit* the target. (The direct object *target* receives the action of hitting.) Subject + verb ———→ object

All the food *had been eaten.* (The subject *food* receives the action of eating.) Subject ←—— verb

An intransitive verb may be an action verb or a verb of being. Since the word *intransitive* means "not transitive," all verbs that do not transfer their action to a noun or pronoun must be intransitive.

B. 1. she did; 2. you did buy; 3. we shall have shown;
4. they are catching; 5. it will grow; 6. I have been
wearing; 7. it had fallen; 8. he goes; 9. you had forgotten; 10. I swung

An intransitive verb is a verb that does not pass an action to a noun or a pronoun. [30]

There are two kinds of intransitive verbs: *complete intransitive* and *linking intransitive*.

A complete intransitive verb is an action verb that is complete in itself. It does not pass an action to a noun or a pronoun. [30a]

In each of the following sentences the action of the verb is complete in itself. The verbs are, therefore, complete intransitive verbs.

> The ship *sank* slowly.
> A crowd *collected* at the scene of the accident.

A linking intransitive verb shows the relationship of the subject to a noun, pronoun, or adjective in the predicate. Since both transitive and linking intransitive verbs are completed by other words (complements), they are often confused. Remember that the complement of a transitive verb is a direct object; the complement of a linking verb is a predicate noun, pronoun, or adjective.

Review subject, predicate verb, and complement.

A linking intransitive verb is a verb that links, or joins, a predicate noun, a predicate pronoun, or a predicate adjective to the subject of the sentence. [30b]

> The barometer *is* an *instrument* for measuring atmospheric pressure. (*Is* links the predicate noun *instrument* to the subject *barometer*.)
> The girl in the play *was she*. (*Was* links the predicate pronoun *she* to the subject *girl*.)
> The dahlias *grew* unusually *tall*. (*Grew* links the predicate adjective *tall* to the subject *dahlias*.)

The most common linking verb is *be* in its various forms: *be, am, is, are, was, were, been, have been, had been,* etc. Since *be* may be an auxiliary verb as well as a main verb, you must be certain that the form of *be* used in a sentence is a main verb in order for it to be a linking verb.

> Kim *has been* angry all day. (*Has been* is a linking verb completed by the predicate adjective *angry.*)
> Kim *has been sulking* all day. (*Has been sulking* is a complete intransitive verb. *Sulking* is the main verb; *has* and *been* are auxiliary verbs.)

Students should memorize all the forms of the verb be to aid them in recognizing the most common of the linking verbs.

Other commonly used linking verbs include the various forms of *seem, become, appear, remain, grow, sound, feel, taste,* and *smell.*

Many verbs may be used either transitively or intransitively. If an action verb is completed by a direct object or passes its action to the subject, it is used transitively; if it is complete in itself, the verb is used intransitively.

Mr. Franklin *ran* his office efficiently. (Transitive)

She *ran* to the window to see what had happened. (Intransitive)

 DEVELOPING YOUR SKILL

A. List on a sheet of paper the verbs in the following sentences. After each verb write whether it is *transitive, complete intransitive,* or *linking intransitive.* If the verb has a complement, write the complement and label it *direct object, predicate noun, predicate pronoun,* or *predicate adjective.* Underscore indicates verb; parentheses indicate complement.

LI, PA 1. He always seems(amiable.)

T, DO 2. Unfortunately, many people don't practice good(manners)at home.

T, DO 3. Mary packed an unusually large picnic(lunch)for us all.

CI 4. We slept soundly in spite of the storm.

T 5. A medal for heroism is awarded at the firemen's ball.

CI 6. Have you been invited to Pat's wedding reception?

LI, PN 7. Corrine and I have remained good(friends)despite our differences of opinion.

LI, PA 8. Everybody has been (anxious)about the results of the examination.

T, DO 9. By the end of next week, Tom will have completed his research (paper.)

CI 10. The supplies had been left at the last camping spot.

B. Write fifteen sentences, five of which contain transitive verbs; five, complete intransitive verbs; and five, linking intransitive verbs.

VOICE AND MOOD

Transitive verbs are further classified as to *voice,* the distinction in the form of a verb to indicate whether the subject performs the action or receives the action.

Voice indicates whether the subject of a sentence completes the action or receives the action of a verb. Only transitive verbs have voice. [29]

There are two voices—*active* and *passive.*

A verb is in the active voice if a direct object is the receiver of its action. [29a]

A verb is in the passive voice if its subject is the receiver of its action. [29b]

The mechanics *repaired* the motor. (Active voice)
The motor *was repaired* by the mechanics. (Passive voice)

The passive voice of a verb is formed by adding forms of the verb *be* to the past participle of a verb. The tense is shown in the form of the auxiliary. Study the following synopsis of *know* in the first person singular, active and passive voices. Notice particularly the logical progression of the forms of the auxiliary in the passive voice.

	ACTIVE VOICE	PASSIVE VOICE
Present	I know	I *am* known
Past	I knew	I *was* known
Future	I shall know	I *shall be* known
Present Future	I have known	I *have been* known
Past Perfect	I had known	I *had been* known
Future Perfect	I shall have known	I *shall have been* known

In most sentences active verbs are more natural than passive verbs and lend greater force to the writing. Compare the following sentences:

All the costumes for the play *were designed* by me. (Passive voice)
I *designed* all the costumes for the play. (Active voice)

The first sentence, which contains a passive verb, sounds rather stilted and awkward; the second, which contains an active verb, has vigor and naturalness. Notice that the object of the preposition in the first sentence *(me)* becomes the subject of the verb in the second sentence *(I).*

The use of the passive voice should be natural to the situation.

Sentence Skill

There are, however, some situations in which the passive voice is preferred to the active voice. If you wish to emphasize the receiver of the action rather than the doer, use the passive voice.

Mr. Donaldson *chose* the selections for the program. (Active voice— the emphasis is on *Mr. Donaldson,* the doer.)

The selections for the program *were chosen* by Mr. Donaldson. (Passive voice—the emphasis is on *selections,* the receiver of the action.)

If the doer is unknown, unnamed, or obvious, use the passive voice.

The new highway *was completed* last year.
That model *has been discontinued.*
Mr. Harrison *was elected* mayor of his town.

When determining whether to use the active or the passive voice in your writing, decide what the emphasis is to be and use the verb form that will make your writing clear and natural.

Both transitive and intransitive verbs have *mood.* Mood shows the state of mind of the speaker or the speaker's intention.

The mood of a verb shows the mood or manner in which the speaker thinks of the action. [29c]

There are three moods in English: *indicative, imperative,* and *subjunctive.*

A verb in the indicative mood states a fact or asks a question. [29d]

The politician *made* an inflammatory speech.
What *was* his topic?

A verb in the imperative mood expresses a command or makes a request. [29e]

Leave the table at once.
Help me put up the chairs for the meeting.

A verb in the subjunctive mood expresses a condition contrary to fact or a wish. [29f]

If I *were you,* I should study harder. (*But I am not you* is implied; the statement expresses a condition contrary to fact.)
I wish I *were* there. (Wish)

Although it is true that many clauses requiring the subjunctive mood begin with *if,* do not assume that all *if* clauses require a subjunctive.

If she *was* absent, she must have been ill. (The speaker is willing to accept the fact that she was absent.)

If he *was* angry, he probably decided to walk home. (The speaker accepts the idea that he probably was angry.)

There is very little difference between the forms of the indicative mood and the subjunctive mood (see the complete conjugation on pages 216 to 219 except for the third person singular, which does not add *s* in the subjunctive mood, and the present and past of the verb *be* in the subjunctive mood. Learn to recognize the subjunctive forms of the verb *be*.

Distinguish between the situations illustrated here and the use of the subjunctive to express condition contrary to fact.

PRESENT INDICATIVE		PRESENT SUBJUNCTIVE	
I am	we are	(if) I be	(if) we be
you are	you are	(if) you be	(if) you be
he, she, it is	they are	(if) he, she, it be	(if) they be

PAST INDICATIVE		PAST SUBJUNCTIVE	
I was	we were	(if) I were	(if) we were
you were	you were	(if) you were	(if) you were
he, she, it was	they were	(if) he, she, it were	(if) they were

Notice that *be* is used with all persons in the present subjunctive of the verb *be,* and *were* is used with all persons in the past subjunctive.

Use the subjunctive in clauses beginning with *that* and expressing necessity, mild command, or a parliamentary motion. [29g]

It is essential that he *be present* when we discuss the matter.
I insist that he *make* his position clear.
I move that the matter *be referred* to committee.

Use the subjunctive were after as though or as if to express doubt or uncertainty. [29h]

She acted as though she *were* completely indifferent to the outcome.
He acts as if he *were* the only one concerned about her.

The following is a complete conjugation of the verb *see.* The first form given is the *simple* form; the second, the *progressive* form, and the third, the *emphatic* form. Not all tenses have emphatic and progressive forms.

Conjugation of the Verb *To See*

Principal Parts: see   saw   seen

INDICATIVE MOOD, ACTIVE VOICE

PERSON	SINGULAR	PLURAL

PRESENT TENSE

First	I see, am seeing, do see	we see, are seeing, do see
Second	you see, are seeing, do see	you see, are seeing, do see
Third	he, she, it sees, is seeing, does see	they see, are seeing, do see

PAST TENSE

First	I saw, was seeing, did see	we saw, were seeing, did see
Second	you saw, were seeing, did see	you saw, were seeing, did see
Third	he, she, it saw, was seeing, did see	they saw, were seeing, did see

FUTURE TENSE

First	I shall see, shall be seeing	we shall see, shall be seeing
Second	you will see, will be seeing	you will see, will be seeing
Third	he, she, it will see, will be seeing	they will see, will be seeing

PRESENT PERFECT TENSE

First	I have seen, have been seeing	we have seen, have been seeing
Second	you have seen, have been seeing	you have seen, have been seeing
Third	he, she, it has seen, has been seeing	they have seen, have been seeing

PAST PERFECT TENSE

First	I had seen, had been seeing	we had seen, had been seeing
Second	you had seen, had been seeing	you had seen, had been seeing
Third	he, she, it had seen, had been seeing	they had seen, had been seeing

Students of superior ability should understand the
shall-will distinction. You may wish to point out the
fact that current informal usage sanctions the use of
will in all persons.

FUTURE PERFECT TENSE

First	I shall have seen, shall have been seeing	we shall have seen, shall have been seeing
Second	you will have seen, will have been seeing	you will have seen, will have been seeing
Third	he, she, it will have seen, will have been seeing	they will have seen, will have been seeing

INDICATIVE MOOD, PASSIVE VOICE

PRESENT TENSE

First	I am seen, am being seen	we are seen, are being seen
Second	you are seen, are being seen	you are seen, are being seen
Third	he, she, it is seen, is being seen	they are seen, are being seen

PAST TENSE

First	I was seen, was being seen	we were seen, were being seen
Second	you were seen, were being seen	you were seen, were being seen
Third	he, she, it was seen, was being seen	they were seen, were being seen

FUTURE TENSE

First	I shall be seen, shall be being seen	we shall be seen, shall be being seen
Second	you will be seen, will be being seen	you will be seen, will be being seen
Third	he, she, it will be seen, will be being seen	they will be seen, will be being seen

PRESENT PERFECT TENSE

First	I have been seen	we have been seen
Second	you have been seen	you have been seen
Third	he, she, it has been seen	they have been seen

PAST PERFECT TENSE

First	I had been seen	we had been seen
Second	you had been seen	you had been seen
Third	he, she, it had been seen	they had been seen

Re-emphasize the logical progression of auxiliaries through all the tenses.

FUTURE PERFECT TENSE

First	I shall have been seen	we shall have been seen
Second	you will have been seen	you will have been seen
Third	he, she, it will have been seen	they will have been seen

IMPERATIVE MOOD

Active Voice
(you) see

Passive Voice
(you) be seen

SUBJUNCTIVE MOOD, ACTIVE VOICE

PERSON	SINGULAR	PLURAL

PRESENT TENSE

First	(if) I see	(if) we see
Second	(if) you see	(if) you see
Third	(if) he, she, it see	(if) they see

PAST TENSE

First	(if) I saw	(if) we saw
Second	(if) you saw	(if) you saw
Third	(if) he, she, it saw	(if) they saw

PRESENT PERFECT TENSE

First	(if) I have seen	(if) we have seen
Second	(if) you have seen	(if) you have seen
Third	(if) he, she, it have seen	(if) they have seen

PAST PERFECT TENSE

First	(if) I had seen	(if) we had seen
Second	(if) you had seen	(if) you had seen
Third	(if) he, she, it, had seen	(if) they had seen

SUBJUNCTIVE MOOD, PASSIVE VOICE

PRESENT TENSE

First	(if) I be seen	(if) we be seen
Second	(if) you be seen	(if) you be seen
Third	(if) he, she, it be seen	(if) they be seen

Point out the brevity of the imperative mood and its restriction to sentences of command or request.

PAST TENSE

First	(if) I were seen	(if) we were seen
Second	(if) you were seen	(if) you were seen
Third	(if) he, she, it were seen	(if) they were seen

PRESENT PERFECT TENSE

First	(if) I have been seen	(if) we have been seen
Second	(if) you have been seen	(if) you have been seen
Third	(if) he, she, it have been seen	(if) they have been seen

PAST PERFECT TENSE

First	(if) I had been seen	(if) we had been seen
Second	(if) you had been seen	(if) you had been seen
Third	(if) he, she, it had been seen	(if) they had been seen

The form *(if) I should see* is used in place of the future subjunctive. The subjunctive is used primarily in the present and past tenses.

Call students' attention to this note.

DEVELOPING YOUR SKILL

A. Rewrite the following sentences, changing any verbs that are in the passive voice to the active voice.

1. By the time Mark and Ron arrived to help us, all the work had been finished by Jim and me.   Jim and I had finished
2. Marcia and her sister were seen by me at the movies last night.   I saw
3. I am glad to know that I am considered a friend by you.   you consider me
4. After careful consideration the profession of electrical engineering has been chosen by Kurt.   Kurt has chosen
5. Beth's plans were suddenly announced by her at the dinner table.
   Beth suddenly announced

Students should recognize the increased smoothness and naturalness of the sentences in the exercise above when the verbs are restated in the active voice.

B. Correct any errors in the mood of verbs in the following sentences. If the sentence is correct write *Correct* after the appropriate number on your paper; if the sentence is incorrect, rewrite it correctly.

Correct   1. Even though I was annoyed, I held my tongue.
call   2. It is imperative that he ~~calls~~ me as soon as he returns.
were   3. If it ~~was~~ up to me, I should grant you permission.
Correct   4. If that was his only goal, he has succeeded.
be   5. I move that the meeting ~~is~~ postponed until next week.
Correct   6. If he is so talented, why don't you ask him to perform in the student show?
were   7. If I ~~was~~ you, I wouldn't repeat that rumor.
were   8. As the boat pulled away from the dock, Gerda felt as if she ~~was~~ never going to see her homeland again.
seems   9. If the plot ~~seem~~ rather complicated, remember that most murder mysteries are deliberately written in this style.
were   10. How I wish I ~~was~~ going with you.

C. Write five sentences in which you use active voice verbs and five in which you use verbs in the passive voice. Be prepared to explain why each voice is suited to the situations in which you used it. Sentences will vary.

Diagraming subjects and predicates

Diagraming is a mechanical device to help you analyze sentences. A sentence diagram aids you in identifying the parts of sentences and in seeing the relationships among the parts of sentences.

Since the simple subject and the predicate verb are the basic structures in a sentence, they should always be the first elements diagramed. Both the simple subject and the predicate verb are diagramed on a horizontal line called the *base line*. They are separated by a short vertical line that cuts through the base line. The simple subject always appears to the left of the vertical line; the predicate verb, to the right of the vertical line.

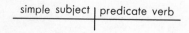

simple subject | predicate verb

Aunt Mary visited us.

Aunt Mary | visited

Diagraming is an aid to illustrating the patterns of sentences. It should never be an end in itself.

The understood *you* in an imperative sentence is diagramed in parentheses in the position of the subject.

Wait for me.

```
(You) | Wait
      |
```

Compound subjects and predicates are diagramed on parallel lines joined by perpendicular dashes or dotted lines. The word that connects the compound parts is written along the broken line.

Ellen and I bought and prepared the food.

DEVELOPING YOUR SKILL See p. T67.

Diagram the simple and compound subjects and predicate verbs in the following sentences.

1. I apparently misinterpreted the story.
2. The officers of the company congratulated the winner and presented him with a check.
3. After only two years in the business, Mr. Webster and his partner decided to expand their interests.
4. The mailman pushed the letters through the slot in the door and left the package on the porch.
5. Stop and think about that more carefully.
6. Everyone in school has been given a copy of the new regulations.
7. Porches, garages, and even fireplaces have become available with prefabricated houses.
8. Don't accept advertising claims blindly.
9. Charles quickly but legibly signed his name to the card.
10. The peoples of the world have not yet learned to live together peacefully.

If you do not teach diagraming, you may wish to have students underscore the subjects and predicate verbs in the exercise above.

MODIFIERS

Modifiers are words that make the meaning of other words more exact by describing or limiting them. There are only two kinds of words that modify—adjectives and adverbs. Any word, phrase, or clause that modifies performs the function of a single adjective or adverb in a sentence.

A modifier is a word or a group of words that describes or limits the meaning of another word or of other words.   [5a]

Adjectives

An adjective is a word that modifies a noun or a pronoun.   [5]

> *That large leather* briefcase belongs to *my* father.
> I didn't have *enough* time to answer *the last four* questions.

Adjectives normally tell *which, what, what kind of,* and *how many.* They are classified according to their use and according to their position in sentences. According to use, adjectives are classified as *descriptive* or *limiting.*

Descriptive adjectives, as their name implies, describe. They may be either common or proper adjectives.

A proper adjective is an adjective formed from a proper noun or is a proper noun used as an adjective. A proper adjective begins with a capital letter.   [5e]

> He drives a *shiny red* convertible. (Common descriptive adjectives)
> Her fluency in the *Spanish* language is the result of her having been
> raised in a *Texas* town. (Proper descriptive adjectives)

Limiting adjectives point out or specify. The most common limiting adjectives are the articles *a, an,* and *the.* Other limiting adjectives include the possessive forms of nouns and of personal pronouns, cardinal numbers *(six)* and ordinal numbers *(sixth).*

> *Mr. Sutton's* grandfather was *the first* mayor of *our* town.

Some words may be used as more than one part of speech, depending upon the way in which the word is used in a sentence.

Some words may be used as adjectives or as pronouns, depending upon their use in a sentence.   [5f]

The following words may be used as adjectives or as pronouns:

all	few	one	these
another	many	other	this
any	more	several	those
both	most	some	what
each	much	that	which
either	neither		

Function determines the part of speech.

Either of the plans should be successful. (Pronoun)
Either plan seems feasible. (Adjective)
What is your purpose in doing that? (Pronoun)
What purpose does it serve? (Adjective)

Adjectives are classified according to position as *attributive, appositive,* or *predicate adjectives.*

An attributive adjective is an adjective that precedes the word it modifies. [5c]

Several large trees were struck by lightning.

An appositive adjective is an adjective that follows the word it modifies. [5d]

Appositive adjectives are set off from the rest of the sentence by commas.

Distinguish between classification according to function and according to position.

The boys, *weary* and *footsore,* made camp at the first clearing they reached.

Most single-word modifiers are placed just before or directly following the words they modify. Some adjectives, however, appear in the predicate of the sentence but modify the subject. Such adjectives are called *predicate adjectives.*

A predicate adjective is an adjective that appears in the predicate part of a sentence but modifies the simple subject. [5b]

Predicate adjectives normally complete the meaning of linking verbs such as *be, seem, become, appear, smell, taste, feel, grow, remain,* and *sound.*

His reluctance to take part became *apparent.*
The warmth of the fire felt *good.*

Adjectives, except predicate adjectives, are diagramed on slanting lines below the words they modify. Each adjective is written on a separate slanting line.

Several dark clouds appeared.

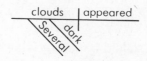

Predicate adjectives are diagramed following the predicate verb on the base line. They are separated from the predicate verb by a diagonal line that slants toward the subject, which is modified by the predicate adjective.

Arlene seems *nervous*. (Predicate adjective)

Arlene | seems \ nervous

DEVELOPING YOUR SKILL   Underscore indicates adjective;
                        arrow points to word modified.

A. Divide a sheet of paper into two columns headed *Adjectives* and *Nouns and Pronouns*. In the first column list all the adjectives in the following sentences. Opposite each adjective write the noun or pronoun it modifies.

1. My friend spent the day studying the surrounding area through his new telescope.

2. After his summer of outdoor work, he was strong, tanned, and healthy.

3. The clear emerald lake became dark and forbidding under the moonless sky.

4. Our parents have assured us that we shall visit several French families while we are in Quebec.

5. Her mother, tired and worried, appeared calmer when Sheriff Mack's men assured her of Elinor's safety.

B. Write a short paragraph in which you describe the street on which you live. Underline the adjectives in your paragraph and draw arrows from the adjectives to the nouns and pronouns they modify. Paragraphs will vary.

C. Diagram the simple and compound subjects and predicate verbs and the adjectives in the following sentences. See p. T68.

1. The old mansion looked deserted.
2. The timid boy was terrified.
3. His kind, genial face beamed.
4. That large black dog can be ferocious.
5. Most Italian music is romantic.

This exercise may be used for oral practice if you prefer. Have students identify the elements to be diagramed.

Possessive case [37]

When the possessive forms of nouns and pronouns are used as adjectives, these forms are called *possessive adjectives*. Pronouns used as adjectives are also called *pronominal adjectives*. Both nouns and pronouns change form to show possession. The possessive case forms of the personal pronouns that may be used as adjectives are these:

	SINGULAR	PLURAL
First Person	my	our
Second Person	your	your
Third Person	his, her, its	their

Please give me *your* telephone number.
That is *my* pencil.

Do not confuse the possessive pronoun *its* with the contraction *it's* (it is). The *its—it's* error is still a common one.
[37h]

The *fledgling* robin spread *its* wings. (Possessive adjective)
It's hard to believe that such a small creature can fly. (Contraction of *It is*)

Out of context, the possessive pronouns are classified as pronouns; within sentences they are usually used as adjectives.

A noun in the possessive case may be used as a limiting adjective. [37i]

That *man's* sister is my *brother's* fiancee.

My parents look forward to their *grandchildren's* visits.

Mr. Johnson's business is flourishing.

Nouns show possession by the use of either an apostrophe and *s ('s)* or just an apostrophe ('). The following rules will help you form the possessive case of nouns correctly:

Form the possessive of a singular noun by adding an apostrophe and an s ('s) to the singular form.   **[37a]**

SINGULAR	SINGULAR POSSESSIVE
boy	boy's
doctor	doctor's
soldier	soldier's
Mr. Jones	Mr. Jones's
aunt	aunt's

Form the possessive of plural nouns ending in s by adding only an apostrophe.   **[37b]**

PLURAL	PLURAL POSSESSIVE
boys	boys'
doctors	doctors'
soldiers	soldiers'
the Joneses	the Joneses'
aunts	aunts'

Form the possessive of plural nouns not ending in s by adding an apostrophe and an s ('s).   **[37c]**

PLURAL	PLURAL POSSESSIVE
people	people's
deer	deer's
geese	geese's

To indicate separate ownership, make all words show possession.
[37d]

Elizabeth's and Jan's eyes are brown. (Each girl has eyes.)

To indicate joint ownership, make only the last word show possession. [37e]

Arthur and Murray*'s* jalopy broke down again. (The two boys own the car jointly.)

Form the possessive of a compound noun by adding an apostrophe and an s ('s) to the last word in the compound. [37f]

SINGULAR	SINGULAR POSSESSIVE	PLURAL	PLURAL POSSESSIVE
son-in-law	son-in-law*'s*	sons-in-law	sons-in-law*'s*
father-in-law	father-in-law*'s*	fathers-in-law	fathers-in-law*'s*

DEVELOPING YOUR SKILL

The following sentences contain errors in the form of the possessive case. Rewrite the sentences, correcting the errors.

1. Her program included selections from ~~Keats~~ and Shelley's works. *Keats's*
2. He has had one year's work in Spanish and two years' work in French.
3. When the Thomas's house was burglarized, the thieves took Mrs. Thomas's furs and jewels, as well as her ~~daughter's-in-law~~ valuables. *daughter-in-law's*
4. The ~~womens'~~ department of ~~Mangus's and Martin's~~ store is noted for its excellence. *women's, Mangus and Martin's*
5. At Mr. Hopkins's suggestion I am sending a photograph of my ~~parent's~~ home after the fire. *parents'*
6. The government used ~~it's~~ influence to secure the ambassador's release. *its*
7. ~~James~~ sister was elected treasurer of her class. *James's*
8. We took our cat to the veterinarian to have ~~it's~~ claws removed. *its*
9. ~~Dennis~~ choice of a profession was the direct opposite of his friends' and relatives' expectations. *Dennis's*
10. Had it not been for the ~~firemens'~~ heroism, the child might have perished. *firemen's*

Adverbs

An adverb is a word that modifies a verb, an adjective, or another adverb. [6]

We *often* walk to the park. *(Often modifies the verb walk.)*

The lecture was *very* enlightening. *(Very modifies the adjective enlightening.)*

The motorcade moved *rather* slowly. *(Rather modifies the adverb slowly.)*

An understanding of single-word functions is essential to the understanding of the functions of word groups.

Students frequently confuse the rule for forming the possessive of compounds with the rules for forming the plurals of compounds. See rules 55f and 55g on pages 364-365.

"WHEN?
WHERE?
HOW MUCH?"

Adverbs tell time (when), place (where), cause (why), manner (how), and degree (how much or to what extent). [6a]

We shall see you *soon*. (Time)
Everywhere we went, we saw children playing. (Place)
She was absent yesterday; *therefore*, she couldn't have known about the meeting. (Cause)
He left *hurriedly*. (Manner)
I *completely* forgot about an appointment. (Degree)

Certain adverbs may be used to connect independent clauses. In this usage they are called *conjunctive adverbs*.

An adverb used as a connective is called a *conjunctive adverb*. [6b]

The most common conjunctive adverbs are *however, moreover, therefore, consequently*, and *nevertheless*. Notice the punctuation in sentences that use the conjunctive adverb as a connective.

We have sold all the cakes; *however,* we still have some cookies left.

Use a semicolon only when a conjunctive adverb connects two independent clauses. In the following sentence *however* is an adverb modifying *have sold*. It does not connect two clauses.

We have sold all the cakes, however, without your help.

Sometimes nouns are used to do the work of adverbs in sentences.

A noun used as an adverb is called an *adverbial objective*. [3f]

Were you *home* yesterday?
The Manns moved here last *year*.

Although an adverbial objective performs the function of an adverb in a sentence, it retains one of its noun characteristics in that it may be modified by an adjective.

He was elected president of his class *this year*.

Stress the point that adverbial objectives, although used as adverbs in sentences, may be modified by adjectives.

(margin note) Conjunctive adverbs retain their adverb usage within dependent clauses.

In the preceding sentence *year* is an adverbial objective modifying *was elected*. The adverbial objective *year* is modified by the adjective *this*.

An adverb that modifies a verb or a predicate adjective is diagramed on a slanting line below the word it modifies.

Simone *always* seems *very* happy.

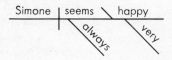

Review the functions of the other parts of speech shown in the diagrams.

Other adverbs are diagramed on slanting lines connected to the lines of the adjectives and adverbs they modify.

An *unusually* extravagant reception was held.

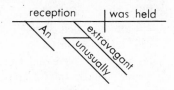

An adverbial objective is diagramed in the same way that an adverb is diagramed. If the adverbial objective is modified by another word, the modifier is diagramed on a slanting line connected to the line of the adverbial objective.

The boys hiked ten *miles*.

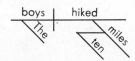

> DEVELOPING YOUR SKILL

    A. List the adverbs, including the adverbial objectives, in the following sentences. After each adverb (and adverbial objective) write the word it modifies and indicate whether that word is a *verb,* an *adjective,* or an *adverb.*

v., v.   1. He speaks well but writes rather confusedly.
adj.   2. His success in that venture seems very doubtful.

You may wish to use Exercise A to review subjects, predicate verbs, and adjectives.

v., adj.   3. Last week several of us spent a completely delightful evening at Bill's home.

adj.   4. Your solution to the problem is highly improbable.

v., adv., v. 5. Tomorrow I shall read the announcement once again.

v.   6. The sun glared blindingly on the hot sand.

v., adv., v. 7. Ray slipped stealthily down the stairs early this morning.

adj., v.   8. After an agonizingly long delay, the train finally started.

adj., adj. 9. The somewhat nasal quality of the oboe makes it an easily recognizable instrument.

adj.   10. I shall not accept this carelessly written theme.

B. Write a paragraph describing a basketball game, a football game, a track meet, or some other athletic contest you have seen. Make your description vivid by using carefully chosen adjectives and adverbs. Underline the adjectives and adverbs in your paragraph and draw an arrow from each to the word it modifies. Paragraphs will vary.

C. Diagram the following sentences. See p. T68.

1. The next step had already been planned.
2. Barbara seemed much better last Sunday.
3. The warmly lighted room looked very inviting.
4. Apparently he does not understand even now.
5. He has never before delayed this long.

Comparison of adjectives and adverbs

Adjectives and adverbs change their forms to indicate differences in the degree to which they modify. These changes in form are called *comparison*.

The three degrees of comparison are the *positive*, the *comparative*, and the *superlative*.   [40]

The positive degree is the simple form of an adjective or an adverb. It is the basis upon which the other degrees are formed. The comparative degree of most adjectives and of adverbs not formed by adding *ly* to an adjective is formed by adding *er* to the positive degree. The superlative degree is formed by adding *est* to the positive degree.

POSITIVE	COMPARATIVE	SUPERLATIVE
wise	wiser	wisest
happy	happier	happiest
soon	sooner	soonest
fast	faster	fastest

Adjectives of more than two syllables and adverbs that end in *ly* usually form the comparative and superlative degrees by prefixing *more* and *most*. In comparisons that indicate a diminishing degree, *less* and *least* are used with all adjectives and adverbs that can be compared.

POSITIVE	COMPARATIVE	SUPERLATIVE
capable	more capable	most capable
capably	more capably	most capably
cool	less cool	least cool
often	less often	least often

Some adjectives and adverbs are compared irregularly and should be memorized.

Emphasize the comparison of irregular adjectives and adverbs.

POSITIVE	COMPARATIVE	SUPERLATIVE
good, well	better	best
bad, ill (adj.), badly	worse	worst
little (quantity)	less	least
many, much	more	most
late (adj.)	latter	last
near	nearer	nearest, next

Use the comparative degree in comparing two persons or things. [40a]

Of the two of us, Judy is the *better* student.
She is more *studious* than I am.

Use the superlative degree in comparing more than two persons or things.
[40b]

She is the *most brilliant* student in our class.

Stress the avoidance of the double comparative and the double superlative.

In comparing a person, place, or thing with the rest of its class, use *other* or *else* with the comparative degree in order to exclude from the class the person, place, or thing compared.   **[40c]**

George is taller than anyone *else* in his family.
New York is more exciting than any *other* city I have seen.

A few adjectives such as *round, square, unique, straight,* and *equal* are incapable of comparison.   **[40d]**

The logic of this rule is apparent. The absolute meaning of each of the adjectives precludes their being compared. If something is unique, for example, it is the only one of its kind; therefore another thing of the same kind cannot be unique. *Unique* has the force of a superlative.

Emphasize the concepts presented in this paragraph.

In current informal usage these words have lost some of their superlative force and one hears such qualifying terms as *rather, somewhat, quite,* and *completely* used with them. This usage is still considered objectionable by many educated speakers and writers and should be avoided, particularly in formal situations. Words such as *almost* and *more nearly* may be correctly used with absolute terms.

DEVELOPING YOUR SKILL

Some of the following sentences contain errors in the use of the degrees of comparison of adjectives and adverbs. If a sentence is correct, write the word *correct* on your paper opposite the appropriate number; if a sentence is incorrect, rewrite it correctly.

other   1. Alaska is larger than any state in the United States.
latter   2. Of the two books you named, I prefer the later.
oftener   3. Whom do you see oftenest, Sue or Tina.
correct   4. That is the worst error you could have made.
an easier   5. There must be a more easy way of doing this.
nearly   6. The margins on your paper should be more equal.
correct   7. The older of the two girls is a college freshman.
worse   8. He plays more badly than anyone else on the team.
straight   9. Hang that picture so that it will be straighter.
latest   10. That was the most late I have ever stayed awake.

COMPLEMENTS

While it is true that the simple subject and the predicate verb are the basic structures in a sentence and express the essential meaning of the sentence, there are times when the meaning requires an additional word or words for completeness and clarity. If, for example, someone were to say to you, "That man is," your immediate reaction might be, "That man is what?" However, if you were told, "That man is honest," there would be no doubt in your mind as to the speaker's meaning. The word *honest* is called a *complement* because it completes the meaning of the verb *is*.

A complement is a word or a group of words that is added to another word or group of words to complete a meaning. [10]

Predicate nouns, predicate pronouns, predicate adjectives, direct objects, indirect objects, objective complements, and retained objects are all complements because each is added to another word or group of words to complete a meaning.

A complement completes the meaning of a verb that, in itself, does not carry out a completed action or predication.

Predicate nouns, pronouns, and adjectives

After such verbs as seem, become, appear, grow, remain, sound, feel, taste, smell, and forms of the verb be, a predicate noun, pronoun, or adjective is used as a complement to complete the meaning of the verb. [10a]

He is my *friend.* (Predicate noun)
It was *I* who telephoned last night. (Predicate pronoun)
She is *unhappy.* (Predicate adjective)

Predicate nouns, pronouns, and adjectives complete linking verbs.

Because predicate nouns and predicate pronouns name the same person or thing named by the subject, they are always in the same case as the subject—the nominative case. Predicate nouns and predicate pronouns are often called *predicate nominatives* because they appear in the complete predicate of a sentence and are in the nominative case. Since nouns do not change form to show the nominative case, your major concern will be with the nominative case forms of pronouns.

A predicate noun or a predicate pronoun is in the nominative case.
[35b]

Stuart is the *boy* on my left.
It was *he* (not *him*) whom I meant.

In teaching predicate adjectives point out distinctions such as <u>He grew tall</u> (predicate adjective) and <u>He grew rapidly</u> (adverb).

Current usage allows "It's me" or "It's him" in spoken language; however, these forms should be avoided in your written work.

Predicate nouns, pronouns, and adjectives are all diagramed in the same manner. A slanting line is used to separate these kinds of complements from the predicate verb.

Linda is my best *friend*. (Predicate noun)

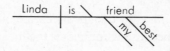

The leading players are *she* and *he*. (Compound predicate pronouns)

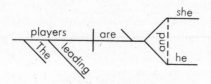

Most animals are *carnivorous*. (Predicate adjective)

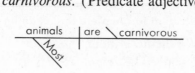

 DEVELOPING YOUR SKILL

A. List on a sheet of paper the complements in the following sentences. Opposite each complement, write whether it is a predicate noun, a predicate pronoun, or a predicate adjective.

PN   1. The other girl was her <u>niece.</u>

PA   2. The dress in that window is relatively <u>inexpensive.</u>

PN   3. I am becoming an avid <u>reader.</u>

PA   4. Outside TV antennas are <u>necessary</u> in many areas.

PN, PP 5. The winners of the contest were <u>Jackie</u> and <u>I.</u>

PA   6. His arguments seemed <u>pointless.</u>

PP   7. The accident victims must have been <u>they.</u>

PA   8. Ken is especially <u>interested</u> in medicine.

PA, PA 9. His manner was <u>expansive</u> and <u>genial.</u>

PN 10. She was a <u>girl</u> from his home town.

(Margin note:) Current informal usage must be acknowledged. However, it need not be accepted in formal written work.

B. Diagram the following sentences. See pp. T68–T69.

See pp. T68-T69.

You may wish to have students identify subjects, predicate verbs, complements, and parts of speech.

1. King Arthur's knights were bold and chivalrous.
2. Our basketball team has been successful this year.
3. Her dog is a miniature poodle.
4. It could not have been Ted or I.
5. I am becoming more confident every day.

Direct and indirect objects

Direct and *indirect objects* are complements that complete the meaning of transitive verbs. Transitive verbs may transfer their action directly or indirectly.

A direct object is a noun or a pronoun that receives the direct action of a verb.   [10b]

They have just built a new *house*.
We saw *Andrew* this morning.

A direct object always answers the question *what* or *whom* after the verb.

An indirect object is a noun or pronoun that receives the indirect action of the verb and answers the question *to whom* or *what* or *for whom* or *what*.   [10c]

I have already given *you* my address.
Ron bought *me* a tie.

In the first of the preceding sentences, the pronoun *you* answers the question *to whom* after the verb *have given. You* is the *indirect* object. *Address* is the *direct* object. In the second sentence, the pronoun *me* answers the question *for whom* and is the indirect object. *Tie* is the direct object. An indirect object always appears between the predicate verb and the direct object. A sentence cannot contain an indirect object without also containing a direct object, but it may contain a direct object without containing an indirect object.

If the preposition *to* or *for* is expressed with an object, the object with its preposition and modifiers is a prepositional phrase, not a complement of the verb.

Show *Miss Hill* your sketches. (Indirect object)
Show your sketches *to Miss Hill*. (Prepositional phrase)

Distinguish between indirect objects and prepositional phrases with <u>to</u> or <u>for</u>.

A direct object is diagramed on the base line, separated from the predicate verb by a short perpendicular line extending up from the base line. An indirect object is diagramed on a line below the verb, with (x) taking the place of the understood preposition *to* or *for*.

Mrs. Robinson offered my friends and me some freshly baked cookies.

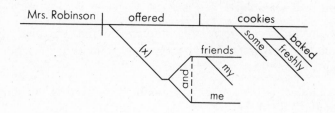

 DEVELOPING YOUR SKILL

A. List and label the direct and (indirect) objects in the following sentences.

If students
continue to
confuse in-
direct and
direct ob-
jects, ask
about sen-
tence 3,
for example,
"Did her
mother
bake
Suzanne
or
the
cake?"

1. A drama coach gave (her) her first opportunity.
2. Lend (me) your assignment notebook.
3. Her mother baked (Suzanne) a birthday cake today.
4. Carl has undoubtedly mailed the cards already.
5. The clerk sold (us) several items.
6. The student council has postponed its annual banquet.
7. James's father has offered (us) his car for the night of the dance.
8. Who will carry these packages for me?
9. My heavy schedule allows (me) little leisure time.
10. Last night I read two short stories and an essay.

B. Diagram the first five sentences in Exercise A. See p. T69.

Objective complements

In some sentences containing direct objects the meaning is further clarified by the inclusion of a word that tells something about the direct object. In the sentence *They named the baby,* the meaning can be made clearer by adding the name given to the baby: *They named the baby Ruth.* *Ruth* completes the meaning of the verb by telling something about the direct object and is called an *objective complement.*

The objective complement names the same thing as or describes the direct object. It always follows the direct object.

An objective complement is a noun or an adjective that completes the meaning of the verb by explaining or describing the direct object. [10d]

We painted the shutters *green*.

In the preceding sentence *green* completes the meaning of the verb by describing the direct object *shutters*.

Objective complements are diagramed on the base line following the direct object and separated from it by a diagonal line that slants toward the direct object.

He calls his dog *Hans*.   They painted their house *white*.

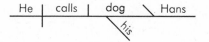

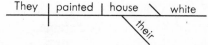

Objective complements usually complete verbs such as elect, consider, name, call, prove, make, believe, and think.

DEVELOPING YOUR SKILL

A. List on a sheet of paper the <u>direct objects</u> and the (objective complements) in the following sentences. Label each.

1. I consider <u>him</u> my best (friend.)
2. Our pastor baptized the <u>infant</u> (*Lisa*.)
3. They wrongly believed <u>him</u> a (traitor.)
4. He has always proved <u>himself</u> (loyal and reliable.)
5. Her long illness made <u>her</u> (thin and haggard.)
6. Miss Green named <u>me</u> temporary (chairman.)
7. The Fine Arts Club has made <u>Mr. Ainsworth</u> an honorary (member.)
8. Her harrowing experience turned Mrs. Loring's <u>hair</u> (gray.)
9. Yesterday the dance committee elected <u>Ray</u> and <u>Peggy</u> (co-chairmen.)
10. The teachers thought this morning's <u>program</u> particularly (worthwhile.)

B. Diagram the first five sentences in Exercise A. See p. T69.

Retained objects

Verbs in the passive voice do not have direct objects; they pass their action to the subjects of sentences. However, verbs in the passive voice may be followed by nouns or pronouns that complete their meaning. Such complements are called *retained objects*. Compare the following pairs of sentences:

His friends gave him a farewell *gift*. (*Gift* is the direct object.)

He was given a farewell *gift* by his friends. (The direct object *gift* from the preceding sentence is retained as the complement of the passive verb *was given* and becomes the retained object.)

They elected David *president*. (President is the objective complement.)

David was elected *president*. (The objective complement *president* from the preceding sentence is retained as the complement of the passive verb and becomes the retained object.)

A noun that completes the meaning of a verb in the passive voice is called a *retained object*.   [10e]

Retained objects are diagramed exactly like direct objects.

We were given a long *assignment*.

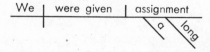

DEVELOPING YOUR SKILL

A. List the retained objects in the following sentences.

1. Jeannette was awarded the first prize.
2. Each boy has already been given a free ticket.
3. Mr. and Mrs. Mason were sold the choice lots.
4. We were offered two different desserts.
5. I was allowed no extra time.

B. List the complements in the following sentences. Label each according to whether it is a *direct object*, an *objective complement*, or a (*retained object*.)

1. The mayor has appointed Mr. Allenby director of traffic and safety.
2. The condemned murderer was not granted a(reprieve.)

Margin note: Emphasize the point that although they are diagramed like direct objects, retained objects are not direct objects. They do not receive the action of the verb.

It is important that students understand that while the retained object completes the meaning of a passive verb, the subject of the sentence receives the action of the passive verb.

3. Our guests considered the <u>arrangements</u> <u>satisfactory</u>.
4. Throughout the storm we heard the <u>crash of falling</u> trees.
5. You have been given every possible (opportunity) to explain.

C. Diagram the sentences in Exercise A. See p. T70.

Objective case   [36]

All nouns and pronouns used as direct objects, indirect objects, objective complements, and retained objects are in the objective case. As with the nominative case, nouns do not change form to reflect the objective case. The personal pronouns, however, do change form with each case. Be sure you use the correct forms of pronouns in objective case usages.

A noun or a pronoun that is a direct object is in the objective case. [36a]

Agnes returned the *wallet* to its owner.
I have recommended *him* for the position.
She sent *Sandra* and *me* as representatives.

A noun or a pronoun that is the indirect object of a verb is in the objective case.   [36b]

David brought his *mother* a beautiful Spanish mantilla.
Mr. Scott taught *us* barbershop harmony.
Aunt Yvonne sent *Bobbi* and *me* jewelry from Iran.

If you are in doubt about which pronoun to use in a compound direct or indirect object, test each part of the compound object separately as follows:

She sent Sandra; she sent *me;* therefore, she sent Sandra and *me.*
Aunt Yvonne sent Bobbi jewelry; Aunt Yvonne sent *me* jewelry; therefore, Aunt Yvonne sent Bobbi and *me* jewelry.

A noun used as an objective complement is in the objective case. [36g]

They considered him their *leader.*

A noun used as a retained object is in the objective case.   [36h]

The pianist was given a standing *ovation.*

The study of the objective case is particularly important as it applies to pronouns. Nouns do not change form to show objective case.

List on a sheet of paper the <u>objective case nouns</u> and <u>pronouns</u> in the following sentences. After each, write the reason for its being in the objective case.

```
                                          DO = Direct Object
                                          IO = Indirect Object
        DO   1. The jury finally reached a verdict.    OC = Objective Complement
        DO   2. We believed him completely reliable.   RO = Retained Object
        RO   3. They had been sent the package by mistake.
    IO, DO   4. Give him one more chance.
        DO   5. Mrs. Benson has engaged an interior decorator.
    DO, DO   6. Chuck and Joyce beat Fred and me easily.
IO, IO, DO   7. Mother bought my sister and me new coats.
RO, DO, OC   8. My sister was christened Roberta, but we call her Berta.
IO,DO, IO, DO 9. Unless you give me her address, I cannot mail her an announcement.
IO, IO, DO  10. I have sent both you and her detailed instructions.
```

CONNECTIVES

Connectives may be used to expand sentence patterns as well as to show relationships among the parts of sentences.

In many languages words change their form to show their relationship to other words in sentences. In English, word relationships are revealed largely through the patterns of sentences. Words that belong together, for example, may be joined by connectives—words that connect other words or groups of words (phrases or clauses) in a sentence.

The two most common kinds of connectives are prepositions and conjunctions.

Prepositions

A preposition is a word that shows the relationship of its noun or pronoun object to some other word or words in the sentence. [7]

The dog ran *around* the house.
The dog ran *under* the house.
The dog ran *into* the house.

In each of the preceding sentences the italicized preposition shows the relationship between the noun *house* and the verb *ran,* showing where the running took place in relation to the house. Notice how the change in preposition changes the relationship expressed.

Impress upon students the changes in relationship expressed with each change of preposition.

Some of the words most commonly used as prepositions include the following:

about	beside	inside	till
above	besides	into	to
across	between	near	toward
after	by	of	under
against	down	off	until
among	during	on	up
around	except	out	upon
at	for	over	with
before	from	since	within
behind	in	through	without

But may be used as a preposition when it has the meaning of *except.* Remember that it is the use of a word in a sentence that determines its part of speech. *Down,* for example, is a preposition in the sentence *He ran down the stairs;* however, in the sentence *Put that down, down* modifies the verb *Put* and is an adverb. When two words that are commonly used as prepositions are used together in a sentence with only one object, the first word is usually being used as an adverb.

You will find Leslie *out in* the yard. *(Out* is an adverb modifying the verb *will find. In* is a preposition showing relationship between its object *yard* and the adverb *out.)*

Some prepositions are composed of more than one word and are called phrasal or compound prepositions. Study the following list of phrasal prepositions:

according to	back of	in front of
ahead of	because of	in place of
apart from	by means of	in spite of
as far as	contrary to	instead of
as to	in addition to	out of

I'll walk with you *as far as* the corner.

Apart from the expense, such a program would be too time consuming.

In addition to the items listed in the brochure, you will need a warm coat and boots.

The exact use of connectives lends clarity and vigor to both oral and written expression.

The noun or pronoun that completes a preposition is the object of the preposition. A preposition must always have an object. A group of words that includes a preposition and its object, together with the modifiers of the object, is called a *prepositional phrase*.

The old ice-cream freezer is stored *in the attic*.

A noun or a pronoun that is the object of a preposition is in the objective case.   [36c]

Each italicized noun and pronoun in the following sentences is the object of a preposition and is in the objective case.

> Most of my *friends* sent me get-well cards.
> They also visited me in the *hospital*.
> All of *them* were very considerate.
> Their visits were good medicine for *me*.

Prepositional phrases usually perform the functions of modifiers in sentences. Each prepositional phrase usually does the work of a single adjective or a single adverb.

> Everyone *in our class* took part. (*In our class* modifies the pronoun *Everyone* and is, therefore, used as an adjective.)
> The old man shuffled *along the street*. (*Along the street* modifies the verb *shuffled* and is, therefore, used as an adverb.)

A preposition and its object are diagramed under the word that the prepositional phrase modifies. The preposition is written on a diagonal line with its object on a connected horizontal line. Modifiers of the object of the preposition are written on slanting lines below the object.

> The skaters swiftly glided *across the frozen lake*.

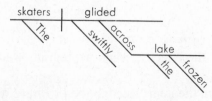

A prepositional phrase may appear at the beginning of a sentence and it may be separated from the word it modifies.

At the festival's climax hundreds *of fireworks* flared *in the sky.*

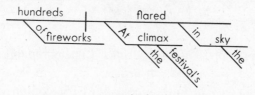

Prepositional phrases are enclosed in parentheses. The first word of the phrase is the prep.; the last word, the object of the prep.

DEVELOPING YOUR SKILL

A. List all the prepositions that appear in the following sentences. After each preposition write the object of the preposition. Then write the word or words that the prepositional phrase modifies.

1. During the night I was awakened by the storm.
2. The last of the races was held in the afternoon.
3. Within two hours everyone but Craig had finished his assigned task.
4. According to the advance publicity the musical will be the best show of the season.
5. Because of the strong tailwind our plane landed thirty minutes ahead of schedule.

B. List on your paper the italicized words in the following sentences. After each write its part of speech.

1. *Before* long Kay and Len drove *up* in *front of* the house.
2. I *like* cold food *on* a day *like* this.
3. *For* the *past* hour I have been walking *past* the theater hoping to catch a glimpse *of* the star.
4. Don't lag *behind!* We are *behind* schedule now.
5. I am going *out for* a walk *along* the shore. Won't you come *along with* me?

C. Diagram the sentences in Exercise A. See p. T70.

Conjunctions

A conjunction is a word used to connect words or groups of words. [8]

Conjunctions join words, phrases, and clauses.

Conjunctions are the links that can promote or destroy the logical progressions of ideas.

Stress the importance of using conjunctions that express relationships exactly.

I plan to serve pizza *and* soft drinks. (The conjunction *and* connects the single words *pizza* and *soft drinks.*)

Put it on the desk *or* in the bookcase. (The conjunction *or* connects the two prepositional phrases *on the desk* and *in the bookcase.*)

Marilyn stopped by, *but* I wasn't ready to leave. (The conjunction *but* connects the two clauses *Marilyn stopped by* and *I wasn't ready to leave.*)

There are three kinds of conjunctions—co-ordinating, subordinating, and correlative.   [43]

One of the tendencies of inexperienced writers is to overuse the conjunctions *and* and *but.* The result is that their writing loses its impact because the exact relationship of ideas is not clearly expressed. Some ideas are of equal value; others are of unequal value. Be sure that you use the appropriate conjunctions to show relationships.

A co-ordinating conjunction joins words, phrases, and clauses of equal rank.   [43a]

All words or word groups connected by co-ordinating conjunctions must be of equal rank.

And, but, or, nor, and *for* are the most important simple co-ordinating conjunctions. *And* is used to connect similar ideas; *but,* to connect contrasting ideas; *or* and *nor,* to connect alternate ideas; and *for,* to introduce evidence for or an explanation of a preceding statement.

Carla wrote the letter, *and* I mailed it. (Similar equal ideas)

I liked the play, *but* I didn't like the leading lady. (Contrasting equal ideas)

Will you call Janet, *or* shall I? (Alternate equal ideas)

Anne will not agree to my suggestion, *nor* will she make one of her own. (Alternate equal ideas)

The boys looked sheepish, *for* they were obviously responsible for breaking the window. (The second clause explains the preceding idea and is equal to it.)

Spend considerable time discussing the precise meanings of various conjunctions and the fine shades of distinction among some of them.

The conjunctions in the preceding sentences join equal independent ideas. Unless the ideas are very short and are closely related, a comma is used with the conjunction.

Certain co-ordinating conjunctions are used in pairs and are called *correlative conjunctions.*

Correlative conjunctions are conjunctions that are used in pairs. [43c]

The most common correlative conjunctions are *both . . . and, either . . . or, neither . . . nor,* and *not only . . . but also.*

> *Both* Jim *and* Roy work after school and on Saturdays.
> I plan to wear *either* my blue *or* my red dress.
> *Neither* Pete *nor* Bill has a badminton racquet.
> We won *not only* the city championship *but also* the state tournament.

Certain adverbs are used to connect equal ideas. Such adverbs are called *conjunctive adverbs* and include such words as *however, moreover, nevertheless, consequently, therefore, so, still, yet,* and *likewise.*

An adverb used as a conjunction is called a conjunctive adverb. [43d]

> There are not enough copies of Macbeth for all the classes in English 3; *therefore,* we shall have to use the available copies on a staggered schedule.

When a conjunctive adverb is used to connect two ideas of equal importance, the ideas are separated by a semicolon.

Some ideas depend upon other ideas for their meaning. They may, for example, express the cause of other ideas; they may express result; or they may exist only if other ideas exist. Such ideas are subordinate to other ideas and are connected to them by conjunctions called subordinating conjunctions. The most common subordinating conjunctions include *because, before, after, since, if, when, while, although, as, as if, unless, where,* and *that.*

A subordinating conjunction joins a dependent, or subordinate, clause to an independent clause.   [43b]

> I ate an extra sandwich at noon *because* I was hungry.
> He has decided to go to Harvard *if* he is accepted.
> *Unless* I receive a letter tomorrow, I shall telephone her.
> *Since* there are eight of us, we had better take both cars.

Emphasize punctuation with the conjunctive adverb. See also rule 58c on page 391.

Students often fail to recognize subordinate conjunctions when the dependent clause is transposed to the beginning of a sentence. Stress this construction.

See also
rule 57b
on page
378.
Notice that when the subordinate idea is first in a sentence, it is followed by a comma.

Conjunctions are diagramed on dotted lines that join the words, phrases, or clauses connected by the conjunctions.

The boys, alone *and* lost, were frightened. (*And* connects single words.)

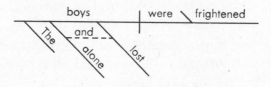

You will find books *both* on the open shelves *and* in the stacks. (*Both . . . and* connects phrases.)

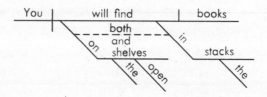

Mr. Carlton is successful, *but* he is not happy. (*But* connects clauses.)

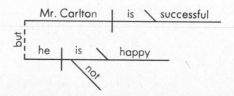

The diagrams may be used to summarize the concepts taught.

Miss Ryan teaches English *although* she was a Latin major. *(Although* connects clauses.)

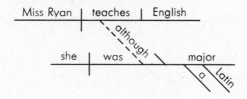

DEVELOPING YOUR SKILL

A. Write the following sentences on a sheet of paper. Underline the conjunctions and put parentheses around the words or word groups that the conjunctions connect.

Example: (Mary,) (George,) and my (cousin) have already left.

1. Carla (wrote) a note of apology and (mailed) it immediately.
2. You may either (leave) a message or (call) back later.
3. The weather was (hot,) (humid,) and generally (uncomfortable.)
4. (Our boat struck an abutment,) but (fortunately the boat didn't overturn.)
5. Everyone considers him both (intelligent) and (talented.)

B. Make as many different sentences as you can by connecting each of the following pairs of ideas with various conjunctions. Sentences will vary.

1. He studies hard. He worries about examinations.
2. George put on a stack of records. The party started to become lively.
3. The flood reached its peak. People scrambled to rooftops for safety.
4. Clare likes to play tennis. She goes to the Y.W.C.A.
5. The band began to play. My feet began to tap out the rhythm.

C. Diagram the sentences in Exercise A. See p. T71.

APPOSITIVES

Sometimes a word or a phrase is used to explain or identify another word in a sentence. Such a word or phrase is called an *appositive* and is said to be in apposition with the word it explains or identifies.

The use of appositives lends clarity to writing and helps to eliminate wordiness. See also page 286, rule 12b.

An appositive is a noun or pronoun—often with modifiers—that follows another noun or pronoun to explain or identify it.   [12]

The appositives in the following sentences are in italics.

May I introduce my cousin, *Frank Sullivan. (Frank Sullivan* is in apposition with *cousin.)*

Mr. Turner chose two girls, *Betsy* and *me,* as his assistants. *(Betsy* and *me* are in apposition with *girls.)*

The degree of separation between a word and its appositive determines whether or not a comma is necessary.

Notice that the appositives in the preceding sentences are set off from the rest of the sentence by commas. If an appositive is closely related to the word it explains or identifies, commas are not necessary.

My cousin *Tim* is here for a visit.

An appositive phrase is made up of an appositive and its modifiers.
                                                                          [12a]

Mr. Thompson, *our new science teacher,* has written several books.

A noun or a pronoun is in the nominative case if it is an apposition with a noun or a pronoun in the nominative case.   [35c]

Mrs. Burton, the *president* of the Parent-Teachers Association, called an emergency meeting. *(President* is in apposition with the subject *Mrs. Burton.)*

That is my math teacher, *Mrs. Lee. (Mrs. Lee* is in apposition with the predicate noun *teacher.)*

A noun or a pronoun is in the objective case if it is in apposition with another noun or pronoun in the objective case.   [36d]

Last year we read *Julius Caesar,* a Shakespearean *tragedy. (Tragedy* is in apposition with the direct object *Julius Caesar.* Since *Julius Caesar* is in the objective case, the appositive *tragedy* is also in the objective case.)

Leave the directions to *us—Martha* and *me.* (In apposition with the object of a preposition)

I shall send *them—Agnes* and *Thea—*a complete list of names. (In apposition with a direct object)

Pronouns followed by appositives often cause confusion in case. The case is determined by the use of the pronoun in the sentence.

The case of a noun or pronoun used as an appositive agrees with the case of the word with which it is in apposition.

We girls (not *us girls*) are planning a fashion show.

Mr. Erwin discussed the problem with *us boys*. (Not *we boys*)

If you are in doubt about which form of the pronoun to use, test the sentence by omitting the appositive. You would not say, "Us are planning a fashion show," nor would you say, "Mr. Erwin discussed the problem with we." The subject of a sentence must be in the nominative case; therefore, the first sentence should begin with *We girls*. The object of a preposition must be in the objective case; therefore, the second sentence should end with the words *with us boys*.

Appositives are diagramed in parentheses immediately following the words they identify or explain.

My sister *Aline* wrote about archery, her current *hobby*.

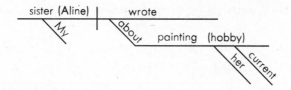

The test for case described here will prove helpful to students who are having difficulty.

> DEVELOPING YOUR SKILL

A. List the (appositive phrases) in the following sentences. Underline the appositive in each phrase. After each phrase write the word which the appositive explains or identifies. Then write the case of the appositive and explain why it is in that case. Arrow points to word explained.

Obj. case 1. This year the Senior class has dedicated the yearbook to Miss Griffith, (our Latin teacher.) Obj. of prep.

Nom. case 2. The word *consensus* is frequently misspelled. Subject

Nom. case 3. Burt Hartmann, our track star, has sprained his ankle. Subject

Obj. case 4. Mr. Dawson gave us—(Ed and me—a make-up test. Indirect obj.

Obj. case 5. Mr. Rice showed Allegra, (a toy poodle,) at the dog show. Direct obj.

B. Diagram the sentences in Exercise A. See T71–T72.

CLAUSES IN SENTENCES

One of the problems that inexperienced writers face is that of choosing the kind of sentence that will best express a specific idea. The writer must make two decisions: what the function of the sentence is to be and what

If students understand the functions of single words in sentences, they should have little difficulty transferring those concepts to the use of clauses in sentences.

structure will give the desired emphasis to his idea. With experience these decisions become automatic.

At the
eleventh-
grade
level,
most of
this
material
can be
used for
review
and
reference.

A sentence may be classified according to its function.   [20]

The four classifications of sentences according to their functions are *declarative, interrogative, imperative,* and *exclamatory.*

A declarative sentence makes a statement. It ends with a period. [20a]

Dr. Drew is a professor at the state university.

He is chairman of the English department.

An interrogative sentence asks a question. It ends with a question mark.
[20b]

When are you leaving on your trip?

Who do you think will be elected prom queen?

An imperative sentence gives a command or makes a request. It ends with a period.   [20c]

Plan to be at the theater by eight o'clock.

Please deliver this package for me.

An exclamatory sentence expresses strong feeling. It ends with an exclamation point.   [20d]

How I wish I could go with you!

What a pleasant surprise this is!

A sentence may be classified according to its structure.   [21]

The second classification of sentences is based upon the number and kinds of clauses a sentence contains. There are two kinds of clauses—*independent,* or *principal,* and *dependent,* or *subordinate.*

A clause is a group of related words that contains a subject and a predicate.   [17]

Some clauses may be used alone as complete sentences; others are used as parts of sentences. An understanding of the difference between independent and dependent clauses will enable you to build more effective sentences and to recognize sentences as being *simple, compound, complex,* or *compound-complex* according to their structure. Knowing how to use these four kinds of sentences will lend variety, interest, and form to your speaking and writing.

Strive for familiarity with types of sentences to the point of naturalness.

A simple sentence is made up of one independent clause. [21a]

An independent clause is a clause that expresses a complete thought and can stand alone as a sentence. [18]

> David has been studying music for the past eight years.
> Last night he attended a concert at Carnegie Hall.

A compound sentence is made up of two or more independent clauses. [21b]

> *Television offers many excellent programs,* but *it presents even more poor ones.*
>
> *Will you tell Elaine about our change of plans,* or *shall I tell her?*

The independent clauses in a compound sentence may be linked by *and, but, or,* or *nor* preceded by a comma. When a word such as *however, moreover, nevertheless,* or *therefore* is used to link the ideas, a semicolon is used between the clauses and a comma follows the connecting word. Sometimes the connecting word is omitted from the sentence, and only a semicolon is used.

A complex sentence is made up of one independent clause and one or more dependent clauses. [21c]

A dependent clause is a clause that depends on the rest of the sentence for its meaning. [19]

> An Italian professor was largely responsible for acceptance of the idea *that disease starts in localized areas of the body.* (One independent clause and one dependent clause)
>
> *Although medicine has made startling advances in recent years,* scientists continue their search for the causes of and cures for many diseases *that still plague mankind.* (One independent and two dependent clauses)

Finding subjects and predicate verbs that are tied together is helpful in determining the number of clauses in
a sentence.
252   *Sentence Skill*

The position of the dependent clauses in a sentence may vary, depending upon the emphasis desired and the relationships expressed. Notice the
position of the italicized dependent clauses in the sentences above.

**A compound-complex sentence is made up of two or more independent
clauses and one or more dependent clauses.**   [21d]

The old courthouse, *which was built in the eighteenth century,* is in
the center of town; the new courthouse stands on a hill at the edge of
town. (Two independent clauses and one dependent clause)

While he was waiting for his cue, Larry felt *that he had forgotten
all his lines;* but *as soon as he was on stage* he gave an excellent performance. (Two independent and three dependent clauses)

 DEVELOPING YOUR SKILL

Reasons depend on number and kinds
of clauses. Independent clauses are
underscored; dependent, in parentheses

A. Read the following sentences aloud. Tell whether each is *simple,
compound, complex,* or *compound-complex* and give a reason. Then
tell whether the sentence is *declarative, interrogative, imperative,* or
exclamatory. Reasons depend on number and kinds of

1, Declarative   1. On our trip to the West we stopped many times to enjoy the beauty
of the scenery.

3, Exclamatory   2. What breathtaking vistas were spread before us when we traveled
through the Rocky Mountains!

2, Declarative   3. The Post Office Department is an enormous business enterprise;
each year it issues money orders amounting to millions of dollars.

4, Interrogative 4. Is the sober-faced person always a serious thinker, or may his
serious expression indicate only that he has forgotten how to laugh?

3, Imperative   5. Please let me know which of your friends and acquaintances you
will want to see when you visit us next month.

B. The following sentences are adapted from Patrick Henry's famous
speech in the Virginia Convention. On a sheet of paper write the numbers 1 to 10. After each number write the classification according
to *function* and *structure* of the corresponding sentence. Follow the
same code as in Exercise A.

2, Declarative   1. I have but one lamp by which my feet are guided, and that is the
lamp of experience.

1, Declarative   2. I know no way of judging the future but by the past.

2, Declarative   3. We have prostrated ourselves before the throne, and we have been
spurned, with contempt, from the foot of the throne.

3, Exclam.4. Three millions of people, armed in the holy cause of liberty, and in such a country as that which we possess, are invincible by any force which our enemy can send against us!

1, Exclam.5. There is no retreat but in submission and slavery!

2, Declar.6. Gentlemen may cry, peace, peace, but there is no peace.

1, Exclam.7. The war is actually begun!

2, Interrog8. Is life so dear, or is peace so sweet, as to be purchased at the price of chains and slavery?

1, Imper. 9. Forbid it, Almighty God!

4, Exclam.10. I know not what course others may take; but as for me, give me liberty, or give me death!

C. Write a short composition on a topic of your own choosing. Make a list, in order, of the kinds of sentences you used, according to function and structure. If you find that you have used too many sentences with the same structure, revise your composition to give it more variety, and make a new list of the kinds of sentences used.

Adjective Clauses

An adjective clause is a dependent clause that modifies a noun or a pronoun. [19a]

An adjective clause is usually introduced by a relative pronoun *(who, whose, whom, which, that)* or by a subordinating conjunction *(where, when, why)*. A relative pronoun may be used as the subject, the direct object, the object of a preposition, or as a possessive modifier in an adjective clause. A subordinating conjunction that introduces an adjective clause usually modifies the verb in that clause.

Adjective clauses are usually the easiest of the dependent clauses for students to recognize and to use in their writing.

. Difficulties sometimes arise with clauses in which
the relative pronoun is preceded by a preposition.
254   *Sentence Skill*

The adjective clauses in the following sentences are in italics.

The people *who had been waiting in line since early morning* carried sandwiches and thermos jugs of coffee.

The woman *whose dog was lost* became hysterical.

Is this the officer *to whom you reported the theft?*

We are planning to have a picnic at the forest preserve, *which is only a mile from our house.*

I intend to buy a microscope *that will last through my four years at college.*

The place *where we saw the accident* is just beyond the next hill.

The time *when we were to leave* finally arrived.

Each of the italicized adjective clauses in the preceding sentences modifies the noun that directly precedes it.

In some sentences containing relative clauses—clauses introduced by relative pronouns and modifying the antecedent of the pronoun—the relative pronoun is not expressed but is understood.

The relative pronoun is sometimes omitted before an adjective clause.

[19e]

The salesman submitted the report *he had prepared.*

One should not believe everything *one hears.*

In the preceding sentences the relative pronoun *that* is understood.

An adjective clause is diagramed below the independent clause. The word modified by the adjective clause is connected to the related word by a broken line.

Don Quixote is the story of a foolish knight *who tried to accomplish impossible tasks.*

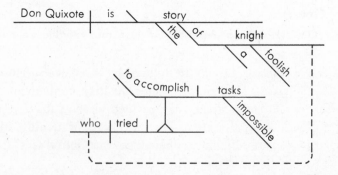

When the relative pronoun is understood, it is written in parentheses in the position that indicates its use in the dependent clause.

The book *I have just finished* is a romantic novel.

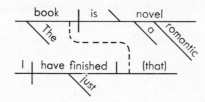

Do you know the reason *why the dance has been canceled?*

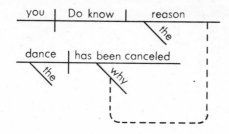

> DEVELOPING YOUR SKILL

A. Copy the following sentences. Enclose the adjective clauses in parentheses. Draw an arrow from the clause to the noun or pronoun it modifies.

1. David, who is the treasurer of the club, keeps accurate records of all income and expenses.
2. The hours that he spent on his hobby have proved profitable.
3. Do you remember the time when your little brother ran away from home?
4. The reason why he changed his mind was funny.
5. He wanted some of the cake your mother had baked that day.

B. Combine each of the following pairs of sentences into a single sentence containing an adjective clause. Make any necessary changes. Then follow the directions for Exercise A. See p. T72 for suggestions.

There will be
some variation
in the sentences.

1. John James Audubon developed an interest in nature study at an early age. He wandered from Labrador to Florida drawing faithful sketches of birds and plant life.
2. Daniel Webster was a great orator. He is ranked with Demosthenes and Cicero.
3. The students concentrated on the mathematical problem. Their teacher had discussed the problem in class on the previous day.
4. He just came back from Mexico. He spent his Christmas vacation there.
5. The television set has not yet arrived. I ordered it last week.
6. This road leads directly to the expressway. It is a branch of the expressway.
7. The corner lot now houses a supermarket. We used to play baseball there.
8. The rain had been pouring down for hours. Suddenly it stopped.
9. Mr. Nelson has proved himself competent. Mr. Carter recommended him for this position.
10. Gary will give a recital in the school auditorium. He has been practicing at least two hours each day.

C. Diagram the sentences in Exercise A.   See pp. T72-T73.

Adverb Clauses

An adverb clause is a dependent clause that modifies a verb, an adjective, or an adverb.   [19b]

Adverb clauses are introduced by subordinating conjunctions such as *when, where, while, before, since, as, as if, if, so, unless, because, in order that, so that, than, though, although*, and *as though*.

She sang in the concert *although she had a cold*. (Adverb clause modifying the verb *sang)*

Gloria is much better *than she was Saturday*. (Adverb clause modifying the predicate adjective *better)*

Rhoda blushes *whenever she is called on for an answer*. (Adverb clause modifying the predicate verb *blushes)*

Adverb clauses are used in the same ways that single-word adverb modifiers are used.

An adverb clause frequently precedes an independent clause.

Although I was angry, I held my temper in check.
Since we had skidded off the road twice, we decided not to drive farther.

Sometimes an adverbial clause is elliptical; that is, some words are omitted but are understood from other parts of the sentence.

An elliptical adverb clause is an adverb clause in which one or more words are understood but not expressed. [19d]

Bob married a girl who is *as tall as he.* (The complete adverb clause is *as tall as he is tall.)*

He reasons more logically *than she.* (The complete adverb clause is *than she reasons.)*

When singing, she closes her eyes. (The complete adverb clause is *When she is singing.)*

The case of a pronoun after *than* or *as* is determined by the use of the pronoun in the understood clause. [39c]

Nobody is more interested in the results of your experiment than *I.*

Nobody is more interested in the results of your experiment than *I am interested.* (The nominative case is used because *I* is the subject of *am,* understood.)

Their antics annoyed him more than *me.*

Their antics annoyed him more than *they did me.* (The objective case is used because *me* is the direct object of *annoyed,* understood.)

Elliptical adverb clauses will be more readily understood if you insist that students complete the intended predication of the elliptical clause.

You can determine the correct case to use after *than* and *as* if you supply the omitted words in the elliptical clause.

An adverb clause is diagramed below the independent clause. A broken line, on which the subordinating conjunction is written, connects the adverb clause to the word it modifies. The understood words in an elliptical clause are written in parentheses in the places where they would normally appear in the diagram if they were expressed.

I shall wait for you *if you are almost ready,* and then we can go together.

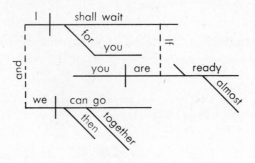

Muttering *as he checked them,* Dad paid the household bills.

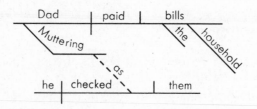

ˈI am even more excited *than she.*

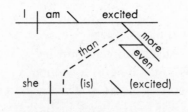

The diagrams incorporate many of the concepts presented earlier in the unit.

DEVELOPING YOUR SKILL

A. Write the following sentences on a sheet of paper. Enclose each adverb clause in parentheses and draw an arrow from the dependent clause to the word it modifies.

1. (Although I understand the point you are making,) I disagree.
2. We stopped and rested (when we were halfway up the hill.)
3. He acted (as if he had solved all the problems of the world.)
4. You have more brothers and sisters (than I.)
5. Is she older or younger (than he?)

B. Write ten sentences containing adjective and adverb clauses. Underline the modifying clauses and draw an arrow from each of them to the word it modifies. Label each underlined clause *adjective* or *adverb* according to its use in the sentence. Sentences will vary.

C. Diagram the sentences in Exercise A. See p. T73.

Noun Clauses

A noun clause is a dependent clause that is used as a noun. [19c]

Noun clauses are usually introduced by words such as *who, which, what, that, when, where, whether, how,* and *why*. Since noun clauses perform the functions of single nouns in sentences, they may be used in the same ways that nouns are used.

The noun clauses in the following sentences are in italics.

Compare the uses of noun clauses with those of nouns.

What he said doesn't interest me. (Subject)

The result of the discussion was *that a committee was formed to investigate local conditions.* (Predicate nominative)

I think *that he has already left his office.* (Direct object)

Give *whoever doesn't have one* a copy of the report. (Indirect object)

He knew the answers to *whatever questions we asked.* (Object of a preposition)

I heard a rumor *that Edith will refuse the nomination.* (Appositive)

You cannot convince me *that I am wrong.* (Objective complement)

He was told *that he could not go with them.* (Retained object)

Sometimes the introductory word *that* is omitted before a noun clause.

I told her *I was sorry. (That* is understood)

The nurse said, "You will have to leave now." *(That* is never expressed before a direct quotation.)

Emphasize the recognition of noun clauses when the introductory <u>that</u> has been omitted.

A noun clause is always a part of an independent clause. In each of the preceding sentences the entire sentence is the independent clause.

A noun clause is diagramed on its own base line but is attached to the main clause at the point where a noun with the same function would be written.

What you are thinking is apparent. (Subject)

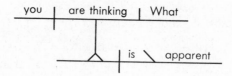

The difficulty is *that both of us want the tickets.* (Predicate nominative)

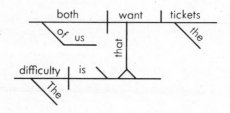

Have you decided *what you will tell her?* (Direct object)

Tell *whoever said that* to stop spreading malicious gossip. (Indirect object)

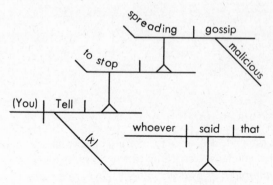

This is the result of *what I told you.* (Object of a preposition)

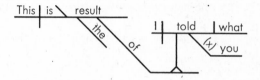

The knowledge *that he was right* gave him satisfaction. (Appositive)

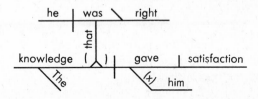

I have convinced her *I was only teasing.* (Objective complement)

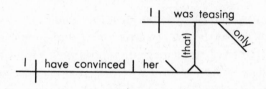

The diagrams will help to illustrate the point made on the preceding page that a noun clause is always part of an independent clause.

She is convinced *that she is not capable.* (Retained object)

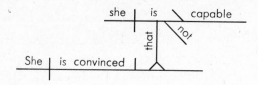

 DEVELOPING YOUR SKILL

A. Write on a sheet of paper the(noun clauses)in the following sentences. Label each clause according to whether it is used as a *subject*, a *predicate nominative*, a *direct object*, an *indirect object*, the *object of a preposition*, an *appositive*, an *objective complement*, or a *retained object*.

Direct object   1. Do you remember (where the car is parked?)

Appositive   2. The fact(that he had traveled extensively)made him an interesting speaker.

Subject   3. (Whether the right-of-way will include our property) has not yet been decided.

Predicate nom.   4. That is(what I meant.)

Object of prep.   5. He told the story to(whomever he saw.)

Retained object   6. Mr. Morgan was asked(whether he had actually seen the accident.)

Direct object   7. I wonder (what he hopes to accomplish by being obstinate.)

Indirect object   8. Did you tell(whoever is in charge of arrangements)(that we shall

Direct object   be late?)

Obj. Complement   9. By trying every method he knew, he convinced himself(that nothing could be done to repair the damage.)

Direct object   10. I said(I would help Elinor with the decorations,)but I now find(I

Direct object   won't be free at that hour.)

B. Diagram the first five sentences in Exercise A. See p. T74.

PHRASES IN SENTENCES

Phrases are word groups that perform the functions of single parts of speech in sentences. Verb phrases, which you studied earlier in this unit, perform the functions of single verbs; prepositional phrases may serve as adjectives or adverbs; and a third group, verbal phrases, may fulfill the functions of nouns, adjectives, or adverbs. The function of a phrase in a

Students frequently experience difficulty with verbal phrases. Lessons about such phrases should be developed carefully.

sentence, like the function of a single part of speech, depends upon the use of the phrase in a sentence.

Prepositional phrases

A prepositional phrase is a group of related words beginning with a preposition and ending with a noun or a pronoun object. [15]

The costumes *for the play* were rented *from a New York company.*

The italicized word groups in the preceding sentence are prepositional phrases. They begin with prepositions and end with nouns that are objects of the prepositions.

When a pronoun is used as the object of a preposition, the pronoun should be in the objective case. [42a]

No one except *me* knows the answer.
No one except Laura and *me* knows the answer.

A prepositional phrase may serve as an adjective in a sentence. [15a]

The rest *of the class* read a story *by Willa Cather.*

The prepositional phrase *of the class* modifies the subject *rest,* a noun, and is therefore an adjective phrase. The phrase *by Willa Cather* is also an adjective phrase; it modifies the direct object *story,* which is a noun.

A prepositional phrase may modify the noun or pronoun object of an immediately preceding prepositional phrase.

The house *at the top of the hill* is theirs. (*At the top* modifies the noun *house. Of the hill* modifies *top,* the object of the preceding prepositional phrase.)

A prepositional phrase may serve as an adverb in a sentence. [15b]

We shall travel *by jet.* (*By jet* modifies the verb phrase *shall travel.*)
On the way we visited Washington D. C. (*On the* way modifies the verb *visited.*)

Remember that prepositional phrases are diagramed below the words they modify. The preposition is written on a diagonal line with its object on a connected horizontal line.

Students who still have difficulty with prepositional phrases should be encouraged to memorize the lists of commonly used prepositions on page 241.

Remind students that prepositional phrases usually modify and that only adjectives and adverbs are used as modifiers.

After the concert meet me *in front of the restaurant at the corner of Broadway and Third Avenue.*

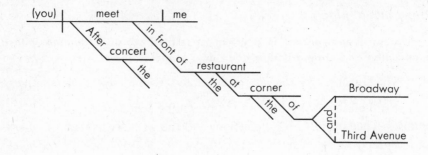

DEVELOPING YOUR SKILL

A. Write on a sheet of paper the (prepositional phrases) in the following sentences. After each, write whether the phrase is used as an adjective or an adverb, and explain why. Adjective phrases modify nouns; adverb phrases, verbs.
1. I should like a position(in the children's department(of Hunter's department store.)
2. (After the election) (of officers) the new president appointed committees (for the dance.)
3. (Around the house) they planted a hedge (of barberry bushes.)
4. (At the end) (of the lecture,) the speaker answered questions (from the audience.)
5. We bought supplies (for the week (at a little country store (in the village.)
6. A pot-luck supper (for the members (of the Parent-Teachers Association) will be held (in the gymnasium (of the high school.)
7. Since the capacity (of the gymnasium) is limited, make your reservation (for the supper) early.
8. (For some reason) Wednesday is always the hardest day (of the week) (for me.)
9. A committee (of irate citizens) appeared (before the mayor) and demanded a solution (to the problem.)
10. One (of the first copies) (of the book) was presented (to the author's secretary (in appreciation (of her hard work.)

B. Diagram the first five sentences in Exercise A. See pp. T74-T75.

Verbals and verbal phrases

Words derived from verbs but used as other parts of speech are called verbals. The verbals are participles, gerunds, and infinitives. [11]

Verbals are verb forms that serve as nouns, adjectives, or adverbs in sentences; they retain their verb characteristics in that they may have complements and may be modified by adverbs. When a verbal has an object or modifiers, the resulting group of words is called a *verbal phrase.*

A verbal phrase is a group of related words that contains a participle, a gerund, or an infinitive. [16]

As you study the three kinds of verbals and verbal phrases, remember that each fulfills the function of a single part of speech in a sentence.

A participle is a verb form used as an adjective. [11a]

The *cheering* crowd rushed onto the field. *(Cheering* is a participle modifying the noun *crowd.)*

The medal *won* by my sister has a place of honor in the living room. *(Won* is a participle modifying the noun *medal.)*

In the preceding sentences, *cheering* (the *ing* form of the verb *cheer)* is a present participle; *won* (the third principal part of the verb *win)* is a past participle. Participles also have perfect forms in the active and passive voices.

Having spoken to him twice, I decided to let the matter drop. (Active)

Having been given a police escort, he arrived at the airport in time. (Passive)

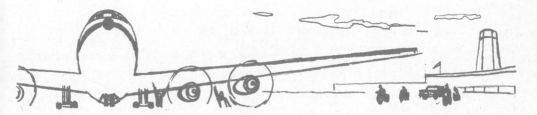

A participle may have a complement and may be modified by an adverb. A participle with its complement or modifiers is called a *participial phrase.*

Students frequently confuse participles with verbs. Impress upon them the fact that a participle may be used as a verb only when it is used with an auxiliary as part of a verb phrase.

(side notes) Emphasize the point made that words in a phrase must be related.

Perfect participles follow the rules of tense formation.

A participial phrase is a group of related words that contains a participle.
[16a]

Singing lustily, the boys marched along the road. *(Singing* is a participle. *Lustily* is an adverb modifying *singing. Singing lustily* is a participial phrase modifying the subject *boys.)*

Leaving the main route, we traveled through the picturesque countryside. *(Leaving* is a participle. *Route* is the object of the participle *Leaving. The* and *main* modify *route. Leaving the main route* is a participial phrase modifying the subject *we.)*

Participles formed from verbs that show state of being may be completed by predicate nouns, pronouns, or adjectives.

Being a capable girl, she assumed all the household duties while her mother was away. *(Girl* is a predicate noun used as the complement of the participle *Being.)*

Feeling depressed, he decided to go for a walk. *(Depressed* is a predicate adjective used as the complement of the participle *Feeling.)*

A second kind of verbal, used as a noun, is called a *gerund.*

Distinguish between gerunds and present participles according to their function in sentences.

A gerund is a verb form ending in *ing* that is used as a noun. It may, then, be the subject of a verb, the direct object of a verb, the indirect object of a verb, a predicate noun, the object of a preposition, or an appositive.
[11b]

Swimming is healthful exercise. (Subject)

I enjoy *swimming.* (Direct object)

She gave *swimming* first place on her list of activities. (Indirect object)

My favorite sport is *swimming.* (Predicate noun)

I don't like any sport except *swimming.* (Object of a preposition)

My favorite sport, *swimming,* is healthful exercise. (Appositive)

A gerund may have a complement and may be modified by an adjective or an adverb. The resulting group of words is called a *gerund phrase.*

A gerund phrase is a group of related words that contains a gerund.
[16b]

Preparing a report often requires research. *(Preparing a report* is a gerund phrase used as the subject of the sentence. *Report* is the complement of the gerund *Preparing.)*

The presentation in the text moves from the verbal to the verbal phrase. The student should have little difficulty if he follows the development of the subject matter step by step.

She enjoys *modeling the new styles* for teenagers. *(Modeling the new styles* is a gerund phrase used as the direct object of *enjoys. Styles* is the complement of the gerund *modeling.)*

Special attention must be paid to the case of a noun or a pronoun before a gerund.

Use the possessive case of a noun or a pronoun before a gerund. [37g]

Have you heard about *his* enlisting in the Navy? (Possessive case pronoun before the gerund *enlisting)*

Would you consider *Mary's* substituting for Helen? (Possessive case noun before the gerund *substituting)*

The third kind of verbal, used as a noun, an adjective, or an adverb, is called an *infinitive.*

An infinitive is a form of a verb that is preceded by the word *to.* Infinitives may be used as nouns, adjectives, or adverbs. [11c]

The infinitives in the following sentences are in italics.

To stay would be pleasant, but I must leave. (Noun—subject)
He plans *to go.* (Noun—direct object)
The only course open to you is *to apologize.* (Noun—predicate nominative)
His plan *to be nominated* did not work out. (Noun—appositive)
I have had several opportunities *to drive.* (Adjective—modifies the noun *opportunities)*
I was delighted *to help.* (Adverb—modifies the adjective *delighted)*

After such verbs as *hear, help, let, make, please* and *see,* the word *to* is usually omitted from the infinitive.

Did you hear him (to) *speak?*
Miss Blake helped me (to) *study* for the special exam.
Please (to) *let* me (to) *use* your notebook.

An infinitive may have a complement and modifiers. A word group built around an infinitive is called an *infinitive phrase.*

An infinitive phrase is a group of related words that contains an infinitive. [16c]

The use of the possessive case before a gerund must be impressed upon students.

Infinitives are the most versatile of all the verbals. They may function as adjectives, adverbs, or nouns, and they may have subjects as well as complements.

The infinitive phrases in the following sentences are in italics.

We took a twenty-mile detour *to see Howe Caverns.* (The noun *Howe Caverns* is the object of the infinitive *to see.)*

You will have *to work faster.* (The adverb *faster* modifies the infinitive *to work.)*

I hope *to be finished by noon.* (The adverbial prepositional phrase *by noon* modifies the infinitive *to be finished.)*

An infinitive used as a noun may have a subject as well as a complement. The subject of an infinitive is part of the infinitive phrase.

A noun or a pronoun that is the subject of an infinitive is in the objective case.   **[36e]**

I asked *Jane* to go with me. *(Jane* is the subject of the infinitive *to go* and is in the objective case. The entire infinitive phrase *Jane to go with me* is the direct object of *asked.)*

Dan expects *me* to be there. *(Me* is the subject of the infinitive *to be* and is in the objective case. The entire infinitive phrase *me to be there* is the direct object of *expects.)*

The following rule applies to all verbals, since they may all be completed by objects.

A noun or a pronoun that is the object of a gerund, a participle, or an infinitive is in the objective case.   **[36f]**

Leaving *him* at the corner, I went on alone. *(Him* is the object of the participle *Leaving.)*

Mr. Harrison would like to meet *her.* *(Her* is the object of the infinitive *to meet.)*

Seeing *them* again was pleasant. *(Them* is the object of the gerund *seeing.)*

Verbals change form to show differences in tense and voice. The fol- You may
lowing list includes all the forms of the verbals formed from the verb *see*. wish to have students include this chart in their note-books.

	ACTIVE VOICE	PASSIVE VOICE
Present Participle	seeing	being seen
Past Participle	seen	(none)
Perfect Participle	having seen	having been seen
Present Gerund	seeing	being seen
Perfect Gerund	having seen	having been seen
Present Infinitive	to see, to be seeing	to be seen
Perfect Infinitive	to have seen, to have been seeing	to have been seen

Verbals are diagramed in the positions of the parts of speech whose functions they perform.

Participles and participial phrases are diagramed below the words they modify. If a participle has an object, the two words are separated by a vertical line. If a participle is completed by a predicate noun, pronoun, or adjective, the two words are separated by a diagonal line. Notice that the participle curves along the angle formed by the modifier line.

The man *just leaving that car* is a newspaper publisher.

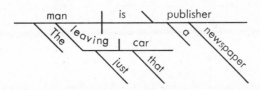

Becoming angry, he stormed out of the house.

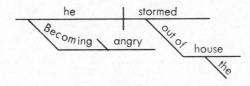

If students think in terms of the function of a verbal or verbal phrase in a sentence, they should have no difficulty with diagraming verbals.

Gerunds and gerund phrases are diagramed along an angled line placed on a stand. The base of the stand appears at the point where a noun fulfilling the same function would appear. The gerund is separated from its object by a vertical line and from its predicate nominative or predicate adjective by a diagonal line.

Selling tickets for the benefit was not easy. (Subject)

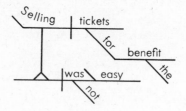

I enjoyed *spending my vacation with my grandparents.* (Direct object)

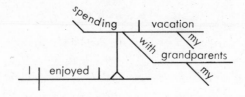

He paid *her continual whining* no attention. (Indirect object)

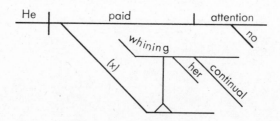

Use the diagrams to illustrate the patterns of sentences that contain verbals.

His error was *parking in a restricted zone.* (Predicate nominative)

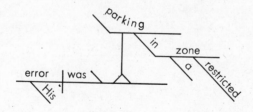

The actress was noted for *being temperamental.* (Object of a preposition)

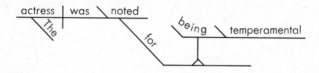

His hobby, *building model rockets to scale,* may lead him to a career. (Appositive)

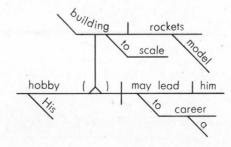

Infinitives and infinitive phrases used as nouns are diagramed along an angled line placed on a stand. The base of the stand appears at the point where a noun fulfilling the same function would appear. Infinitives used as modifiers are diagramed along an angled line below the words they modify.

A comparison of the diagrams will help to illustrate the distinction between present participles and gerunds.

To withdraw is the only solution. (Subject)

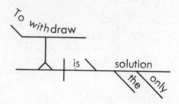

Notice the way the subject and the object of the infinitive in the following sentence are diagramed.

He expects *me to tell her tomorrow.* (Direct object)

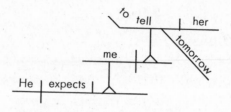

His purpose in life is *to help others.* (Predicate nominative)

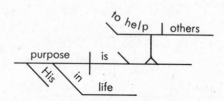

His ambition *to pilot a plane* will soon be realized. (Appositive)

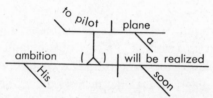

A comparison of the diagrams of infinitives with those of prepositional phrases (see pages 242-243, 264) will illustrate the distinction between the two types of phrases.

Is this the way *to mark a pattern?* (Adjective)

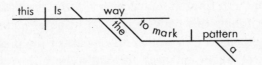

Jeff has gone to Texas *to visit his cousin Neil.* (Adverb)

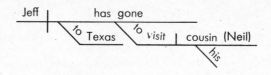

> **DEVELOPING YOUR SKILL**

A. Copy the following sentences on a sheet of paper. Underline each verbal. If the verbal is part of a phrase, enclose the phrase in parentheses. Draw an arrow from the verbals used as modifiers to the words they modify. Above each verbal used as a noun, write its noun function.

                                                     Direct Object

Example.(Exhausted after his ordeal,) he decided(to take a long, much-needed vacation.)

Pred. nom.   1. The understudy's hope is(to appear in the role at least once.)
Dir. obj.   2. The lost child kept (whimpering for his mother.)
              3.(Having made other plans for the evening,)I had(to refuse the dinner invitation.) Direct ojbect.
Dir. obj.   4. Leta's mother wants(her to study singing.) Obj. of infinitive
Appositive   5. Her greatest talent,(mimicking others,) later led her to a career in the field of entertainment.
Subject   6.(Being a good friend)means(being a loyal friend.) Direct object
Pred. nom.   7. His aim has always been(to study art in France.)
              8. There was not enough light(to finish the painting that afternoon.)Dir. obj.
              9. Our neighbors objected to(my playing records so late.) Obj. of prep.
Dir. obj.   10. She tried(to make her voice(heard across the room.)

B. Write a paragraph in which you discuss what you plan to do after high school. When you have revised and polished your paragraph, follow the directions for Exercise A. Paragraphs will vary.

C. Diagram the first five sentences in Exercise A. See p. T75.

Making students conscious of the subject-verb relationships in sentences in inverted order will help them to
avoid the solecism of mixing singular and plural subjects
274 and predicates.   *Sentence Skill*

INVERTED ORDER

Inverted order is often a good stylistic device for emphasis or for variety.

The usual order in English sentences is *subject, predicate, complement.* Sentences that follow this pattern are said to be in *natural order.* Some sentences vary their pattern so that all or part of the predicate verb precedes the subject. Such sentences are said to be in *inverted order.*

A sentence in *inverted order* is one in which all or part of the predicate precedes the subject.   [1k]

There are several kinds of sentences that are often patterned in inverted order.

The subject usually follows the predicate verb in sentences beginning with *there*.   [1g]

There <u>are</u> six thousand <u>people</u> in the stadium.
There <u>goes</u> the starting <u>signal</u>.

When the word *there* is used to introduce an idea, it is called an *expletive.* An expletive is never the subject of a sentence.

Inverted order is usually used in questions and in sentences beginning with words that express or imply negative ideas. It is sometimes used in sentences that start with a prepositional phrase used as an adverbial modifier.

<u>Is</u> there any <u>need</u> for me to go with you? (Question using the expletive *there*)

What <u>do</u> <u>you</u> <u>think</u> of my idea? (Question)

Seldom <u>have</u> <u>I</u> <u>seen</u> a more beautiful sight. (Beginning with a negative word)

Out of the cave <u>tumbled</u> two bear <u>cubs</u>. (Beginning with an adverbial prepositional modifier)

Not all questions are in inverted order. The following examples are in natural order.

<u>Who</u> <u>called</u> me? (The interrogative word *Who* is the subject.)

What <u>film</u> <u>is being shown</u> tonight? (The interrogative word *What* is used as an adjective modifying the subject *film.*)

Sentences in inverted order are diagramed in natural order.

There is no fruit in the refrigerator. (The expletive *There* is an independent element and is diagramed on a line separate from the rest of the diagram.)

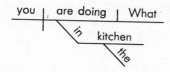

What are you doing in the kitchen?

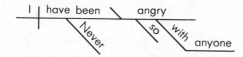

Never have I been so angry with anyone!

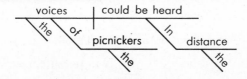

In the distance could be heard the voices of the picnickers.

DEVELOPING YOUR SKILL

Copy the following sentences. Draw one line under the simple subject and two lines under the predicate verb. If the sentence is in natural order, write *N.O.* in the margin beside the number of the sentence; if the sentence is in inverted order, write *I.O.*

I.O. 1. Can there be any other answer to that question?

N.O. 2. What are his plans for next year?

I.O.   3. There <u>are</u> at least two different <u>versions</u> of the ballad "Barbara Allen."
I.O.   4. Seldom <u>have</u> <u>I</u> <u>heard</u> such beautiful music.
I.O.   5. On the stage <u>were</u> two <u>lecterns</u> for the readers.
N.O.   6. <u>Which</u> of these two questions <u>seems</u> the more difficult to you?
N.O.   7. For a short time <u>all</u> <u>was</u> quiet in the dormitories.
I.O.   8. Rarely <u>has</u> <u>anyone</u> <u>accomplished</u> so much in such a short time.
N.O.   9. <u>Who</u> <u>told</u> you about the job opening?
I.O. 10. With whom <u>did</u> <u>you</u> <u>leave</u> the key to the cottage?

ELLIPTICAL SENTENCES

Read the following dialogue.

"Where are you going?"
"Downtown. Want to come?"
"Can't."
"See you later."

Only the first question is a grammatically complete sentence. In the rest of the dialogue, the speakers have omitted words. Despite the omission, the ideas are clear; the omitted words are understood. Such sentences are called *elliptical sentences*. <u>The kind of elliptical sentences illustrated in the preceding examples should be restricted to informal speaking situations or to informal dialogue in writing.</u> There are elliptical sentences, however, that may be correctly used in all speaking and writing.

An elliptical sentence is one in which the complete thought is implied but not stated. [11]

Imperative sentences in which the subject is understood but not expressed are elliptical sentences.

Come here. (The subject *You* is understood.)

In the sentences that follow, the words in parentheses may be omitted without destroying the meaning of the sentences. Such sentences may correctly be used in speaking and writing. Notice that a comma is used to indicate that words have been omitted in the last two sentences.

Did you pack your robe? (Did you pack) Your slippers? (Did you pack) Your shower cap?

Some of the spectators waved pennants; others, (waved) placards; still others, (waved) streamers attached to sticks.

He is in the eleventh grade; his brother, (is) in the twelfth (grade).

Distinguish between grammatically correct elliptical sentences and fragments.

In diagraming elliptical sentences the understood words are diagramed in parentheses in their normal positions in the diagram.

Did you remember the tomato sauce? The cheese? The sausage?

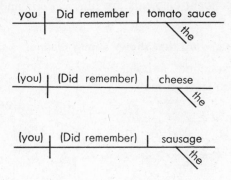

Jean is seventeen years old; her brother, nineteen.

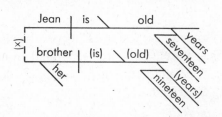

The unexpressed conjunction is represented by an (x) in the diagram.

Since the clauses are separated by a semicolon instead of a conjunction, the connective is represented by (x) on the connecting line.

DEVELOPING YOUR SKILL

A. Rewrite the following sentences, adding the understood words. Enclose the understood words in parentheses.

1. Alice cleaned the living and dining rooms; Barbara, the bedrooms; and I, the kitchen and bathroom. (cleaned), (cleaned)
2. Is his name George? Gerald? Jerome? (Is his name), (Is his name)
3. Tom is studying electrical engineering; Les, mechanical engineering. (is studying)
4. Some of the girls wore skirts and sweaters; others, slacks and wool shirts; and still others, casual dresses with matching sweaters. (wore), (wore)
5. (You) Send me the original, Miss Roberts the first copy, and Mr. Lester the second copy. (You) (send), (You) (send)

B. Diagram the sentences in Exercise A. See p. T76.

INDEPENDENT ELEMENTS

Certain sentence elements have <u>no direct grammatical relationship</u> to the other parts of the sentence and are, therefore, called *independent elements*. Two independent elements are *interjections* and nouns in *direct address*.

An interjection is a word that shows strong feeling.   [9]

> *Oh!* I left my notebook at home.
> *Goodness!* You startled me!

The writer's intention determines whether a comma or an exclamation point is used.

Interjections are sometimes followed by exclamation points, but sometimes they are just unrelated words separated from the rest of the sentence by commas. The difference in punctuation depends upon the strength of the feeling expressed.

> Well, shall we start?
> Oh, I don't think he meant to be rude.

A noun in direct address is one that names the person being spoken to.

A noun of direct address is in the nominative case.   [35d]

Because a noun in direct address is always in the nominative case, it is sometimes called the *nominative of address*. The nominative of address may appear at the beginning, in the middle, or at the end of a sentence. It is set off from the rest of the sentence by commas.

> *Hal,* I think you are making a mistake.
> The solution, *Al,* is obvious.
> Is the cake ready to come out of the oven, *Mother?*
> My *friends,* thank you for your kindness.

In addition to interjections and nouns in direct address, sentences sometimes contain another kind of independent element—an *absolute expression*. Absolute expressions are frequently called *nominative absolutes*.

Although independent elements have no direct grammatical relationship to the other parts of the sentence, students should understand that they are related in meaning.

They have no grammatical relationship to the rest of the sentences in which they appear.

An *absolute expression,* or *nominative absolute,* is a phrase that is composed of a noun or a pronoun and a participle.   [1m]

Both the noun or the pronoun and the participle in an absolute expression may have modifiers.

> *The assembly program having been long,* classes were shortened to twenty-five minutes.
>
> The seals frolicked and cavorted in the pool, *their wet bodies glistening in the sunlight.*

A noun or a pronoun used in an absolute expression is in the nominative case.   [35e]

> The *principal* having finished the announcements, he introduced the master of ceremonies for the program. (The noun *principal* is in the nominative case.)
>
> Vicky spoke to Mr. Raymond, *he* being the personnel director. (The pronoun *he* is in the nominative case.)

Although an absolute expression usually has the force of an adverb clause, it is never a clause. Remember that a clause must have a subject and a predicate.

Do not mistake an absolute expression for a dependent clause.   [19f] Students frequently confuse an absolute expression with a dependent clause.

> *The gas tank being empty,* we had to walk to the nearest service station. (Absolute expression)
>
> *Because the gas tank was empty,* we had to walk to the nearest service station. (Adverb clause)
>
> *While waiting for the bus,* we discussed last night's homework assignment. (Elliptical adverb clause)

An independent element is diagramed on a line that is separate from the rest of the diagram.

> *Ouch!* I cut my finger.

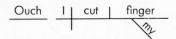

Students should be able to identify and use absolute expressions, particularly in formal writing. In current informal usage a subordinate clause is often preferred.

Come here, *Betty*.   Dinner is ready, *children*.

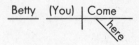   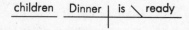

An absolute expression, like all independent elements, is diagramed on a separate line. The noun or pronoun is written on the line. The participle and other modifiers are diagramed below the line.

The fog finally having lifted, he determined his course and headed the boat home.

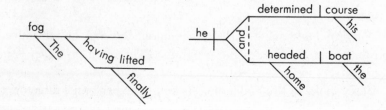

 DEVELOPING YOUR SKILL

    A. List and label the interjections and the nouns in direct address in the following sentences.

Interjection   1. Oh, if only I had listened to you, Carl. `Direct address`
Interj. Dir. Addr. 2. Why, it doesn't seem possible, Rita, that a whole year has passed.
Interjection   3. Wow! Wait until I tell the others!
Direct address   4. Mr. Hansen, who lives next door, is always willing to help out, Bud.
Interjection   5. Oh well, Steve, maybe you'll make it next time. `Direct address`

    B. Write on a sheet of paper and label the absolute expressions and the (adverb clauses) in the following sentences.

      1. My brother having shown a flair for designing, my parents encouraged him to attend an art school.
      2. The buildings in the old part of the city having become dangerously run-down, the planning board decided to raze them and rebuild the area.
      3. (When the children had finished playing) they ran into the house to ask for milk and cookies.
      4. Geri asked my advice, I having had a similar disagreement with Lenore recently.

Exercise B provides practice in distinguishing between absolute expressions and subordinate clauses.

  5. (While looking through old magazines,) Gail hit upon an idea for her research paper.

  6. (While pushing their carts through the streets,) the old vendors used to call out chants advertising their wares.

  7. Larry hopes to be accepted at State University, <u>it having an excellent school of agriculture</u>.

  8. <u>The meteorologists having charted the course of the hurricane,</u> the radio stations broadcast warnings to the inhabitants of the island.

  9. <u>The weather being cold,</u> we took blankets to the football game.

  10. (While introducing Elaine and Lance,) I suddenly couldn't remember Elaine's last name.

C. Diagram the following sentences. See p. T77.

  1. Now, Sandy, don't be a spoilsport.
  2. Oh, I hadn't heard about that before, Scott.
  3. My! You look just beautiful, Lynne.
  4. Those cookies, my dear, were made for the baked goods sale.
  5. What! I can hardly believe that, Pat.

D. Diagram the first five sentences in Exercise B. See pp. T77–T78.

Review Exercises—Structure in Sentences

A. Write the numbers 1 to 10 on a sheet of paper. After each number write the form of the verb in parentheses that will make the sentence correct.

  1. When the bell (ring), Miss Bennett dismissed the class. rang
  2. After I (finish) washing the dishes, I suddenly remembered that it was my sister's night to do them. had finished
  3. The convicted criminal was sentenced to be (hang). hanged
  4. I am certain I (know) by tomorrow. will know
  5. We sat around and talked after we (eat). had eaten
  6. At this rate he (swim) twenty lengths of the pool before you get ready to dive. will have swum
  7. Although the process (teach) thoroughly, Hank still doesn't understand it. has been taught
  8. Grandmother (bring) us gifts each time she has visited us. has brought
  9. Hal (drink) three cokes in the last thirty minutes. has drunk
  10. (Choose) your sister the bridesmaids for her wedding yet? Has....chosen

Exercise A in the Review Exercises may be used for oral practice as well as for written review.

C.1. Inf.-mod. <u>letters</u>; 2. Part.-mod. <u>man</u>, part.-mod.
<u>man</u>, inf.-mod <u>entered</u>; 3. ger.-subj.; 4. inf.-mod. <u>ready</u>,
ger.-appos.; 5. inf-dir. obj., inf.-obj. of <u>to help</u>, part.-
282 mod. <u>notebook</u>.   *Sentence Skill*

See p. B. Write synopses of the following verbs in the third person singular, mascu-
T78.   line gender, indicative mood, active and passive voices: *think, drive, freeze,*
          give, swing.

C. List the verbals in each of the following sentences. After each write whether
   it is a *participle*, a *gerund*, or an *infinitive*. Then write the function of each
   verbal. See also top margin.

   1. The letters <u>to be mailed</u> are lying on my desk.
   2. <u>Gritting</u> his teeth, the <u>determined</u> young man entered his employer's
      office <u>to ask</u> for a raise.
   3. His <u>reasoning</u> seems to be sound.
   4. Cathy is always ready <u>to discuss</u> her favorite subject, modern <u>dancing</u>.
   5. Try <u>to help</u> him <u>find</u> his <u>missing</u> notebook.

D. Copy the following sentences. Enclose each dependent clause in parentheses.
   Draw an arrow from each adjective and adverb clause to the word it modifies. Above each noun clause write its function in the sentence.

Appositive   1. The very idea (that anyone could do such a thing) is unbelievable.
Direct Obj.   2. I assure you (we shall try to make your visit pleasant.)
Direct Obj.   3. (When I reached home,) I found the gloves (I thought I had lost.)
Subject   4. (Whatever you want to do) is agreeable to me.
               5. The consultant (who spoke to us last year) is the one (I mean.)

1=Simple   E. Copy the following sentences. Draw one line under the simple and the com-
2=Compound   pound subjects; two lines under the predicate verbs. Label the complements
3=Complex   of verbs *D.O.* (direct object), *I.O.* (indirect object), *P.N.* (predi-
4=Compound-   cate nominative), *P.A.* (predicate adjective), *O.C.* (objective comple-
   Complex   ment), and *R.O.* (retained object). If the complement is a phrase or a
               clause, enclose it in parentheses. Above each italicized word write its part
               of speech. Following each sentence write its classification according to
               function and according to structure. See also p. T78.

1, declar.   1. The *price* <u>increases</u> <u>are</u> effective *immediately* and <u>apply</u> to *all brands.*
3, interrog.   2. <u>Has</u> <u>anyone</u> <u>heard</u> (*whether* Selma <u>has decided</u>) *what* she <u>will do?</u>)
2, declar.   3. This <u>book</u> <u>is</u> difficult to read; *nevertheless* <u>I</u> <u>am</u> determined to finish it.
3, declar.   4. *If* <u>you</u> <u>give</u> the boy <u>I</u> <u>pointed</u> out the *master* sheet, *he* <u>will run</u> *off* copies
                  on the *duplicating* machine.
(You)   5. <u>Give</u> Shelley and me *some* idea of what <u>you</u> <u>mean.</u> 3, imper.
1, declar.   6. Our work being finished, <u>Tom</u> and <u>I</u> <u>decided</u> (to spend the *afternoon*)
                  tobogganing.
4, exclam.   7. *Oh, how* beautiful the <u>leaves</u> <u>are</u> when *they* <u>turn</u> color, *but* how ugly
                  they <u>seem</u> when <u>they</u> <u>have</u> (to be raked *up* for *burning!*)

8. *After* an examination of our *proposal,* you will *readily* see its advantages *over* the *others submitted.*   1, decl.
9. *Going so far* from *her* family made(Shirley feel *adult* and *adventurous.*)1, decl.
10. Alex has been given *no* encouragement, but he is a *determined young* man and he intends(to send his manuscript to a publisher.) 2, decl.

2. Style in Sentences

The style of your writing determines whether your reader can grasp your meaning immediately or whether he must reread your material several times before he can comprehend its content. Awkward structures and wordiness detract from the effectiveness of your ideas. Good style in writing requires that sentences be complete, clear, and unified.

COMPLETENESS IN SENTENCES

A complete sentence in English contains a subject and a predicate, either expressed or understood. In elliptical sentences the subject or the predicate, or both, may be understood. Such sentences occur primarily in conversation.

"Where are you going?"
"To the store."

The words *To the store* in the preceding example would normally be considered a fragment—a part of a sentence written as though it were a complete sentence. *To the store* is a prepositional phrase; it has no subject and no predicate verb. However, within the example given, the words *I am going* are understood from the context of the conversation. In this usage *To the store* is an elliptical sentence and is therefore complete. This kind of elliptical sentence is correct only in informal spoken and written conversations.

Since the aim in studying grammar is better speech and better writing, the study of style in sentences comes appropriately after the study of the formal aspects of grammar.

Experienced writers sometimes use fragments deliberately to achieve particular effects or for emphasis. Such fragments are called *stylized fragments.*

They had been walking for hours before they finally came to a farmhouse. *What a welcome sight!*

Steve was determined to succeed. *And he did.*

In the first of the preceding examples, the subject and the predicate verb have been omitted. In the second example, the second clause is detached from the clause to which it is related. In both cases the use of the stylized fragment emphasizes the writer's ideas. Since this usage requires skill and an extensive knowledge of writing techniques, it should be avoided, except by very talented writers.

Elliptical sentences and stylized fragments are correct structures; all other sentence fragments are incorrect. What you have learned about sentence structure and sentence elements will help you avoid writing fragments instead of complete sentences.

Prepositional phrases and other phrases cannot be used as complete sentences. [22]

More people are needed in scientific fields. *According to recent statistics.* (Fragment)

More people are needed in scientific fields *according to recent statistics.* (Complete sentence)

Verbal phrases cannot be used as complete sentences. [23]

Having had no time to develop outside interests. Mr. Barclay was at a loss when he retired from his business. (Fragment)

Having had no time to develop outside interests, Mr. Barclay was at a loss when he retired from his business. (Complete sentence)

Sentence fragments may occur when a sentence is carelessly divided. [24]

I enjoy walking in the country. *Especially during the spring and the autumn.* (Fragment)

I enjoy walking in the country, *especially during the spring and the autumn.* (Complete sentence)

Dependent clauses cannot stand alone as sentences. [25]

Students should be cautioned to avoid even the stylized fragments unless they are especially gifted in their use of language.

The sentence fragment error should disappear as students understand and apply their knowledge of sentence structure.

If you receive a formal invitation. You must send a formal reply of acceptance or regret. (Fragment)

If you receive a formal invitation, you must send a formal reply of acceptance or regret. (Complete sentence)

DEVELOPING YOUR SKILL   Slash through cap. letter indicates lower-case letter; through period, deletion.

Some of the following word groups are complete sentences; some are fragments. If a group of words is a sentence, write *complete* on your paper opposite the appropriate number. If a word group is a fragment, rewrite it so that it becomes a complete sentence.

1. Eleanor Farjeon, who is an English author, has received many awards for her books for children. Complete
2. Entering a new school and getting acquainted with new people all on the same day. Sentences will vary.
3. The room was filled with chattering children, Some of whom had met on the school bus.
4. First of all, the courses that are required for graduation. Sentences will vary.
5. Driving on holiday weekends has become very dangerous, Especially on the first and last days of a long weekend.
6. Although roads are better constructed than ever, reckless drivers continue to cause accidents. Complete
7. While Sybil was in the hospital, she received many gifts, One of which was a beautiful robe.
8. At present more gold is taken each year near Dawson City in the Yukon Territory/ Than was taken during the gold rush of 1898.
9. At Wisconsin's highest waterfall, Big Manitou Falls. Sentences will vary.
10. After a time I began to develop an appreciation of modern art, An appreciation based on understanding.

The exercise above requires that students not only recognize sentence fragments but also apply their knowledge of the patterns of complete sentences.

CLARITY IN SENTENCES

Students who have learned to write grammatically complete sentences are now ready to learn some of the refinements of style.

Grammatical completeness in sentences is only one element of style; in fact, it is possible to write correctly and still have an uninteresting style. In order to achieve interest in your writing, you must learn to write clearly. Clarity is essential to good writing, for good ideas may lose their force if they are not clearly expressed. One way of achieving clarity is by avoiding wordiness.

Wordiness

Avoid wordiness by reducing clauses to appositives. [12b]

Don Simmons presented the petition to Mr. Leonard. *Don is president of the student council. Mr. Leonard is our principal.*

Don Simmons, *the president of the student council,* presented the petition to Mr. Leonard, *our principal.*

Avoid wordiness by reducing clauses to prepositional phrases. [15c]

There were many people taking examinations. *The examinations were for Civil Service appointments.*

There were many people taking examinations *for Civil Service appointments.*

Avoid wordiness by reducing clauses to verbal phrases. [16d]

I washed the dinner dishes. Then I sat down to watch my favorite TV program.

Having washed the dinner dishes, I sat down to watch my favorite TV program (Participial phrase)

I can't decide *what I should tell him.*

I can't decide *what to tell him.* (Infinitive phrase)

Sentences that present too many details are often called *rambling sentences. And* and *so* are frequently used to add details that would be better in a separate sentence. By the time a reader has finished such a sentence, he has often lost interest.

Avoid the use of too many details in a single sentence. [74d]

Emphasize the point that lack of clarity can destroy the force of one's ideas.

The disease that is destroying many of our most beautiful trees can be arrested if it is discovered early, *and so* the people of our town have launched a vigorous campaign to save the trees. (Rambling)

The disease that is destroying many of our most beautiful trees can be arrested if it is discovered early. Knowing this, the people of our town have launched a vigorous campaign to save the trees. (Improved)

The and so error is a common one. Work to eliminate it.

Effective writers avoid the use of words that are not essential to the meaning of their writing.

Avoid the use of superfluous words.   [74e]

Redundancy is the term used to refer to the use of unnecessary repetition in a sentence.

> Each and every one of you is responsible for the assignment. (Redundant)
> Each of you is responsible for the assignment. (Clear)

Other kinds of wordiness include talking around the point (circumlocution), putting emphasis on unimportant details (prolixity), and using many words where a few words would do (verbosity).

> When he was still in his boyhood, Mr. Sheldon performed many of the duties associated with his male parent's food and household-supply establishment. (Circumlocution)
> When he was a boy, Mr. Sheldon worked in his father's grocery store. (Clear statement)

Students often feel that the more words they use in a sentence, the more impressive their ideas. Work for direct, concise use of language.

Mary suddenly realized that she had forgotten her short white gloves with the pink flowers embroidered on them. (Prolix statement)

Mary suddenly realized that she had forgotten her gloves. (Clear statement)

It is highly evident that Joe is not interested in music. (Verbose statement)

Joe obviously is not interested in music. (Clear statement)

Keeping writing interesting also involves using language that is fresh and up-to-date. Some expressions have been so overworked that they are no longer effective. Such terms are called *trite expressions*.

Avoid trite expressions.   [74f]

Many trite The following list includes expressions that should be avoided.
expressions
have become
part of in-   add insult to injury   easier said than done
formal speech.   all work and no play   fools rush in
Caution stu-   at a loss for words   goes without saying
dents to avoid   beat a hasty retreat   good as gold
such usages,   beautiful but dumb   green with envy
particularly   brave as a lion   hungry as wolves
in writing.   brown as a berry   ignorance is bliss
                       cold as ice   pretty as a picture
                       cool as a cucumber   sings like a bird
                       deadly earnest   wee, small hours

Figures of speech are often used to add color and effectiveness to writing. You must be careful, however, not to mix the figures you use; that is, do not start a sentence with one comparison and finish it with a totally different comparison.

Avoid mixed figures of speech.   [74g]

Steer a straight course along the road to success.

According to the preceding sentence, the way to success is a road along which you are to steer a ship. The ideas would be more consistent as follows:

Follow a direct route along the road to success.

Once again remind students that figures of speech, to be effective, must be fresh and appropriate and must not seem obviously contrived.

▶ DEVELOPING YOUR SKILL

A. Rewrite the following sentences in concise English. Use appositives, prepositional phrases, and verbal phrases to overcome the problem of wordiness.

1. People are being made to want more things than they can afford. ~~Advertising is largely responsible for this attitude.~~ Through advertising,
2. The route ~~you should follow~~ is marked on the map. to follow
3. Mr. Moore, ~~is~~ our newly-appointed vice-president, ~~He~~ majored in business administration at college and spent ten years out in the field.
Having 4. ~~Bob has~~ explored all the job possibilities near his home, ~~Now he is~~ looking farther afield. Bob is now looking...
5. Reese hopes ~~that he will be~~ able to make the honor roll. to be
6. They have decided to give three performances. ~~They expect the variety show to be a huge success.~~ Expecting... success,
7. College enrollments will continue to rise for many years. ~~Recent studies indicate this to be a fact.~~ As indicated by recent studies,
8. Miss LaRue asked two boys to help her. ~~She asked~~ Paul and me,
9. ~~Denise and I were~~ looking through old yearbooks, ~~We~~ found pictures of our parents when they were our age. Denise and I
10. James expects ~~that he will join~~ his father's college fraternity. to join

B. Rewrite the following sentences, in simple, clear language. conquered it

1. He swam against the river of opposition and finally ~~plowed it under.~~
2. Collect ~~together~~ all your books and papers.
3. Be sure to sign the letter ~~at the bottom.~~
Yes 4. Carl's answer was ~~in the affirmative.~~
5. I am of the persuasion that you did not give your attention to my discourse. I believe you were not listening to me.
marry 6. Bill and Alice are planning to ~~enter into the state of matrimony.~~
very late 7. We didn't get home until ~~the wee hours of the morning.~~
All lights 8. ~~It is required that all illumination~~ in the dormitories ~~be extin-~~
must be out ~~guished~~ at ten o'clock.
9. Mr. Miller, who has taught at Park High School for the past thirty years, is going to retire at the end of the year, ~~and so~~ the students have planned a farewell party for him and are collecting money for a gift which they will present to him at the party.
10. Nancy Benson, ~~who is tall, dark-haired, and attractive and who always has a pleasant smile for everyone,~~ won the journalism award.

There may be some variation in the methods used to rewrite the sentences above.

Misplaced and dangling modifiers

Clarity is often a matter of word order, particularly in the placement of modifiers. When modifiers are placed in sentences so that they seem to modify words other than those intended, the modifiers are said to be *misplaced* or *dangling*.

Words such as *only, not only, nearly, hardly,* and *even* are frequently misplaced in sentences, with the result that the meaning of the sentence becomes vague.

Awareness of the meanings of the sentences they write will help students to eliminate these errors.

Place modifiers as close as possible to the words they modify.   [41g]

I *only* plan to invite a few friends. (Vague)
I plan to invite *only* a few friends. (Clear)

The company *only* sent two representatives. (Vague)
The company sent *only* two representatives. (Clear)

Misplaced prepositional phrases may make the meaning of a sentence ludicrous.

Place a prepositional phrase as close as possible to the word it modifies.
[42l]

I bought a stuffed bear for my baby sister *with large shoebutton eyes.* (I bought a stuffed bear *with large shoebutton eyes* for my baby sister.)

The hero of the game agreed to ride in an open convertible *with an embarrassed grin. (With an embarrassed grin,* the hero of the game agreed to ride in an open convertible.)

Squinting modifiers are often less apparent to students
than are misplaced modifiers. Develop this section carefully.

Style in Sentences 291

When a modifier may refer to either of two parts of a sentence, it is said to be *squinting*.

Avoid squinting modifiers. [41h]

Students who daydream in class *frequently* miss what is going on.
The preceding sentence may mean either of two things:

Students who *frequently* daydream in class miss what is going on.
Frequently, students who daydream in class miss what is going on.

A modifier is said to be *dangling* when it does not refer logically to some other word in the sentence. Participial phrases, gerund phrases, and infinitive phrases used to begin sentences are sometimes left dangling in sentences. Logically, such a phrase should be attached to the subject of the clause that follows.

Avoid dangling verbal phrases. [41i]

Entering the house, the smell of freshly baked bread greeted me. Students
(According to this sentence, the smell was entering the house.) should
under-
There are two ways of correcting the preceding sentence. stand both

Entering the house, I was greeted by the smell of freshly baked bread. methods of
(The participial phrase is related to the subject *I*.) correcting
As I was entering the house, the smell of freshly baked bread greeted dangling
me. (The dangling participial phrase has been changed to a clause.) construc-
After proving my point, Tom apologized. (Dangling gerund phrase) tions.

After proving my point, I received an apology from Tom. (Related
to the subject *I*)

When I had proved my point, Tom apologized. (Changed to a
clause)

DEVELOPING YOUR SKILL

The following sentences contain misplaced and dangling modifiers.
Rewrite the sentences correctly.

1. After being awakened at 5:30 A. M., breakfast ~~wasn't served~~ until
   8:00 A. M. we weren't served
2. ~~I not only saw~~ the Statue of Liberty but also the Empire State Building
   and Rockefeller Center. I saw not only

In the exercise that begins above and continues on page
292, possible changes are suggested. The actual methods of
correction used by students may vary.

3. The antique gold locket (belonged to my great-grandmother) with the removable secret compartment.

we discovered 4. By studying the map carefully, our mistake ~~became evident.~~

After I had 5. ~~Having~~ convinced Mr. Datton of my ability, he let me take the advanced course.

we lowered 6. To prevent the boat's capsizing, the sails ~~were lowered~~.

hardly 7. We ~~hardly~~ had enough refreshments for the crowd that arrived.

they found 8. Arriving early in the morning, everyone ~~was~~ still asleep.

9. The old man liked to sit in a comfortable chair and tell stories about his boyhood (in front of the fire)

10. Established in 1836, ~~the Lawson family has always owned the local newspaper.~~ *the local newspaper has always been owned by the Lawson family.*

Illogical constructions

Clarity frequently depends upon sentence sense and form. Each element of a sentence must have a logical relationship to the other parts of the sentence.

The subject of a sentence must be clearly defined.   [74a]

Jet travel is an exciting period. (The subject *Jet travel* is not clearly related to the rest of the sentence.)

The twentieth century is an exciting period of jet travel. (The subject is now clearly defined.)

The subject of a sentence must make sense in relation to the predicate.
[74b]

The time will be seven o'clock in the school gymnasium and will be informal. (According to this sentence, the time will be informal.)

The dance will be held in the school gymnasium at seven o'clock and will be informal. (Clear relationship of subject to predicate)

Stress the point that each element of a sentence must have a logical relationship to the other sentence elements.

Adjust the form of an indirect quotation to the rest of the sentence. [74c]

Sandy wanted to know was I downtown last night. (Illogical)
Sandy wanted to know whether I was downtown last night. (Clear)

 DEVELOPING YOUR SKILL   Possibilities are suggested. Methods of correction may vary.

Rewrite the following sentences, correcting all illogical constructions.

1. After the hurricane the local reserve troops were reinforced with troops from neighboring areas and ~~with~~ authority to arrest looters. were given
2. Laura's note said that she would be delighted to take part in the festival and ~~"I am~~ looking forward to seeing all of ~~you~~ again.~~"~~ that she was, us
3. Tomorrow is our English examination. the day of
4. ~~By~~ being considerate of others, both in and out of school, helps one to make lasting friends.
Having 5. ~~With~~ two books to read makes it impossible for me to go out this week.
6. I don't know ~~was he~~ serious or not. whether he was
7. Hearing shouts from the football practice field has become a familiar ~~sound.~~ experience.
8. Next month ~~will be~~ my parents' twentieth wedding anniversary. will celebrate their
9. The first meeting of the club was held three years ago, and is still in existence today. the club
10. By working nights and weekends ~~was the way~~ he financed his college education.

UNITY IN SENTENCES   A sentence must be thought of as a unit in which one main purpose is achieved.

In addition to completeness and clarity, sentences must have unity if they are to be effective.

A sentence has unity when all the ideas expressed are closely related and contribute to a single impression.   **[75]**

The *New Yorker* is my favorite magazine, and it contains many clever cartoons. (Faulty)

Glen is a talented pianist, his oldest sister being a gifted artist. (Faulty)

If the ideas expressed are related, they may be connected in such a way that the relationship is clear.

Grammatical completeness, clarity, and unity are the essential characteristics of a sentence.

Students
should
under-
stand
co-ordi-
nation,
subordi-
nation,
and
separa-
tion of
ideas to
achieve
a mature
style of
writing.

Unity is sometimes achieved by subordinating one idea to the other.

[75a]

The *New Yorker,* which is my favorite magazine, contains many clever cartoons. (Improved)

Sometimes the ideas expressed are not closely enough related to be written in the same sentence. In such cases they must be written as separate sentences.

Unity is sometimes achieved by the complete separation of ideas. [75b]

Glen is a talented pianist. His oldest sister is a gifted artist. (Two distinct ideas)

Sometimes it is possible to show the relationship between two separate ideas as follows:

Glen, who is a talented pianist, has an older sister who is a gifted artist.

DEVELOPING YOUR SKILL

Methods may vary.

Rewrite the following sentences to achieve unity.

1. My brother has decided to be a policeman and he is six years old. (who)
2. A committee was appointed by the mayor, and they were to investigate the buying of contracts for the construction of public buildings.
3. My cousin lives in Philadelphia, and his name is Dwight.
4. Tourists in New York City usually want to see the Broadway shows, and the view from the top of the Empire State Building is also a popular tourist attraction. (who
5. Mr. Stapleton offered me a part-time job, and he is a business partner of my uncle's.)
6. The mascot of the team is a small terrier, and it is named "Touchdown."
7. *The Count of Monte Cristo* is an exciting story of a young sea captain, and it was written by Alexandre Dumas.
8. I was just about to go out the door and I realized that I had forgotten my key. when
9. Atlanta is the capital of Georgia, and it is one of the fastest-growing cities in the South.
10. Guidance counselors have been added to the staffs of many large high schools, and their main purpose is to give advice to students.

Review Exercises—Style in Sentences

Rewrite the following sentences, making improvements in style.

1. Determined to win all rounds, the young lawyer ~~plunged~~ into the political ~~current~~. `climbed` `arena.`
2. Leaving his parents for the first time and going off to camp. `Sentences will`
3. Tell Henry (when he gets here) I want to talk to him. `vary.`
4. I met an old seaman who had a hook for a hand (named Tom Bates.)
5. Lew believes that ~~there are many obstacles to comprehension in the science that treats of exact numerical relationships~~. `mathematics is difficult.`
6. ~~It goes without saying that~~ her walking out before I could answer was ~~just adding insult to injury~~. `rude.`
7. My father is a tall man. He is a physician. He has dark hair and gray eyes. `See below.`
8. ~~Coming~~ into the house, the warmth felt good. `When we came`
9. ~~It is often the case that~~ interns are on duty for thirty-six hours at a stretch. `often`
10. Tuesday will be the Honors Society tea and it will be at four o'clock. `See below.`

7. `My father, who is a physician, is a tall man with dark hair and gray eyes.`

10. `The Honors Society tea will be held on Tuesday at four o'clock.`

UNIT SUMMARY

Mastery of grammar is an aid to good writing. Your understanding of structure and good style in sentences will enable you to express your ideas logically, clearly, and effectively.

English would be a stilted language were it not for the variation possible in sentence types and structure. The four types of sentences according to function and according to structure enable you to express your ideas in the form best suited to them. The various sentence types also permit you to combine related ideas, to separate unrelated ideas, and to emphasize or subordinate ideas, according to their importance.

A knowledge of sentence structure is essential to good writing. You must understand the basic subject—predicate structure of English sentences and be able to add to the basic structure the complements, modifiers, connectives, appositives, and independent elements that add meaning to a sentence. Since sentences are made up of words—used singly or in groups—it is essential that you understand the functions of words in

`Mastery of this unit should result in grammatically and stylistically improved speech and writing.`

sentences. The following chart summarizes the functions of the parts of speech and their substitutes in sentences.

STRUCTURE	PART OF SPEECH	SUBSTITUTE FOR PART OF SPEECH
Subject	noun pronoun	gerund or gerund phrase (n.) infinitive or infinitive phrase (n.) clause (n.)
Predicate	verb	verb phrase (v.)
Modifier	adjective adverb	prepositional phrase (adj., adv.) participle or participial phrase (adj.) infinitive or infinitive phrase (adj., adv.) clause (adj., adv.) adverbial objective (adv.)
Complement	noun pronoun adjective	gerund (n.) infinitive (n., adj.) prepositional phrase (adj.) clause (n., adj.)
Connective	conjunction preposition	conjunctive adverb (conj.)
Appositive	noun	gerund or gerund phrase (n.) infinitive or infinitive phrase (n.) clause (n.)
Independent elements Direct address Expletive Nominative absolute	interjection noun	

Good style in writing involves completeness, clarity, and unity. Sentence fragments, except for stylized fragments, detract from the interest and clarity of writing. Even stylized fragments must be used sparingly and judiciously. Wordiness is a flaw in style. Superfluous words often make meanings obscure and make the style of the writing heavy and pompous. Illogical constructions and unrelated ideas cause the reader confusion and sometimes make the writer appear illiterate.

Your goal in writing should be the writing of grammatically correct, forceful sentences that say what you intend your reader to understand.

You may wish to duplicate the chart or have students copy it into their notebooks. This summary chart will prove helpful in demonstrating to students the relationships among single words, phrases, and clauses that function interchangeably in sentences.

A. Permits one to express more complex ideas and relationships
and to communicate ideas clearly. B. Other elements include
interest, clarity, logic, and unity.
Unit Review 297

UNIT REVIEW EXERCISES

DISCUSSION TOPICS

A. In what ways can a knowledge of sentence structure help you improve
your writing? See top margin.

B. Discuss the following statement: "Grammatical completeness in sentences
is only one element of style." See top margin.

C. What verb characteristics do verbals retain? What verb characteristic do
they not have? May be modified by adverbs and may be completed
by complements. May not be used as predicate verbs.

D. Your teacher may wish to select a passage from your literature text for this
exercise. Discuss the kinds of sentences the author has used. Analyze the
patterns of the sentences. Try to restate the passage, using simple sentences
in natural order. What is the effect? Analyses will vary.

WRITTEN WORK
Paragraphs will vary.

A. Write a paragraph beginning with the following topic sentence: In effective
sentences, form and style are blended to produce clear meaning and interesting expression. Leave a full line of space after each line of writing.

B. Use the paragraph you wrote for Exercise A for this exercise. Draw one
line under each subject and two lines under each predicate verb. Enclose
the complements of verbs in parentheses. Above each word write the abbreviation for its part of speech.

VOCABULARY

Did you know the meaning of all the words in this unit? The following sentences use some of the words in different contexts. Write the numbers 1 to 5
on your paper. After each number, write the letter of the word or phrase that
could best be substituted for the italicized word in each sentence. Before making your choice, find the word on the page indicated to see how it is used in
the unit.

1. The appeal of the show lay largely in its humorous *elements*.   [p. 193]
 c (*a*) characteristics; (*b*) situations; (*c*) components; (*d*) speeches

2. Ken's strong *assertion* concerning local politics left us gasping.   [p. 195]
 b (*a*) attitude; (*b*) declaration; (*c*) declamation; (*d*) oration

3. There was a *perpendicular* drop to the base of the cliff.   [p. 221]
 a (*a*) sheer; (*b*) direct; (*c*) difficult; (*d*) treacherous

4. The *impact* of his ideas showed clearly in the faces of his listeners.   [p. 244]
b   (*a*) importance; (*b*) force; (*c*) immediacy; (*d*) futility
5. His excessive use of symbolism makes his meaning *obscure*.   [p. 296]
c   (*a*) unmistakable; (*b*) unimportant; (*c*) vague; (*d*) senseless

SPELLING

The following spelling words appeared in the unit or were chosen because they are commonly misspelled. Study these words so that you will be prepared to write them from dictation.

1. elements	11. illegibility
2. assertion	12. transmitted
3. perpendicular	13. mercenary
4. impact	14. eliminate
5. obscure	15. extraordinary
6. traits	16. miscellaneous
7. judiciously	17. unconscious
8. superfluous	18. unnecessary
9. illogical	19. soliloquy
10. sparingly	20. eminent

UNIT SELF-TEST
Brackets are used for clauses used as complements when the clauses themselves contain complements.
A. Divide a sheet of paper into three columns. List all the *Subjects* in the following sentences in the first column, the *Predicate Verbs* in the second, and the *Complements* in the third. Label each complement to indicate whether it is a *direct object,* an *indirect object,* a *predicate nominative,* a *predicate adjective,* an *objective complement,* or a *retained object.* See also
                                          bottom margin.
1. Both Jim and I told Phil our plans for doing volunteer work at the community center.
2. I know that Susan considers me her friend and would not refuse to help.
3. His interest in doing advanced work is evident; I hope his ambition matches his interest.
4. Each soldier was given a survival kit before setting out on the mission.
5. Bicycling has become their favorite Saturday activity.
6. Mrs. Stone doesn't know whether Jean will take the early plane or the later one.

A.1. Phil–IO, plans–DO; 2. clause–DO, me–DO, friend–OC, to help–DO; 3. evident–PA, clause–DO, interest–DO; 4. kit–RO; 5. activity–PN; 6. clause–DO, plane–DO, one–DO.

Unit Review   (·You)   299

7. Since only a limited <u>number</u> of these books <u>will be published</u>, <u>place</u> your   See
   (order) for one now.   above.

8. There <u>are</u> several secondhand <u>bookstores</u> where <u>you</u> <u>can find</u> usable
   inexpensive (copies) of the novel.

9. (Which) of your courses <u>do you enjoy</u> most, or <u>haven't you decided</u> yet?

10. If <u>Mac</u> <u>weren't</u> so (obstinate,) <u>he</u> <u>would tell</u> (Rita) [that <u>he</u> <u>was</u> (wrong.)]

B. Write the numbers from 1 to 10 on a sheet of paper. After the appropriate
   number write the form of the verb in parentheses that will make the sentence correct.

   1. You have never (write) a better composition. written
   2. Alice and I (swim) out to the raft. swam
   3. Has anyone (speak) to Jack about the job opening? spoken
   4. Our star football player has (tear) a ligament in his leg. torn
   5. You should have (take) a sweater with you. taken
   6. When I (see) him, he was on his way to school. saw
   7. Do you think the judge will sentence him to be (hang)? hanged
   8. The wool sweater (shrink) when I washed it. shrank
   9. Seeing the way his arm (hang) at his side, we were afraid it was broken. hung
   10. Everyone at the picnic was (bite) by mosquitoes. bitten

C. Copy the following sentences. Enclose each dependent clause in parentheses. If the clause is used as a modifier, draw an arrow from the clause to
   the word it modifies. If the clause performs the function of a noun, write
   the function above the clause.

   1. (Whatever you decide to do) is all right with me. Subject
   2. (Before we can make final plans for the election campaign,) we must get
      the approval of Mr. Rogers, (who is in charge of student activities.)
   3. The fact (that I don't agree with you) shouldn't make you change your
      mind. Appositive
   4. (Since the cabins of planes are pressurized,) most people with heart
      diseases can travel in comfort.
   5. The stockbroker (to whom I talked) said (that a crash like that of 1929
      can never happen again.) Direct object
   6. (What he said) was not (what we had expected to hear.) Predicate Nominative — Subj.
   7. He always gives (what he is doing at the moment) his full attention. Indirect Object
   8. The author (I mean) is the one (who wrote *My Antonia.*)
   9. (Before you leave,) remind me to give you the notes (I borrowed yester-
      day.)
   10. You will be judged by (what you say) and (how you say it.) Both obj. of
                                                                  prep.

D. Write the numbers 1 to 5 on your paper. After each number write the classification of the corresponding sentence according to function and structure.

1. After considering your request carefully, the directors of the bank have decided to grant you a loan. `Declarative, Simple`
2. Do you think you will have time to write all those letters, or do you want me to appoint someone to help you? `Interrog., compound-com-`
3. If you are in no hurry and want an inexpensive means of travel, arrange `plex` to go by freighter. `Declarative, complex`
`Exclam.` 4. Oh, if he were only here now, what a performance he would give!
5. The new highway has not yet been completed; however, two lanes in each direction have been opened to traffic. `Declarative, compound`

E. List the italicized words on a sheet of paper. After each word write its part of speech. `See below.`

1. *Neither* Marge nor Jack has seen your new *painting*.
2. *This* exam *has been* more difficult than I expected.
3. Put your packages *down on* that chair.
4. *Well,* I am not sure, but I am afraid that *neither* of them will be here.
5. By *listening* carefully, I was able to detect a trace of a *French* accent in her speech.

```
E. 1. Neither-conj., painting-n.
   2. This-adj., has been-v.
   3. down-adv., on-prep.
   4. Well-interj., neither-pron.
   5. listening-n., French-adj.
```

Unit 9

Usage Skills

Your goal in communicating ideas is to be able to choose words and structures that will express your ideas clearly and correctly. This goal would be relatively simple to achieve if there were only two kinds of English—right and wrong. However, since correct usage varies according to time, place, and situation, it is necessary that you be able to communicate at several different levels.

Although most of your communication is at the informal level, for which your usage of language is probably adequate, there are many occasions on which it is necessary to speak and write more formally. It is this level of usage that is emphasized in this unit. Wherever acceptable informal variations exist, such variations are indicated.

Before you begin your study of usage, complete the following Check Yourself section to determine how much you already know about correct usage.

CHECK YOURSELF

Write the numbers from 1 to 25 on a sheet of paper. After each number write the word from the parentheses that will make the sentence correct.

1. Mrs. Lawrence, accompanied by her two daughters, (is, are) vacationing in Mexico.
2. Neither Mary nor her brother (play, plays) a musical instrument.
3. It (don't, doesn't) matter.

Permit students to complete the Check Yourself
exercise before discussing it.
302   *Usage Skills*

Do not
discuss
the
answers
in great
detail
at this
point.
The pur-
pose of
the ex-
ercise
is pri-
marily
diag-
nostic.

4. Each of the members (is, are) entitled to two tickets.
5. Where (was, were) you last night when I called?
6. If someone calls me, ask (him, them) to leave a message.
7. Mathematics (is, are) my favorite subject.
8. I don't know (if, whether) I can go with you.
9. Neither the cookies nor the cake will lose (its, their) freshness in the refrigerator.
10. That is the candidate (who, whom) I believe is best qualified for the the office.
11. Have they (lain, laid) the foundation for the new school yet?
12. Larry would (of, have) gone with us if he had known sooner.
13. This is just (between, among) the three of us.
14. He was rewarded (by, with) a trip to Washington, D. C.
15. This sweater is different (than, from) the one I ordered.
16. I am (continuously, continually) being interrupted in my work.
17. The (famous, notorious) criminal escaped from prison.
18. Are you (implying, inferring) that you doubt me?
19. As soon as he comes (in, into) the room, everyone will shout, "Surprise!"
20. The sight of blood always makes me feel (nauseous, nauseated).
21. I cannot (except, accept) your invitation since I shall be out of town.
22. The club secretary wrote to the British (consul, counsel, council) for information.
23. There are (fewer, less) people here than there were last year.
24. The man (who, whom) you mean is my uncle.
25. We can hardly see (anything, nothing) from these seats.

1. Usage in Sentences

SUBJECT-VERB AGREEMENT

Do you ever use sentences like the following ones:

He don't think so.
There is several people absent.
Either they or I are wrong.
The most beautiful sight are the rose gardens.

Each of the preceding sentences is incorrect because the subject and the verb do not agree. Errors in agreement of subject and verb are among

Errors in subject-verb agreement spring largely from poor
speech habits. In classes where students carry over good speech
patterns into written work, much of this unit may be used
primarily for review and reference.

Usage in Sentences   303

the most common errors made in the use of English. Occasionally, such
errors slip into the speech even of well-educated persons. In writing, however, there is no excuse for making an error in agreement since a writer
has the opportunity to reread and revise what he has written.

Study the following facts about subjects and verbs, and apply the rules
to your speaking and writing.

A verb must agree with its subject in person and number.   [45]

She always *thinks* clearly. (Third person singular subject and third
person singular verb)

Have you heard from Lorraine? (Second person plural subject and
second person plural verb)

A singular subject requires a singular verb.   [45a]

A prepositional phrase that comes between the subject and the verb
does not affect the number of the verb. A verb always agrees with its subject, never with the object of a preposition.

Representatives from the university *are coming* to interview candi-
dates.

One of the representatives *is* Dr. Brown, the head of the service department.

The word *doesn't*, which is a contraction of *does not*, is third person,   The "he
singular number. The word *don't*, which is a contraction of *do not*, must   don't"
never be used with a singular subject in the third person.   [45m]   error
                                                                                is still
    He *doesn't* understand.   *I don't* agree.   a com-
    She *doesn't* like cabbage.   *You don't* have to leave.   mon one.
    It *doesn't* seem possible.   *They don't* see us.   Stress
                                                                                this
Words joined to a subject by *with*, *together with*, *including*, *accompanied*   this
by, *in addition to*, or *as well as* do not change the number of the subject.   rule.
If the subject is singular, the verb is singular.   [45b]

My *parents,* as well as my brother, *were* present.

His entire *collection,* including many valuable albums, *was* lost in
the fire.

Singular subjects joined by *or* or *nor* require a singular verb.   [45c]

Neither the *exterior nor* the *interior* of the building *was* attractive.

Plural subjects joined by *or* or *nor* require a plural verb.   [45d]

Neither the *books nor* the *papers are* where you said they should be.

Develop this rule carefully; it is frequently confusing to students.

If two subjects connected by *or* or *nor* differ in person or number, the verb agrees with the nearer subject.   [45e]

Either a *stadium* or *dormitories* are to be built next year.
Either *dormitories* or a *stadium is* to be built next year.

Subjects joined by *and* usually require a plural verb.   [45h]

Lew and *Helen have* already *left.*
Where *are you* and *Stelle going?*

Singular subjects joined by *and* and preceded by *every* require a singular verb.   [45i]

Every desk drawer *and* bookshelf *was* searched.
Every office *and* conference room *is* occupied.

In sentences having inverted order, the subject must be kept clearly in mind.   [45k]

There *go Michael* and *Dean.*
Is there any *alternative?*

A compound subject considered as a unit rather than as two distinct things takes a singular verb.   [45o]

Bacon and eggs is my favorite breakfast food.
Pot roast and noodles is on the menu tonight.

In a compound subject if one subject is used affirmatively and the other negatively, the verb agrees with the subject that is used affirmatively.   [45p]

She, not I, *is* at fault.
Doug, not Scott or Ed, *deserves* credit for the victory.

When the subject and the predicate nominative are different in number, the verb agrees with the subject, not the predicate nominative.   [45q]

My favorite *fruit is* apples.
Apples are my favorite fruit.

Point out to students that the subject and predicate nominative in a sentence need not be in the same number. The verb always agrees with the subject.

Each, each one, either, neither, everyone, everybody, anybody, and no-body are singular and require a singular verb. [45f]

> *Neither* of the applicants *was* qualified for the position.
> *Everyone* in both groups *likes* your idea.

All, none, and some may be either singular or plural. [45g]

None is no longer always con-sidered singular.

> *All* of them *were* anxious to go to the game, (Several, plural)
> *All* of it *was* gone. (Amount, singular)
> *None* of them *were* ready. (Several, plural)
> *None* of the corn *was* saved. (Amount, singular)
> *Some* of the students *are* absent. (Several, plural)
> *Some* of the wheat *was* saved. (Amount, singular)

Another word used in the same way is *number*. When *number* is used to mean *many,* it takes a plural verb; when it is used to refer to an arithmetical number, it takes a singular verb. When *number* is preceded by the article *a,* it is usually plural; when it is preceded by *the,* it is usually singular.

This state-ment provides a memory aid.

> A *number* of guests *have* already arrived. (Plural)
> The *number* of people present *makes* the room seem small and crowded. (Singular)

Words that are plural in form but singular in meaning take a singular verb. [45n]

Words affected by this rule fall into the following categories:

1. Words such as *physics, mathematics, mumps, news,* and *politics.*

> *Mathematics* is my favorite subject.
> The *news is* good.

2. Subjects that are plural in form but describe a quantity or number and are considered as a unit.

> *Ten dollars is* too much to pay.
> *Seven from twelve leaves* five.

3. The titles of books, plays, paintings, musical compositions, or other such works.

> *"Pomp and Circumstance" is* frequently used as a graduation march.
> *"The Killers" is* a story by Ernest Hemingway.

Discuss the three categories of words that are plural in form but singular in meaning. Draw from students as many additional examples as necessary to establish the rule firmly in the students' minds.

The pronoun *you*, even when it refers to one person, requires a plural verb.   [45j]

> *Have you seen* that movie, Jan?
>
> *You are* all welcome.

Meaning
deter-
mines
number.

A collective noun requires a singular verb if the group is thought of as a unit; a plural verb is required if the individuals in a group are considered.   [45l]

> My *family* is planning to move to Florida. (Unit)
>
> My *family differ* in their political views. (Individuals)

 DEVELOPING YOUR SKILL

A. Write the numbers 1 to 10 on a sheet of paper. After each number write the verb from the parentheses that will make the sentence correct. After each verb write whether the subject is singular or plural.

1. He (don't, doesn't) like to speak in public.
2. Neither Les nor his brothers (like, likes) dancing.
3. Beth, (was, were) you with them last night?
4. Cake and milk (taste, tastes) good after an evening of studying.
5. The flowers for the table (was, were) a welcome gift.
6. There (come, comes) the Harding twins.
7. Every one of the girls (thinks, think) the dance should be formal.
8. All the flour (has, have) been sold.
9. Five miles (is, are) a long distance to walk.
10. The folders, not the notebook, (is, are) what I asked for.

B. Rewrite the following sentences, correcting any errors in agreement. If the sentence is correct, write *C* after the appropriate number.

C   1. Do you agree that physics is a difficult subject?

   2. When the leading performers in a play appears on stage for the first time, the audience always applaud. s

has 3. Measles ~~have~~ reached epidemic proportions in our city.

is 4. The corned beef and cabbage ~~are~~ particularly good tonight.

Is 5. ~~Are~~ either of you planning to nominate anyone for office?

C   6. Mother, as well as Dad, is firm about my being home early on week nights.

have 7. None of these points ~~has~~ anything to do with the proposal.

is 8. The number of tickets already sold this year ~~are~~ greater than last year's total.

   9. If each of you receive a weekly allowance in addition to what you earn, you should be able to save some money.

C 10. Either you or I am to let her know when the plans are definite.

The exercises above may be used for oral as well as written practice.

PRONOUN-ANTECEDENT AGREEMENT

Pronouns have meaning in sentences only when they clearly refer to antecedents and agree with their antecedents. Unless the reader can understand the reference of all the pronouns you have used, your writing loses clarity and meaning.

Every pronoun should refer clearly to a definite antecedent.   [39a]

Notice the ambiguity in the following sentence because of the unclear reference of the pronoun.

> Geri argued with Pat about *her* history assignment.

In the preceding sentence the reference of the pronoun *her* is not clear. The reader does not know whether the argument was over Geri's or Pat's assignment. The sentence can be made clear by repeating the name of the person whose assignment is meant.

> Geri argued with Pat about *Pat's* history assignment.
> Geri argued with Pat about *Geri's* history assignment.

Sometimes changing the structure of the sentence makes the meaning clearer and avoids awkwardness.

> Geri and Pat argued about Pat's history assignment.

Study the following examples:

> Sue was talking with Jean, and *she* looked very worried. (Ambiguous)
> Sue, who was talking with Jean, looked very worried. (Clear)
> When she was talking with Jean, Sue looked very worried. (Clear)

> Mr. George told Les that *he* would have to work overtime. (Ambiguous)
> Mr. George said, "Les, you will have to work overtime." (Clear)

The repetition of the name often creates an awkward sentence. Stress clarification through a change in structure.

The amount of teaching, review, and practice necessary will vary according to the backgrounds and capabilities of your students.

Vague-
ness
of refer-
ence can
destroy
the ef-
fective-
ness of
ideas.

The antecedent of a pronoun should always be definitely stated. [39b]

I enjoyed my visit to San Francisco. They are courteous and helpful to tourists. (Vague)

In the preceding sentence, the antecedent of *they* may have been in the mind of the writer, but it is not expressed. No people, other than the speaker, are mentioned.

I enjoyed my visit to San Francisco. *San Franciscans* are courteous and helpful to tourists. (Clear)

Even in sentences in which the pronoun has a clearly stated antecedent, the meaning will not be clear unless the pronoun agrees with its antecedent.

A pronoun must agree with its antecedent in person, number, and gender.   [46]

Larry will get better work from *his* committee members if *he* plans *their* duties with *them*.

In the preceding sentence, *his* and *he* refer to *Larry*. *Larry* is third person singular, masculine; therefore, *his* and *he* are third person singular, masculine. *Their* and *them* refer to *members*. *Members* is third person plural, common gender; therefore, *their* and *them* are third person plural, common gender. *(Their* and *them* are used in all genders.) A pronoun does not have to agree with its antecedent in case. The case of a pronoun is determined by the pronoun's function in a sentence.

When the antecedent of a pronoun is a noun or pronoun of common gender, the masculine pronoun should be used, unless it is clear that a girl or a woman is meant.   [46h]

Every *student* was asked to list *his* outside interests. *(Student* is common gender. It may mean either boys or girls, or both.)

Each *member* of the girls' fencing team did *her* best. (In this sentence it is clear that the members are all girls.)

Pronouns referring to the singular pronouns *each, everyone, anyone, one, no one, nobody, someone, somebody, anybody,* and *everybody* must be singular.   [46a]

Has *everyone* been issued *his* books?

Impress upon students that it is not necessary to say "his or her" when the antecedent of a pronoun is in the common gender.

A pronoun must be in the third person if its antecedent is a noun or an indefinite pronoun. [46g]

Unless they are used in direct address or in apposition with pronouns in the first or second person, all nouns and indefinite pronouns are in the third person. Notice the lack of agreement in the following sentence:

If a *boy* wishes to be trusted, *you* must develop a sense of responsibility. (The noun *boy* is the antecedent and is in third person; *you* is a second person pronoun.)

The following sentence is improved.

If a *boy* wishes to be trusted, *he* must develop a sense of responsibility. *(Boy* and *he* are both in third person.)

Do not be misled by a phrase such as *of you* coming between the pronoun and its antecedent. The following sentence is incorrect:

Neither of you has paid *your* dues. *(Neither,* the antecedent, is an indefinite pronoun in the third person. *Your* is a second person pronoun.)

The following sentence is improved:

Neither of you has paid *his* dues. (Both *Neither* and *his* are in the third person.)

A singular pronoun is used to refer to nouns like *mumps, measles, news,* and *mathematics,* all of which are plural in form but singular in meaning. [46b]

Although *mumps* is contagious, I didn't get *it.*

A plural pronoun is used to refer to two antecedents joined by *and.* [46c]

Don and Al brought *their* guitars.

A singular pronoun is used to refer to singular antecedents joined by *or* or *nor.* [46d]

Either *Betty or Linda* will lend you *her* notes.

A plural pronoun is used to refer to plural antecedents joined by *or* or *nor.* [46e]

Neither the *reporters nor* the *photographers* met *their* deadlines.

Mastery of clear pronoun reference and pronoun-antecedent agreement is essential to mature use of language.

This is an important rule and one that is frequently difficult for students to remember. Emphasize it in your teaching of agreement.

A pronoun should agree with the nearer of two antecedents joined by or or nor. [46f]

Neither the roses nor the *camellia* has lost *its* freshness.

The pronoun *what* is an exception to the pronoun-antecedent rules. The antecedent of *what* is implied in the meaning of *what—that which;* therefore, *what* does not require an antecedent.

Do not use *what* to refer to an expressed antecedent. [46i]

The dress *what (that which)* you sent was the wrong size. (Incorrect)
The dress *that* you sent was the wrong size. (Correct)
I don't understand *what (that which)* you mean. (Correct)

  DEVELOPING YOUR SKILL

After stu-
dents
have
com-
pleted
this
exer-
cise,
you may
wish to
discuss
with
them the
reasons
for the
changes.

The following sentences contain errors in pronoun-antecedent agreement. Rewrite the sentences, making any changes necessary to make the sentences correct. In some sentences you may have to change the form of a verb.

1. The company gives a guarantee to each of its customers when ~~they~~ `he` buy s new merchandise.
2. Frank told Charles that he was sure ~~he~~ `Charles (See also below.)` would be elected class president.
3. Everyone is welcome to attend the lecture if t~~hey wish.~~ `he wishes`
4. Each of us has signed ~~their~~ name to the petition. `his`
5. Since the toaster is broken, we can't have ~~it~~ for breakfast. `toast`
6. I haven't finished the report ~~what~~ is due today. `that`
7. You must submit the plan to your teachers or to the principal for ~~their~~ `his` approval.
8. The little boy asked his father how tall he was. `See bottom margin.`
9. Every employee was asked to make ~~their~~ contribution as generous as possible. `his`
10. Somebody must have put ~~their~~ coat in my locker. `his`

OTHER USAGE PROBLEMS

Usage errors often indicate careless thinking. Sentences that contain usage faults are awkward and unclear. If you wish to make your writing clear, learn to use the accepted forms and constructions that follow. Avoid substandard usage.

2. Frank said, "I am sure I will be elected class president."
8. The little boy asked, "Father, how tall are you?" or "Father, how tall am I?"

Using pronouns correctly [39]

In standard English reflexive and intensive pronouns are used only to refer to other words in sentences or for emphasis.

Avoid using reflexive and intensive pronouns in place of personal pronouns. [39e]

That message was intended for Claire or *me*. (Not *for Claire and myself*)

Avoid using the illiterate pronoun forms *hisself*, *theirself* and *theirselves*. [39f]

He decided to do the work *himself*. (Not *hisself*)

They *themselves* are not sure what they will do. (Not *theirself* or *theirselves*)

When you use personal pronouns in a compound construction, always mention the person spoken to (second person), the person spoken about (third person), and the speaker (first person), in that order. Courtesy requires that the pronoun that you use to refer to yourself *(I, my, mine, me, we, our, ours, us)* be given last in a compound element.

This is a matter of courtesy rather than of grammatical usage.

The order of personal pronouns in compounds is second person, third person, first person. [39g]

You, she and *I* have been chosen for the pageant.
These sandwiches are for *you, Bob,* and *me*.

Empha-
size
this
rule. **Avoid using them as a demonstrative pronoun.**   [39h]

Those are my books. (Not *Them are my books*)

Redundancy is a common error in the use of pronouns. Be particularly careful not to add unnecessary pronouns when you use the contraction *let's*. *Let's* means *let us*.

"Let's
us" is
a par-
ticu-
larly
common
error. **Avoid using redundant pronouns.**   [39i]

Let's decide about this now. (Not *Let's* us *decide about this now.*)

The two sweaters are identical. (Not *The two sweaters are* both *identical.*)

My aunt gave me a puppy. (Not *My aunt* she *gave me a puppy.*)

It is sometimes used impersonally to introduce an idea, as in the sentences *It was he who directed the play* or *It was sunny this afternoon.* Expressions such as *it is true, it is certain, it is imperative,* and *it is necessary* are also correct. In all other uses, *however,* the pronouns *it* and *they* should not be used indefinitely; they should have clearly expresed antecedents.

Avoid the indefinite use of you, it, and they.   [39j]

In this novel *it* shows the way people lived during the Middle Ages. *(It* has no antecedent.)

This novel shows the way people lived during the Middle Ages. (Improved)

Nowadays *you* don't find many blacksmith shops in operation. *(You* doesn't have a clear antecedent.)

Nowadays *one* doesn't find many blacksmith shops in operation. (Improved)

They say that more teachers are needed at the college level. *(They* has no antecedent.)

It is said that more teachers are needed at the college level. (Improved)

They have good roads in that section of the state. *(They* has no antecedent.)

That section of the state has good roads. (Improved)

There is an increasing tendency to use what someone has called "the great anonymous they." Students should be cautioned to avoid this usage.

2. Instrumental groups will be featured in our annual concert.

Usage in Sentences 313

> DEVELOPING YOUR SKILL   This exercise may be used for oral as well as written practice.

The following sentences contain errors in the use of pronouns. Rewrite the sentences, correcting the errors.

1. ~~Phil, you,~~ and I should plan to study together. *You, Phil,*

See 2. In our annual concert, they plan to feature the instrumental groups.

top 3. Five of the students ~~all~~ worked together to prepare the debate brief.

margin 4. Did he do all the redecorating ~~hisself~~? *himself*

Those 5. ~~Them~~ are the dresses I like.

6. I read an article on hypnotism, but I still don't understand how ~~they~~ can make people insensitive to pain. *hypnotists or hypnotism*

C 7. Let's work together on the oral report for history. *3.   1.   2.*

8. Of all the drawings submitted, the judges selected mine, yours, and his.

9. My aunts, uncles, and cousins ~~they all~~ came to the family reunion.

The 10. ~~In the~~ paper ~~it~~ lists all the schools in which adult education classes will be held.

Using modifiers correctly [41]

An error in usage that is frequently heard—particularly in informal usage—is the substitution of adjectives for adverbs.

Learn to distinguish between adjectives and adverbs. [41a]

Jack sings *well*. (Not *good)*
That story is *very* interesting. (Not *real)*
I am *surely* glad you could come. (Not *sure)*
Are you *almost* ready? (Not *most)*
It is not *too* late to change your mind. (Not *two)*

Well may be used as an adjective when it refers to someone's state of health.

I don't feel *well* today.

Do not misuse adverbs for predicate adjectives. Verbs such as *be, seem, become, appear, grow, remain, sound, feel, taste,* and *smell* are often completed by predicate adjectives. Determine whether the modifier refers to the subject (predicate adjective) or to the verb (adverb).

The corn in our garden grew *tall* last summer. (Predicate adjective)
The corn in our garden grew *rapidly* last summer. (Adverb)

Students may raise the point that they constantly hear real and sure substituted for very and surely. Although their objection has some validity, point out to students that these usages have not yet been accepted into the standard vocabulary of English.

Many of the errors made in the use of modifiers are made in the comparison of adjectives and adverbs. When comparing adjectives and adverbs do not use *more* and *most* with words to which *er* and *est* have been added. Be careful, too, not to create double comparatives and superlatives with irregular adjectives and adverbs.

You may
wish to
teach
this rule
when you
teach
compari-
son of
adjec-
tives
and
adverbs
(pages 230-
232).

Avoid double comparatives and superlatives. [40e]

I see you *oftener* (or *more often*) than I see Lila. (Not *more oftener*)
Sandy made the *best* possible choice. (Not *most best* or *bestest*)

Words such as *not, hardly, scarcely, never,* and *only* (when *only* means *no more than*) are negative words. A single verb should not be modified by more than one negative adverb. Also avoid using the negative *not* with words such as *no, nothing, no one, nowhere,* and *neither.*

Avoid using a double negative construction in sentences. [41c]

I have *never* seen an opera. (Not *haven't never*)
We couldn't find him *anywhere*. (Not *couldn't find him nowhere*)
Adverbs such as *again, back, ever, over, up,* and *with* are frequently used where they are not necessary. The result is redundant speech or writing.

Avoid using unnecessary adverbs. [41d]

He *rarely* participates in social activities. (Not *rarely ever*)
Jim had to *rework* the problem. (Not *rework the problem over*)

 DEVELOPING YOUR SKILL

Rewrite the following sentences correcting any errors in the use of modifiers.

1. Nobody didn't realize ᵈwhat was happening at the time.
2. I haven't only enough paper for myself.
3. The view was even more lovelier than I had remembered.
4. Clay is real happy about his appointment and we are sure glad for him. very, surely
5. One seldom ever meets up with such a distinguished person.
6. She spoke very quietly, but she didn't look calmly.
7. I don't never expect to see a more better match.
8. It was two dark to see good, but I am real sure it was Carl. very too, well
almost
9. He appeared suddenly and disappeared most as sudden. ly
10. Has everyone paid up his dues for this year?

You may wish to use this exercise for oral as well
as written practice.

Using conjunctions correctly   [44]

Connectives can change the meaning of a sentence by changing the You may
relationships expressed. Learn to use connectives to express exact rela- wish to
tionships. corre-

Co-ordinating conjunctions may be used to *add* one word or idea to late
another, to point up *contrast*, to indicate *choice*, and to show *result*. The the
following list of conjunctions show the relationships indicated: teach-
ing of

> Addition: *and, both . . . and, also, besides, furthermore, likewise,* this
> *moreover, then* mate-
> Contrast: *but, however, nevertheless, still, yet* rial on
> Choice: *or, nor, either . . . or, neither . . . nor, otherwise* conjunc-
> Result: *therefore, consequently, accordingly, hence* tions

Use connectives that express relationships between co-ordinate ideas with
the pres-
exactly. [44e] entation

Both Hank *and* Ben are interested in electronics. (Addition) of

I have sent an application to a university in England; *however,* I conjunc-
don't know yet whether I shall be able to go to school overseas. (Con- tions on
trast) pages

Don has to make up a history course; *otherwise,* he will not graduate 243–247.
with our class. (Choice)

There are no playgrounds in some neighborhoods; *therefore,* the
children play in the streets. (Result)

Use *that*, not *because*, to introduce a noun clause. Use *because* to intro-
duce an adverb clause. [44b]

The reason the doctor was delayed was *that* (not *because)* he had an
emergency call. (Noun clause)

The doctor was delayed *because* he had an emergency call. (Adverb
clause)

Use *that*, not *where* or *as*, in sentences such as the following. [44c]

Did you read *that* (not *where)* the strike has been settled?

I don't know *that* (not *as)* I believe his story.

Use *if* to introduce a conditional clause. Use *whether* to introduce a noun
clause used as the direct object of a verb. [44d]

I could finish this job more quickly *if* I weren't interrupted so often.
(Conditional)

I wonder *whether* there will be room for all of us. (Noun clause)

The <u>whether-if</u> distinction also seems to be disappearing
from informal speech. However, students should be taught the
difference and should be required to make the distinction.

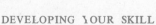

DEVELOPING YOUR SKILL

This
exer-
cise
may also
be used
for oral
practice.

A. Write the numbers 1 to 10 on a sheet of paper. After each number write the word or words from the parentheses that will make the sentence correct.

1. I don't know (as, whether) I want to enter the contest.
2. The reason he gave for his rudeness was (because, that) he was tired and upset.
3. Did you see in the paper (that, where) the entire athletic program is being revised?
4. Al says he doesn't know (as, that) he wants to run for office.
5. It is hard to tell (if, whether) he is serious.
6. Have you heard (where, that) activity fees are going to be increased?
7. (If, Whether) you enjoy music, you will like the new program on FM radio.
8. The reason for tabling the motion is (because, that) we need more information.
9. I wonder (whether, if) the dance will be a success.
10. I don't know (as, whether) anyone is home.

See p.
T79
for this
exercise.

B. Combine each of the following pairs of sentences into a single sentence, using a connective that shows the exact relationship between the ideas.

1. Laura plays tennis well. Ed plays tennis well.
2. Marilyn passed the scholarship exam with the highest grade ever received. She is sure to be granted a full tuition scholarship.
3. Ed's accident will keep him from playing football this year. He plans to work for the team in any way he can.
4. We didn't have a quorum present at the meeting. The result was that the meeting was postponed until next week.
5. Howard has to decide about the job offer today. If he doesn't, the offer will be withdrawn.

Using prepositions correctly [42]

Do not confuse a preposition with a conjunction. Use a preposition to introduce a phrase and a conjunction to introduce a clause. [44a]

We won't leave *without* you. (Preposition)
We won't go *unless* (not *without*) you go too. (Conjunction)
Your dress looks just *like* mine. (Preposition)
It looks *as if* (not *like*) I shall have to do it myself. (Conjunction)

If students consider function in the sentence, they should not confuse prepositions with conjunctions.

In colloquial English *like* is frequently used as a conjunction. However, the best speakers and writers prefer to use *as* or *as if* to introduce a clause.

Mother still treats us *like* we were babies. (Colloquial)
Mother still treats us *as if* we were babies. (Formal)

Did you give him the message *like* I asked you to? (Colloquial)
Did you give him the message *as* I asked you to? (Formal)

As may be used as a preposition when it means "in the role of." Notice the difference in meaning between *like* and *as* when both are used as prepositions.

She acted *like* a spoiled child.
She acted *as* a spoiled child in the play.

Do not use *like* in place of the conjunction *that*.

He feels *that* (not *like*) he is capable of the work.

Avoid redundant prepositions such as *at* and *to* with *where*, and *of* with *off, inside, outside,* and *had*.

Do not use unnecessary prepositions.   [42m]

Where is Joel? (Not *Where is Joel at?*)
Where did he go? (Not *Where did he go to?*)
The lamp was knocked off (not *off of*) the table.
If I had (not *had of*) known sooner, I should have called you.

> DEVELOPING YOUR SKILL

Write the numbers 1 to 10 on a sheet of paper. After each number write the word or words from the parentheses that will make the corresponding sentence correct. Select the terms that are accepted formal usage.

1. She never makes a decision (without, <u>unless</u>) she first finds out what her friends think.
2. It looks (like, <u>as if</u>) I was mistaken.
3. Joan wants to be an actress and, (<u>as</u>, like) many aspiring actresses, is working with a little theater group.
4. The contestants dived (<u>off</u>, off of) the edge of the pool.
5. Everyone treated us (<u>like</u>, as) royalty during our visit.
6. It looks (like, <u>as if</u>) it might rain. I don't know (as, <u>that</u>) it will, though.

This exercise may also be used for oral practice.

The decision to use colloquial English in a given situation should be a deliberate one; it should not be the result of lack of knowledge concerning more formal usage. Impress this point upon students.

7. He said that if he (had, had of) been responsible, he would have admitted it.
8. We have been looking everywhere for you. Where did you (go, go to)?
9. The operation cannot be performed (without, unless) the patient has a blood transfusion first.
10. Tie your dog (outside, outside of) the garage.

Review Exercises—Usage in Sentences

Most of the following sentences contain errors in usage. Rewrite the incorrect sentences correctly. If a sentence is correct, write the word *correct* after the appropriate number.

1. He don't have no money for lunch.   doesn't, any
2. Never in my life had I been so surprised before.
has 3. Neither the cookies nor the coffee have been delivered yet.
C 4. Nothing, not even the threat of failure, stirs him to action.
C 5. The old man's chief support was his son and daughter.
unless 6. You won't have time to eat lunch without you hurry.
was 7. Fifteen dollars were our total expenses.
has 8. Athletics have become increasingly important in this country.
Were 9. Was you there when Lorraine won the state competition?
has 10. The committee have recommended a course of action.
Has 11. Have either of you written for college catalogs?

The Review Exercises on this page and on the following page may also be used for oral review.

12. Miss Wilson told Irene that she would have to postpone ~~her~~ interview. `Irene's`
13. ~~They have~~ many beautiful vacation spots in New York State. `There are`
14. The reason I didn't tell you before was ~~because~~ I wasn't sure of all the facts. `that`
15. Has everyone received ~~their~~ share of the inheritance? `his`
16. If a man hopes to succeed in business, ~~you~~ must be willing to work hard. `he`
17. The painting ~~what~~ you bought is an excellent reproduction. `that`
18. Arthur and Jim will have to settle their problem ~~theirselves.~~ `themselves`
C 19. It is imperative that you do this immediately.
20. ~~In this~~ magazine article ~~it~~ discusses new techniques in cancer detection. `This`
21. Let's ~~us~~ arrange a surprise birthday party for Ray. `or Let us`
C 22. The plane accident was the worst in the history of aviation.
23. I am ~~real~~ anxious to visit New York City again; ~~however,~~ I shall spend at least a week of my vacation there. `very, consequently or therefore`
24. When he returned ~~back~~ from Europe, he found that many of his friends had moved away.
25. Did you report the incident ~~like~~ I suggested? `as`

2. Specific Word Forms

There are in English many words that are easily confused because the user is aware of their similarities but fails to recognize their differences. Selective use of language requires that you learn to distinguish between words that are similar in some respects but unlike in others.

TROUBLESOME PRONOUNS

Use *who* in the objective case, *whose* in the possessive case, and *whom* in the objective case.   **[39d]**

`The who-whom problem is approached through an analysis of the construction of the sentence.`

The relative and interrogative pronouns *who*, *whose*, and *whom* follow the same rules as the personal pronouns. The nominative case form *who* may be used as the subject of a verb or as a predicate nominative.

The clerk *who* sold me the shoes was very patient. (*Who* is the subject of *sold*.)

Who gave you that information? (*Who* is the subject of *gave*.)

We don't yet know *who* our new neighbors are. (*Who* is the predicate nominative after *are*. The natural order of the relative clause is *our new neighbors are who*.)

`Review with students the parts of the sentence, the functions of words in sentences, and the principles of agreement.`

The possessive case form *whose* is used as a modifier.

The family *whose* house this is moved here from Wisconsin. *(Whose modifies house.)*

Whose side are you on? *(Whose modifies side.)*

Empha-
size
the
point
that in
formal
usage
the
object
of a
prep-
osi-
tion
is al-
ways
in the
objec-
tive
case
re-
gard-
less
of the
place-
ment
of the
prep-
osi-
tion.

Do not confuse the possessive case form *whose* with the contraction *who's*. *Who's* means *who is*.

Whose books are these? (Possessive case)

Who's going with you? (Contraction)

The objective case form *whom* may be used as a direct object, an indirect object, the object of a preposition, the subject of an infinitive, or the complement of an infinitive.

This is the girl *whom* I met at camp last summer. *(Whom* is the direct object of *met*. The natural order of the relative clause is *I met whom.)*

The man *whom* you sent the letter is president of the company. *(Whom* is the indirect object of *sent*. The natural order of the relative clause is *you sent [to] whom the letter.)*

My parents insist upon knowing the boys with *whom* I go out. *(Whom* is the object of the preposition *with.)*

Sometimes sentences are smoother when the preposition is placed at the end. In formal usage the object of the preposition must still be in the objective case even though it precedes the preposition.

Whom did you vote for? (The natural order of this sentence is *You did vote for whom?)*

In informal conversation *who* is often accepted when the pronoun precedes the preposition; however, this usage should be avoided in writing and in formal speaking situations.

Who did you ask for? (Informal conversation)

Whom did you ask for? (Formal usage)

The following sentences illustrate the use of *whom* with infinitives.

Whom do you expect to sign the petition? *(Whom* is the subject of the infinitive *to sign.* The natural order of this sentence is *You do expect whom to sign the petition?)*

Whom do you plan to see in Los Angeles? *(Whom* is the object of the infinitive *to see.* The natural order of the sentence is *You do plan to see whom?)*

The subject of an infinitive is in the objective case.

In sentences containing relative pronouns, do not be misled by parenthetical clauses that come between the relative pronoun and the rest of the clause. If the sentence makes sense without the parenthetical clause, such a clause does not affect the case of the relative pronoun. In the following sentences the parenthetical clauses are enclosed in parentheses.

Who (do you think) came to see me last night? *(Who* is the subject of *came.)*

He is a boy *whom* (I am sure) everyone respects. *(Whom* is the direct object of *respects.)*

Whoever, whosever, and *whomever* follow the same rules as *who, whose,* and *whom.*

Eric shows his stamp collection to *whoever* comes to the house. (The entire relative clause *whoever comes to the house* is the object of the preposition *to. Whoever* is the subject of *comes.)*

Whosever car that is, it must be moved immediately. *(Whosever* modifies *car.)*

She can get along with *whomever* she meets. *(Whomever she meets* is the object of the preposition *with. Whomever* is the direct object of *meets.)*

 DEVELOPING YOUR SKILL

Write the numbers 1 to 10 on a sheet of paper. After each number write the word from the parentheses that will make the sentence correct formal usage. Following each word you select, write its use in the sentence.

1. I can't imagine (who, whom) could be calling at this hour. Subject
2. Please let me know (who, whom) you would like to see when you come to visit. Object of infinitive

If you use the exercise that begins on this page for oral practice, insist upon distinct enunciation. If there is any doubt as to whether students are saying who or whom, ask them to spell the words.

3. (<u>Whose,</u> Who's) invitation have you accepted? Modifies <u>invitation</u>
4. (Who, <u>Whom</u>) do you consider to be the outstanding student in our class? Subject of infinitive <u>to be</u>

Direct obj.   5. Are you sure it was she (who, <u>whom</u>) you saw at the drugstore?

Subject   6. Miss Berman is a teacher (<u>who,</u> whom) everyone agrees makes history an interesting subject.

Obj. of prep.   7. Do you know (who,<u> whom</u>) the flowers came from?

Direct obj.   8. Give the chairmanship to (whoever, <u>whomever</u>) you think capable.

Direct obj.   9. I tried to get in touch with the decorator (who, <u>whom</u>) you recommended.

10. The judges won't announce (<u>who,</u> whom) the winner is until tomorrow. Predicate nominative

TROUBLESOME VERBS

Certain verbs in English cause confusion because of similarities in spelling or in meaning. When you have mastered the following usage problems, you will have overcome some of the most common errors made in the use of English.

Using verbs correctly   [31]

Learn the meanings and the principal parts of the verbs *lie* and *lay* and *sit* and *set* to use the verbs correctly.   [31a]

Lie and *sit* are complete intransitive verbs. They never take direct objects nor are they used in the passive voice. *Lay* and *set* are transitive verbs. They may take direct objects or they may be used in the passive voice. Study the forms of these four verbs.

Insist upon students' learning the principal parts of these verbs.

PRESENT	PAST	PAST PARTICIPLE	PRESENT PARTICIPLE
lie (to recline)	lay	lain	lying
sit (to rest)	sat	sat	sitting
lay (to put into place)	laid	laid	laying
set (to put into place)	set	set	setting

A successful approach to teaching the <u>lie-lay</u>, <u>sit-set</u>, and <u>rise-raise</u> distinctions is often from the point of view of intransitive and transitive verbs.

Specific Word Forms   323

Yesterday I *lay* down for an hour after school.   Intransitive
Mother *had* just *lain* down when the doorbell rang.   Intransitive
Have you *been sitting* here long?   Intransitive
The patient *sat* up for an hour today.   Intransitive
Lay your books on the desk and come help me.   Transitive   Transi-
The foundation for our new house *was laid* last week. (Passive voice) tive
Ronni *set* her new plants in front of the picture window.   Transitive
Their umbrellas *were set* outside the door. (Passive voice)   Transitive

**Rise is a complete intransitive verb. It never has a direct object. *Raise*
is a transitive verb and may have a direct object or may be in the passive
voice.**   [31b]

		PAST	PRESENT
PRESENT	PAST	PARTICIPLE	PARTICIPLE
rise (to go up)	rose	risen	rising
raise (to cause	raised	raised	raising
something			
to go up)			

The sun *rises* in the east.   Intransitive
The sun *had* not yet *risen* when he started out.   Intransitive
Mrs. Coleman *raises* herbs in her garden.   Transitive
She *has been raising* herbs for many years.   Transitive
All the herbs *are raised* for her own use. (Passive voice)   Transitive

Ear
train-
ing
in the
correct
forms
is as
impor-
tant as
prac-
tice in
writing
the cor-
rect
forms.

Learn to use *borrow* and *lend* correctly. *Borrow* implies receiving; *lend* implies giving. [31f]

May I *borrow* one of your pencils?
Will you *lend* me one of your pencils?

Learn to distinguish between *bring* and *take*. *Bring* implies motion toward the speaker or listener; *take* implies motion away from the speaker. [31g]

Bring me the report you wrote. (Motion toward the speaker)
I shall *bring* you the report in a moment. (Motion toward the listener)
Take these records to the filing room, please. (Motion away from the speaker)

Do not confuse the meanings of *learn* and *teach*. *Learn* means "to receive knowledge"; *teach* means "to impart knowledge." [31h]

My mother *taught* me to bake an apple pie.
She says I *learned* my lessons well.

Learn to use *let* and *leave* accurately. *Let* means "to allow" or "to permit"; *leave* means "to go away" or "to allow to remain." [31i]

Let me help you with that.
We shall *leave* in an hour.
Leave your package here until we return.

Learn the correct use of *may* and *can*. *May* implies permission; *can* implies physical or mental ability. [31j]

You *may* leave now if you have finished your work. (Permission)
He *can* do the work if he applies himself. (Ability)

May is also used to express possibility or a wish.

It *may* snow this afternoon. (Possibility)
May you be successful in your new venture! (Wish)

Might is the past form of *may*. *Might* is used after a verb in the past tense; *may*, after a verb in the present tense.

She *said* that she *might* be willing to serve on the committee.
She *says* that she *may* be willing to serve on the committee.

The verbs on this page are frequently confused
because of similarity in meaning.

► DEVELOPING YOUR SKILL

The following selection contains errors in the use of verbs. Rewrite the selection, correcting the errors. Underline the changes you make.

lying   I had been ~~laying~~ across my bed listening to my new album. Sud-
  sat   denly I ~~set~~ up and thought, "I've ~~got~~ to raise some money if I'm   have
 take   going to ~~bring~~ Sandra to the dance Friday night." I thought about
        whether I could talk my brother into ~~borrowing~~ me some money,   lending
        but then I decided there was no point in asking him. I already owed
taught him a dollar, and experience had ~~learned~~ me that he wouldn't ~~bor-~~   lend
        ~~row~~ me any more money until after I had paid my debt. I knew that
  let   Dad wouldn't ~~leave~~ me have my next week's allowance in advance.
teach   He was trying to ~~learn~~ me to live within a budget. What could I do?
might   I thought I ~~may~~ tell Sandra that I didn't feel well Friday afternoon.
        But that wouldn't be fair. There was only one solution. I ~~raised~~ from   rose
        my bed and went down to the kitchen. "Mom, what were those jobs
        you said the Ladies' Auxiliary would pay me for doing?"

Using auxiliary verbs correctly

Current informal usage tends to accept *will* and *would* in all persons to express future tense. Most good speakers and writers, however, make distinctions in the use of *shall* and *will* and *should* and *would*.

With slower classes, you may wish to avoid the shall-will distinction. More advanced students, however, should be aware of the differences in usage.

Use *shall* in the first person and *will* in the second and third persons to express a simple future (expectation). *Should* is usually used like *shall*, and *would*, like *will*.   [27a]

> I *shall* be seventeen in April.
> If you don't hurry, you *will* be late.
> I *should* like to talk further about this matter.
> John *would* be glad to help you if you asked him.

Use *will* in the first person and *shall* in the second and third persons to express strong feeling, command, determination, or promise on the part of the speaker.

> I *will* see that she sends you the information this afternoon. (Determination)
>
> He promises that he *shall* write every day. (Promise)

Use *should* in all persons to express obligation, duty, or a condition.
                                                                [27b]

> I *should* get more sleep than I do. (Obligation)
> If he *should* ask you, tell him I have gone shopping. (Condition)

Use *would* in all persons to express habitual action.   [27c]

> When I was a child, I *would* sit looking out the window for hours.
> Bob *would* always tease me about wearing out the window seat.

Empha-
size
this
point
with
all
classes.

The following facts will help you avoid illiterate usage of auxiliary verbs.

Avoid using *better* for *had better* as a synonym for *ought to*.   [31c]

> I *had better* (not *better*) study harder.

Do not use an auxiliary with *ought*.   [31d]

> You *ought* (not *had ought*) to explain the situation to Rita.

Do not use the preposition *of* for the verb *have* after *could*, *should*, *would*, *may*, *might*, or *must*.   [42d]

> I *could have* (not *could of*) gone had I wanted to.
> She *must have* (not *must of*) misunderstood you.

Do not use *would have* in an *if* clause.   [31e]

> If you *had* (not *would have*) told me, I might have been able to help you.

Stress the rules that teach the avoidance of illiterate usage. Training in the use of correct forms should be auditory as well as visual.

DEVELOPING YOUR SKILL

Write the numbers 1 to 10 on a sheet of paper. After each number write the word or words from the parentheses that make the sentence correct.

1. I give you my word that I (shall, <u>will</u>) be there on time.
2. We (<u>should,</u> would) like to see you soon again.
3. Alex (better, <u>had better</u>) stop wasting so much time.
4. The others (<u>must have,</u> must of) left already.
5. They (hadn't ought, <u>ought not</u>) to have repeated that slanderous gossip.
6. I (should, <u>would</u>) never have let you borrow my notebook if I (would have, <u>had</u>) known you would be so careless.
7. He is determined that he (shall, <u>will</u>) go to college.
8. We (<u>shall,</u> will) send you the information as soon as possible.
9. You (<u>ought,</u> had ought) to apologize for your rudeness.
10. I told you I (should, <u>would</u>) do it, and I (shall, <u>will</u>).

This exercise may be used for oral practice also.

TROUBLESOME MODIFIERS

<u>Errors in the use of modifiers are frequently the result of carelessness.</u> <u>Bad speech habits are sometimes picked up from listening to others and then are transferred to writing.</u> Do not mar your speech and writing with illiterate modifier usage.

Less refers to a quantity of something and is always used to modify singular nouns. Fewer refers to the number of something and is always used with plural nouns. [41b]

There is *less* cake left than I thought.
He has *fewer* chickens this year than he had last year.

Use *this* and *that* to modify singular nouns and *these* and *those* to modify plural nouns. [41e]

This kind of apple is my favorite.
Have you ever eaten *that* kind of chocolate.
These types of reports are long and involved.
Those types of people always look for trouble.

Do not use *here* or *there* after the adjectives *this* or *that*.

This (not *this here)* kind of land is good for farming.

When the ear recognizes the correct forms, errors tend to disappear.

These
usages
are
sub-
standard
and
should
be
avoided.

Do not use *a* or *an* after *this kind, this sort,* or *this type.*

This kind of (not *this kind of a*) program interests people.

Avoid the illiterate use of modifiers. [41f]

Right should never be used as an adverb of degree.

He seems *very* (not *right*) capable.

We are *very* (not *right*) pleased with your work.

Do not add *s* to words such as *anywhere, nowhere, somewhere, every-where.*

I couldn't find him *anywhere* (not *anywheres*).

Do not use *nohow* for *at all.*

I can't do the work *at all* (not *nohow*).

Do not use *worse* to mean *more* or *in the worst way* to mean *very much.*

I want a new dress *more* (not *worse*) than ever.

I want that dress *very much* (not *in the worst way*).

Do not use *never* to mean *did not.*

I *did not see* (not *never saw*) her once today.

   DEVELOPING YOUR SKILL

Rewrite the following sentences, correcting any errors in modifier usage.

1. I always try to avoid these kind of people.

fewer 2. I made less errors this time than I did on the last test.

3. You will have to look somewheres else for your sweater.

at all 4. Trudy says that she doesn't like the idea nohow.

fewer 5. There are less opportunities for error in this kind of an operation.

very much 6. Hal wants a new car in the worst way.

7. This here blouse matches my skirt exactly.

did not 8. I never remembered to eat lunch today.

very 9. Your dog seems right friendly.

fewer 10. There would be less absentees if the meetings were more interesting.

The problem of regional usage may arise with the use
of modifiers. Again, point out to students the standard
usage.

TROUBLESOME CONNECTIVES

Specific connectives frequently cause difficulties in usage, either because they are similar in meaning or because they are idiomatic. The following facts will help you to overcome problems in the use of such connectives.

Use *between* when the object or objects of the preposition refer to two persons or things; use *among* when the object or objects refer to three or more. [42b]

Mother divided the cookies *between* my sister and me.
The prize money was divided *among* the three winners.

Do not confuse the preposition *in* with the preposition *into*. *In* expresses being within a place; *into* expresses entrance to a place. [42c]

She sat waiting *in* the library.
He ran *into* the house to tell his parents the good news.

Use *beside* to mean *at the side of*. Use *besides* to mean *in addition to*. [42e]

Come sit *beside* me.
Who was there *besides* the usual crowd?

Use *at* to show *where* something or someone is. Use *to* to show the idea of *motion toward* someone or something. [42f]

My father is *at* (not *to*) home.
Are you going *to* the movies with us?

Distinguish between the prepositions *to* and *with* when used with the verb *agree*. You agree *to* a proposal and *with* a person. [42g]

Although I agree *with* you in principle, I cannot agree *to* such a plan.

Use *from*, not *than*, with the adjective *different*. [42h]

This painting is different *from* (not *than)* any other I have seen.

Distinguish among the prepositions *by*, *for*, and *with* when used with the verb *reward*. You are rewarded *by* a person, *for* something, *with* a gift. [42i]

Our class was rewarded *by* the principal *for* our co-operation in the clean-up campaign.

We were rewarded *with* (not *by)* a record hop in the gymnasium.

The emphasis in this section is on the use of easily confused prepositions and idiomatic prepositional phrases.

Each rule should be discussed thoroughly and then practiced until students use the forms easily and naturally.

Use the preposition *for* with the verb *blame*.   [42j]

Do not blame me *for* what happened. (Not *blame what happened on me).*

Use *in* and *on* with the verb *live* to mean to live *in* a town or city but *on* a street.   [42k]

David lives *in* New York *on* East Fifth Street.

Use *with*, not *to*, with *identical*.   [42n]

Your jacket is identical *with* (not *to)* mine.

Use *for*, not *on*, with *wait* when the meaning is *to await*.   [42o]

What's your hurry? Wait *for* (not *on)* me.

Distinguish among the prepositions *with*, *from*, *about*, and *over* when used with *differ*. One differs *with* a person *about* or *over* a question. Something differs *from* something else.   [42p]

I must differ *with* you *about* your interpretation of the question.
My opinion differs *from* (not *with)* yours.

Distinguish among the prepositions *for*, *with*, *of*, and *at* when used with *impatient*. One is impatient *for* something desired, *with* someone else, *of* restraint, and *at* someone's conduct.   [42q]

She is impatient *for* the day of the party to arrive.
Miss Brown was impatient *with* us today.
Jack is impatient *of* any kind of delay.
I am impatient *at* such childish behavior.

Distinguish among the prepositions *for*, *with*, and *against* when used with *contend*. One contends *for* a principle, *with* a person, and *against* an obstacle.   [42r]

He was willing to contend *for* what he believed in.
The two salesmen contended *with* each other for the managerial position.
She had her own shyness to contend *against*.

Distinguish between the prepositions *to* and *with* when used with *compare*. One compares something *to* something similar and *with* something dissimilar.   [42s]

The speaker compared the poetry of Shelley *to* that of Keats.
As compared *with* you, I am tall.

If you have any foreign-born students in your classes, they will probably need special help in the use of idioms. The same connectives are often used in different ways in different languages.

Write the numbers 1 to 10 on a sheet of paper. After each number write the word from the parentheses that will make the sentence correct. *This exercise may also be used for oral practice.*

1. The emphasis in education is different (than, <u>from</u>) what it was fifty years ago.
2. When Larry came (in, <u>into</u>) the room, he found several of his friends gathered (<u>in</u>, into) one corner.
3. No one (beside, <u>besides</u>) me knows the results of the election yet.
4. If you will wait (on, <u>for</u>) me for a few minutes, I'll walk home with you.
5. Jane doesn't agree (<u>with,</u> to) you and says she won't agree (with, <u>to</u>) your recommendations.
6. Your choice is identical (<u>with,</u> to) mine.
7. As compared (<u>with,</u> to) mine, your hair is long.
8. The work was divided (among, <u>between</u>) the two classes.
9. There was nobody (<u>at</u>, to) home when I telephoned.
10. Ron lives (in, <u>on</u>) Fullerton Parkway (<u>in</u>, on) Chicago.

EASILY CONFUSED WORDS [76]

Some words are confused because they have the same pronunciation but differ in meaning. Such words are called homonyms: *bear, bare; compliment, complement; cereal, serial.* Other words are frequently confused because of similarities in appearance; *respectively, respectfully; illusion, allusion; quiet, quite.* Other pairs of words are confused because of apparent similarities in sound as a result of careless pronunciations: *accept, except; affect, effect; devise, device.* Still other words are confused because of similarities in meaning: *continual, continuous; famous, notorious; fewer, less.* <u>The only way to overcome difficulties in the use of such words is to master each word—its spelling, pronunciation, and meaning.</u> The following explanations of the differences that exist among easily confused terms will help you to use the terms correctly.

about around

About means "approximately."

We walked *about* two miles.

Around means "along the circumference of; on all sides of."

We walked *around* the block.

Stress the point made in the introduction that each word must be mastered.

Accept means "to receive [a thing offered] with a consenting mind."

She *accepted* the gift graciously.

accept
except

Except as a verb means "to omit." As a preposition it means "with the exclusion of."

Honor students were *excepted* from the final examination (verb).

Everyone left *except* John (preposition).

Adapt means "to adjust to meet a new condition."

They found it difficult to *adapt* to a new way of life.

adapt
adopt

Adopt means "to take and apply as one's own [what is not so naturally]."

English has *adopted* many words from other languages.

Advice is a noun meaning "recommendation regarding a decision."

He sought professional *advice.*

advice
advise

Advise is a verb meaning "to recommend a course of action to someone."

I cannot *advise* you until I know the entire situation.

Note: Avoid using *advise* to mean "inform" or "tell."

Please *inform* us when your train will arrive.

(Not *Please* advise *us when your train will arrive.*)

Affect is used as a verb meaning "to influence" or "to assume the character of; to feign."

Will his decision *affect* our plans?

He *affected* a British accent.

affect
effect

Effect may be used either as a verb or a noun. As a verb it means "to bring about; to accomplish." As a noun it means "a result; consequence."

The incident *effected* a change in his attitude.

What *effect* will that have on our plans?

The words, their definitions, and examples of the words in sentences are so arranged as to serve as a ready reference for both teachers and students.

aggravate
annoy

Aggravate means "to make worse."

The hot weather *aggravated* the child's skin rash.

Annoy means "to disturb or irritate, especially by repeated acts."

The child's whining *annoyed* his mother.

all ready
already

All ready means "completely ready" or "everyone or everything ready."

I am *all ready* for the dance.

The marchers are *all ready* for the start of the parade.

Already means "previously."

I have *already* seen that movie.

all together
altogether

All together means "everyone or everything in one place."

There were ten of us present *all together*.

Altogether means "wholly."

That is an *altogether* different situation.

amount
number

Amount is used to refer to a total quantity that cannot be counted.

The flood did a vast *amount* of damage.

Number is used to refer to countable units.

An unusually large *number* of people were present at the meeting.

capital
capitol

Capital means "first" or "chief". It is used to refer to the principal city of a state or country.

Washington, D. C. is the *capital* of the United States.

Capitol (written with a capital letter) refers to the building in which Congress holds its sessions. It may also refer to the building in which a state legislature meets (often not capitalized).

We attended several sessions at the *Capitol*.

The state legislature will convene at the *capitol* building at 9:00 A.M.

Distinguish between words that are confused because they are homonyms and words that are misused because of carelessness in pronunciation.

character
reputation

Character means "the total of an individual's distinctive qualities." A person's character is formed through nature, education, and/or habit.

Mr. Nelson is a person of irreproachable *character*.

Reputation means "the opinions others hold of one's character."

Mr. Nelson's *reputation* was damaged by malicious gossip.

complement
compliment

Complement means "that which completes."

That hat would be the perfect *complement* to your outfit.

Compliment means "a flattering speech or attention."

Your new outfit should win you many *compliments*.

consul
council
counsel

Consul means "an official who represents his government in a foreign country."

We wrote to the French *consul* for information about the French Riviera.

Council means "an advisory or legislative body."

Ruth was elected secretary of the student *council*.

Counsel as a noun means "advice" or "adviser." As a verb it means *"to advise."*

His *counsel* would be valuable in this situation. (Advice)

The court appointed the defendant's *counsel*. (Adviser)

If you will explain the problem, I shall try to *counsel* you. (Advise)

continual
continuous

Continual means "occurring in steady, rapid, but not unbroken succession; repeated often."

The *continual* interruptions made it difficult to work.

Continuous means "occurring without interruption."

The *continuous* noise of the machines made conversation impossible.

Encourage students to work out mnemonic devices to help them distinguish between similar words; for example, in <u>complement</u> the <u>ple</u> corresponds to the <u>ple</u> in <u>complete</u>.

Device as a noun means "a mechanical apparatus" or "a scheme."

device
devise

The new *device* was intended to cut production costs.

Devise as a verb means "to think out, invent, or plan."

It took them several months to *devise* a new system for reporting progress.

Discover means "to find or find out about something not previously known but already in existence."

discover
invent

Columbus *discovered* America.

Invent means "to produce for the first time; to create something new."

Eli Whitney *invented* the cotton gin.

Epic refers to a narrative poem that deals with heroic action and is written in an elevated style.

Beowulf is an eighth century *epic* poem.

Epoch means "any event or time of an event marking the beginning of a relatively new development" or "a period of time characterized by a distinctive event or series of events."

epic
epoch

Chaucer is frequently called the "father of English literature." His poetry marks an *epoch* in English literature.

This is the *epoch* of space development.

Famous means "well-known," generally for admirable achievement.

famous
notorious

Ezio Pinza was a *famous* opera star.

Notorious means "well-known," generally for an unfavorable reason.

They captured the *notorious* criminal.

Formally means "in a conventional or ceremonious manner."

formally
formerly

He made the presentation very *formally*.

Formerly means "in time past."

He was *formerly* a member of our club.

Hanged refers to the death penalty.

hanged
hung

He was *hanged* for his crimes.

Hung refers to objects that have been suspended.

They *hung* their coats in the hall closet.

Healthful means "serving to promote health of body or mind."

Arizona's climate is considered *healthful* for people with respiratory diseases.

healthful
healthy

Healthy means "being in a state of health; well," "showing good health," or "conducive to health."

The doctor's report showed Ann to be *healthy*.
She has a *healthy* complexion.
Swimming is *healthy* exercise.

Human means "characteristic of man."

His mistake only made him seem more *human*.

human
humane

Humane means "kind" or "benevolent."

The A.S.P.C.A. advocates *humane* treatment of animals.

Illusion means "an unreal or misleading image; a deceptive appearance."

illusion
allusion

Vertical stripes give the *illusion* of height.

Allusion means "an indirect reference by passing mention or by quotation to something generally familiar."

His research paper contained several *allusions* to Shakespeare's plays.

imply
infer

Imply means "to express indirectly; to hint or hint at."

Do you mean to *imply* that you don't trust her?

Infer means "to draw a conclusion from facts or premises."

I *infer* from what you say that you don't trust her.

liable
likely
apt

Liable means "answerable" or "exposed to the danger or risk of something undesired."

He is *liable* for damages he caused.

Man is *liable* to many diseases.

Likely means "probable."

It is *likely* that he will telephone tonight.

Apt means "suitable" or "quick to learn."

He used an *apt* quotation to illustrate his point.

Reese is an *apt* pupil.

maybe
may be

Maybe is an adverb meaning "perhaps."

Maybe we'll join you later.

May be is a verb form.

We *may be* there later.

most
almost

Most as a noun means "the greatest or largest quantity or amount." As an adjective it means "greatest in number, quantity, size or extent" or "nearly all." It may also be used to form the superlative of an adjective or adverb.

Most of the students attended the variety show. (Noun)

Most teen-agers enjoy dancing. (Adjective)

That is the *most incredible* idea of all. (Superlative form)

Almost is an adverb meaning "nearly."

Are you *almost* ready to leave?

nauseated
nauseous

Nauseated means "disgusted" or "sick at the stomach."

I was *nauseated* by the odors in chemistry lab.

Nauseous means "disgusting" or "causing nausea."

The odors in chemistry lab were *nauseous*.

Some of the distinctions in meaning are very fine and should be discussed carefully and thoroughly.

persecute
prosecute

Persecute means "to cause to suffer because of belief" or "to annoy, harass."

Throughout history various groups have been *persecuted* because of their beliefs.

Prosecute means "to carry out legal action against."

The commissioner said he would *prosecute* all traffic violators.

precede
proceed

Precede means "to go before."

Spring *precedes* summer.

Proceed means "to go forward; to advance."

As soon as everyone has arrived, we shall *proceed* with the discussion.

principal
principle

Principal as an adjective means "first" or "chief." As a noun it may mean "a sum of money due as a debt or used as a fund" or "the chief executive officer of a school."

Her *principal* ambition is to be a doctor.

He paid the interest on his note, but was unable to decrease the amount of the *principal*.

Mr. Hayes is the *principal* of Southwest High School.

Principle means "a fundamental truth or rule."

The basic *principle* involved is the same for all these machines.

prophecy
prophesy

Prophecy is a noun meaning "a prediction."

Macbeth saw each *prophecy* of the witches come true.

Prophesy is a verb meaning "to predict."

It is difficult to *prophesy* the outcome of this race.

The four pairs of words on this page are among those that are most commonly misused.

Quiet as an adjective means "free from noise." As a noun it means "silence."

quiet
quite

> Please be *quiet;* the baby is sleeping.
> The *quiet* soothed his irritation.

Quite is an adverb that means "completely" or "wholly." Avoid using *quite* to mean "very" or "somewhat."

> I am not *quite* satisfied with the results.

Respectfully means "in a respectful or deferential manner."

respectfully
respectively

> He *respectfully* requested permission to attend the conference.
> She signed the letter to her congressman, *"Respectfully* yours."

Respectively means "each in the order given."

> Jan and Pat won first and second prizes, *respectively.*

To is a preposition expressing "direction toward."

> We are going *to* the movies.

to
too
two

Too is an adverb meaning "also."

> They are going *too.*

Two is a number.

> There are *two* magazines in the rack.

Weather as a noun means "state of the air or atmosphere, with regard to temperature, humidity, or any other meteorological phenomena." As a verb it means "to come safely through."

> The *weather* has been stormy for the past week.
> They *weathered* their financial difficulties and built a successful business.

weather
whether
if

Whether is a conjunction used to introduce an indirect question.

> They asked *whether* they might go with us.

If is a conjunction meaning "supposing that" or "in case that."

> We shall attend *if* the weather is good.

The weather-whether confusion is largely the result of mispronouncing whether (hwĕth´ĕr).

DEVELOPING YOUR SKILL

Rewrite the following sentences, correcting the errors in usage. If the sentence is correct, write *Correct* after the appropriate number.

principal's   1. I couldn't help wondering what I had done when I was called to the ~~principle's~~ office.
whether   2. She doesn't know ~~if~~ she can go with us.
correct   3. Scientists are studying the effects of radiation from fall-out.
formally   4. We have spoken to each other, but we haven't been ~~formerly~~ introduced yet.
famous   5. Mrs. Brady is ~~notorious~~ for her good deeds.
imply   6. What you have said seems to ~~infer~~ that you think him guilty.
allusions   7. When you use literary ~~illusions~~, be sure you use them correctly.
likely   8. You are ~~liable~~ to be injured if you go near that construction project.
correct   9. When I have the flu, the thought of food makes me feel nauseated.
continually   10. The special news bulletins interrupted the program ~~continuously~~.

Review Exercises—Specific Word Forms

Rewrite the following sentences, correcting all errors in formal usage.

Take   1. ~~Bring~~ these reports with you when you go to the meeting.
shall   2. I ~~will~~ try to let you know what time his train leaves.
who   3. The man ~~whom~~ I believe is the best speaker is the one sitting at Mr. Johnson's right.
taught   4. My father ~~learned~~ me to drive.
fewer   5. There are ~~less~~ complications than the doctors expected.
precede   6. Has anyone determined which act will ~~proceed~~ the finale?
whomever   7. You may invite ~~whoever~~ you like.
notorious   8. He was a ~~famous~~ leader of the underworld.
me for   9. Don't blame the failure of the plan ~~on me~~.
adapt   10. When visiting a foreign country, you must ~~adopt~~ yourself to other customs.
from   11. My ideas on the subject are different ~~than~~ yours.
affected   12. Arthur ~~effected~~ an air of nonchalance, but we were not convinced by it.
very   13. I was ~~right~~ pleased to have met him at last.
besides   14. How many people ~~beside~~ us will be present?
number   15. The increased ~~amount~~ of cars on the road has created a serious traffic problem.

Both the Developing Your Skill exercise and the Review Exercises may be used for oral as well as written practice and review. It will be necessary to have students spell some of the words if the sentences are to be read aloud.

16. I don't understand this kind of a~~ problem.   omit a
17. He is impatient ~~with~~ any kind of delay.   of
18. ~~Who~~ do you plan to ask for help? Whom
19. Your attitude seems to ~~infer~~ that you are in doubt about the practicality of the plan. imply
20. What new ~~devise~~ have they suggested? device

UNIT SUMMARY

A knowledge of acceptable usage, combined with a knowledge of grammar, will give your speaking and writing the distinction that is evident in the language of successful persons. Mastery of the principles presented in this unit will enable you to overcome such common errors as subject-verb agreement and pronoun-antecedent agreement. By application of the facts you have learned, you should be able to eliminate illiterate usages from your speaking and writing. Finally, by paying close attention to the spelling, pronunciation, and meaning of easily confused words, you will become precise in your use of language.

A. Correct usage is a mark of an educated person. One is judged by his use of language in social and business situations in which one must communicate orally.

UNIT REVIEW EXERCISES

B. Parenthetical expressions may be dropped to test the correct form.

C. Similarities in pronunciation are often apparent rather
DISCUSSION TOPICS   than real. Careless pronunciation leads to careless spelling and usage. Meanings, too, must be learned.

A. People are often judged by their use of language. See above.

B. Parenthetical expressions, such as *I believe, I think,* and *I am sure,* need not cause difficulties in the use of *who* and *whom.* See above.

C. Much of the confusion that exists in the use of specific words is the result of carelessness. See above.

D. Each person must be able to communicate at several different levels. See below.

E. Errors in agreement sometimes slip into the speech even of well-educated persons. There is, however, no excuse for making errors in agreement in writing. See below.

D. Different levels of language are appropriate to different situations. Each person should be able to adapt his language to the situation.

E. A writer has the opportunity to reread and revise what he has written.

WRITTEN WORK

A. Write sentences in which you use the following forms:

lay	1. The past form of *lie*	Sentences for this
lie, lies	2. The present form of *lay*	exercise will vary.
lain	3. The past participle of *lie*	The correct verb forms
sat	4. The past form of *sit*	are given.
set	5. The past participle of *set*	
lying	6. The present participle of *lie*	
laying	7. The present participle of *lay*	
rose	8. The past form of *rise*	
risen	9. The past participle of *rise*	
raised	10. The past form of *raise*	

B. Write the numbers 1 to 10 on a sheet of paper. After each number write the expression from the parentheses that will make the sentence correct.

1. Neither John nor Tom (want, <u>wants</u>) to come with us.   (agree-
2. There (was, <u>were</u>) several projects going on at the same time.   ment)
3. Each of my friends always (call, <u>calls</u>) before (<u>he</u>, they) comes to visit.
4. The idea (what, <u>that</u>) you suggested sounds workable to me.
5. Physics (<u>is</u>, are) difficult for me to understand.
6. The most unusual fruit I have eaten (<u>is</u>, are) mangoes.
7. Was that letter addressed to Ellen or to (yourself, <u>you</u>)?
8. I am (sure, <u>surely</u>) glad that the play was (real, <u>very</u>) successful.
9. We won't go (without, <u>unless</u>) you go with us.
10. Miss Thompson always speaks to us (like, <u>as if</u>) we were equals.

C. Write original sentences in which you use the following pairs of words correctly.

1. accept, except   Sentences for this
2. affect, effect   exercise will vary.
3. among, between
4. complement, compliment
5. continual, continuous
6. discover, invent
7. famous, notorious
8. fewer, less
9. imply, infer
10. quiet, quite

Vocabulary

Did you know the meaning of every word in the unit? In the following sentences, some of the words are used in different contexts. Write the numbers 1 to 5 on your paper. After each number write the letter of the word or phrase that could best be substituted for the italicized word in each sentence. Before making the choice, find the word on the page indicated to see how the word is used in this unit.

b

1. What he said was *relatively* unimportant; it was the way he said it. [p. 301]
   (*a*) completely; (*b*) comparatively; (*c*) somewhat; (*d*) totally

a

2. She always tries to stereotype people and to separate them into specific *categories*. [p. 305]
   (*a*) classifications; (*b*) catalogs; (*c*) groups; (*d*) relationships

c

3. His speech was so filled with *ambiguity* that we couldn't understand what point he was trying to make. [p. 307]
   (*a*) errors; (*b*) cliches; (*c*) double meanings; (*d*) illiterate usages

c

4. The materials used in the building project were found to be *substandard*. [p. 310]
   (*a*) adequate; (*b*) above standard; (*c*) inferior; (*d*) superior

d

5. Such an incident can *mar* your record to such an extent that you will be ineligible for a scholarship. [p. 327]
   (*a*) mark; (*b*) improve; (*c*) affect; (*d*) spoil

Spelling

The following spelling words appeared in the unit or were chosen because they are commonly misspelled. Study these words so that you will be prepared to write them from dictation.

1. relatively	11. abhorrence
2. categories	12. dissipate
3. ambiguity	13. intercede
4. substandard	14. hypocrisy
5. mar	15. disappointment
6. reflexive	16. carburetor
7. intensive	17. visible
8. antecedent	18. serviceable
9. indefinite	19. unanimous
10. demonstrative	20. paralyzed

Continue to co-ordinate spelling study with vocabulary study.

UNIT SELF-TEST

Write the numbers 1 to 25 on a sheet of paper. After each number write the term from the parentheses that will make the sentence correct.

1. He (could, couldn't) hardly lift the package.
2. The books have (laid, lain) on the desk for several days.
3. Her hair, which is light brown, looks blond as compared (with, to) mine, which is black.
4. They would not agree (to, on, with) his proposal for a new gymnasium.
5. I am sorry I cannot (except, accept) your invitation.
6. My sister's (continuous, continual) interruptions are beginning to (affect, effect) my nerves.
7. You didn't say that you doubted him, but your tone of voice (inferred, implied) that you did.
8. We have invited Mr. Harding, (who, whom) you all know, to act as one of our chaperones.
9. Madame Curie (discovered, invented) radium.
10. Lisa is the one (who, whom) I think should be held responsible for the escapade.
11. You are (liable, likely, apt) to meet everyone you know at her house to-night.
12. Anyone who damages this property will be (persecuted, prosecuted).
13. Neither the teachers nor the principal (is, are) in the building.
14. He (don't, doesn't) agree (with, to) your ideas for raising money.
15. If anyone asks for me, tell (them, him) that I (shall, will) be back in a few minutes.
16. Do you know (whether, if) Mr. Black has arrived yet?
17. Jack, who is president of the student council, was (formally, formerly) vice-president of that organization.
18. Would you (of, have) spoken so harshly if you had known all the facts?
19. Mother has been (lying, laying) down most of the afternoon.
20. Where (was, were) you when the accident occurred?
21. Anne is to be (complemented, complimented) on the excellence of her performance.
22. Please (sit, set) the groceries on the kitchen table.
23. He was rewarded (for, with, by) ten dollars (for, with, by) Mrs. Dalton (for, with, by) returning her wallet to her.
24. Can you (prophecy, prophesy) the outcome of this matter?
25. The (imminent, eminent) artist was taken ill suddenly.

Students who do not score well on this test should be directed to review the rules, examples, and practice exercises that apply to the areas of usage in which the students failed.

Unit 10

Mechanics in Writing

The ideas presented in the introduction are important. Read the introduction aloud and discuss the points made. Emphasize the statements that are underscored.

Clarity is essential to good writing. <u>Correctness in the mechanics of writing can help you to achieve clarity</u>. The mechanics of writing include the form of paragraphs, outlines, and letters; spelling; capitalization; punctuation; and syllabication. All these elements—when correctly used —work together to make your ideas clear to the reader.

<u>The form</u> of your writing serves to attract the reader's attention and to indicate to him the type of writing you are doing <u>and the general plan of the written material</u>. <u>Correct spelling is the mark of a careful writer,</u> as are correct <u>capitalization, punctuation,</u> and <u>syllabication</u>. Accurate <u>capitalization</u> and <u>punctuation</u> serve, further, as signals to the reader to <u>help</u> him correctly <u>interpret your meaning</u>. The person who writes with his reader in mind pays close attention to mechanics in writing.

Before you begin your study of this unit, complete the following Check Yourself questions to determine how much you already know about mechanics in writing.

Spoken English relies partly on pitch, tone, emphasis, pause, and gesture to reveal meaning. Mechanics must help compensate for these elements in written language.

CHECK YOURSELF

A. Write the numbers 1 to 10 on a sheet of paper. After each number write the word or words that belong in the corresponding blanks.

indented 1. Every paragraph should be—approximately three-fourths of an inch from the left-hand margin.

topic, sentence 2.-3. Two kinds of outlines are the—outline and the—outline.

block, indented 4.-6. Letters may be written in—style,—style, or—style. semiblock

heading 7. The—of a letter contains the sender's full address and the date.

inside address 8. The—, which is used only in business letters, contains the recipient's full name and address.

salutation 9. The—is the sender's greeting to the recipient of the letter.

complimentary 10. The—is a concluding expression of regard for the recipient of the close letter.

B. Find the misspelled words in the following sentences and write them correctly after the appropriate numbers on your paper.
all right, scheme, provided, stretch, extra

1. Father has said "alright" to our <u>sceme</u>, <u>pervided</u> we can <u>strech</u> our allowance over the <u>exter</u> two days.

2. Please <u>except</u> my <u>opology</u> for <u>failling</u> to return the records <u>immediately</u>. accept, apology, failing, immediately

3. The members of the <u>planing</u> <u>comittee</u> were concerned, since they had received no sign that Dr. Braun intended to <u>acknowlege</u> the invitation. planning, committee, acknowledge

4. The rolling hills and fertile <u>vallies</u> were a welcome <u>releif</u> after the flat <u>planes</u>. valleys, relief, plains

5. His <u>couragous</u> deed <u>affected</u> an <u>improvment</u> in the <u>atitudes</u> of the other students toward him. courageous, effected improvement, attitudes

C. Write each of the following sentences, correcting all errors in capitalization.

1. the speaker of the house has raised his gavel to open the session; the senate is already in session.

2. the lancasters and the yorks waged the wars of the roses.

3. the beatitudes and the lord's prayer are both found in the new testament.

4. the man exclaimed, "oh, but that isn't true!"

5. "how would you know that a roman coin stamped 100 b. c. could not be real?" asked brother.

D. Write the numbers 1 to 10 on a sheet of paper. Mark a plus sign (+) after the appropriate number if the sentence is correctly punctuated; mark a zero (0) if the sentence is incorrectly punctuated.

0   1. Poe, Harte, Mark Twain and O. Henry made important contributions to the short story in America.

0   2. Poe was born in Boston, Massachusetts, January 19, 1809 and died in Baltimore, Maryland, October 7, 1849.

+   3. "Yes, Jean," replied her teacher, "he who wishes to learn history may turn to literature."

0   4. The Gulf of Mexico, the largest gulf in the world, makes the topography interesting, moreover, there are two other gulfs on Mexico's coast line.

0   5. The governor of the state, who was campaigning for re-election, made some startling charges concerning his opponent.

+   6. I intended to call you sooner but—well, you know how it is.

+   7. The *Americana* states: "The ancient galley (the warship of the Greeks) was a narrow vessel about 100 feet in length."

0   8. The two opposing nominees for the office met at the Municipal Auditorium to debate at 830 P.M., October 10.

0   9. The story of Jonah's adventures may be found in Jonah 2: 1-10; the account of Paul's in Acts, 27: 1-44.

0 10. Until they left, the party was a great success.

E. Copy the following words on a sheet of paper. If the word is hyphenated where it may correctly be broken at the end of a line, mark a check (✔) before the number of the word; if the word is incorrectly hyphenated, write a minus sign (—) before the number of the word.

—   1. transfer-red   one syllable   ✓ 6. bat-tal-ion

✓   2. un-doubt-edly   — 7. spag-hetti   gh single sound

✓   3. dis-tinc-tion   ✓ 8. oc-ca-sion-ally

—   4. e-lect   single letter   ✓ 9. pas-ture

—   5. bi-cy-cle   silent vowel   —10. mos-sy   two letters

1. Form in Writing

The first impression that a reader receives from your written work depends upon the form and neatness of your work. Poor form can detract from the effectiveness of your writing, no matter how excellent the content.

Emphasize the point that the form of writing indicates the writer's plan to the reader.

PARAGRAPHS

Paragraphs are the thought divisions of your writing. They show your reader the various phases of your thinking on a subject. The form of your writing indicates your plan to your reader.

A paragraph is an orderly arrangement of sentences, all of which are related to a single topic.   [71]

Stress
the
three
essen-
tials
of a
para-
graph.
If you are in doubt about whether you have written a complete paragraph, check your writing for the three essentials of every paragraph: *unity, coherence,* and *emphasis.* If all the sentences develop a single topic, the paragraph has unity; if the sentences are arranged in logical order, the paragraph has coherence; and if the sentences are so arranged as to give the ideas the greatest possible force, the paragraph has emphasis. Unless a group of sentences has all three essentials, it is not a paragraph.

Indent the first line of every paragraph, except in letters written in block form.   [71a]

A change of paragraph signals your reader that you are going to talk about a new topic or about a different aspect of the topic you are discussing. Unless the form of your writing clearly signals such changes, your reader is likely to be confused.

In most of your writing, including letters written in indented style and in semiblock style, indent each paragraph approximately three-fourths of an inch from the left margin. Letters written in block form are not indented. Each paragraph begins at the left margin. When using block form, you must be particularly careful to space between paragraphs.

Do not leave blank space in a line unless a new paragraph is to begin on the next line.   [71b]

Begin each line of a paragraph, after the first line, at the left margin and continue to write until the line is filled. Plan your writing so that no words are crowded at the right margin or so that only a minimum of blank space is left at the right. If necessary, do not hesitate to syllabicate words correctly at the ends of lines. Try to keep your left and right margins symmetrical. Only the last line of a paragraph may correctly have a large amount of blank space.

Insist upon margins, indention, and a single topic in all paragraphs. If you reject work that is not up to standard, students will learn to meet your high standards.

The following sentences comprise a paragraph, but the sentences have been shifted from their logical order. Write the paragraph, arranging the sentences in the order that will present the ideas logically and effectively. Pay particular attention to the form of your writing.

Check for form as well as logical order.

2.   1. Every morning, promptly at six o'clock, I am awakened by a soft whirring, as of a small motor.

5.   2. The whirring gets louder, and if I don't respond, four feet are firmly planted on my chest, and a cold nose nudges my cheek.

1.   3. I have the gentlest, but most insistent, alarm clock known to man.

3.   4. But this is an alarm clock that I can't shut off.

6.   5. Finally, I open my eyes to find the blue eyes of Mali, my Siamese cat, looking down at me reproachfully.

4.   6. Usually I open one eye, grunt, and settle deeper into my pillow.

OUTLINES   [72]

An outline is a plan of the material to be included in a speech or in a written theme. It shows the sequential arrangement of the ideas to be discussed and the relative importance of each idea.

The main headings of an outline are started at the left margin of the paper and are labeled with Roman numerals. Subtopics are indented and are given letters and numbers. The first order of subtopics are labeled with capital letters; the second, with Arabic numerals; and the third, with lower-case letters. If further subdivisions are necessary, Arabic numerals in parentheses and, finally, lower-case letters in parentheses are used. Usually, three kinds of subheadings are sufficient. The arrangement of numbers and letters in an outline is as follows. Notice that topics and subtopics are so arranged that all numbers and letters of the same kind are aligned with each other throughout the outline.

You may wish to correlate the teaching of this material with the teaching of the outline for the research paper (pages 138-140).

Title

Point out
particularly
the align-
ment of
correspond-
ing numbers
and letters
and the
punctuation
used.

I.

   A.

   B.

     1.

     2.

       a.

       b.

         (1)

         (2)

           (a)

           (b)

II.

   A.

     1.

     2.

   B.

Empha-
size
this
para-
graph.   Since subtopics are divisions of larger topics, there must always be at least two subtopics. If a topic cannot be broken down into two or more parts, use no subtopics. You cannot divide anything into one part.

Notice that the title is written above the outline. It is not one of the numbered or lettered headings. All the topics and subtopics are divisions of the broad subject indicated in the title. Notice, too, the punctuation in the preceding example. All numbers and letters are followed by periods, except those in parentheses.

There are two kinds of outlines that are commonly used: the *topic outline* and the *sentence outline*.

A *topic outline* is one in which each heading and subheading is a word, a phrase, or a dependent clause.   **[72a]**

In writing a formal topic outline, it is important that you express parallel ideas in parallel form; that is, that you state in the same grammatical structure all headings that are divisions of the same major idea. If the first main heading, for example, is *To prevent accidents,* all the other

Make clear the idea of parallelism in outlining.

main headings must be infinitives or infinitive phrases. The same rule applies to each category of subtopics under each main topic. All those labeled with capital letters must be in the same construction; those labeled with Arabic numerals must be in the same construction; and so on. Parallel structure in your outline will help make clear the relationships between ideas.

Compare the following lists of ideas to be used as main topics in an outline on the topic *How to Decrease Automobile Accidents*. The first group of topics is not in parallel form.

1. Good driving habits
2. Pedestrians have to observe the laws
3. Improving road conditions

Notice how the relationship of the ideas becomes clear when the topics are written in parallel construction.

1. Good driving *habits*
2. *Observance* of the laws by pedestrians
3. Improved *road conditions*

The following is a sample topic outline. <u>Notice that each topic begins with a capital letter</u>. No other words are capitalized unless they are proper nouns or proper adjectives.

`Stress this point.`

Barter in North America

I. Early American trading posts
  A. Indian trade
    1. Furs and hides
    2. Wampum
      a. Types of beads
      b. Value
  B. Community trade
    1. Products
      a. Furs and hides
      b. Food
      c. Cloth
    2. Services
II. Modern trading posts

`The sample outline may be used as a basis for the discussion of form, punctuation, capitalization, and parallelism in outlines.`

There are times when you may wish to have an outline that gives <u>more detailed information</u> about each topic and subtopic. In such cases you will find the sentence outline helpful.

A sentence outline is one in which each heading and subheading is a complete sentence.   **[72b]**

The numbering and lettering in a sentence outline is exactly the same as in a topic outline. Since each topic and subtopic is a complete sentence, each one must begin with a capital letter and end with a terminal punctuation mark, usually a period.

The following sentence outline has been developed from the topic outline that illustrates rule 72a.

Barter in North America

I. Barter was the usual medium of exchange in the early American trading posts.

    A. The early traders were particularly anxious for Indian trade.

       1. The Indians exchanged valuable furs and hides for other articles.

       2. The Indians also used beads called *wampum* for trading.

          a. Wampum was made of three different colors of beads —white, purple, and black.

          b. In the Colonial period, a standard of monetary value for wampum was established.

    B. Communities often grew up around trading posts.

       1. Citizens of the community frequently bartered for supplies they needed.

          a. Trappers exchanged furs and hides for supplies and equipment.

          b. Farmers exchanged produce for supplies and equipment.

          c. Housewives exchanged homespun cloth for household supplies.

       2. Skilled workmen frequently exchanged their services for supplies and equipment.

    II. Today barter is still carried on in trading posts in the southwestern United States.

> DEVELOPING YOUR SKILL

A. Rewrite the following items so that they are in parallel form. The subject is *Good Study Habits.* One possibility follows:

    1. Plenty of sleep is necessary   Sufficient sleep

P 2. Review the previous day's assignment

    3. Physical conditions for study

D 4. Ignore distractions such as TV, radio, and the telephone

    5. Assignment notebook

B. Write a topic outline, using one of the following titles as your subject or using a subject of your own choosing.

Why Curfew?   Topic outlines will vary.

The Value of Intramural Sports

We Need an Invention

What Our Town Is Proud Of

Tyrant in the Home—TV

C. Expand the topic outline you wrote for Exercise B to a sentence outline.   Sentence outlines will vary.

LETTER WRITING [73]

Although the telephone has somewhat decreased the need for writing letters, there are times when a letter is the most satisfactory means of communication. Well-written friendly letters allow for leisurely conversation and an exchange of opinions and experiences between friends. Good business letters enable you to transact business efficiently and effectively.

There are three general styles in use for both social and business letters: *indented, block,* and *semiblock.* Any of the three styles may correctly be used for social and business letters; however, <u>the indented style is usually used for social correspondence</u> and the <u>block or semiblock style for business correspondence.</u> This is a matter of custom rather than one of rule.

In letters written in *indented style*, the second and third lines of the heading, the first word in each paragraph in the body, and the signature are indented. [73a]

Letters written in *block style* have no indentions in any part of the letter. [73b]

Letters written in *semiblock style* have only the first word in each paragraph in the body indented; the rest of the letter is in block style. [73c]

The following diagrams illustrate the indented, block, and semiblock styles:

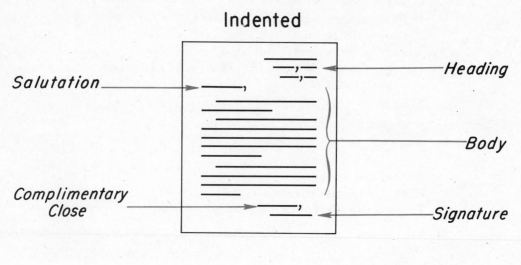

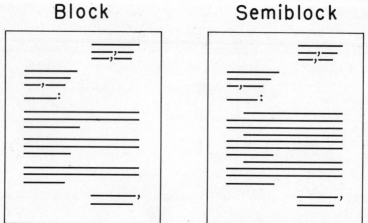

The block style illustrated in the diagram is sometimes referred to as *modified block style* since there is another style called *full block style,* which is used by some business firms. In full block style there are no indentions and all parts of the letter, including the heading and the complimentary close and signature, begin at the left margin.

The diagrams on these pages provide a quick reference for the form and punctuation of letters.

The following diagram illustrates full block style:

Full Block

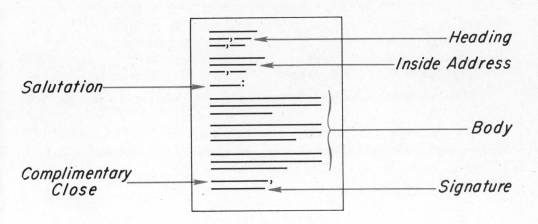

The following labels appear on the diagram: Heading, Inside Address, Salutation, Body, Complimentary Close, Signature

All letters are divided into parts, each of which serves a particular purpose. The social letter contains five parts; the business letter, six.

The *heading* of a letter contains the sender's street address, city, zone number (if any) and state, and the date. **[73d]**

INDENTED STYLE   BLOCK STYLE

1112 Ricewood Avenue   649 State Street
Portland 6, Maine   Cleveland 12, Ohio
March 3, 19—   February 1, 19—

Business letters are often written on stationery that contains the letterhead of the company. Since the letterhead includes the complete address of the company, only the date need be written in the place of the heading.

When a business letter must be carried over to a second page, use a plain sheet of paper of the same size and quality as the first sheet. The heading should contain the name of the person to whom the letter is directed, the number of the page, and the date, as follows:

Mr. L. M. Jones   2.   December 6, 19—

Stress the importance of using a good quality stationery for all letters.

**The *inside address*, which is used only in business letters, contains
the name of the person (or company) to whom the letter is written, the street
address, the city and zone number (if any), and the state.**   [73e]

INDENTED STYLE

Mr. J. E. Cobb
  North Atlantic Company
    18 Constance Street
      Trenton 4, New Jersey

BLOCK STYLE

Dr. Wilbur H. Holding
Superintendent of Schools
400 City Hall
Dalton 23, Wisconsin

The salutation is the writer's greeting to the recipient of the letter.
[73f]

In a social letter the salutation is informal and is followed by a comma;
in a business letter the salutation is followed by a colon. The salutation
always begins at the left margin. The first word and all nouns in the
salutation are capitalized.

SOCIAL LETTERS

Dear Father,
Dear Uncle Howard,
Dear Andy,
Dear Marilyn,

BUSINESS LETTERS

Dear Sir: or Dear Mr. Cobb:
Dear Madam: or Dear Miss Cooke:
Gentlemen:
My dear Sir:

**The *body* of a letter is that part in which the sender writes his message
or states his business.**   [73g]

The body of a friendly letter should be informal, but you should not
let informality degenerate into illiteracy and illegibility. Letters can be
friendly and informal and still be in good taste. You do not need to resort
to an overuse of slang, to gaudy stationery, and to unconventional shades
of ink. Take the time and trouble to make your personal letters not only
interesting and friendly, but attractive and in good form.

Your letters will vary in content, depending upon the person to whom
you are writing and your own interests. There is no rule that can tell you
what to say in a friendly letter, but the following suggestions will help
you to write better friendly letters:

1. Begin your letter with a lively and interesting subject. Do not say,
"I have intended writing but have been too busy."

2. Keep in mind the person to whom you are writing and tell what
you think he will enjoy hearing.

3. Be sincere. Your letter should sound like you.

4. Stop when you have finished. Do not make excuses by saying, "It's time for lunch, so I must close now."

5. Be sure your letter is correct in form, sentence structure, punctuation, and spelling.

Business letters are frequently written to strangers. It is your letter that tells the recipient what kind of person you are. Business letters should be clear, courteous, and concise. The language of the business letter should be formal, without being stilted. Avoid such expressions as *kindly inform, enclosed please find, at your earliest convenience,* and *thanking you in advance.*

Since business letters are written for specific purposes, their content will vary according to their individual purposes. The following standards, however, apply to all business letters:

1. Make your letter clear, courteous, and concise.
2. Get to the point of your letter quickly.
3. Be sure to include all the necessary information.
4. Avoid trite, hackneyed expressions.
5. Be sure your letter is correct in form, sentence structure, punctuation, and spelling.

The *complimentary close* is a concluding expression of regard for the recipient of the letter. [73h]

The wording of the complimentary close should be suited to the tone of your letter and to your relationship with the person who is to receive the letter. Some generally accepted closes for social and business correspondence follow. Notice that only the first word of the complimentary close begins with a capital letter and that the last word is followed by a comma.

Social Letters	Business Letters
Sincerely,	Sincerely yours,
Yours sincerely,	Yours truly,
Affectionately yours,	Very truly yours,
With love,	Respectfully yours,

Stress the capitalization and punctuation in the complimentary close.

The *signature* is the sender's handwritten name.   [73i]

The sig-   Whether your letter is written by hand or is typewritten, sign it with a
nature   pen. In a social letter, your signature may be your first name alone, pro-
must   vided you are certain that the person receiving the letter can identify you
always   by your first name. In a business letter, you must always sign your full
be   name. If the letter is typewritten, type your name four spaces below the
hand-   complimentary close and write your signature above the typewritten name,
written.   as in the following examples:

INDENTED STYLE   BLOCK STYLE

Yours very truly,   Yours very truly,

Marianne Lewis   *Richard M. Davis*

Marianne Lewis   Richard M. Davis

The title *Mr.* is never used in a signature, but a woman may indicate
the title to be used in replying to her letter. An unmarried woman may
write *Miss* in parentheses before her signature; a married woman may
write *Mrs.* in parentheses before her signature or she may write her married name below her signature. If no title is given, it is assumed that a
woman is to be addressed as *Miss.*

INDENTED STYLE   BLOCK STYLE

Yours truly,   *Yours truly,*
Ellen Davis   *Joan Miller,*
                                            (Mrs. John R. Miller)

or   *or*

Yours truly,   *Yours truly,*
(Miss) Ellen Davis   *(Mrs.) Joan Miller*

Point out to students the confusion that may arise as
a result of an improperly signed letter or of an illegible
signature.

These examples show women's signatures in typewritten letters:

Yours truly,

Ellen Davis

(Miss) Ellen Davis

Yours truly,

Joan Miller

(Mrs. John R. Miller)

> Point out the difference in the use of parentheses.

Two addresses appear on the envelope—the return address and the mailing address. These should be in the same style as is used in the letter.

The *return address* on the envelope contains the sender's full name and address.   [73i]

The return address is usually placed in the upper left-hand corner of the envelope. The name of the city, the zone number (if any), and the state should be written on the same line. Abbreviations may be used in the return address. Do not use commas at the ends of lines.

The *mailing address* on the envelope contains the full name and address of the person (or company) to whom the letter is being sent.   [73k]

The mailing address is usually placed about halfway down the envelope and begins a little left of center. Do not use abbreviations in the mailing address, except when they are part of a name. Postal authorities prefer that the name of the state be written out in full on a separate line. Do not use commas at the ends of lines.

> Discuss the need for a return address.

Henry L. Prentess
148 Breckenridge St.
Boston 6, Mass.

Mr. Joseph P. Manning
683 Washington Avenue
Minneapolis 12
Minnesota

A. Write the heading, inside address (where applicable), salutation, complimentary close, and signature for each of the following letters. Draw lines to indicate the body of the letter.

Use diagrams on p. 354 as guide.

1. From your home address, write to Mr. Alan J. Wood, Curtiss Seafood Company, 1297 William Street, Bangor 16, Maine. Use block style. Check to be sure there are no indentions.

2. Mary Stone, 591 Seventeenth Street, El Paso 17, Texas, is writing to her friend, Karen Dickinson, 410 Main Street, Newark 4, New Jersey. Use indented style. Inside address not applicable.

3. The president of Kempner Brothers, Inc., Mr. Robert J. Kempner, receives a letter from Nancy Cummings (Mrs. Arthur J. Cummings), 1240 East Lexington Avenue, New York 10, New York. Kempner Brothers is located at 19 Bellevue Boulevard, San Francisco 24, California. Use semiblock style. Paragraph indentions in body only.

See diagram p. 359.

B. Draw an outline of an envelope on a sheet of paper. Address the envelope to The Craft Shop, 418 Columbia Street, Greenwood 9, South Carolina. Use your name and address for the return address. State to be written on separate line.

Review Exercises—Form in Writing

A. Prepare a topic or a sentence outline for one of the following subjects (or choose a subject of your own): Outlines will vary.

Going steady
Progressive jazz
Hi-fi equipment
Hands

If I had three wishes
Cats
Dogs
The Peace Corps

B. Write a composition based on the outline you prepared for Exercise A. Pay particular attention to paragraphing and to the form of your composition. Compositions will vary.

C. Using appropriate writing materials and giving attention to punctuation and to placement on the page, copy the following letter in semiblock style.

2500 Rosemont Avenue, Estes Park 4, Colorado, December 20, 19--, The Boulder Appliance Company, 840 Broad Street, Boulder 26, Colorado, Gentlemen, On December 10 I purchased from you a twelve-foot Standard Refrigerator which has so far proved to be very satisfactory. However, the instructions for caring for the refrigerator were not in the box. Will you please send me the booklet of instructions? Sincerely yours, David R. Jones. Check for form. Only paragraphs in the body of the letter should be indented. See the diagram on page 354.

2. Spelling

English is a varied language derived from a variety of sources. Unfortunately, it is this same variety that has made English spelling complex. However difficult you may find spelling, the problems are not insurmountable if you will practice the following procedures:

1. Pronounce words correctly.
2. Visualize words accurately.
3. Make and use mnemonic (memory) devices.
4. Learn and apply spelling rules. (A few simple rules control the spelling of thousands of words.)
5. Write words carefully.

These proce- dures, if ap- plied dili- gently, will help poor spellers to im- prove.

Learn to pronounce words correctly. [51]

Pronounce words carefully so that you do not omit vowels, consonants, or syllables. [51a]

The omission of sounds frequently causes misspellings such as the following:

minature for min*i*ature
accidently for accident*all*y
quanity for quan*t*ity
satiricly for satiric*all*y

Pronounce words carefully so that you do not add extra vowels. [51b]

Do not say *artharitis* for *arthritis, attackded* for *attacked,* or *hinderance* for *hindrance.* If you pronounce such words correctly, you are less likely to misspell them.

Pronounce words carefully so that you do not transpose sounds. [51c]

Pronounce words such as *children, introduce* and *modern* correctly. Do not say *childern, interduce,* and *modren.*

Visualize words in your mind. [52]

Learn to take accurate mental pictures of words. One of the most frequent errors made in visualizing words is mistaking a word for another word whose spelling is similar. Do not confuse words such as *access* and *excess, stationary* and *stationery,* and *conscious* and *conscience.* Pay particular attention also to words that contain silent letters: g*host,* p*neu-* matic, p*sychology.*

Impress upon students the importance of correct pronunciation.

Encour-
age stu-
dents
to de-
vise
mne-
monic
aids.

Use memory devices to help remember correct spellings.   [53]

Mnemonic devices are intended to help you spell correctly. Since they are intended for your own use only, they may be any associational devices that will work for you, no matter how silly they may seem. For example, since the word *conscience* includes the word *science*, a sentence such as the following may help you to remember the correct spelling: My con*science* tells me that I should study for the *science* test. Other helpful sentences may be these: His private *secret*ary knew every *secret* of the business. *We* were *at her* house when the rainy *weather* started. Work out mnemonic devices of your own, and use them.

Learn and apply the rules for spelling.   [54]

This is
an im-
portant
point.
Excep-
tions
to the
rules
do not
make
the
rules
in-
valid.

An understanding of the spelling rules included here will help you to overcome many of the most common errors made in spelling. Although there are exceptions to the rules, the exceptions are few as compared with the number of words governed by the rules. If you know and can apply the rules, you will find that you can recognize the exceptions more easily.

Avoid confusing *ei* and *ie*.   [54a]

Write *ie* when the sound is long *e* (as in *see*).

relieve	grief	fiend	piece
believe	thief	field	priest

Exceptions: either, neither, leisure, weird, seize

Write *ei* after *c* or when the sound is not long *e*, especially when the sound is long *a* (as in *ate*).

receive	neighbor	heir	height
conceit	weigh	freight	foreign

Exceptions: friend, mischief, handkerchief, financier, sieve, fiery

Drop the final e before a suffix beginning with a vowel.   [54b]

shine + *ing* = shining   grieve + *ous* = grievous
advise +*er* = adviser   exaggerate + *ion* = exaggeration

Exceptions: dyeing, singeing, tingeing

Words ending in ce or ge usually keep the e before suffixes that begin with a, o, or u.   [54g]

In words such as *noticeable* and *courageous* the silent *e* is retained to keep the *s* sound of *c* and the *j* sound of *g*.

Point out to students that the e is retained in dyeing, singeing, and tingeing to prevent confusion with dying, singing, and tinging as well as to keep the sound of j in the last two words (rule 54g).

Retain the final e before a suffix beginning with a consonant.   [54c]

care + ful = careful   sincere + ly = sincerely
fierce + ness = fierceness   amaze + ment = amazement

Exceptions: duly, argument, ninth, awful, wholly, truly. Judgment
and *acknowledgment* are preferred forms.

**Double a final consonant before a suffix beginning with a vowel (a) if
the consonant ends a word of one syllable or a word that is accented on
the last syllable *and* (b) if the consonant is preceded by a single vowel.**
[54d]

stop (The final consonant is preceded by a single vowel in a single-
syllable word.), *stopped, stopping*

refer (The final consonant is preceded by a single vowel in a word
with the accent on the last syllable.), *referred, referring*

Exceptions occur in derivatives in which the accent is thrown back
to another syllable; as *refer', ref'erence; defer', def'erence.*

**Words ending in y preceded by a consonant usually change y to i before
any suffix except one beginning with i.**   [54e]

y preceded by a consonant: *happy, happiest, happiness; hungry,
hungrily; merry, merrier, merrily, merriment*

y preceded by a consonant before a suffix beginning with *i: hurry,
hurrying; busy, busying*

Exceptions: One-syllable adjectives usually retain the *y* before *ly*
and *ness;* as *shy, shyly, shyness.*

   Before *ship* and *like;* as *secretaryship, citylike.*
   The *y* is retained in the plural of proper names; as the
    Bradys.
   The *y* is retained in the possessive case; as, *nobody's.*

**Words ending in y preceded by a vowel generally retain the y un-
changed before any suffix.**   [54f]

*Examples: delay, delayed, delaying; annoy, annoyed, annoying; joy,
joyful*

Exceptions: day, daily; lay, laid; say, said; slay, slain

Words ending in c usually add k before a suffix beginning with e, i, or y.
[54h]

Refer students to their dictionaries to check the preferred forms.

Emphasize particularly the plural of proper names ending in y.

When discussing rule 54d, emphasize the point that the final
consonant is doubled only when the accent remains on the last
syllable of the root word.

Empha-
size
the need
for k in
terms of
pronun-
ciation.

The purpose of the added *k* is to keep the hard sound of *c;* as *shellac, shellacked; picnic, picnicking; panic, panicky.*

Exceptions: arc, arced, arcing; disc, disced, discing

Words ending in c usually add *ally* to form an adverb.   [54i]

basic, basically   sarcastic, sarcastically
enthusiastic, enthusiastically   realistic, realistically

Only three English words end in ceed; one in sede. All others with the same pronunciation end in cede.   [54j]

ceed: exceed, proceed, succeed
sede: supersede

Learn the following rules that will help you to form the plural of nouns correctly.   [55]

To form the plural of most nouns, add an s to the singular.   [55a]

book, books; pin, pins; toy, toys

To form the plural of nouns ending in s, x, z, ch, and sh, add es.   [55b]

gas, gases; bush, bushes; tax, taxes; waltz, waltzes

To form the plural of nouns ending in y preceded by a consonant, change the y to an i and add es. Most nouns ending in y preceded by a vowel add an s.   [55c]

y preceded by a consonant: penny, penn*ies;* city, cit*ies*
y preceded by a vowel: boy, boy*s;* alloy, alloy*s*

To form the plural of many nouns ending in f or fe, change the f or fe to ves.   [55d]

half, hal*ves;* thief, thie*ves;* calf, cal*ves*

To form the plural of letters, figures, and signs, add the apostrophe and s ('s).   [55e]

t's, 5's, %'s

Words discussed as words also add an apostrophe and *s* ('s) to form the plural.

His speech is filled with *and's* and *uh's.*

To form the plural of many compound words, make the most important words plural.   [55f]

mother-in-law, mothers-in-law
board of education, boards of education

Distinguish carefully between plurals of compound words and possessive case of compound words. (See p. 227.)

To form the plural of nouns compounded with *ful*, add s at the end of the word. [55g]

cupful, cupful*s;* handful, handful*s*

If in doubt about the plural of nouns ending in o, use your dictionary. [55h]

Nouns ending in *o* preceded by a vowel add *s* only.

cameo, cameo*s;* studio, studio*s;* zoo, zoo*s*

Nouns ending in *o* preceded by a consonant vary.

solo, solo*s;* pueblo, pueblo*s;* silo, silo*s*
embargo, embargo*es;* tornado, tornado*es;* veto, veto*es*

The plurals of some nouns are formed irregularly. If in doubt about a plural form, use your dictionary. [55i]

foot, *feet*	ox, *oxen*
mouse, *mice*	tooth, *teeth*
woman, *women*	child, *children*
man, *men*	goose, *geese*

Some nouns have the same form in both the singular and the plural. [55j]

sheep, deer, fowl, trout, gallows, species, Siamese

Some nouns taken from foreign languages retain their foreign plurals, some have English plurals, and some have both. [55k]

Foreign plurals: alumnus, alumn*i;* alumna, alumn*ae;* crisis, cris*es;* parenthesis, parenthes*es;* datum, dat*a;* chateau, chateau*x*

English plurals: bonus, bonus*es;* encyclopedia, encyclopedia*s;* campus, campus*es,* forum, forum*s*

In the following list of words, the foreign plural is given before the English plural:

Both: formula-formula*e,* formula*s;* index, ind*ices;* index*es;* curriculum-curricul*a,* curriculum*s;* radius-radi*i,* radius*es*

Because of the variation in spelling words ending in o preceded by a consonant, caution students to check in their dictionaries.

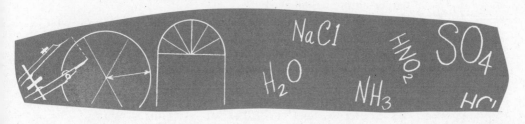

Proofread carefully everything that you write.   [56]

Careful proofreading of everything you write can help you to find and eliminate spelling errors that are the result of carelessness or haste. When you have completed a piece of written work, proofread it one time solely for the purpose of finding and correcting spelling errors. If you are in doubt about the spelling of any word you have used, check the spelling in a good dictionary.

DEVELOPING YOUR SKILL

A. Write the numbers 1 to 5 on a sheet of paper. After each number write the word from the parentheses that is appropriate to the meaning of the sentence.

1. Hearing the spectators cheer is good for team (morale, moral).
2. How does the schedule change (effect, affect) you?
3. When did you (loose, lose) your wallet?
4. I was so (scared, scarred) I could hardly speak.
5. Helen was not (quiet, quite) ready when we arrived.

B. Write correctly the misspelled words in the following sentences. After each word write the number of the specific rule that applies to the spelling of that word. See also top and bottom margins.

1. Each girl recieved a compact as a rememberance of the occasion.
2. Represeratives of both companys interveiwed canidates for part-time employment.
3. We saw many amuseing sites at the circus.
4. My brothers and thier wifes are hopping to visit the Henries when they are in California.
5. All the datas for the report are being assembled.
6. There is a noticable diffrence in everybody's atitude since the alumnuses have agreed to help with the campain.
7. I have been getting *B*s in English ever since I began working harder on my writen work.
8. It is a releif to know that the dayly quizzes will count toward our midsemester grade.
9. The couragous policemen recieved special awards.
10. The recipe calls for two teaspoonsful of baking powder.

C. Add the suffixes indicated to the words in the following list. Make any changes that are necessary to the correct spelling of the words.

referred   1. refer + ed
profited   2. profit + ed
truly   3. true + ly
merciless   4. mercy + less
dyeing   5. dye + ing

6. propel + er   propeller
7. desire + ous   desirous
8. courage + ous   courageous
9. move + able   movable
10. panic + y   panicky

D. Form the plurals of the following words and write a sentence using each plural form.   Sentences will vary.

1. leftover s
2. Hardy s
3. ally ies
4. wolf ves
5. tooth teeth
6. Englishman men
7. & ' s
8. alumnae
9. crisis es
10. alto s
11. valley s
12. leaf ves
13. curio s
14. great-aunt s
15. box es

Review Exercises—Spelling

A. Write the following words on a sheet of paper, inserting *ie* or *ei* in the spaces where letters have been omitted.

ei   1. dec--t
ie   2. financ--r
ei   3. d--gn
ei   4. w--ght
ie   5. s--ge

6. for--gn   ei
7. t--r   ie
8. n--ther   ei
9. pr--st   ie
10. l--sure   ei

B. List the following words on a sheet of paper. Following each word write the plural form and the number of the rule that applies to the formation of the plural.

55c   1. journeys
55b   2. church es
55a   3. squirrel s
55h   4. radio s
55j   5. species same
55k   6. parenthesis es
55g   7. handful s
55c   8. summary ies
55i   9. fireman men
55h   10. cameo s

55d   11. knife ves
55c   12. duty ies
55i   13. tooth teeth
55d   14. leaf leaves
55f   15. commander in chief s
54e   16. Mary s
55c   17. agency ies
55e   18. S 's
55b   19. bus es
55a   20. chief s

1. inviting, friends, listen, program; 2. surprised, hear;
3. difficult, complimentary, signature, address; 4. disappointed,
mentioning, occurred; 5. tries, persuade, swimming, appreciate

C. The following sentences contain misspelled words. Write the numbers 1
to 5 on a sheet of paper. After each number write correctly the misspelled
words in the corresponding sentence. See also top margin.

1. I am inviteing all my freinds and relatives to lissen to a radio pogram.
2. The family was both suprized and pleased to here from you.
3. The names of the parts of a letter that are dificult to spell are the salutation, the complementary close, the signiture, and the adress.
4. How dissapointed we were! Not an event worth mensioning ocurred
on the journey.
5. Father trys to presuade us that we must go swiming with him at dawn
to apreciate the real beauty of the lake.

D. Write on your paper the words in the following list. Form as many words
as you can by adding the suffixes *ed, ing, ous, able, ible, ness, ance, ment,*
and *ly.* Write the new words beside the words from which they are formed.

See p. T79.

1. acquit	11. excite
2. argue	12. happen
3. begin	13. manage
4. believe	14. marriage
5. benefit	15. note
6. courage	16. recognize
7. debate	17. rebel
8. desire	18. refer
9. drastic	19. silly
10. endure	20. value

3. Capitalization

Usage has established specific rules and exceptions for the use of
capital letters in English. While it is true that many modern writers tend
to ignore the rules of capitalization, such deviations from standard usage
are not generally accepted and should be avoided. The incorrect use of
capital letters gives the impression of carelessness and often of illiteracy.
Make a conscious effort to master the rules of capitalization. After a time
you will find that you will apply the rules effortlessly.

You may wish to use the exercise on page 375 to determine
which of your students still have difficulty with capitalization.

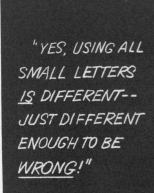

Capitalize the first words in most situations. [47]

Capitalize the first word in every sentence. [47a]

*M*y father bought a new car yesterday.
*W*ho will preside at the meeting?

Capitalize the first word in a quotation. [47b]

Al agreed, "*A*ll of us will have to work hard to make the safety campaign a success."

Selma asked, "*H*ow many people will be working on the committee?"

Do not capitalize the first word in a continuing quotation that does not begin a new sentence. [47c]

"I don't know," she said, "*w*hether I fully understood the problem."
"I think you are wrong," I objected. "*W*hat good will such action accomplish?"

Capitalize the first word of a line of poetry. [47d]

*L*ike as the waves make towards the pebbled shore,
*S*o do our minutes hasten to their end.

—WILLIAM SHAKESPEARE

Some modern poets disregard this rule. If you use a quotation from a poem in one of your papers, copy the lines exactly as they are written.

Capitalize the pronoun *I* and the interjection O. [47e]

Usually *I* spend my vacations on my grandparents' farm.
Roll on, *O* mighty ocean!

The E. E. Cummings poem on page 26 is an example of a modern poem in which the first word is not capitalized.

369

Point out to students that not all publishing and printing houses use exactly the same style of capitalization, but that essentially the practice of capitalization in English language publications follows the rules prescribed in this text.

The interjection *O* is rarely used in modern writing. When it is used, it is always used in direct address and is always capitalized. The more commonly used interjection *oh* is capitalized only at the beginning of a sentence or when it stands alone.

Oh, I don't know about that.
Oh! I forgot my English assignment!
I am certain—*oh* no, I see now.

Capitalize the first letter of each main point and each subhead in an outline.   **[47f]**

   I. *T*he trade fair
      A. *A*merican exhibits
         1. *A*rts and crafts
         2. *B*usiness and industry
      B. *F*oreign exhibits

Capitalize the first word of a formal statement following a colon.
[47g]

The ruling of the student court was as follows: *T*hat all students who are found guilty of breaking school rules shall be penalized according to the seriousness of the violation.

Capitalize the first word of a resolution following *Resolved* or *Whereas*.
[47h]

Resolved: *T*hat the Federal government should award scholarships to all qualified students.

Whereas is usually used in the preamble to a formal document.

Whereas: *T*he parties of both parts have agreed to the conditions stated herein. . . .

Capitalize the first word in each item of a list.   **[47i]**

The survey reveals the following conditions to be prevalent:
         1. *I*nadequate housing
         2. *F*ire hazards
         3. *P*oorly lighted streets
         4. *L*imited recreational facilities

You will probably want to correlate the teaching of the rules for capitalization with the teaching of specific areas of study to which they apply.

In letter writing capitalize the first word and all nouns in the salutation. Capitalize only the first word of the complimentary close. [48]

Dear Bob,	*Dear Mrs. Johnson,*	*My* dear *Mrs. Lee,*
Gentlemen:	*Dear Sir:*	*My* dear *Madam:*
Yours very truly,	*As* always,	*With* love,

Capitalize all proper adjectives. [49]

Joanne speaks Spanish with an *American* accent.

Mr. Wells has a very *British* sense of humor.

Capitalize all proper nouns. [50]

Capitalize the names of the days of the week, the months of the year, and holidays. Do not capitalize the names of the seasons of the year. [50a]

Monday, Tuesday, Wednesday, Thursday, Friday, Saturday, Sunday

January, February, March, April, etc.

Christmas, Thanksgiving Day, Veteran's Day, Fourth of July

spring, summer, autumn, winter

The names of the seasons are capitalized only if they are personified.

Next came *Autumn* wearing a coat of brilliant colors.

The snow wrapped *Winter* in a blanket of white.

The seasons of the year are capitalized only when they are personified.

Capitalize all specific geographical or place names, as well as sections of the country. Do not capitalize directions of the compass. [50b]

Times Square	*Lake Superior*	*Missouri River*
State Street	*Manhattan*	*Yosemite Valley*

North, south, east, and *west* are capitalized when they refer to sections of the country or when they precede the name of a street. When they refer to directions of the compass, they are not capitalized.

The dialects of the *North* are different from those of the *South.*

She lives on *North* Clark *Street* near *West* Fullerton *Parkway.*

Turn *east* at the next corner and walk two blocks. The building is on the *north* side of the street.

Do not capitalize a common noun used with a proper noun unless the common noun is a part of the specific name.

Jets cross the Atlantic *Ocean* from New York to Paris in six hours and fifteen minutes.

Distinguish between nouns that are parts of proper names and those that retain their common noun reference.

America is bounded by the Atlantic and Pacific *o*ceans. *(Oceans* is not a part of the specific names in this sentence.)

There are many beautiful shops on *F*ifth *A*venue.

I shall meet you at Fifth and South *a*venues. *(Avenues* is not a part of the specific names in this sentence.)

Capitalize personal titles and all titles of officials in government, business, and the professions when those titles precede the name of the person.   [50c]

<table>
<tr><td>Develop</td><td>*M*rs. Jackson</td><td>*S*uperintendent Cooke</td></tr>
<tr><td>care-
fully</td><td>*P*rincess Grace</td><td>*C*hief *J*ustice Hughes</td></tr>
<tr><td>the dis-</td><td>*M*ajor Elian</td><td>*S*enator Bradley</td></tr>
<tr><td>tinc-</td><td>*D*r. Sullivan</td><td>*P*resident Washington</td></tr>
</table>

Develop care- fully the dis- tinc- tions dis- cussed under this rule.

A title that follows a name or that is used alone is not capitalized unless it refers to a high government official or is used in place of a name.

Nelson A. Rockefeller, *G*overnor of New York State, was elected to his office in 1958. (High government official)

The *S*ecretary of *S*tate appeared on television last night. (High government official)

Dr. Cooke, the *s*uperintendent of schools, spoke in assembly yesterday. (Title not capitalized)

The words *President* and *Vice-President* are always capitalized when used to refer to the President and Vice-President of the United States. The prefix *ex* and the adjective *elect* are not capitalized when they are used with titles.

ex-President Truman   Senator-*elect* Norman

Capitalize the first word, the last word, and all important words of titles of books, plays, poems, songs, short stories, and essays. Do not capitalize articles, short conjunctions, or short prepositions unless they are the first or last words in the title.   [50d]

*S*mall *S*ounds in the *N*ight (Book)

*R*iders to the *S*ea (Play)

"*S*topping by *W*oods on a *S*nowy *E*vening" (Poem)

"*I*'m in *L*ove with a *W*onderful *G*uy" (Song)

"*B*y the *W*aters of *B*abylon" (Short Story)

"*T*he *A*utocrat of the *B*reakfast *T*able (Essay)

Students frequently capitalize all words in a title. Emphasize the part of the rule that applies to articles, short conjunctions, and short prepositions.

The words *a, an,* and *the* before a title are capitalized only when they are part of the title.

Emphasize this point.

The book T*he Sea Around Us* presents a scientific subject in informal, non-technical language. *(The* is part of the title.)

I enjoy the cartoons in *the New Yorker. (The* is not part of the title.)

Capitalize the names of famous historical events and documents. [50e]

Battle of *B*unker *H*ill   *W*ar *B*etween the *S*tates

World War *II*   Treaty of *V*ersailles

Capitalize references to the Deity and the names of religions and races. [50f]

| God | Jehovah | Allah | Roman Catholic | Protestant |
| Judaism | Moslem | Negro | Caucasian | Mongolian |

The word *god* is not capitalized when it refers to pagan deities. The word *goddess* is not capitalized.

Mount Olympus was the dwelling place of the *g*ods and *g*oddesses, according to Greek mythology.

Asgard was the home of the *g*ods and of slain heroes in Norse mythology.

Pronouns used to refer to the Deity are capitalized.

When God created the world, *He* rested on the seventh day.

Capitalize the names of religious books of all religions. Do not underline or use quotation marks. [50g]

| the *B*ible | the *O*ld *T*estament | the *N*ew *T*estament |
| the *K*oran | the *T*orah | the *H*oly *S*criptures |

Capitalize the words *father, mother, brother, sister,* and other family relationships whenever they are used in place of the person's name or in connection with that name. [50h]

The names of religious books are not treated as titles of other books are.

Mother   Uncle *J*im   Brother *A*ndrew   *S*ister *N*atalie

I promised *M*other I would go shopping with her.

Do not capitalize a mere relationship: *my mother, your uncle, his cousin Fred, our sister Bea.* Such relationships are preceded by a possessive pronoun.

I promised *my m*other I would go shopping with her.

Distin-
guish
between
course
titles
and
common
nouns
that
describe
various
courses.

In the names of school subjects, capitalize specific subjects offered in the curriculum (Algebra 1A or Radio 2) and all names derived from proper names of countries or languages (English, Latin, German). [50i]

Spanish   *French*   *Italian*

I find this course in *office practice* rather difficult.

I find *Office Practice 2* rather difficult.

Capitalize the names of political parties and of specific governmental bodies, departments, bureaus, or other divisions. [50j]

Democratic Party   *Republican Party*   the *Senate*
State Department   *Congress*   the *Supreme Court*

Capitalize the names of buildings, business firms, and brand names of products. [50k]

the *Empire State Building*   *Benson Brothers, Inc.*

The common noun that follows a brand name is not capitalized except in advertising.

Glow toothpaste   *Bunberry bread*

Capitalize the names of organizations, institutions, and special groups. [50l]

American Medical Association Art Institute South High Glee Club

Do not capitalize such words as *high school, college, university, hotel,* and *theater* unless they are part of proper names.

My brother is studying medicine at Johns Hopkins *University*.
My brother is studying medicine at a *university* in Baltimore.

Jeanne plans to stay at the Martha Hannibal *Hotel*.
Jeanne plans to stay at a women's *hotel*.

Names of school classes are capitalized only when the word *class* accompanies them.

The *Junior* class elected officers yesterday.
The *juniors* are planning a class party.

Capitalize the names of special events. [50m]

World Series   *Junior Prom*   *Class Day*

You may wish to have students compare the various styles of capitalization used in newspapers and magazines with each other and with the standard conventions presented in this unit.

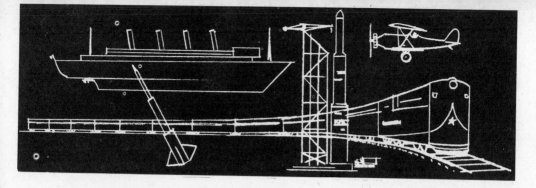

Capitalize the names of ships, trains, planes, missiles, and rockets.

[50n]

Titanic *Lone Star State* Express *A*strojet
Nike-Zeus *Freedom Seven* *Spirit of* St. Louis

> DEVELOPING YOUR SKILL

Write the numbers 1 to 10 on a sheet of paper. After each number write correctly the words and word groups that should be capitalized in the corresponding sentence. Underscore indicates capital letter.

1. when laura hamilton and i were in washington, d.c. last spring we visited the lincoln memorial, the capitol, the white house, and the library of congress.
2. all the students in the junior high school are studying either french or spanish.
3. during book week this year, miss levitt, the librarian, prepared a special exhibit.
4. in english class this year we have read *macbeth* and *giants in the earth,* as well as poetry of the romantic period and the victorian period.
5. after living in the southeastern part of the country for three years, my mother and father moved to the northwest.
6. mr. david reed, founder of reed and sons, incorporated, has decided to move the company's offices to the new whitehall building at webster and seventh streets.
7. the parent-teachers association held its annual banquet at the allyson hotel.
8. the american astronaut, commander alan b. shepard, made his historic flight into space in the spaceship *freedom seven.*
9. the marshall plan, which was put into effect after world war II, was named for its originator, general george c. marshall, who was then secretary of state.
10. the nobel prizes were established under the will of alfred bernhard nobel, a swedish chemist and engineer who died on december 10, 1896.

375

Review Exercises—Capitalization

Rewrite the following sentences, correcting any errors in capitalization. If a sentence is correctly capitalized, write a plus sign (+) following the number of the sentence. Underscore indicates capital letter; slash, lower-case letter.

1. The new york yankees, the boston braves, and the cincinnati reds are famous ball clubs.

+ 2. "The Discus Thrower" and many other Greek statues give evidence of the athletic interests of the Mediterranean peoples.

3. Ann began her letter "My Dear Uncle," and ended it "Affectionately, Your Niece."

4. *The Tyranny Of Words* by stuart chase contains such chapter headings as "a Writer in Search of his Words" and "cats And Babies."

5. The president of the United States conferred with the governor of New Jersey, the assistant secretary of the navy, and rear admiral frank g. johnson.

6. The reverend Grant Seabrook of the Anglican Methodist Church said: "This is the important Commandment: 'Thou shalt love thy neighbor as thyself.'"

7. The world series has become an important american institution.

8. Governor-Elect Hamilton and Ex-Senator Roberts conferred with the leaders of the democratic and republican Parties.

9. New York university is opposite washington square in greenwich village.

+ 10. The president of the student council called a special meeting to discuss the problem.

You may wish to read the introduction aloud and discuss it in class. Emphasize the point made that overpunctuation is just as bad as too little punctuation.

4. Punctuation

Punctuation is the system of marks used to make the meaning of written material clear. Prior to the sixteenth century, there was no systematic use of punctuation. Punctuation marks were omitted completely or were used according to the wishes of the writer. In some early writings not only was no punctuation used, but words were also run together to save space or precious writing materials.

In the sixteenth century a Venetian printer, Aldus Manutius, systematized the use of punctuation. It is Manutius's system that is the basis for the system of punctuation used today.

Punctuation is particularly important as an aid to revealing meaning in written language.

Just as there are certain conventions that you must follow in grammar, usage, writing, spelling, and capitalization, so are there conventions in punctuation. Your readers will expect your writing to be punctuated according to standard usage. Departures from standard usage can lead to misreading and misunderstanding.

Punctuation has come to serve two purposes, both of them related to clarity: (1) to make the meaning of the writing clear and (2) to conform with the conventions established by standard usage. These are the only two reasons for which punctuation should be used. Overpunctuation is just as bad as too little punctuation.

Like capitalization, punctuation is a printer's device to help make meaning clear.

COMMA

The comma is probably the most used of all punctuation marks. Usage has established a number of rules for the use of commas in writing, all of them designed to make the writer's meaning clear. Study the rules and apply them in the exercises given for practice. Then be sure you apply the rules to your own writing.

Use commas in your writing in all the situations established through usage.   [57]

Insert a comma between sentence elements when the thought might be incorrectly interpreted if no punctuation were used.   [57a]

A speaker uses pauses, change of pitch, gestures, and facial expression to help make his meaning clear. A writer must depend upon punctuation to achieve clarity. Even when the construction of a sentence is completely correct, the meaning can be destroyed by a lack of punctuation. Notice, for example, the confusion that results from the omission of commas in the following sentences:

When I said I would cook my father decided to take us out for dinner.
Instead of twenty nine appeared at the meeting.
Just a week before we had cautioned Rob about his carelessness.
Ever since she has refused to speak to Jim.
Debbie spends her summers in Oregon; her sister in Maine.

These sentences, when spoken, would be clear.

Each of the preceding sentences becomes clear with the addition of a single comma.

Students tend to use commas indiscriminately, particularly when commas are equated with pauses in speaking. Unless you plan to present a detailed discussion of juncture, teach commas solely from the point of view of logical meaning and clarity.

Written
language
requires
punctuation.

When I said I would cook, my father decided to take us out for dinner.

Instead of twenty, nine appeared at the meeting.

Just a week before, we had cautioned Rob about his carelessness.

Ever since, she has refused to speak to Jim.

Debbie spends her summers in Oregon; her sister, in Maine.

In the last sentence the comma indicates the omission of the words *spends her summers.*

Use a comma to set off an introductory adverbial clause.   [57b]

When we were almost at our destination, I realized that I had forgotten the picnic lunch.

When he saw that I would not be dissuaded from my position, he launched into a violent tirade.

The comma may be omitted after a short introductory adverb clause if there is no danger of the sentence's being misread.

If it rains we shall hold the exercises in the auditorium.

When plans go awry everyone is disappointed.

Use a comma to set off introductory participial phrases and introductory infinitive phrases used as adjectives or adverbs.   [57c]

Coming suddenly upon a group of soldiers, the officer stopped to question them.

To be successful, you must work hard.

Hovering in the air, the helicopter looked like a giant bird.

You may wish to correlate the teaching of many of these rules with the teaching of related areas of study; for example, rule 57b with the teaching of adverbial clauses.

Use a comma to set off a succession of prepositional phrases at the beginning of a sentence. [57d]

At the end of the day, he sought shelter.

Newspapers and magazines frequently differ in their use of the comma after introductory elements. If you follow the general rule of inserting a comma after all introductory elements of five words or more, you will not have to worry about overpunctuation.

In the morning the grass was fresh with dew. (No comma needed)
Before deciding upon a specific course of action, investigate the possibilities thoroughly. (Correct use of the comma)

Use a comma to set off a single word like *yes, no, well, indeed, alas,* or single words obviously out of their natural order in the sentence. [57e]

Yes, I agree with you.
Well, this is a pleasant surprise.
Finally, I remembered what Bill had said.

Use a comma to set off words of direct address, whether they come at the beginning, the middle, or the end of the sentence. [57f]

Remember that a word of direct address may be either the name of the person spoken to or a substitute for the person's name, as "my friend" or "my boy." Notice the use of the comma with words of direct address. When the expression of direct address comes in the middle of a sentence, two commas are needed.

Emphasize the point that words in direct address may be substituted for persons' names.

Gretchen, your work in English is improving.
It was right here, *Mother,* that I saw it last.
I have only this to say to you, *Hank Sullivan.*
Come here, my *friend,* and listen to some good advice.
The error, *ladies and gentlemen,* is mine.

Use commas to set off parenthetical words and phrases. [57g]

Parenthetical expressions are those inserted by the writer to help make his meaning clear. Since parenthetical expressions interrupt the thought of the sentence and are not necessary to the meaning of the sentence, they are separated from the rest of the sentence by commas. Some of the most common parenthetical expressions are *however, in fact, indeed, on the*

Discuss the point that parenthetical expressions help to clarify meaning but are not necessary to the meaning of a sentence.

other hand, as a matter of fact, nevertheless, and *therefore.* You will un-doubtedly be able to think of many more parenthetical expressions that are frequently used.

There was, *on the other hand,* nothing we could do.

We agreed, *therefore,* to hold a special meeting.

Sometimes the punctuation of parenthetical expressions depends upon the writer's intention. If he intends that an expression should be par-enthetical, the writer inserts commas; if not, he omits commas. Some-times, however, the use of commas with such expressions depends upon the placement of the parenthetical expression in the sentence. Study the following sentences:

Discuss
these
three
examples
in de-
tail.
We *therefore* chose to ignore his rudeness. (The writer intends that there be no pause.)

We, *therefore,* chose to ignore his rudeness. *(Therefore* is intended to be parenthetical.)

We chose, *therefore,* to ignore his rudeness. *(Therefore* is out of its natural order and should be set off by commas.)

Use commas to set off words used in apposition.   [57h]

Another type of expression that may interrupt the thought of a sen-tence is an appositive. An appositive is a word or phrase that explains or identifies the noun or pronoun it follows.

Mr. Lester Rinehart, *the vice-president of the company,* will retire at the end of the year. *(Vice-president* identifies *Mr. Lester Rinehart.)*

Last year we had two cars, *a Buick and a Ford. (Buick* and *Ford* identify *cars.)*

Let us, *the living,* not forget our obligations. *(Living* identifies *us.)*

Sometimes an appositive is so closely related to the word it explains or identifies that no commas are necessary. Such appositives are called *restrictive appositives* and are usually one-word appositives.

My aunt Dorothy is coming to visit us next week. *(Dorothy* is in apposition with *aunt.)*

The word *ain't* is considered substandard usage. *(Ain't* is in apposi-tion with *word.)*

The poem "Sea Fever" was written by John Masefield. *("Sea Fever"* is in apposition with *poem.)*

Rule 57h may be correlated with the teaching of
appositives (pages 247-249).

Use a comma to set off a final clause when the thought turns aside; if the thought continues, use no comma. [57i] The relationship of the final clause to the rest of the sentence determines whether or not a comma is needed.

If you have difficulty determining whether a comma should precede a final subordinate clause, ask yourself whether the final statement introduces a new idea or whether it continues the idea presented in the main clause. Study the following examples and their explanations:

Margaret was glad she had invited Nancy, the new girl, to the party, especially since Nancy proved to be such a likable person. (The final clause introduces a new idea and is therefore set off by a comma.)

He must be here, although I don't see him in the room. (A comma is used to set off the final clause, which introduces a new idea.)

I will call you as soon as I get home. (The final clause completes the idea begun in the main clause; therefore, no comma is needed.)

She spoke as though she were an authority. (No comma is necessary.)

Use commas to set off the elements of a series of words, phrases, or clauses. [57j]

A series is a group of three or more related words, phrases, or clauses arranged in the pattern A, B, and C. If you substitute the elements of a series for the letters used to designate the pattern of a series, you should have little difficulty with punctuating this construction.

The stone was round, rough, and porous. (Words in a series)

He wore the same old hat in winter, in summer, in spring, and in fall. (Phrases in a series)

We asked him where he was going, how he planned to travel, what he intended to do there, and when he expected to return. (Clauses in a series)

Some writers today omit the comma before *and* in a series. Since the omission of the comma can result in confusion, it is better to develop the habit of including the comma. Read the following sentences:

The following officers were elected: president, vice-president, secretary, and treasurer. (Four officers were elected)

The following officers were elected: president, vice-president, secretary and treasurer. (The punctuation in this sentence seems to indicate that only three officers were elected, the office of secretary and treasurer being a combined office held by one person.)

Impress upon students that the omission of the comma before <u>and</u> in a series may result in confusion. It is never wrong to inclu<u>de</u> the comma in this usage.

Empha-
size
these
points.

Words that are usually used in pairs are set off as a single item in a series. Such expressions include such terms as *bacon and eggs, hat and coat, bread and butter, pen and ink,* etc.

For the examination you will need paper, pen and ink, an eraser, and a ruler.

Do not insert a comma before the first word or after the last word in a series.

I am taking sandwiches, fruit, and cookies for my lunch. (Not *I am taking, sandwiches, fruit, and cookies, for my lunch.*)

No commas are used in a series when each of the elements is preceded by *and* or *or.*

I can't decide whether to serve ham or chicken or beef.
His clothes were tattered and torn and ill-fitting.

Use a comma before the co-ordinating conjunction that connects two independent clauses. [57k]

Two independent clauses joined by a co-ordinating conjunction form a compound sentence. A comma usually precedes the conjunction *and, but, or, for,* or *nor* in a compound sentence.

Listen to me, or I shall burst with excitement!
The wind is blowing off the lake, but the day is still oppressively hot.

You may wish to correlate the teaching of rule 57k with the teaching of compound sentences (page 251).

Do not confuse compound subjects or compound verbs with compound sentences. No commas are necessary in the following sentences.

He *turned* the car skillfully into the drive and *drove* it into the garage. *(And* joins the verbs *turned* and *drove.)*

Doing his homework and *reviewing for a history test* took most of the evening. *(And* joins two gerund phrases used as a compound subject.)

If the clauses in a compound sentence are very short or if the subjects of the clauses remain the same, the comma may be omitted, especially before the conjunctions *and* or *or,* as in the following sentences:

I have made my decision and I intend to stick to it.

Will you lead or shall I?

Be sure you use a comma before a co-ordinating conjunction if there is any danger of misreading.

I couldn't wait any longer for the bell was about to ring. (Confusing)

I couldn't wait any longer, for the bell was about to ring. (Clear)

If either or both of the clauses in a compound sentence contain commas, a semicolon is usually used before the co-ordinating conjunction, as in the following sentences:

Susan packed her dresses, skirts, and blouses; but she forgot to include her shoes, sweaters, and accessories.

I am, I must confess, frightened at the risks involved; but I am tempted to try my luck.

Use commas to set off nonrestrictive phrases and clauses.   [571]

Restrictive phrases and clauses limit the meaning of the words they modify by telling *which one* or *what kind*. Since they are essential to the meaning of the sentences in which they appear, restrictive phrases and clauses are not set off by commas.

The train *leaving at three o'clock* will get you there in time for dinner. (Restrictive phrase)

Americans *who travel abroad* must learn to adapt themselves to the customs of the people of foreign countries. (Restrictive clause)

The use of commas with nonrestrictive elements should be developed carefully and thoroughly.

[side margin note:] Distinguish carefully between compound elements in sentences and compound sentences.

Nonre-
stric-
tive
ele-
ments
are
paren-
theti-
cal in
meaning.

In the first of the preceding examples, the participial phrase *leaving at three o'clock* tells which train is meant. If the phrase were omitted, the meaning of the sentence would be incomplete. In the second example sentence, the clause *who travel abroad* tells which Americans are meant. If the clause were omitted, the sentence would mean that all Americans must adapt themselves to the customs of the people of foreign countries. Since both the phrase and the clause are necessary to the meaning of the sentences in which they appear, they are not set off by commas.

Nonrestrictive phrases and clauses simply give additional information about the words they modify. Nonrestrictive phrases and clauses are not necessary to the meaning of the sentences in which they appear and therefore are set off by commas.

> My brother Murray, *exhausted after his ordeal,* spent several days in the hospital. (Nonrestrictive)

> The president of the company came out of his office, *which was separated from the outer offices by a partition.* (Nonrestrictive)

In both the preceding sentences, the italicized words could be omitted without changing the meaning of the sentences. The participial phrase in the first sentence and the relative clause in the second sentence are nonrestrictive and must be set off by commas.

Sometimes only the writer of a sentence can determine whether a phrase or a clause is restrictive. In such cases, it is up to the writer to punctuate the sentence correctly so that its meaning will not be misconstrued.

> Our club is sponsoring a Halloween dance. The club members, *who have worked hard,* will be given free tickets.

By setting off the italicized clause in the preceding sentence, the writer has indicated that all the club members have worked hard and will receive free tickets to the dance. Notice how the omission of the commas changes the meaning:

> Our club is sponsoring a Halloween dance. The club members who have worked hard will be given free tickets.

In the preceding example, the writer has indicated that only those club members who have worked hard will receive free tickets to the dance.

Impress upon students the importance of making the intended meaning clear through the use of punctuation when a sentence element may be either restrictive or nonrestrictive.

A simple test to help you determine whether a modifying phrase or clause should be set off by commas is to omit the modifier in question and read the sentence. If the meaning of the sentence is clear without the phrase or clause, the modifier should be set off by commas.

The first man *who served as President of the United States* was George Washington.

The italicized clause obviously is essential to the meaning of the sentence. Without it the sentence becomes ridiculous. The clause is restrictive and should not be set off by commas.

The following points will help you recognize nonrestrictive phrases and clauses:

You may wish to duplicate these five points for inclusion in students' notebooks.

1. They add information; they do not limit.
2. They may be removed without changing the meaning of the sentence.
3. Phrases and clauses that modify proper names are usually nonrestrictive and should be set off by commas.
4. The use of a possessive pronoun with the modified noun often indicates that the phrase or clause is nonrestrictive and should be set off by commas.
5. Most dependent clauses beginning with *that* are restrictive.

Use commas in letter writing between the day and the year, between the city and the state, after the salutation in a social letter, and after the complimentary close. [57m]

October 3, 1962
Buffalo, New York
Dear Jerry,
Sincerely yours,

If a zone number is used between the city and state, insert the comma after the zone number.

Buffalo 11, New York

Avoid using only a comma to splice, or join, two independent clauses.
[57n]

The comma splice error occurs when two or more main clauses are written as a single sentence with only a comma to separate the clauses. The independent clauses in the following sentence are incorrectly joined by a comma.

> That hat is particularly becoming to you, you ought to buy it.

The comma splice may be corrected in several ways, depending upon the emphasis you wish. If you wish to give the ideas equal emphasis, you may use a period or a semicolon in place of the comma, or you may use a co-ordinating conjunction with the comma. If you wish to emphasize one idea more than the other, you may subordinate one idea by using a subordinating conjunction.

> That hat is particularly becoming to you. You ought to buy it. (Use a period at the end of the first clause, and capitalize the first word of the second clause.)

> That hat is particularly becoming to you; you ought to buy it. (Use a semicolon to join the clauses.)

> That hat is particularly becoming to you, and you ought to buy it. (Use a co-ordinating conjunction with the comma.)

> *Since that hat is particularly becoming to you,* you ought to buy it. (Subordinate one idea.)

Use a comma between co-ordinate adjectives.   [57o]

Two or more adjectives that modify the same noun and that are of equal rank are called *co-ordinate adjectives*. The co-ordinate adjectives in the following sentences are italicized.

> He drove cautiously on the *dark, narrow* road.
> A *tall, slender* girl walked into the office of the modeling agency.

In some sentences the adjectives are not co-ordinate, and no comma should be used.

> Martha bought a *red wool* coat.

In the preceding sentence, *wool* modifies coat. *Red* describes the com- Be sure
bined idea *wool coat. Red* and *wool* are not co-ordinate adjectives and that
should not be separated by a comma. Notice the punctuation of the ad- stu-
jectives in the following sentence: dents

> Martha has a *new, red wool* coat. *(New* and *red* are co-ordinate with
> each other, but not with *wool.* Both *new* and *red* describe the *wool*
> coat.)

If you are in doubt about whether to use a comma between adjectives,
try inserting the conjunction *and* between the adjectives. If the conjunction fits the meaning naturally, a comma should usually be used.

under-
stand
this
dis-
tinc-
tion.

Use commas to separate the parts of an address.   [57p]

> Steve and his family moved to *436 Humboldt Parkway, Rochester
> 15, New York,* last week.

Notice that a comma follows the last item in the address when the address does not come at the end of the sentence.

Use commas to separate the parts of a date.   [57q]

> Mark was born on *December 6, 1946,* in Portland, Oregon.

Notice that a comma follows the year when the date does not conclude
the sentence.

When only the month and the day are given, no comma is used.

> November 19 is my parents' wedding anniversary.

When only the month and the year are given, commas are usually used,
although some modern writers tend to omit the commas in this usage.

> It was in April, 1960, that Mr. Miller became president of the
> company.

Do not use commas when the items in a date are joined by a preposition.

> He last visited us in March *of* 1961.

**Use a comma to set off the exact words of a speaker from the rest of
the sentence, except when a question mark or an exclamation point is
required.**   [57r]

> She said, "Your reasoning does not seem valid to me."
> "Your reasoning does not seem valid to me," she said.

You may wish to correlate the teaching of rule 57r with the
teaching of writing direct quotations (page 400).

"In that case," he replied, "you haven't been listening to me."

"What are your plans?" he asked. (The meaning requires a question mark instead of a comma.)

Use a comma to set off a short final clause that changes a statement to a question.   [57s]

He said he would be here, *didn't he?*

I haven't told you this story before, *have I?*

Use a comma to separate contrasted co-ordinate elements in a sentence.
[57t]

The co-ordinate elements in the following sentences are in italics.

The author of that story is *Hemingway,* not *Lardner.*

He spoke *quietly,* but *emphatically.*

Use a comma or commas to set off transposed modifiers.   [57u]

It was a dull meeting, *long* and *tiring.*

His tone of voice, *sharp* and *businesslike,* brought everyone to attention.

This rule
may be   **Use a comma or commas to separate an absolute expression from the**
taught   **rest of a sentence.**   [57v]
when
absolute   *The rain having stopped,* we decided to walk downtown.
expres-   During the trial, *the courtroom being filled,* many people waited out-
sions   side the courthouse for news.
are taught. (See pages 278–280.)

> DEVELOPING YOUR SKILL

    A. Determine where commas are necessary in the following sentences. After the appropriate number on your paper, write the words that should be followed by commas, and place a comma after each word. If the sentence is written correctly, write + after the appropriate number.

      1. If sufficient food, water, and cover are not available, wild game will not be plentiful.

 + 2. His first day's selling experience convinced him that he had the wrong approach and that he must try again.

3. When I could no longer see, the fishermen were still out on the lake.

4. The old lady said, "Thank you for your help, young man."

5. Bret Harte, an American author, wrote stories about life in mining camps.

6. The cost, however, is more than I can afford.

7. This plan, when you consider all the possibilities, is the best one for our purposes.

+   8. With everyone's help we can make this project a success.

9. I did understand you correctly, didn't I?

10. Our cottage having been flooded, we spent the night at a motel, twenty miles away.

+   11. The roads that I like to travel are the side roads.

12. Mr. McCormick, who has his office at 33 South Michigan Avenue, Nashville 5, Tennessee has been elected to the school board.

13. His short story has a clever, unusual plot.

14. He was born in Atlanta, Georgia, on April 25, 1901, at seven o'clock in the evening.

15. Children's diseases, a principal concern of UNICEF, have received special medical attention only since the turn of the century.

16. We started out on a bright, sunny August afternoon.

17. You will be glad you decided to take the extra math courses, even though you may not realize it now.

18. My little sister received ten bright new, silver dollars for her birthday, one for each year of her life.

19. Just when he was ready to begin eating, the telephone rang.

20. He was a peevish, selfish, irascible old man, if I ever saw one.

B. Some of the following sentences contain nonrestrictive elements that should be set off by commas. If a sentence requires commas, write the sentence after the appropriate number on your paper, inserting commas where necessary. If the sentence does not require commas, write *C* after the appropriate number.

C   1. The building being constructed at the corner of Seventh Avenue and Twelfth Street will house the new community center.

2. Her new dress, which she bought for the dance, is a beautiful shade of blue.

C   3. All cities which have a population of at least 100,000 are considered in the report.

C   4. People who have not developed hobbies are often bored and lonely when they retire.

These exercises are sufficiently objective in nature to be checked by students in class. The teacher may read the correct answers or may call upon students to give the answers.

5. Our cottage, which is located at the foot of Big Lake, is a favorite gathering spot for our friends and relatives.
6. Milk, which is a complete food, should be in everyone's diet.

C 7. The sports that I like best are football and track.
8. Laura, left alone in the house, locked all the doors and windows.
9. U. S. Highway 30, which spans the country from ocean to ocean, passes through mountain ranges and plains.
10. A plan that will expedite fire drills has been submitted to the faculty committee, which will consider it at the next meeting.

C. Correct the comma-splice errors in the following groups of words.

1. You had better leave an hour earlier, traffic to the airport is heavy at that time of day.   since
2. Carl is working hard to complete his research paper by Friday, as he wants to have the weekend free.
3. One of my friends was injured in an automobile accident, according to the report, his injuries were not serious.
4. Everyone was relaxed and in good spirits; consequently, the party was a success.
5. I always like to throw several pine cones into the fire; they give off a fragrant, woodsy scent.
6. I had planned to be here early, however, I was delayed in traffic.
7. That is your own fault, if you had been more careful you wouldn't have made the error.
8. I won't be eligible to join the Reserves until after my birthday in February; nevertheless, I am going down tomorrow to get all the necessary information.
who 9. Pete is the boy who played the lead in the play, he is very talented.
10. When Pete was eight years old, he was playing small parts in the Studio Workshop productions; he still appears in many of their plays.

390

There may be some variation in the methods used to correct the comma-splice errors. Those given are suggestions.

SEMICOLON

A semicolon is used where a mark of punctuation stronger than a comma is needed. It is most often used in sentences that have two or more parts of equal rank. **[58]**

Use a semicolon to separate related independent clauses that are not connected by a co-ordinating conjunction (*and, but, or, for, nor*). **[58a]**

Please don't mention that incident again; I want to forget it as quickly as possible.

I suddenly realized that this was not a lake; the whole area had been flooded.

Use a semicolon between independent clauses connected by a co-ordinating conjunction if the clauses contain commas or are long. **[58b]**

We spent two weeks traveling through Connecticut, Massachusetts, Vermont, and New Hampshire; and everywhere we went the autumn foliage was spectacular.

Our neighbors, the Johnsons, have invited us to their daughter's wedding; but we cannot go, since my cousin is being married that same day.

The reasons for this rule can be illustrated by writing one of the example sentences with a comma instead of a semicolon.

Use a semicolon to separate independent clauses connected by such conjunctive adverbs as *however, therefore, consequently, nevertheless, and moreover*. **[58c]**

Jim is a credit to the team; moreover, he is an honor student.

The proposal involved the entire student body; therefore, representatives from each class were invited to attend the meeting.

Words that are used as conjunctive adverbs may also be used parenthetically. Do not confuse the two uses of these words. When they are used to connect clauses, they are conjunctive adverbs and should be preceded by a semicolon; when they are used as parenthetical adverbs, they are usually set off by commas.

I am not convinced, *however,* that he is the man for the job. (Parenthetical adverb)

I shall, moreover, prove that I am right. (Parenthetical adverb)

Use a semicolon between items in a series if any of the members of the series contain commas. **[58d]**

Point out to students that two independent clauses that are linked only by a semicolon could also be written as two single sentences, but that the ideas frequently lose force when they are separated.

In this usage the semicolon prevents confusion. Notice the difficulty in reading the following sentence in which only commas are used:

The members of the dance band include John Wilson, piano, Bob Lawson, drums, Andy Montgomery, saxophone, Stan Slocum, trumpet, and Dick Miller, guitar.

The use of semicolons between the items in the series makes the meaning clear:

The members of the dance band include John Wilson, piano; Bob Lawson, drums; Andy Montgomery, saxophone; Stan Slocum, trumpet; and Dick Miller, guitar.

 DEVELOPING YOUR SKILL

Write the numbers 1 to 10 on a sheet of paper. After each number write the word or words in each sentence that should be followed by a semicolon instead of a comma. Write the semicolon after each word that should be followed by this mark of punctuation.

him; 1. Since he has won the election, I shall support him, however, I was opposed to his candidacy.

them; 2. If you think you can use the tickets, I should like you to have them, but if you can't go, I shall give the tickets to Agnes and David.

area; 3. The storm slowed traffic throughout the area, the school buses, consequently, were late.

fire; 4. Many of his records were destroyed in the fire, consequently, the investigation will take several months.

university; 5. My parents would like me to attend the local university, I should prefer to go out of town.

Commerce; 6. The panel consisted of Mr. Alan Canfield, the president of the Chamber of Commerce, Mrs. Ruth Hartwell, the vice-president of the
Association; Parent-Teachers Association, Mr. Anthony Pinto, a member of the
Education; Board of Education, and Miss Janice Levitt, the head librarian of the Wilson Library.

year; 7. There is to be a meeting of the Student Council on Friday, June 1, to elect officers for the coming year, all representatives are asked to attend.

8. When I talked with Bill yesterday, he was enthusiastic about directing the show, but when I saw him today, he seemed indifferent. show;
9. Down the street came the high-stepping, smartly uniformed drum major-
   majorettes, the combined high-school bands, many floats, and riding in ettes;
   an open convertible, the queen of the festival and her attendants.   bands;
10. Napoleon never completed his empire, he had scarcely made more floats;
    than a beginning when he was overthrown. empire;

COLON

The chief function of a colon is to introduce something that will follow.
[59]

The colon is a formal mark of punctuation and is used primarily in
formal situations and in certain conventional usages.

**Use a colon to introduce a list when the items follow such words as
the following and *these*.**   [59a]

The following students have been awarded music scholarships: Margaret Bradley, Dennis Thompson, and Yvonne Hartmann.

Be sure to include these items: a raincoat, waterproof boots, and a
warm sweater.

Avoid using the colon after a form of the verb *be* when a simple series
follows or before a list that follows immediately after any other verb.
Notice the punctuation in the following sentences:

My hobbies are stamp collecting, fishing, and building model rockets.
The Red Cross sent food, clothing, and other supplies into the disaster area.

Use a colon after the salutation in a business letter.   [59b]

Gentlemen: Dear Madam:

**Use a colon to separate hours from minutes when expressing a time in
figures.**   [59c]

8:17 A.M.   11:40 A.M.   9:30 P.M.

Use a colon before a long, formal statement or a formal quotation.
[59d]

Most uses of the colon are obvious and will be learned
readily.

The principal issued the following statement: All students who are found loitering in the corridors will be brought to the office for disciplinary action. (Notice that quotation marks are not necessary in this construction.)

The speaker concluded his talk with Shakespeare's words: "This above all: to thine own self be true."

This use of the colon is more subtle than most of the other uses.

Use a colon after a statement which is followed by an explanatory clause or expression.   [59e]

There is only one kind of person I dislike: a dishonest man.

Colleges are becoming increasingly selective: there is a shortage of qualified teachers, and classrooms are already overcrowded.

Use a colon to separate the act from the scene of a play.   [59f]

The lines he quoted were from *Macbeth* I: 2. (Act I, scene 2 of *Macbeth*)

Use a colon to separate chapter and verse when referring to a specific Biblical selection.   [59g]

The minister took his sermon from Luke 16:10. (Chapter 16, verse 10 of Luke)

DEVELOPING YOUR SKILL

Rewrite the following sentences, inserting colons where they are needed. If a sentence is correctly punctuated, write + after the appropriate number.

1. This is his schedule for the morning a sales meeting at nine o'clock, an art conference at ten-thirty, an interview at eleven-fifteen, and a luncheon meeting with the heads of divisions at twelve-thirty.
2. His letter began Gentlemen I am sending the photographs you requested for use in your advertising brochure.
3. Samuel Johnson once wrote "It is better to live rich, than to die rich."
4. I was sure the quotation was from Proverbs 9 8, but it turned out to be Isaiah 25 5.
5. Mr. Richards, who was a Shakespearean actor, not only can quote long passages but can even give the exact sources, such as *King Henry V*, III 6, *All's Well That Ends Well* V 3, or *Othello*, II 1.
+ 6. The three requirements are a high-school diploma, a minimum age of eighteen, and a certificate of health from your family doctor.

Students should understand the difference between the semicolon used in balanced structure and the colon used to introduce a conclusion, a result, or an effect.

7. The plane was scheduled to leave at 1:50 P.M., but it was delayed until 2:35.
8. I am pleased with the progress you have made: your classwork has improved, your written work is better, and your grades are higher.
9. The notice posted on the bulletin board read: "All students not in their homerooms when the final bell rings are to be considered late."
+ 10. Representatives of all the community service organizations canvassed the city's businesses to collect medical supplies, clothing, books, toys, and food for shipment overseas.

END PUNCTUATION

The period, the question mark, and the exclamation point are called *end,* or *terminal, punctuation* because they usually mark the ends of sentences. The period, however, has several additional uses.

Use a period at the end of a statement.   [60]

George Gershwin wrote "Rhapsody in Blue."

The period may also be used to end mild imperative sentences, indirect questions, and certain requests.

Use a period to end a mild imperative sentence.   [60c]

Close the window; it's cold in here.

Use a period at the end of an indirect question.   [60d]

He asked whether we would help him.
I wonder who he is.

Use a period at the end of a simple request that is stated in the form of a question for the sake of courtesy.   [60e]

Would you please take this message to the office.
Will you please give me your attention.

395

Terminal punctuation should present no problems for the eleventh-grade student.

The prob-
lem of
fused
sen-
tences
should
be elim-
inated
as stu-
dents
master
the
grammar
of the
sen-
tence.

Avoid writing *run-on* sentences caused by the omission of a period.
[60a]

A *run-on sentence,* which is sometimes called a *fused sentence,* consists of two independent clauses that have been fused together without a connecting link. Such sentences are usually the result of carelessness in writing and in proofreading.

The following is an example of a fused sentence:

Choose a different movie that one received unfavorable reviews.

The period may be used to correct a run-on sentence. Insert a period after the first clause and capitalize the word that follows the period.

Choose a different movie. *T*hat one received unfavorable reviews.

A run-on sentence may also be corrected by using a semicolon or a comma and a co-ordinating conjunction or by subordinating one idea.

Choose a different movie; that one received unfavorable reviews.
Choose a different movie, for that one received unfavorable reviews.
Since that movie received unfavorable reviews, choose a different one.

Use a period after abbreviations.   [60b]

Although abbreviations should generally be avoided in writing, there are certain standard abbreviations that are considered good usage.

1. The titles *Mr., Mrs., Dr., St.,* and *Mt.,* may be used with a name to form a proper noun.

2. The titles *Jr.* and *Sr.* may be correctly used after a proper noun— *Mr. Sidney Wadsworth, Sr.* A title placed after a proper noun is separated from the proper noun by a comma.

3. Titles such as *M.D., D.D.S., B.A., M.A., Ph.D., D.D.* and *LL.D.* may be correctly abbreviated after a person's name.

4. Certain titles, such as *Rev.* (Reverend) and *Hon.* (Honorable), are usually abbreviated when used as part of a name, except in formal announcements. They are never correctly used without a first name or initials.

The *Rev. Clifford J. Woods* pronounced the benediction. (Not *Rev. Woods pronounced the benediction.*)

Insist upon the use of periods with abbreviations,
except where the letters form a pronounceable unit.

5. The titles *Professor, Senator,* and *General* should always be written out in full.

6. Such abbreviations as *R.R.* (Rural Route) and *P.O. Box* (Post Office Box) may be correctly used in addresses. <u>Do not abbreviate the names of streets, avenues, cities, states, or countries in an address.</u> The *St.* in *St. Louis,* however, is correct. <u>Abbreviations are also permissible in return addresses.</u>

Emphasize these points.

Abbreviations of the names of some government agencies and of some international organizations are frequently written without periods, especially if the letters form a pronounceable unit.

NATO   USAFI   UNESCO

Use a period after each number or letter in an outline, except for those enclosed in parentheses.   **[60f]**

You may wish to teach this rule with the teaching of outlines (pages 138–140, 349–352).

I.

   A.

     1.

     2.

       a.

       b.

         (1)

           (a)

           (b)

         (2)

   B.

II.

Use periods to indicate ellipses.   **[60g]**

An ellipsis is an omission of words. Periods are used to show ellipses in quotations or in material in which the omitted words are not understood from the sense of the rest of the sentence. Use three periods to indicate an ellipsis within a sentence. When an ellipsis occurs at the end of a sentence, add the sentence period to the ellipsis marks.

It was Lincoln who said: " . . . Our fathers brought forth on this continent a new nation . . . dedicated to the proposition that all men are created equal."

Correlate the teaching of ellipsis with the teaching of the research paper. (See page 136.)

Change the last sentence to read as follows: Therefore, it is our decision that . . . . (The ellipsis here indicates that the rest of the sentence is to remain as it was originally written.)

Use a question mark at the end of a question.   [61]

When will you let me know?

How many extra chairs will have to be brought from the other classrooms?

Use a question mark enclosed in parentheses to express uncertainty or doubt.   [61a]

He was born on February 28 (?), 1920. (The day of his birth is uncertain.)

Hernando De Soto, the Spanish explorer, lived from 1500 (?) to 1542. (The year of his birth is uncertain.)

Stress this point.

<u>This use of the question mark should be reserved for situations in which it is impossible to find exact information.</u> The use of the question mark in a sentence such as the following is a mark of laziness. It would be relatively simple to find out whether there is such a book by Masefield.

The two books he wants are *The Old Man and the Sea* by Hemingway and *Live and Kicking Ned* (?) by Masefield.

Use question marks after elliptical questions in a series.   [61b]

Did you take your notebook? Your lunch? Your bus fare?

Use an exclamation point at the end of an exclamatory sentence.   [62]

How beautiful the trees are!

Bob shouted, "Man overboard!"

Rule 61b may be correlated with the teaching of elliptical sentences (pages 276–277).

An exclamation point may also be used after an interjection.

Ouch! Be careful!
Goodness! Must you make so much noise?

An imperative sentence may be followed by either an exclamation point or a period, depending on the intensity of the emotion expressed. A mild imperative sentence is followed by a period; a strong imperative sentence is followed by an exclamation point.

The intention of the writer determines the choice of punctuation.

Please stop that foolishness. (Mild imperative)
Stop that foolishness! (Strong imperative)

 DEVELOPING YOUR SKILL

A. Rewrite the following sentences, inserting periods and capital letters wherever they are needed.   Underscore indicates capital letter.

1. Dr. and Mrs. Burton are visiting their daughter in Sault Ste. Marie.
2. The article signed "James B. Doyle, PhD" was reprinted in all the local newspapers. Ph.D.
3. The Hon. Winthrop P. Hodges, Sr. presided over the trial.
4. There is *(words omitted)* danger of an epidemic breaking out.
5. Address the letter to P.O. Box 40. it will surely reach me.

B. Rewrite the following word groups, inserting periods, question marks, exclamation points, and capital letters wherever necessary.

1. The return address on the letter read as follows: "Martin S. Steiner, DDS, 436 Linwood Ave, Boston, Mass." Ave.   D.D.S.
2. Oh! What a mess you've made of things!
3. Professor Conrad J. Smith, PhD is to be the main speaker. his subject will be "What Does the Future Hold for You"?"   Ph.D.
4. Would you please take a message for Linda.
5. Marie asked me whether I would walk home with her after school.
6. I know you're there. why are you hiding?
7. Have you brought the popcorn? the candy? the nuts?
8. If we are to succeed *(words omitted)* we must all work together.
9. He was born on April 29, 1730 (Indicate that the year of his birth is uncertain.)   1730 (?)
10. If Jack can't have the car, how will we get to the dance? will your father drive us?

QUOTATION MARKS

Quotation marks are used to enclose direct quotations—a speaker's exact words.   [63]

Refer
stu-
dents
to the
patterns
fre-
quently.

Quotation marks are a device used by writers and printers to separate direct quotations from narrative, description, or explanation. Sentences containing quotation marks fall into the following four patterns:

Type A: " — ," he insisted.
Type B: He replied, " — ."
Type C: " — ," he went on, " — ."
Type D: " — ," he concluded. " — ."

If you follow the pattern given, you should have no difficulty learning to use quotation marks. These patterns cover almost every situation in which quotation marks are used to indicate conversation.

The first word of a direct quotation is capitalized. Do not capitalize the second part of a broken quotation (Type C). A direct quotation is separated from the rest of the sentence by one or more commas, a period, an exclamation point, or a question mark.

Empha-
size
this
rule.

Do not use quotation marks with indirect quotations.   [63a]

Phyllis said, "I am leaving now." (Direct quotation)
Phyllis said that she was leaving. (Indirect quotation)

Quotation marks always follow commas and periods and precede semi-colons and colons. The position of quotation marks with exclamation points and question marks varies with the particular situation.   [63b]

By the time Tom said, "Let's go inside to get warm," I could no longer feel my toes and fingers.

Mary said, "I'm cold too."

Mother asked, "Who is hungry?" (Only the quotation is a question.)

Did he really say, "I'm not hungry"? (The question mark applies to the entire sentence.)

Dick shouted, "Hooray!" (Only the quotation is an exclamation.)

How annoyed I was when he said, "I won't help"! (The exclamation point applies to the entire sentence.)

He finally said, "I'll do what I can"; but by this time, no one wanted his help. (The semicolon applies to the entire independent clause.)

You may wish to teach the use of quotation marks for
direct discourse in conjunction with writing short stories
or narratives.

Begin a new paragraph each time the speaker changes in dialogue (two or more persons speaking). [63c]

Quota-
tion
marks
serve
as a
guide
to the
reader.

"The Halloween masquerade was such fun, wasn't it?"

"I don't think I have ever attended a better dance, Pat," replied Geri.

"Didn't Carl look funny with that bearskin and club?" interjected Sue. "I laughed so hard I had to sit down."

"Carl was a good sport about all the teasing," said Pat. "After the dance he took Geri, Stan, and me to the drive-in for hamburgers."

If you write a single long quotation that includes several paragraphs, use quotation marks at the beginning of each paragraph and at the end of the last paragraph only.

Use quotation marks to set off titles of poems and titles of chapters, articles, and other parts of books and magazines. [63d]

Have you read Robert Frost's poem "Birches"?

The chapter entitled "Coral Formations" is particularly interesting.

His short story "Twins" first appeared in a magazine.

Use single quotation marks to set off a quotation within a quotation. [63e]

"When I talked to him last," said Greg, "he said, 'I'll be there in an hour.' "

"Were his actual words 'You have my permission to go'?" asked Ned.

Use quotation marks to enclose words or expressions used in a special sense. [63f]

Words used in a special sense include technical terms used in non-technical writing, coined words, ironical expressions, and words that suggest a different level of usage when used in formal writing.

The "folio" is the number of a page in a book. (Technical term)

The wheels of the train whispered a rhythmic "pocketa-pocketa-pocketa" all through the night. (Coined word)

You're the "genius"; you fix it. (Ironical usage)

The audience "came to life" when the barbershop quartet began to sing. (Colloquial usage)

Emphasize the use of single quotation marks. This usage is frequently confusing to students.

You may wish to stress the first paragraph by
reading it aloud in class.

402   *Mechanics in Writing*

Be careful not to overdo the last usage illustrated. The quotation
marks indicate that the writer knows that the level of usage is not up to
the level of the rest of the sentence. It would be better to substitute an
expression that is appropriate to the level of the sentence.

The audience became attentive when the barbershop quartet began
to sing.

DEVELOPING YOUR SKILL

Rewrite the following sentences, punctuating them correctly. Insert
capital letters wherever they are needed.

1. I said boldly "I have already read *Hamlet* three times do I have to read
   it again? I am growing tired of to be or not to be.

2. "Have you read the article Charles Darwin in the *Encyclopaedia Britannica* asked Miss Graham.

3. "Don't tell me to face the music said Harry I am as frightened as you are.

4. "I have just read the chapter In Secret from *A Tale of Two Cities* she
   said; are you familiar with the episode?

5. "Do not said the teacher use the word ain't.

6. Keats's poem On a Grecian Urn is one of the outstanding poems in
   the English language.

7. The guard shouted halt.

8. What did you mean when you said People who live in glass houses . . . ?

9. The cameras dollied in for a close-up of the star.

10. The Closed Door is an important chapter in Hardy's *Return of the
    Native.*

11. It is rather uphill work initiating my brother Tommy into the mys-
    teries of table manners; Tommy's motto has always been Food
    Above All.

12. When we sat down at the table Mother said Tommy don't reach for
    the bread until your sisters are all served and it is passed to you.

13. "But I'm hungry protested Tom.

14. After the meat and vegetables were served, Tommy was not heard
    from until he broke out with hey sis shove the jelly this way.

15. "Ask for that in the right way Tom said Mother. Betty don't pass it
    until he does.

16. "Please sister pass me the jelly said Tommy in a high-pitched voice.
    It was plain that he thought this business pretty silly.

17. "Young man in about six or seven years you'll begin to appreciate all
    this said Father.

18. By this time Tom was holding his fork in what is known as the "banjo grip," and someone had to remind him about that.
19. "Don't use your fork like a shovel," said Mother; "put one kind of food on it at a time."
20. Having a brother in the "tough stage," as you might say, is surely hard on the rest of the family.

APOSTROPHE

The apostrophe is used primarily for two purposes: to show possession and to indicate that letters have been omitted in a word. There are, in addition, several other uses of apostrophes. Close attention to the following facts will enable you to master the correct use of the apostrophe.

Use the apostrophe (') to indicate omitted letters, to indicate certain possessives, and to form certain plurals. [64]

The apostrophe is used to indicate that one or more letters have been omitted in a contraction. [64a]

they have	becomes	*they've*
do not	becomes	*don't*
is not	becomes	*isn't*
he will	becomes	*he'll*

Notice the change in spelling when *will not* is contracted to *won't*. Be sure you spell contractions correctly.

Use the apostrophe with a noun to indicate possession. [64b]

SINGULAR	PLURAL
boy's	boys'
Jones's	Joneses'
child's	children's

The formation of possessive nouns is presented on pages 226–227.

Remember that all singular nouns and all plural nouns that do not end in *s* add an apostrophe and *s* (*'s*) to form the possessive; all plural nouns that end in *s* just add an apostrophe (').

For a more detailed discussion of possessive case forms, see rules 37a through 37f, pages 226 to 227.

Use the apostrophe to form certain plurals. [64c]

An apostrophe and *s* (*'s*) are used to form the plural of a letter, a figure, a symbol, or a word considered as a word.

The apostrophe, strictly speaking, is an adjunct of spelling rather than a mark of punctuation. It is so frequently misused that it should receive considerable attention.

I have three *A*'s on my report card.
You have two *3*'s in your numbering.
Do not use *&*'s in your writing.
I counted ten *so*'s in your composition.

In formal English only nouns that indicate living things are used in the possessive case. There are, however, certain other acceptable possessive usages.

Develop
this
rule
care-
fully,
stres-
sing
the
point
that
of is
used
with
most in-
animate
things
to show
posses-
sion.

Some organizations of living persons may be considered possessive.
[64d]

The *club's* program has been planned for the year.
The *company's* pension plan provides for retirement after twenty-five years of service.
The *city's* new ordinance went into effect yesterday.

<u>Most nonliving things show possession with the preposition *of*.</u>

The *roof of the house* (not *the house's roof*) needs new shingles.
The *top of the desk* (not *the desk's top*) needs refinishing.

Certain expressions of time, words indicating amount in dollars and cents, and certain idiomatic expressions may be possessive.   [64e]

Singular	Plural
an hour's work	two hours' work
a day's pay	three days' pay
one cent's worth	ten cents' worth

Idiomatic expressions include *today's news, for goodness' sake, a hair's breadth,* and *for pity's sake.*

 DEVELOPING YOUR SKILL

A. In the following passage you will find uses for apostrophes to indicate possession, omissions of letters, or plurals of letters and figures. List on a sheet of paper the words that require apostrophes and insert the apostrophes.

   When you're touring the country and everyone's tired of making conversation, try the alphabet game. The object of the game is to go through the alphabet from beginning to end, taking one letter at a time from signs along the road. The one who finishes first, of course, wins the game. My father's rules are rather strict, and you'll probably

Students should memorize the idiomatic expressions that are commonly expressed in the possessive form.

want to make up your own. He won't let us take any letters from signs within the town's limits. We've insisted on using letters on truck licenses and on mailboxes, but to no avail. The twins, who are too young to know *d*'s from *z*'s, spend their time counting horses and cows. My mother always tells us about the trips she took back in the 1930's, when she wasn't any older than I am now. Her family used to play this game for hours, she says. My brother Charles's pet peeves are the *j*'s and *q*'s. They're almost impossible to find unless you're lucky enough to come to a highway junction when you need a *j,* or to be passing a service-station sign for Quaker State oil when you're look- ing for the letter *q.* The twins' final reaction to our game is usually, "When can we stop for an ice-cream cone?"

B. Rewrite the following sentences, inserting apostrophes wherever they are needed.

1. The children's eyes followed the cake as it was brought to the table.
2. Weaver's Variety Store sells women's and men's clothing.
3. There are four *s*'s and two *t*'s in *Massachusetts.*
4. The first four years' salary was the hardest to earn.
5. You may use *&*'s when you are taking notes, but do not substitute them for *and*'s in your themes.
6. The *A*'s through *E*'s are filed in the first drawer.
7. The company's policies are clearly stated in these pamphlets.
8. Bob's and John's coats are almost identical.
9. If you'll give my secretary your telephone number, she'll call you when we've made a decision.
10. Ruth and Isabel's brother is dating my brother-in-law's sister.
11. Mabley and Carew's Department Store had a special sale to cele- brate the store's many years' service to the community.
12. Since our parents' birthdays both come in June, my brother and I decided to buy them a joint gift.
13. I wanted to get two pictures for Mother's new early American room.
14. Don's idea was a new radio for Mother and Dad's bedroom.
15. If a boy's father is my father's sister's brother, what relation is the boy to me?
16. Betty's and Arlene's new coats were bought at the same store.
17. I'll take hers, with its sheep's wool lining, any time she'll trade.
18. Television is still comparatively new, and its use is still limited; its significance, however, may be far-reaching.
19. "For goodness' sake!" she exclaimed. "I can't believe it's really you!"
20. I don't understand all the *why*'s of the situation.

These exercises may be checked by students in class. Insist that the position of apostrophes in relation to the words be clearly indicated.

DASH

The dash is a dramatic punctuation mark, often used to indicate sudden breaks in speech or quick changes of subject. These uses of the dash make it particularly valuable for reproducing the speech patterns of characters in a story; the dash allows the writer to approximate the actual speech habits of his characters.

Too frequent use of the dash is undesirable. <u>Do not use the dash as a substitute for a period, a semicolon, or a colon.</u>

Use the dash (—) to show changes or interruptions in the thought of a sentence.   [65]

Use the dash to indicate a sudden change in the direction of thought.   [65a]

She is the most self-centered—but I said I wouldn't talk about the incident any more.

His name—if anyone told me what it was—has completely escaped me.

Use a dash to indicate a suddenly interrupted bit of conversation.   [65b]

When a line of dialogue is broken off in the middle of a sentence or in the middle of a word, a dash is the only mark of punctuation needed at the end of the speech, except for quotation marks to indicate that the speaker has finished.

I tried to thank her. "Ann, I can't begin to tell you how grateful I —"

Use the dash to set off long, complicated appositives that are themselves punctuated with commas.   [65c]

Dad's favorite chair—an old, somewhat battered armchair with deep cushions and a high back—is an eyesore in our living room.

Copies of the letter have been sent to three of the executives—Mr. Lawson, Mr. Hamilton, and Mr. Dodd.

If a comma were used in place of the dash in the second sentence, the reader might think that copies of the letter had been sent to six people, rather than three.

Copies of the letter have been sent to three of the executives, Mr. Lawson, Mr. Hamilton, and Mr. Dodd.

DEVELOPING YOUR SKILL

Rewrite the following sentences, inserting dashes wherever they are required. Do not change any of the punctuation marks already in the sentences.

1. With only a minute left to play I still get excited thinking about it Pete took the ball down the field for a touchdown.
2. "I was coming around the corner you know, the one near our house when Andy appeared, apparently out of nowhere."
3. At the beginning of the story right in the first sentence, in fact the author tells you what his theme is to be.
4. "You may believe you are right," she began, "but" —"
5. Mrs. Bailey's entry a colorful, intricately designed hooked rug on which she had worked for a year won first prize.

HYPHEN

The hyphen is a device that helps to make writing clear by showing that two words or two parts of a word belong together. The hyphen is a mark that is about half the size of the dash. Since hyphens are used within words, they are often considered more marks of spelling than of punctuation.

Use the hyphen in compound adjectives, after certain prefixes, and in words that must be divided at the ends of lines. [66]

Use the hyphen between the parts of compound numbers from twenty-one to ninety-nine. [66a]

thirty-five one hundred thirty-five

Use a hyphen between the numerator and denominator of a fraction used as an adjective. [66e]

He won by a *three-fourths* majority. (Used as an adjective)
Three fourths of the students attended the game. (Used as a noun)

Use the hyphen between the words in a compound adjective—words that, used together, form a single modifier of a noun or pronoun. [66b]

an I-told-you-so look an awe-inspiring sight
a door-to-door salesman greenish-blue eyes

The use of the hyphen is rather fluid; students should be directed to consult new dictionaries for the most recent authority in the spelling of compound words.

If two or more compound adjectives are formed from the same base, the base word may be given once only.

> second- and third-place winners
> 3- by 5-inch cards

Use a hyphen between certain prefixes and the proper nouns or adjectives that are used with them.   [66c]

self-centered	all-star
ex-President Eisenhower	pro-British
inter-American	Senator-elect

Use the hyphen to divide a word between syllables at the end of a line.

                                               [66d]

radia-	syllabi-	manu-
tion	cation	script

For a more detailed discussion of syllabication, see rules 70 through 70e, pages 414 to 416.

Use a hyphen to join the parts of certain compound nouns, adverbs, and verbs.   [66f]

NOUNS	ADVERBS	VERBS
producer-director	full-throatedly	dry-clean
mother-in-law	left-handedly	quick-freeze
merry-go-round	sky-high	double-tongue

Since there is no simple rule for the hyphenation of compound words and since usage varies, consult your dictionary when you are in doubt.

DEVELOPING YOUR SKILL

Write on your paper the words that should be hyphenated in the following sentences, writing the hyphens where they belong.

1. The ill-assorted group of forty-six recruits quick-stepped through the army post to their barracks.
2. The slow-moving traffic caused a tie-up on the expressway.
3. By the time I had written twenty-five references on 3- by 5-inch note cards, I began to see the advantages of using a source number.
4. The well-known actor and his agent-manager wore dark-colored glasses in an effort to escape recognition.
5. With an I-dare-you-to-contradict-me attitude, she launched into an antiart, antimusic tirade.

Distinguish between word forms that are hyphenated as adjectives, but not as nouns—eleventh-grade students, eleventh grade.

ITALICS (UNDERLINING)

<u>Underlining in handwritten and typewritten material corresponds to *italic type* in material that has been printed.</u>

Empha-size this point.

Italic type (in which the letters slant upward and to the right) is simulated by underlining in writing and typing. [67]

Use italic type for the titles of books, newspapers, magazines, works of art—such as statues, musical compositions, pictures—and the names of airplanes, ships, and trains. [67a]

He reported on *Under the Sea Wind* by Rachel L. Carson. (Title of a book)

I always read the Sunday edition of the *New York Times*. (Title of a newspaper)

Do you subscribe to the *Saturday Evening Post?* (Title of a magazine)

Swan Lake is a beautiful ballet. (Title of a ballet)

The second manned American capsule was the *Liberty Bell*. (Name of a spaceship)

The *Exodus* was the name of the ship around which the plot of the story revolved. (Name of a ship)

We took the *Comet,* which is an express train. (Name of a train)

Use italic type for words, letters, and numerals referred to as such. [67b]

Your *k*'s look like *h*'s.

Do not use *seen* where you should use *saw*.

That is a *2* not a *Z*.

Use italic type for foreign words and phrases. [67c]

He is an *ex-officio* member of the committee.

Dr. Carson is president *emeritus* of the university.

 DEVELOPING YOUR SKILL

List on a sheet of paper and underline the words, letters, and figures that should be in italics.

1. She has all her clothes designed and made by a French couturier.
2. You have written the word there, when you intended to write their.
3. The Burlington line's Zephyr goes through my home town.
4. One of the expressions for good-by in French is au revoir.

Certain foreign words have become so much a part of the standard vocabulary of English that they are no longer italicized. Direct students to consult a dictionary if they are in doubt about a word.

5. I have just finished reading The Stranger by Albert Camus.
6. Anna Maria Alberghetti was an immediate success in the lead role in Carnival.
7. The Atlantic Monthly, the Saturday Review, and the Chicago Daily News all carried reviews of his new book.
8. The numbers 2, 9, 3, and 4 are in his phone number, but I can't remember their sequence.
9. The motto of Scotland is nemo me impune lacessit.
10. The Nautilus was the world's first nuclear-powered submarine.

PARENTHESES   [68]

Parentheses are used to enclose comments that are added to a sentence but that are not considered of major importance.

Use parentheses to enclose material that is explanatory or incidental.
[68a]

One of the first English novels (Samuel Richardson's *Pamela)* is written as a collection of letters.

The new yearbook adviser (we hope it will be Miss Brady; however, we haven't heard yet) will have a good staff to work with.

Notice the punctuation of the parenthetical material in the preceding sentences. Parenthetical comments that come within a sentence are not capitalized nor are they ended with periods, even when they are complete sentences. Commas and semicolons, however, are used just as they usually are.

When the parenthetical material is interrogative or exclamatory, a question mark or an exclamation point is used within the parentheses.

Someone (was it you?) sent me an unsigned birthday card.

Last Sunday (what a beautiful day it was!) we spent the afternoon raking and burning leaves.

Parentheses may be used in a wide range of materials from informal personal messages to formal research-type treatises.

Punctuation marks that apply to the sentence follow the second parenthesis; such marks never precede the first parenthesis.

> If I decide to ask him (and I think I shall), do you think he will give me a direct answer?

Parentheses and dashes may be used interchangeably to set off an incidental comment within a sentence. Parentheses show that the comment is only slightly relevant to the rest of the sentence; dashes give the parenthetical comment greater emphasis.

A complete parenthetical sentence that follows the main sentence begins with a capital letter and ends with a terminal mark of punctuation —a period, a question mark, or an exclamation point.

> Miss Blackwell asked me to see her after class. (What had I done this time?) When I stopped at her desk, she said, "I am very pleased with the improvement in your work this quarter, Richard."

Do not use parentheses to enclose words that are to be omitted from a sentence. If you cannot erase such words neatly, draw a single line through them.

Use parentheses to enclose material that gives directions or references.
[68b]

> Dr. Conrad's research (see Chapters 5-9) took him to remote areas of the world.

> Do not use *what* to refer to an expressed antecedent. (See rule 46i.)

Use parentheses to mark numbered or lettered divisions within sentences or paragraphs.
[68c]

Numbers and letters enclosed in parentheses are not followed by periods.

> When you write a business letter, consider the following items: (1) placement on the page, (2) form, (3) clarity, (4) conciseness, and (5) courtesy.

> Mr. Enwright made the point that only two elements were necessary to the success of the program: (a) community interest and (b) community action.

Emphasize particularly the discussion of punctuation and capitalization of parenthetical material on this and the preceding page.

Write the following sentences on a sheet of paper, enclosing any parenthetical material in parentheses.

1. The man in question (I hope that you will consider this information confidential) is not worthy of your trust.
2. Pearl Harbor Day (December 7) will long be remembered.
3. The famous first Battle of the Marne lasted nearly a week (September 6-12, 1914).
4. The story is based on the belief that at midnight on Christmas Eve animals have the power of speech and kneel to pray. (Incidentally, Thomas Hardy's poem "The Oxen" is based on the same theme.)
5. Your outside reading assignments will consist of the following items from the list I have just given you: (1) two novels, (2) one full-length play or three one-act plays, and (3) twenty short stories.
6. According to the English system of weights, a pound of feathers would weigh (16 ounces avoirdupois weight); however, a pound of gold would weigh only 12 ounces (troy weight).
7. Dorothy did not suspect (or did she?) that we were planning a surprise party for her.
8. The lines he quoted were from the Bible (Matthew 2:5).
9. His theory (everyone seems to have a theory!) is that the money was not stolen; it was merely misplaced.
10. *Generalization, elevation, degeneration,* and *transference* (see Unit 4) are processes by which words change meaning or acquire new meanings.

BRACKETS   [69]

Brackets are usually used to set off comments, explanations, or corrections that are inserted into the text by someone other than the original author. They differ from parentheses in that brackets are used to enclose the writer's additions to quoted material, whereas parentheses enclose the writer's own words.

Use brackets to enclose material that has been interpolated by someone other than the original writer or speaker.   [69a]

"More than 50,000 Huguenots [French Protestants] were killed in the Massacre of St. Bartholomew."

Students should know the two main uses of brackets, particularly before they write an investigative paper.

"Virginia Dare was the first child born in America of English parents [1587, on Roanoke Island, North Carolina]."

Use brackets enclosing the word *sic* to show that an error in quoted material is one that occurs in the original material. [69b]

The first sentence of her theme read: "Henry Wordsworth [*sic*] Longfellow is noted for his poetry." (The bracketed *sic* after *Wordsworth* indicates that the quoted sentence is reproduced exactly as it was written and that the error occurs in the original sentence.)

DEVELOPING YOUR SKILL

Write the following sentences, inserting brackets or parentheses where they are needed.

1. "As cold water is to a thirsty soul, so is good news from a far country [Proverbs: Old Testament."
2. In English football (Rugby the ball may be passed, dribbled with the feet, or carried.
3. The review read: "His [Robert Burnett] new novel fulfills the prediction made by this reviewer (see August, 1959 issue) when the talented young writer's first book was published."
4. Her note ended: "I hop [sic] you will be able to come to see us soon."
5. Yesterday's game (and what a game it was!) put our team in first place.

Review Exercises—Punctuation

A. Write each of the following sentences, inserting all necessary punctuation marks. Underline words that should be in italic type. <u>All the sentences are correctly capitalized.</u>

1. As a result of the long drought the grass was brown and the cattle hunted in vain for food.
2. President Barnes Ph.D. left this morning for Texas his home state.
3. When Jack London was a young man he went to Alaska he later incorporated his experiences into many of his short stories.
4. An I-dare-you-to-teach-me-something attitude prevents some students from being successful in school.
5. These October Saturdays and Sundays are autumn's finest days
6. "Whenever I have planned an unusually good dinner it seems that some member of the family usually you Tom is late complained Mother.

7. Dad gave only two reasons for not wanting me to have a car (1) insurance costs are too high and (2) studies have shown that high-school students who drive cars tend to neglect their school work

8. "Benjamin Franklin said Save the pennies and the dollars will take care of themselves John quoted

9. Les the editor of the school paper concluded his editorial with the following quotation The battle Sir is not to the strong alone it is to the vigilent sic the active and the brave

10. Included among the foreign newspapers in the library are the Manchester Guardian the French Ce Soir (Evening) and the German Frankfurter Allgemeine Zeitung (Frankfort General Newspaper).

B. Rewrite the following selection, inserting all required punctuation marks and paragraphing correctly. The capitalization is correct. See p. T79.

Put dots not circles over your is Betty said Miss Martin Two women I know use circles said Betty and I think their writing is pretty But this is a class in business English and it is not businesslike to make circles replied Miss Martin She continued If youre planning a business career students make your writing as simple and legible as possible Nowadays employers are too busy to waste time on fancy touches

5. Syllabication

Occasionally, you may find it necessary to break words at the ends of lines in order to keep the right-hand margin of your paper reasonably even. Such breaks should be made between syllables only; a hyphen is used at the end of the first part of the broken word. Avoid carrying over fewer than three letters.

Syllabication is the division of words into syllables.　　　　[70]

Stress
this
point.
　　The following rules will help you determine the correct syllabication of words. If you are in doubt about where to divide a particular word, consult your dictionary.

The rules for syllabication given in this part of the unit are basic to correct syllabication and are almost infallible.

Divide a word at the end of a line only between syllables. A one-syllable word may not be divided. [70a]

width (not wid-th)   I've (not I-'ve)

talked (not talk-ed)   wrong (not wro-ng)

Do not divide a word so that a single letter stands by itself at the end of a line or at the beginning of the next line. [70b]

alarm (not a-larm)   pity (not pit-y)

erupt (not e-rupt)   area (not are-a)

Do not carry over a group of letters that contains only a silent vowel sound. [70c]

double (not dou-ble)   reli-able (not relia-ble)

muscle (not mus-cle)   vis-ible (not visi-ble)

Usually, divide a word after a prefix or before a suffix. [70d]

pre-fer   amaze-*ment*

inter-fere   change-*able*

mis-spell   merci-*ful*

Usually, divide a word between two consonants. [70e]

Words that contain double consonants are usually divided between the double consonants.

ha*p-py*   reco*m-m*end

wo*r-ry*   co*m-m*is-*s*ion

bu*t-t*er   recu*r-r*ence

Words that contain a double consonant as a result of adding a suffix, carry the second consonant over with the suffix.

ho*p-p*ing   refe*r-r*al

prefe*r-r*ing   swi*m-m*ing

pla*n-n*er   occu*r-r*ence

Double consonants that are part of the root word are not divided.

ca*ll*-ing   spe*ll*-ing

pa*ss*-able   bu*zz*-ers

gue*ss*-ing   cro*ss*-ing

Discuss each of the exceptions to rule 70e thoroughly. Point out to students that each exception is governed by a rule of its own.

Two consonants that appear between two vowels may be divided if each of the consonants is pronounced separately.

aba*n-d*on	ho*s-p*ital
pa*r-t*icular	desi*g-n*ate
my*s-t*erious	ki*n-d*er-*g*ar-*t*en

If two consonants are pronounced as a single sound, do not divide them.

no*th*-ing	ca*sh*-ier
assi*gn*-ment	so*ph*-omore
deta*ch*-able	dri*nk*-ing

DEVELOPING YOUR SKILL

Hyphenate the following words to show where they may be broken at the ends of lines. Some words may be broken at more than one place. If a word should not be divided, write the word without hyphens after the appropriate number.

Example: 1. com-mit-tee
2. alone

asked	1. asked	6. dressers	dres-sers
des-sert	2. dessert	7. indispensable	in-dis-pen-sabl
ir-rel-e-vant	3. irrelevant	8. although	al-though
ath-lete	4. athlete	9. excelling	ex-cel-ling
ac-com-mo-date	5. accommodate	10. trouble	trouble

Review Exercises—Syllabication

Write the following words on a sheet of paper, inserting hyphens to indicate where the words may be divided at the ends of lines. If a word should not be divided, put a check mark (✔) before the number of the word.

stop-per	1. stopper	6. occurrence	oc-cur-rence
man-u-script	2. manuscript	7. tossing	toss-ing
✓	3. equal	8. syllable	syl-lable
wor-ri-some	4. worrisome	9. swimmer	swim-mer
de-sign-ers	5. designers	10. psychological	psy-cho-log-i-ca

You may wish to have students cite the rule that applies to the syllabication of each word in the exercises above.

UNIT SUMMARY

Good writing is a blend of content, style, grammar and usage, and mechanics. In this unit you have studied mechanics in writing—form, spelling, capitalization, punctuation, and syllabication—the devices by which a writer makes his plan and his intended meaning clear to the reader. It is these devices which should receive careful consideration when you proofread any piece of written work.

Correct form in paragraphs, outlines, and letters not only makes a good first impression upon the reader, but also permits him to see at a glance the design of the writing. Correct spelling and syllabication lend clarity to writing by eliminating the confusion that results from misspelled words and incorrectly divided words. The correct use of capital letters and punctuation prevents misreading and misunderstanding of the writer's ideas. The use of parentheses, brackets, and underlining (for words that should be set in italic type) makes clear the relationship of words so marked to the rest of the text.

The Unit Review Exercises that follow will enable you to determine your strengths and weaknesses in the areas studied in this unit.

UNIT REVIEW EXERCISES

DISCUSSION TOPICS

A. How does form in the paragraphing of a theme indicate the plan of the theme to the reader? How does the statement apply to an outline? To a letter? See pp. T79-T80.

B. In what way does a business letter differ from a friendly letter? See p. T80.

C. How do misspellings and incorrect capitalization and syllabication detract from the clarity of writing? See p. T80.

D. How does punctuation make writing more intelligible? Give specific examples to support your answer. See p. T80.

E. How can careful proofreading improve the quality of your writing? See below.

Careful proofreading helps one to find and eliminate errors that are the result of carelessness or of haste. The elimination of such errors improves the quality of the writing.

Paragraphs begin at The Mountains ..., "Whichever are ...,"
"That's the way ...."
418   Mechanics in Writing

WRITTEN WORK

A. Rewrite the following passage, inserting all required capital letters and
punctuation marks, and paragraphing correctly. Underscore indicates
capital letter.

the mountains, which we saw on all sides, were an attraction to those of
us from the mississippi valley. the berkshires are not overwhelming, but
they are filled with delightful winding roads and pretty farms. as we drove
along, the small boys smile grew wider and wider, and the freckles on his
face seemed to be farther apart. his brother norman asked, "which state
do you prefer illinois or massachusetts? whichever one im in," came the reply.
"thats the way to have a good time," said norman. See also top margin.

B. Rewrite the following topic outline, correcting all errors in form, capitalization, and punctuation. Constructions used will vary; the form,
however, should be exact.

How to Write a Theme

I Preparation for Writing the Theme   I.
                                                              A.
    A Selecting a topic.   B.
    B Narrow the topic.   C.
    C Collect the materials you will need for writing   1.
        (1) yellow paper and pencils   2.
        (2) theme paper and pen (or typewriter)   3.
        (3) eraser

II Writing a good theme requires time and effort   II.
    A You will have to make a plan or outline   A.
    B Actual Writing   B.
    C Reading the theme aloud   C.
        a Checking sentence structure   1.
        b To catch grammatical errors   2.
    D Proofreading silently   D.
        (a) Checked spelling   1.
        (b) Corrected punctuation   2.
    E Final copy on theme paper.   E.
        Margins   1.
        Heading   2.
    F Proofread the final copy for errors.   F.

III Value of a well-written theme   III.
    1. You have the satisfaction that comes from work that is done well.
    2. training for future   A.
                                                            B.

C. Rewrite the following business letter in semiblock form, paying attention to capitalization, punctuation, and paragraphing. See diagram p. 354 for form. Short underscore indicates capital letter. Slash indicates lower-case letter.

2113 twentieth street

new orleans 12 louisiana

september 18, 1961

the metropolitan museum of art

255 gracie station

new york 28 new york

gentlemen:

please send me a copy of your new catalog of christmas cards as advertised in the september 16 issue of the new yorker. I have enclosed twenty-five cents to cover mailing costs.

Yours Truly,

Sidney R. Lewis

D. Rewrite the following sentences, correcting all spelling errors. See bottom margin.

1. The plan of student goverment in our school is similar to that in quiet a few high schools.

2. In the science labatory the instructer cautions us not to brake the fragile containers.

3. Finaly, our principle decided to seperate the childern who were involved in the fight and to take away there priveleges.

4. On the advise of the camp councilor, Bob and I have desided that we'll procede with our original plans.

5. Nobody can tell whether the weatherman will favor the picnic on the nineth, but we are all hopping for a fare day.

E. Rewrite the following passages, inserting all necessary capital letters and punctuation marks.

"The differences between great books and good books" said professor murray "are not always obvious time alone can make the final decision but there are certain standards that help guide our opinions we can in applying these standards consider the relative merits of the two books we have been discussing bennetts the old wives' tale and tolstoys war and peace is one of these books great and the other merely good I should apply first the test of universality which book more nearly portrays the life and hopes of universal man and thus tells the truth about mankind I should say war and peace however there are other tests some of them equally valid.

D. 1. government, quite; 2. laboratory, instructor, break; 3. Finally, principal, separate, children, their, privileges; 4. advice, counselor, decided, proceed; 5. ninth, hoping, fair.

the tones of the voices of ones parents bring a special comfort it is always easy to recognize mothers voice aunt alices words are easily recognized also.

the brents house stands on the corner of westmore and gladstone you have passed it many times when out walking their yard is one of rare beauty mrs brent is a woman of charm the term a real lady seems to me to be meant especially for alice brent.

well said alice I enjoyed the lecture well enough but I found some of the speakers mannerisms rather annoying his scowl for example though meant to be impressive seemed to me a bit silly also I was bored by his frequent use of such expressions as now I tell you in all truth and get this this is important and perhaps you will find this hard to believe but dont you find such expressions tedious however on the whole it was a good talk

many writers have contributed to the fame of the middle west in literature among the first of these was edward eggleston with whose stories of the hoosier schoolboys you may be familiar perhaps you have read lewiss novel main street one of the best books reflecting life in a small town in this region. willa cather too with her stories and novels of pioneer times in nebraska has created fine regional literature with iowa as his background phil stongs tales have been very successful these writers and many others have made the middle west a region familiar to all who read good books

VOCABULARY

Did you know the meaning of every word in this unit? In the following sentences, some of the words are used in different contexts. Write the numbers 1 to 5 on your paper. After each number write the letter of the word or phrase that could best be substituted for the italicized word in each sentence. Before making your choice, find the word on the page indicated to see how the word is used in this unit.

1. His gestures and mannerisms *detract* from the impact of his speech. [p. 347]
   (*a*) enhance; (*b*) diminish; (*c*) dramatize; (*d*) exaggerate

2. Her flower arrangements are always *symmetrical*.   [p. 348]
   (*a*) beautiful; (*b*) symbolic; (*c*) balanced; (*d*) unusual

3. You seem to have *aligned* them on your side.   [p. 349]
   (*a*) decided; (*b*) ranged; (*c*) won; (*d*) influenced

b

c

b

4. He has completely *misconstrued* my meaning. [p. 384]

d   (*a*) understood; (*b*) misquoted; (*c*) interpreted correctly; (*d*) misinterpreted

5. She tends to use commas and semicolons *interchangeably* in her writing.

[p. 411]

b   (*a*) similarly; (*b*) one for the other; (*c*) incorrectly; (*d*) haphazardly

SPELLING

The following spelling words appeared in the unit or were chosen because they are commonly misspelled. Study these words so that you will be prepared to write them from dictation.

1. detract	11. continuously
2. symmetrical	12. ecstasy
3. aligned	13. susceptible
4. misconstrued	14. diphtheria
5. interchangeably	15. ptomaine
6. contrasted	16. clique
7. ellipses	17. commendable
8. idiomatic	18. permissible
9. superfluous	19. sarcastically
10. transposed	20. ameliorate

B. I.
A.
1.
2.
a.
b.
(1)
(a)
(b)
(2)
B.
II.
A.
B.
C.

UNIT SELF-TEST

See diagram p. 354.

A. Write the form for a three-paragraph letter that you would send to a friend. Draw lines to represent the body of the letter. Use indented style.

B. Write the following numbers and letters in correct outline form. Do not change the sequence of the numbers and letters.

I, A, 1, 2, a, b, 1, a, b, 2, B, II, A, B, C   See above.

C. Write the form indicated in parentheses after each of the following words:

families   family (Plural)
interfering   interfere (Add *ing*)
sincerely   sincere (Add *ly*)
truly   true (Add *ly*)
peaceable   peace (Add *able*)

mother-in-law (Plural) mothers-in-law
happy (Add *ness*) happiness
alumnus (Plural) alumni
alto (Plural) altos
compel (Add *ing*) compelling

Insist that the Unit Self-Test be completed without any reference to the rules and examples in the unit.

D. Rewrite the following sentences, inserting all necessary capital letters and marks of punctuation.

1. during the last weeks of august we went to the dentist consulted the oculist and purchased clothing suitable for school.

2. we spent the christmas holidays in new england with grandfather who has just celebrated his sixty-eighth birthday.

3. was it rudyard kipling who wrote the poems if and boots?

4. no said peggy i dont agree when you say that all books that older people recommend are dry.

5. every time i say he dont my mother cringes said tom.

6. how different this part of the country is from the east but you know that without my telling you.

7. the discussion of nuclear power for peacetime use (see chapters 4-6) is encouraging.

8. her letter began you deserved everything that happened to you i have no intention of comiserating [sic] with you.

9. e pluribus unum the motto of the united states appears on the great seal

UNESCO   10. unesco which was established on november 4, 1946 has its headquarters at 19 avenue kléber paris 16 france.

E. Copy the following words on a sheet of paper, inserting hyphens to show where the words may be broken at the ends of lines. If a word may not be divided, underline the word.

	1. city	6. hedge	
par-al-lel	2. parallel	7. ricochet	ri-co-chet
in-vis-ible	3. invisible	8. chapter	chap-ter
mer-ri-ment	4. merriment	9. enough	
fall-ing	5. falling	10. they're	

Students who continue to have difficulty with mechanics in writing should review areas of weakness before trying the final Unit Test.

INDEX

References in red type indicate pages on which instructional material appears.

424

429

431

432

Question mark, 395, 398, 399, 402, 418, 419, 420, 422
Quiet, quite, 339, 342
Quotation
  capitalization of, 369, 418, 419, 420, 422
  direct, 400, 402-403, 418, 419, 420, 422
  indirect, 293, 400
  paragraphing, 401, 414, 418
  punctuation of, 387-388, 389, 400-402, 403, 413, 414, 418, 419, 420, 422
Quotation marks, 400-402, 403, 413, 414, 418, 419, 420, 422

Raise, rise, 323, 325, 342
Rambling sentence, 286, 289
Readers' Guide, 4, 8, 40, 76, 128, 137
Reading, 89-93, 94, 95-97, 98-99, 100-114, 115-116
  Check Yourself, 90
  figurative language, 90-93, 94, 99, 115, 116
  irony, 95-97, 98-100, 111, 115, 116
  short story
    analysis of, 105-113, 114, 115, 116
    analysis, method of, 101-105, 114, 115, 116
    atmosphere, 103, 105, 108, 114, 115, 116
    background, 102, 105, 106, 114, 115, 116
    character development, 103, 105, 107, 114, 115, 116
    climax, 103, 105, 113, 114, 115, 116
    clues in, 103, 106, 114, 115, 116
    complication in, 104, 105, 106, 109, 114, 115, 116
    conflict, 103, 105, 107, 114, 115, 116
    denouement, 104-105, 113, 114, 115, 116
    exposition, 102, 105, 106, 114, 115, 116
    focus of narration, 102, 105, 106, 114, 115, 116

Reading *(continued)*
  foreshadowing in, 103, 106, 114, 115, 116
  key moment, 104, 105, 113, 114, 115, 116
  moment of illumination, 104, 105, 113, 114, 115, 116
  mood, 103, 105, 114, 115, 116
  point of view, 102, 105, 106, 114, 115, 116
  resolution, 104-105, 113, 114, 115, 116
  setting, 102, 105, 106, 114, 115, 116
  style, 100, 114, 115, 116
  suspension of disbelief, 101, 106
Real, very, 313, 314, 319, 342
Reasoning, deductive, 54, 60
  syllogism in, 54
Reasoning, inductive, 53-54, 60
Reasoning, logical
  in debate, 53-55, 56, 59, 60
  deductive, 54, 60
  inductive, 53-54, 60
  in discussion, 41, 42
  fallacies in, 54-55, 56, 59
    faulty analogy, 45, 56
    faulty dilemma, 55, 56
    hasty generalization, 54, 56
    mistaken causal relationship, 55, 56
    post hoc fallacy, 54, 56
Rebuttal, 46, 56-57, 58, 60
Reciprocal pronoun, 203, 204
Redundancy, 287, 289
Reference books. *See* Research paper
Referents, of words, 63, 68, 71, 76
Reflective essay, 169-171, 172
Reflexive pronoun, 202, 203-204
  not substitute for personal pronoun, 311, 342
Regular verb, 205, 207
Relative clause, 254, 255, 256, 282, 299
Relative pronoun, 201, 203-204
Reputation, character, 334
Request slips, library, 121, 129
Research paper, 117-150, 151-152

434

438